ANIMAL LAND

4

By Makoto Raiku

Translated and adapted by Stephen Paul

Lettered by Eve Grandt

KODANSHA
COMICS

When the weather is nice, the best thing to do is take Riku out on a walk. When I throw Riku's octopus toy, he runs to fetch it, panting, "heh heh, heh heh." Do ho ho, do ho ho.

Makoto Raiku

ANIMAL LAND

4

Makoto Raiku

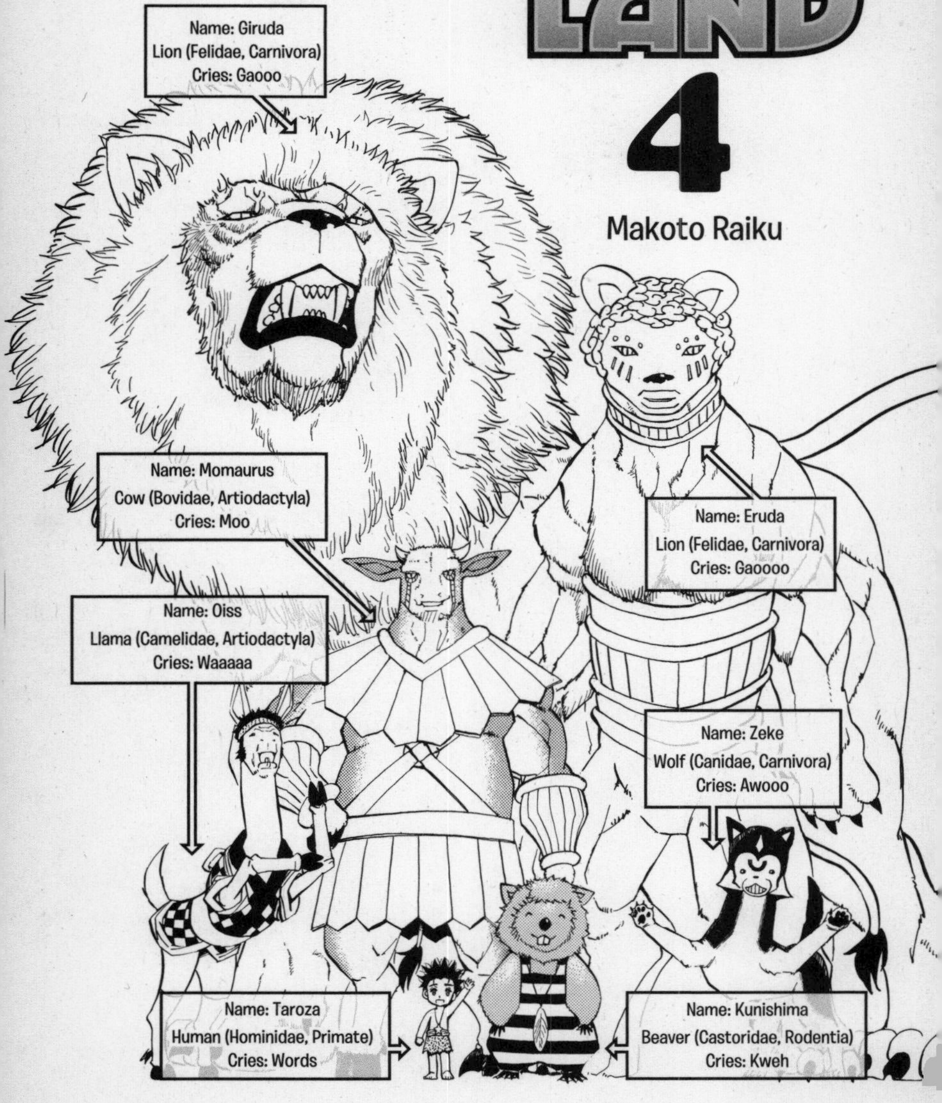

Name: Giruda
Lion (Felidae, Carnivora)
Cries: Gaooo
Name: Eruda
Lion (Felidae, Carnivora)
Cries: Gaoooo
Name: Momaurus
Cow (Bovidae, Artiodactyla)
Cries: Moo
Name: Oiss
Llama (Camelidae, Artiodactyla)
Cries: Waaaaa
Name: Zeke
Wolf (Canidae, Carnivora)
Cries: Awooo
Name: Kunishima
Beaver (Castoridae, Rodentia)
Cries: Kweh
Name: Taroza
Human (Hominidae, Primate)
Cries: Words

ANIMAL LAND
Character Profiles

Taroza

A human baby whose cries (speech) enable him to communicate with all different species of animal. Raised from a baby by Monoko. We thought he was the only human in Animal Land, but...

Did his birth mother abandon her own baby?

Taroza grows from a baby to a boy!

Monoko

A female tanuki and Taroza's mother. When a wildcat ate her parents, she was all alone until she met Taroza. It was at this point that she decided to be a mother.

Zeke

A wolf pup whose family was attacked and killed by a bear. He now lives in the tanuki village and considers Taroza and Monoko part of his family.

Kurokagi

A large wildcat with misgivings about the "survival of the fittest" laws of the world. When Taroza's words save his life, he makes it his duty to protect the boy. Even now, he is a valuable warrior protecting Taroza's village.

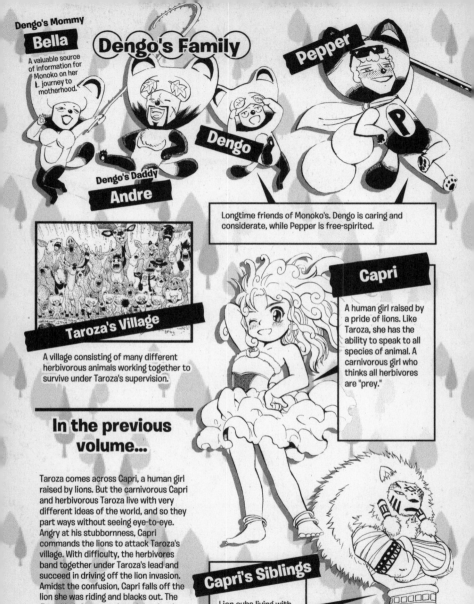

Dengo's Family

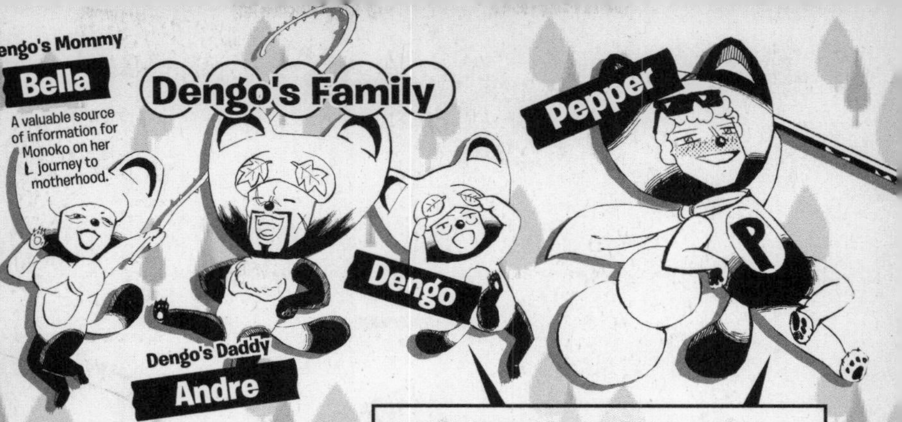

Dengo's Mommy
Bella
A valuable source of information for Monoko on her journey to motherhood.

Dengo's Daddy
Andre

Dengo

Pepper

Longtime friends of Monoko's. Dengo is caring and considerate, while Pepper is free-spirited.

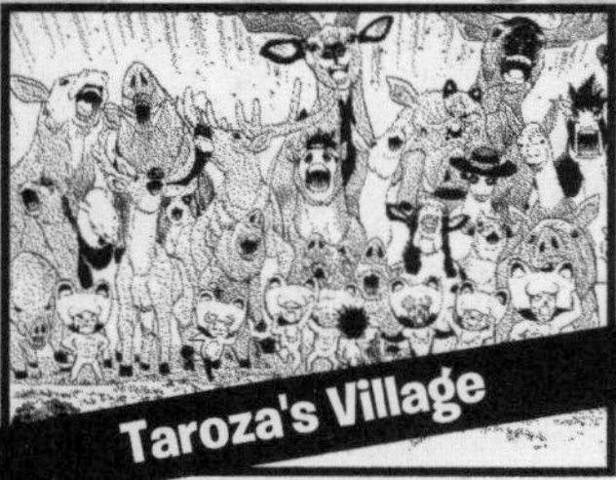

Taroza's Village

A village consisting of many different herbivorous animals working together to survive under Taroza's supervision.

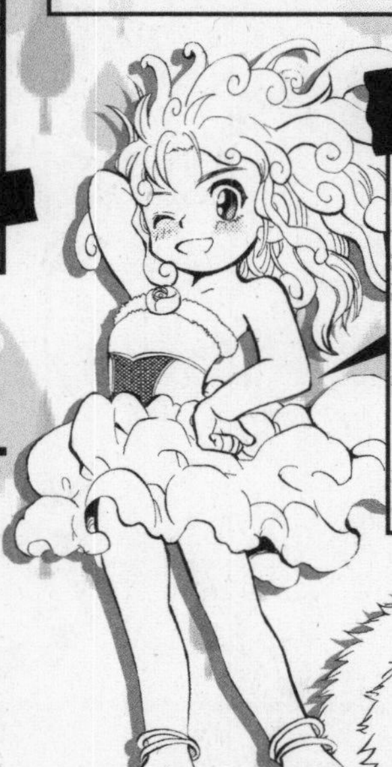

Capri

A human girl raised by a pride of lions. Like Taroza, she has the ability to speak to all species of animal. A carnivorous girl who thinks all herbivores are "prey."

In the previous volume...

Taroza comes across Capri, a human girl raised by lions. But the carnivorous Capri and herbivorous Taroza live with very different ideas of the world, and so they part ways without seeing eye-to-eye. Angry at his stubbornness, Capri commands the lions to attack Taroza's village. With difficulty, the herbivores band together under Taroza's lead and succeed in driving off the lion invasion. Amidst the confusion, Capri falls off the lion she was riding and blacks out. The first thing she sees when she wakes is Taroza's face...

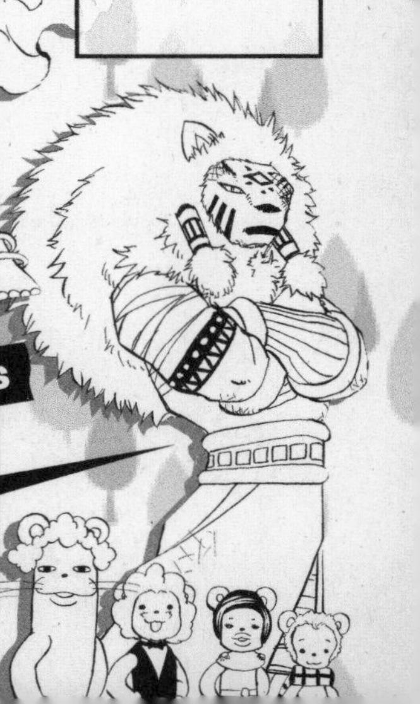

Capri's Siblings

Lion cubs living with Capri, whom they protect and adore.

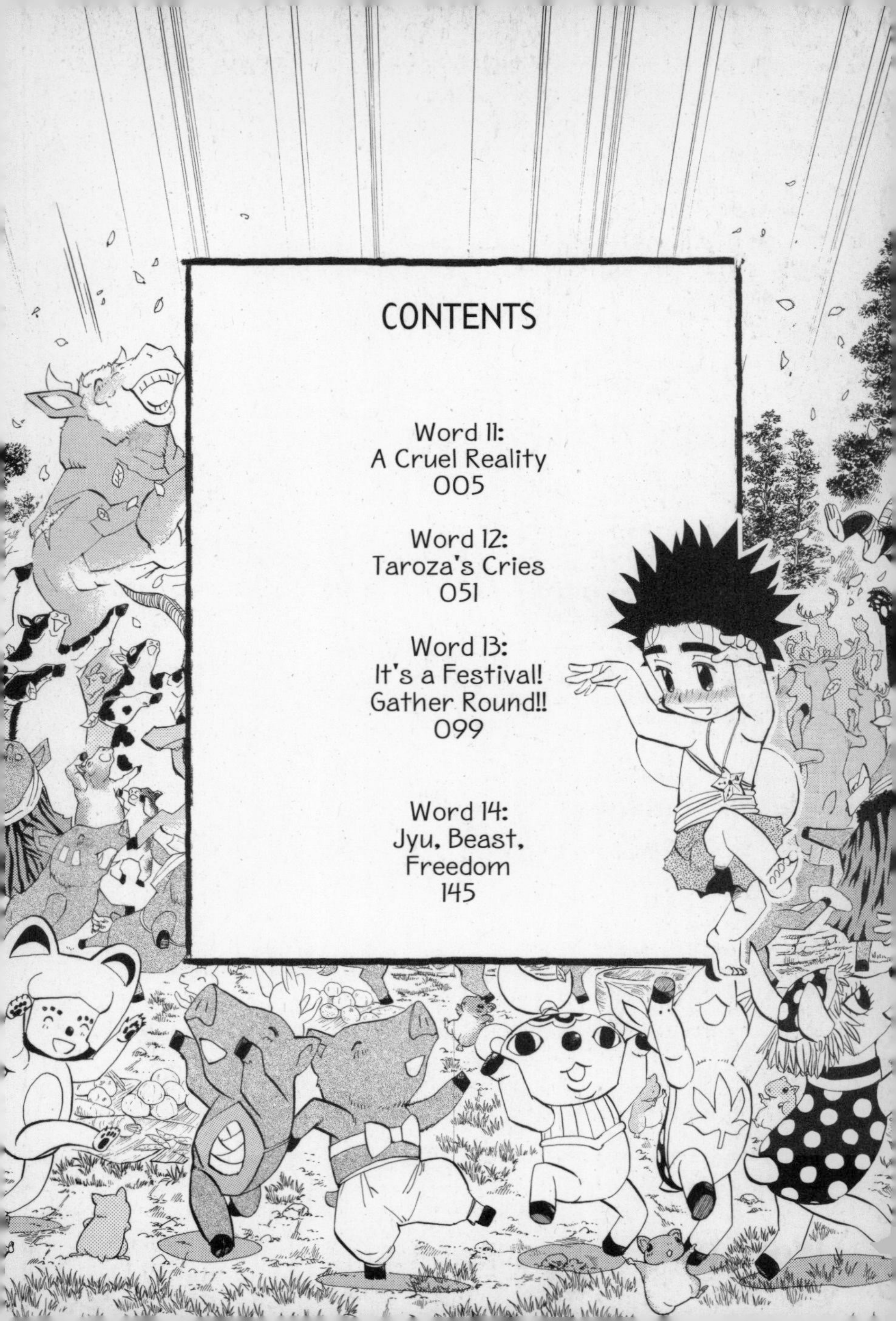

CONTENTS

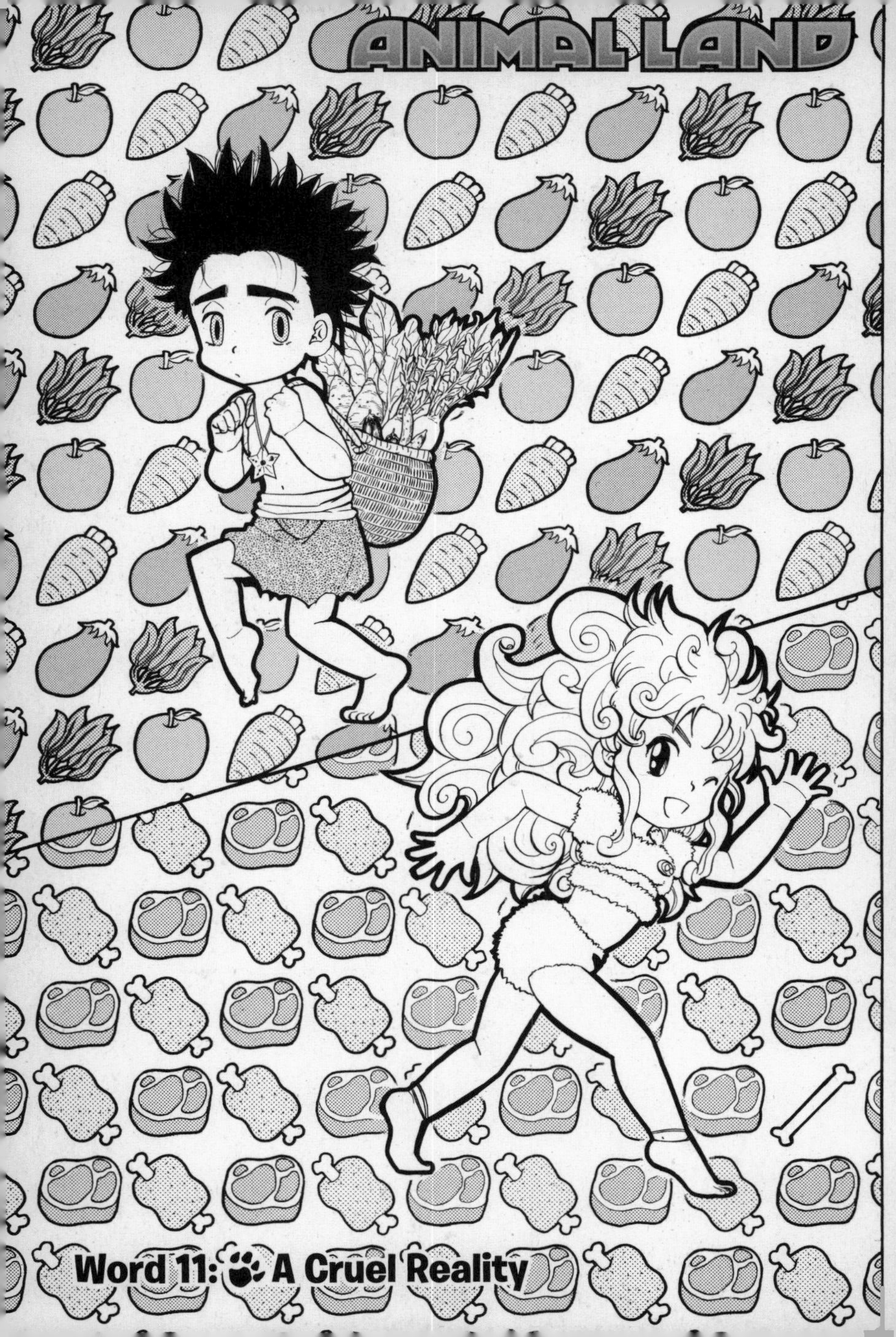
ANIMAL LAND
Word 11: A Cruel Reality

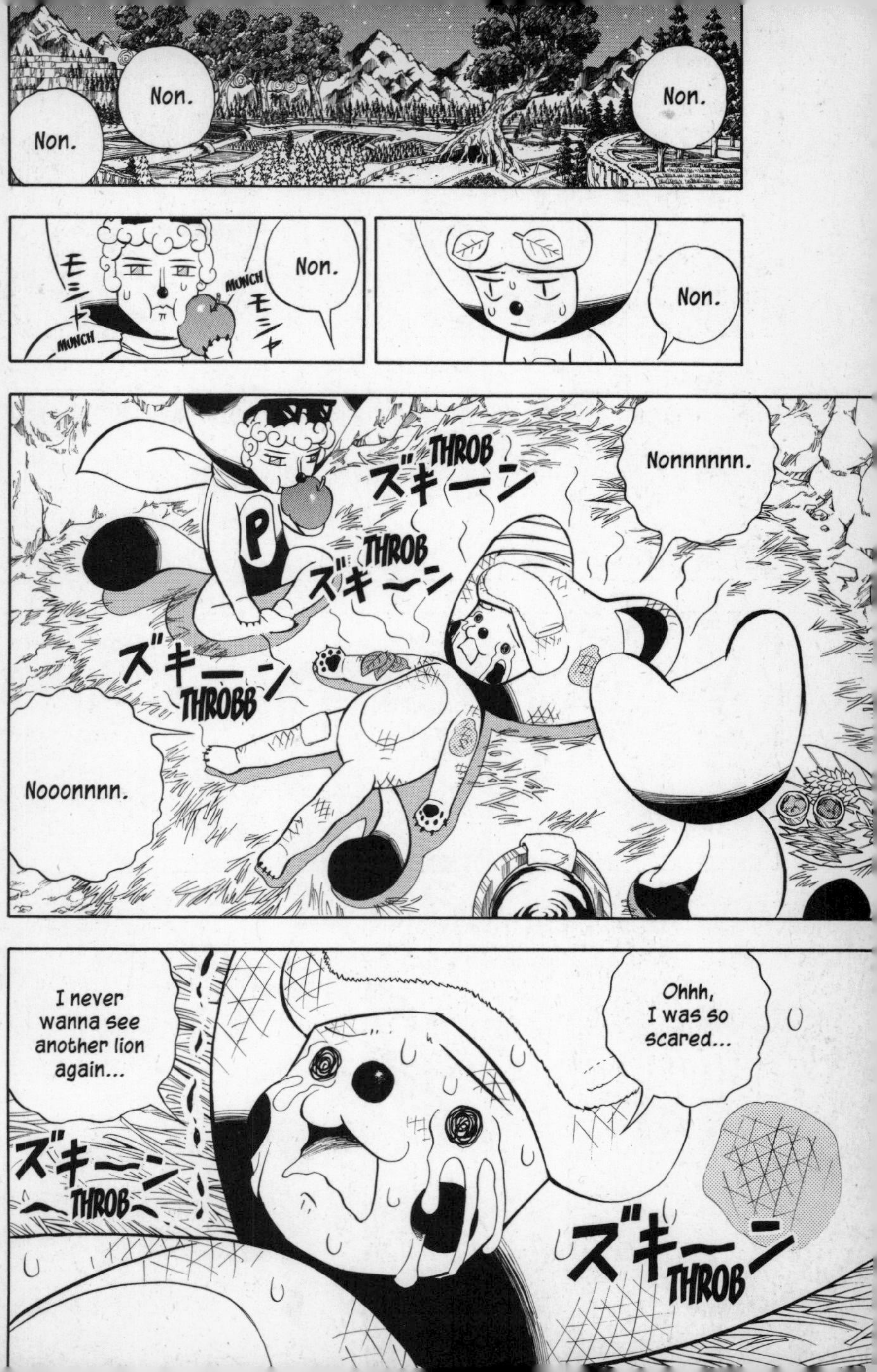
Non.
Non.
Non.
Non.
Non.
モシャ MUNCH
モシャ MUNCH
Nonnnnnn.
ズキーン THROB
ズキーン THROB
ズキーン THROBB
Nooonnnn.
Ohhh, I was so scared...
I never wanna see another lion again...
ズキーン THROB
ズキーン THROB

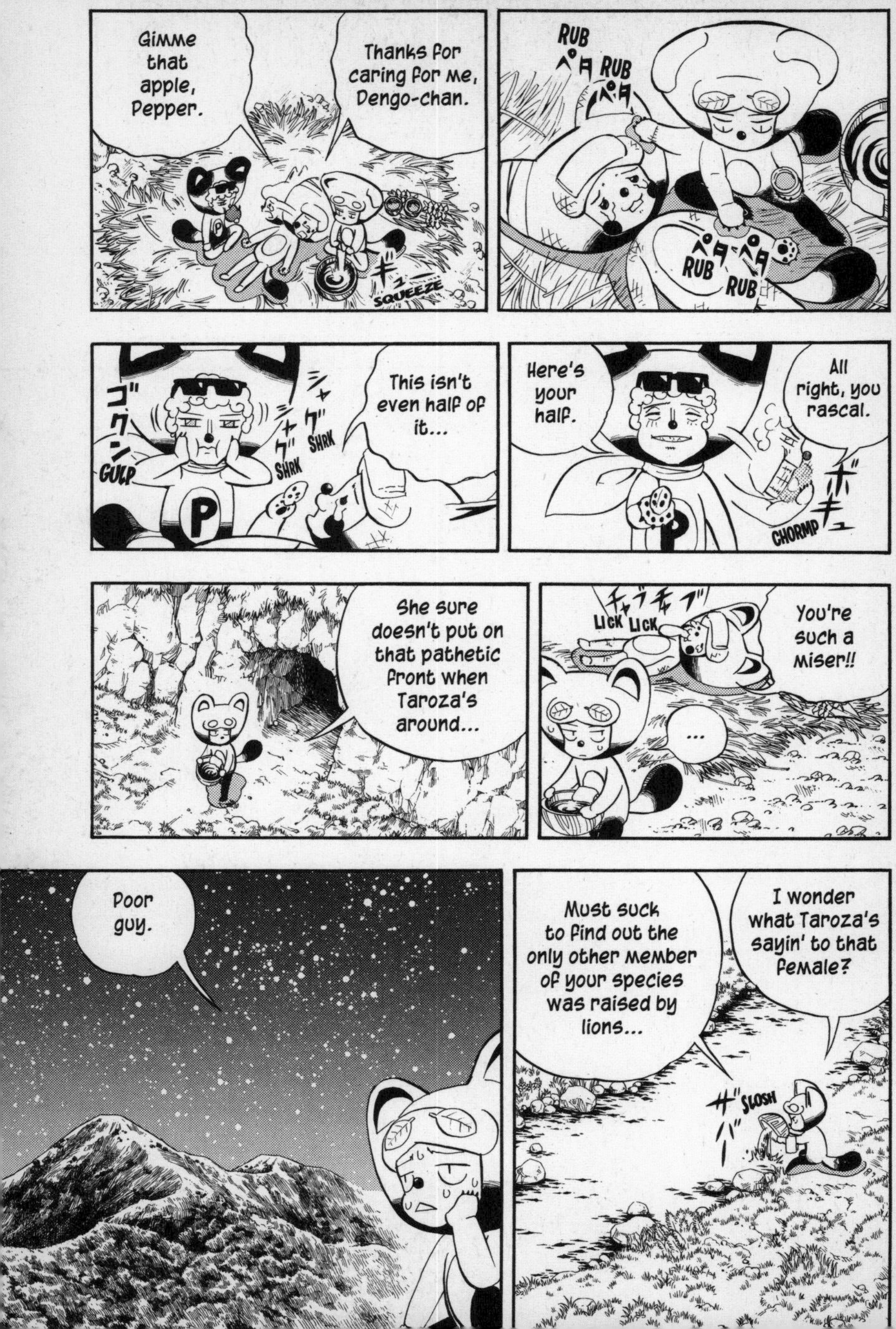
RUB
RUB
RUB
RUB
Thanks for caring for me, Dengo-chan.
Gimme that apple, Pepper.
SQUEEZE
All right, you rascal.
Here's your half.
CHORMP
This isn't even half of it...
SHRK
SHRK
GULP
You're such a miser!!
LICK LICK
...
She sure doesn't put on that pathetic front when Taroza's around...
I wonder what Taroza's sayin' to that female?
Must suck to find out the only other member of your species was raised by lions...
SLOSH
Poor guy.

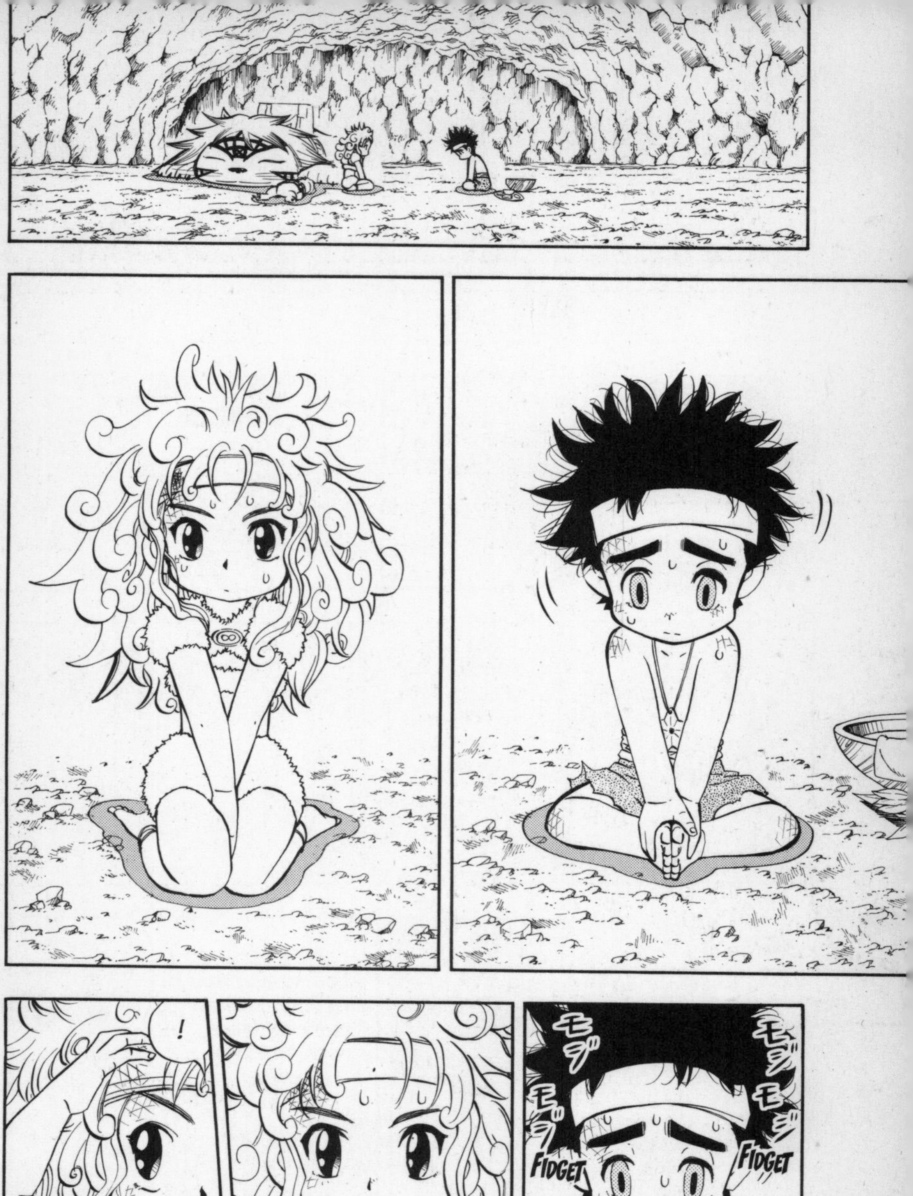
モジモジ
FIDGET
モジモジ
FIDGET
!

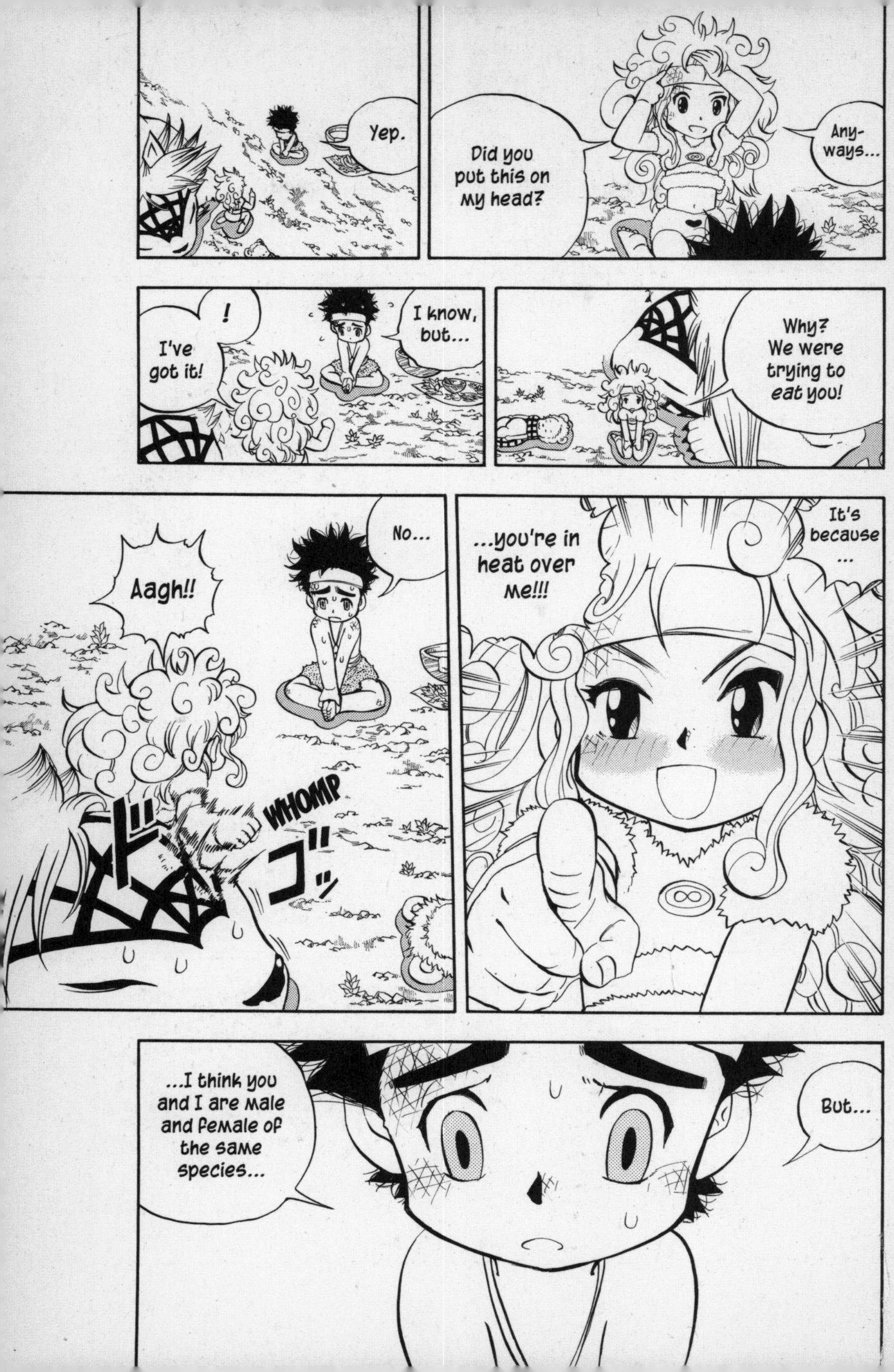
Any-ways...
Did you put this on my head?
Yep.
Why? We were trying to eat you!
I know, but...
!
I've got it!
It's because ...
...you're in heat over me!!!
No...
Aagh!!
WHOMP
ドゴッ
But...
...I think you and I are male and female of the same species...

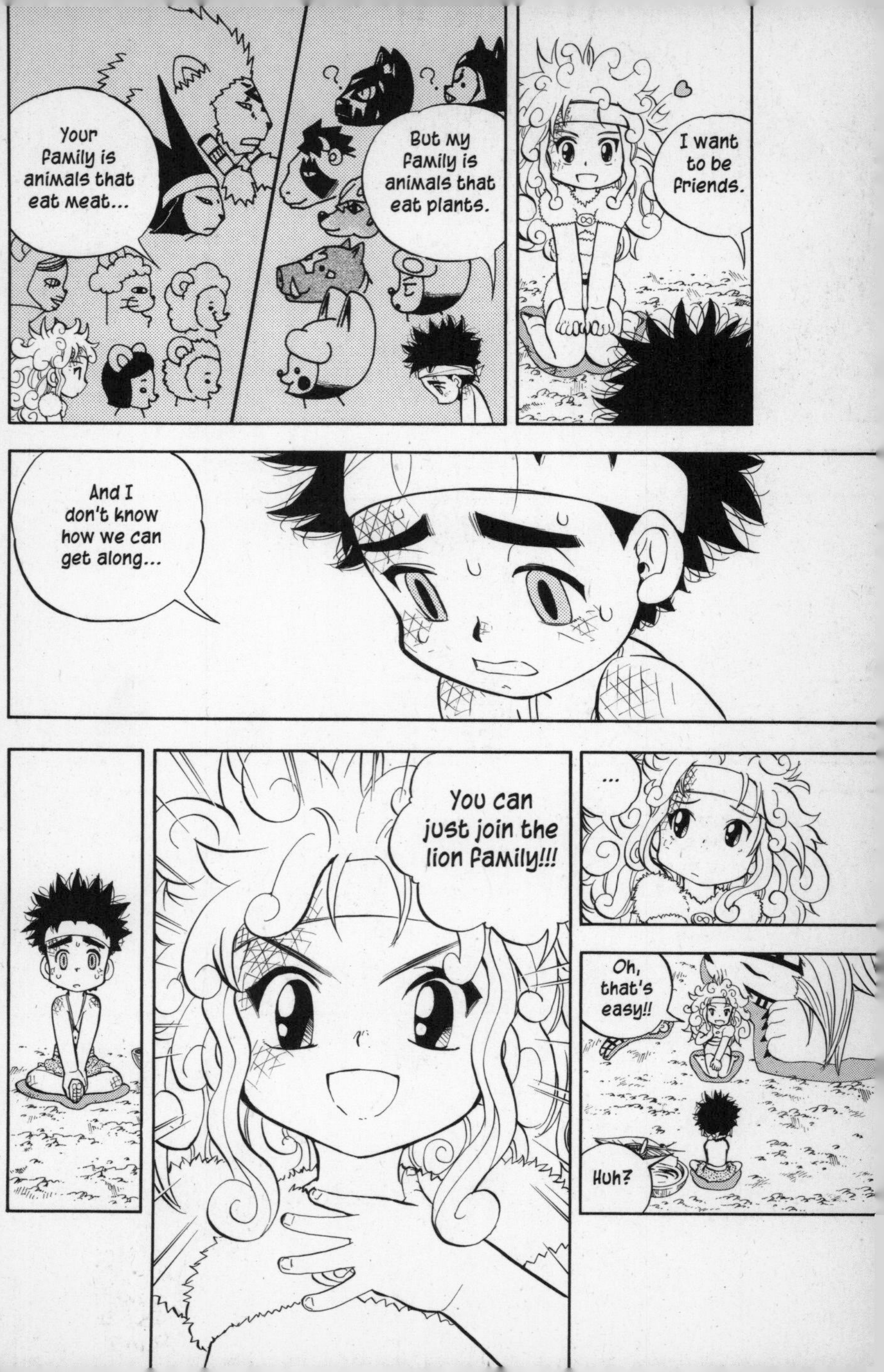
I want to be friends.
But my family is animals that eat plants.
Your family is animals that eat meat...
And I don't know how we can get along...
...
Oh, that's easy!!
Huh?
You can just join the lion family!!!

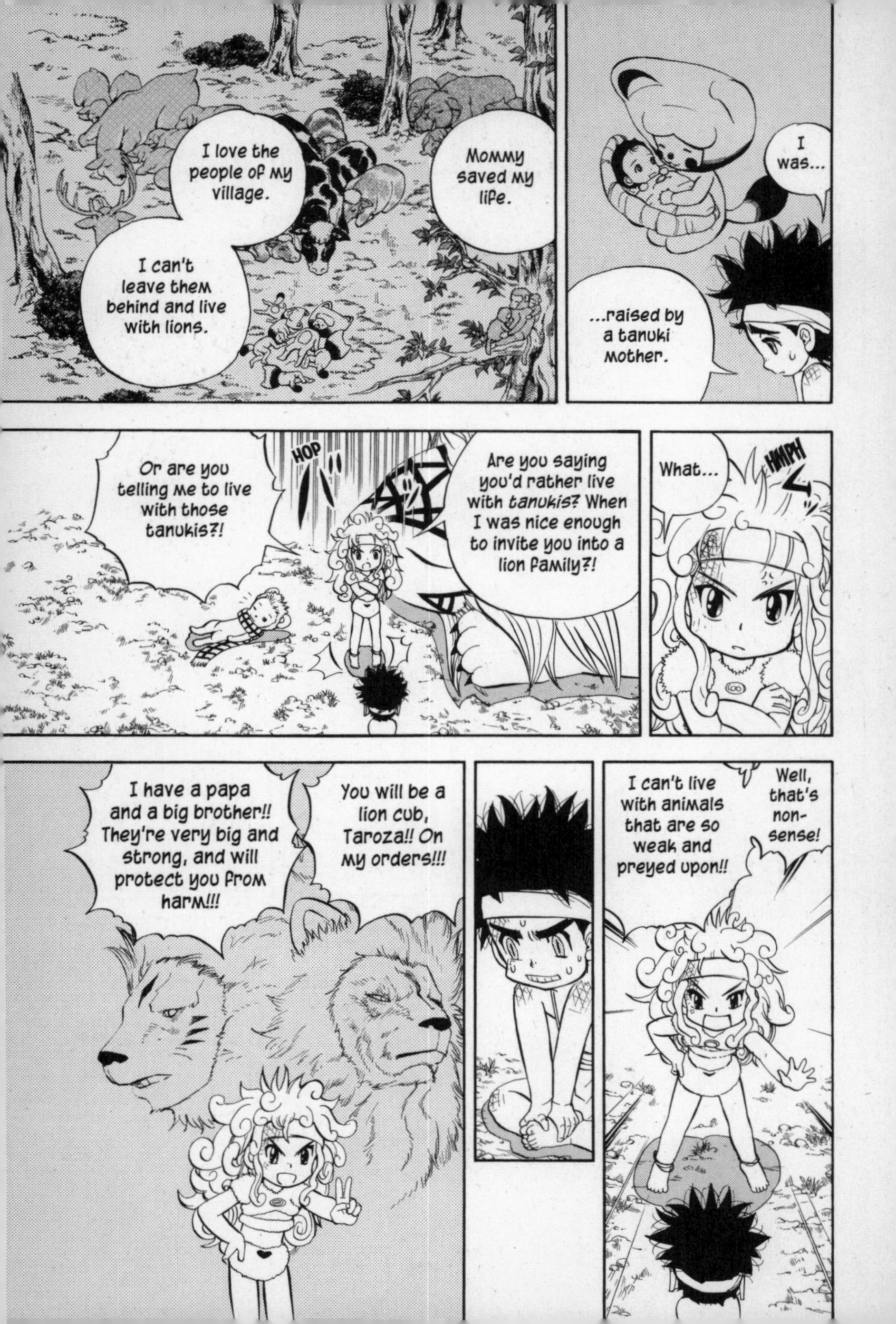

I was...
...raised by a tanuki mother.
Mommy saved my life.
I love the people of my village.
I can't leave them behind and live with lions.
What...
HMPH
Are you saying you'd rather live with *tanukis*? When I was nice enough to invite you into a lion family?!
HOP
Or are you telling me to live with those tanukis?!
Well, that's non-sense!
I can't live with animals that are so weak and preyed upon!!
You will be a lion cub, Taroza!! On my orders!!!
I have a papa and a big brother!! They're very big and strong, and will protect you from harm!!!

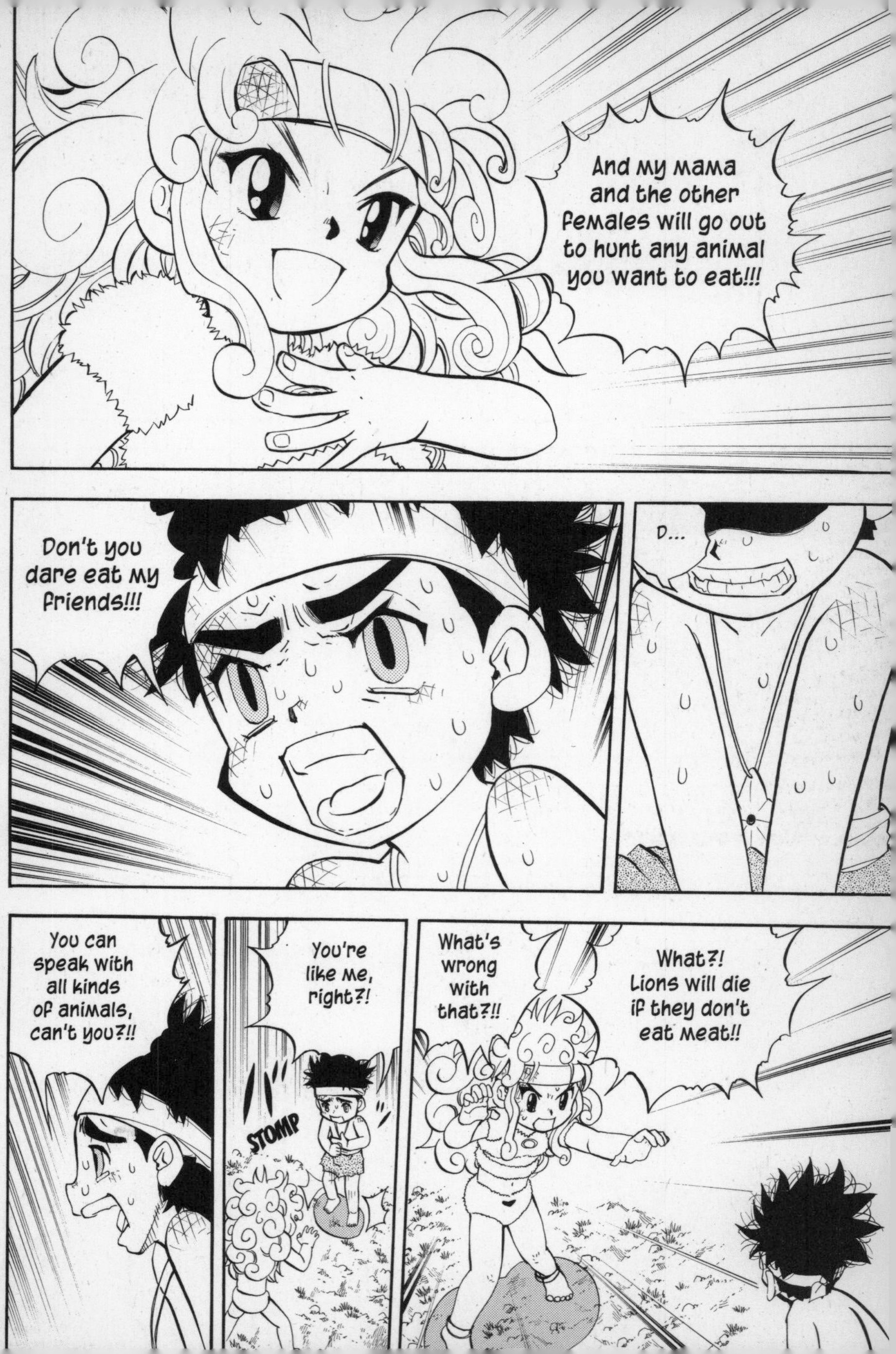
And my mama and the other females will go out to hunt any animal you want to eat!!!
D...
Don't you dare eat my friends!!!
What?! Lions will die if they don't eat meat!!
What's wrong with that?!!
You're like me, right?!
STOMP
You can speak with all kinds of animals, can't you?!!

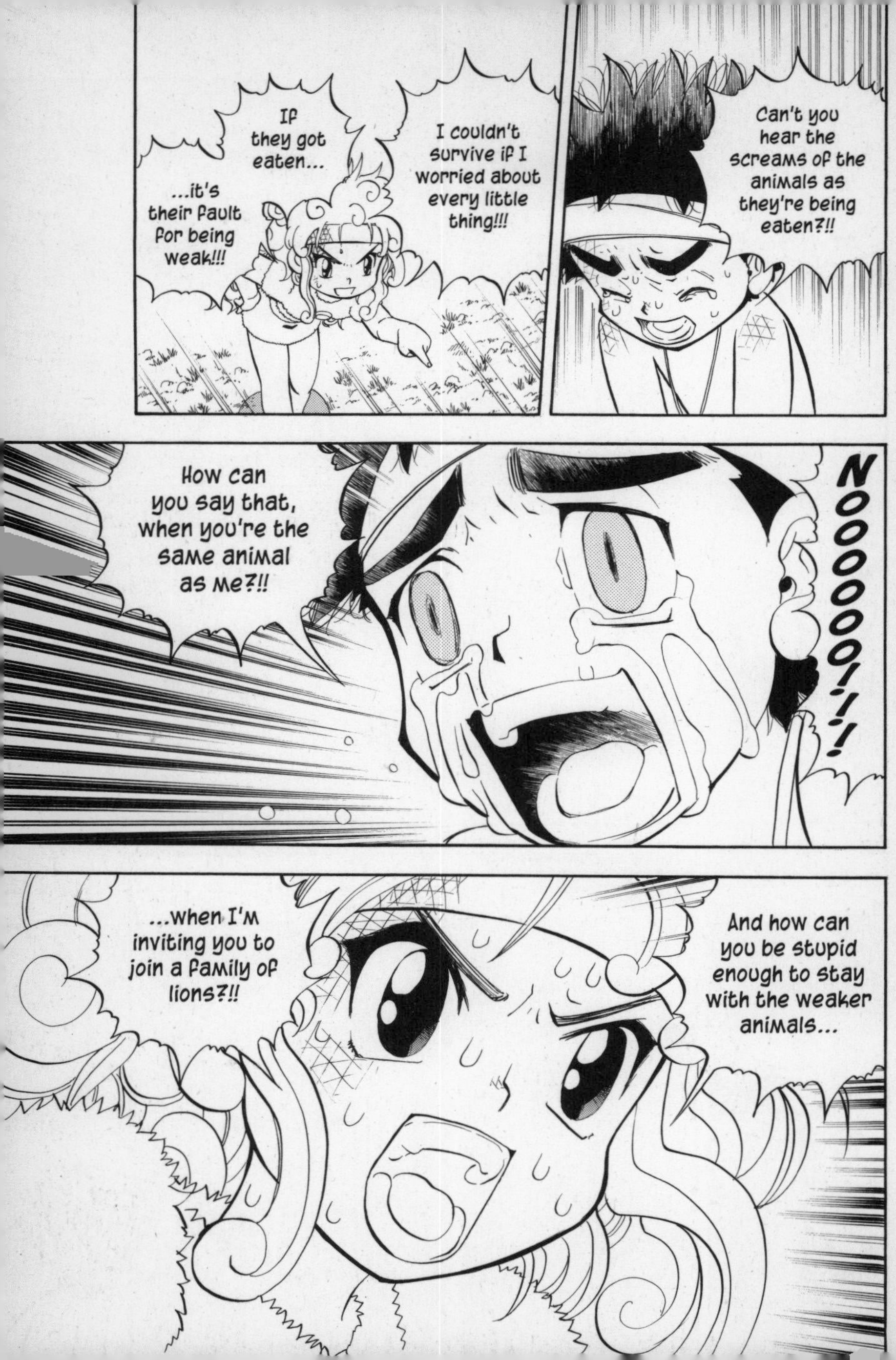
Can't you hear the screams of the animals as they're being eaten?!!
I couldn't survive if I worried about every little thing!!!
If they got eaten...
...it's their fault for being weak!!!
NOOOOOOO!!!
How can you say that, when you're the same animal as me?!!
And how can you be stupid enough to stay with the weaker animals...
...when I'm inviting you to join a family of lions?!!

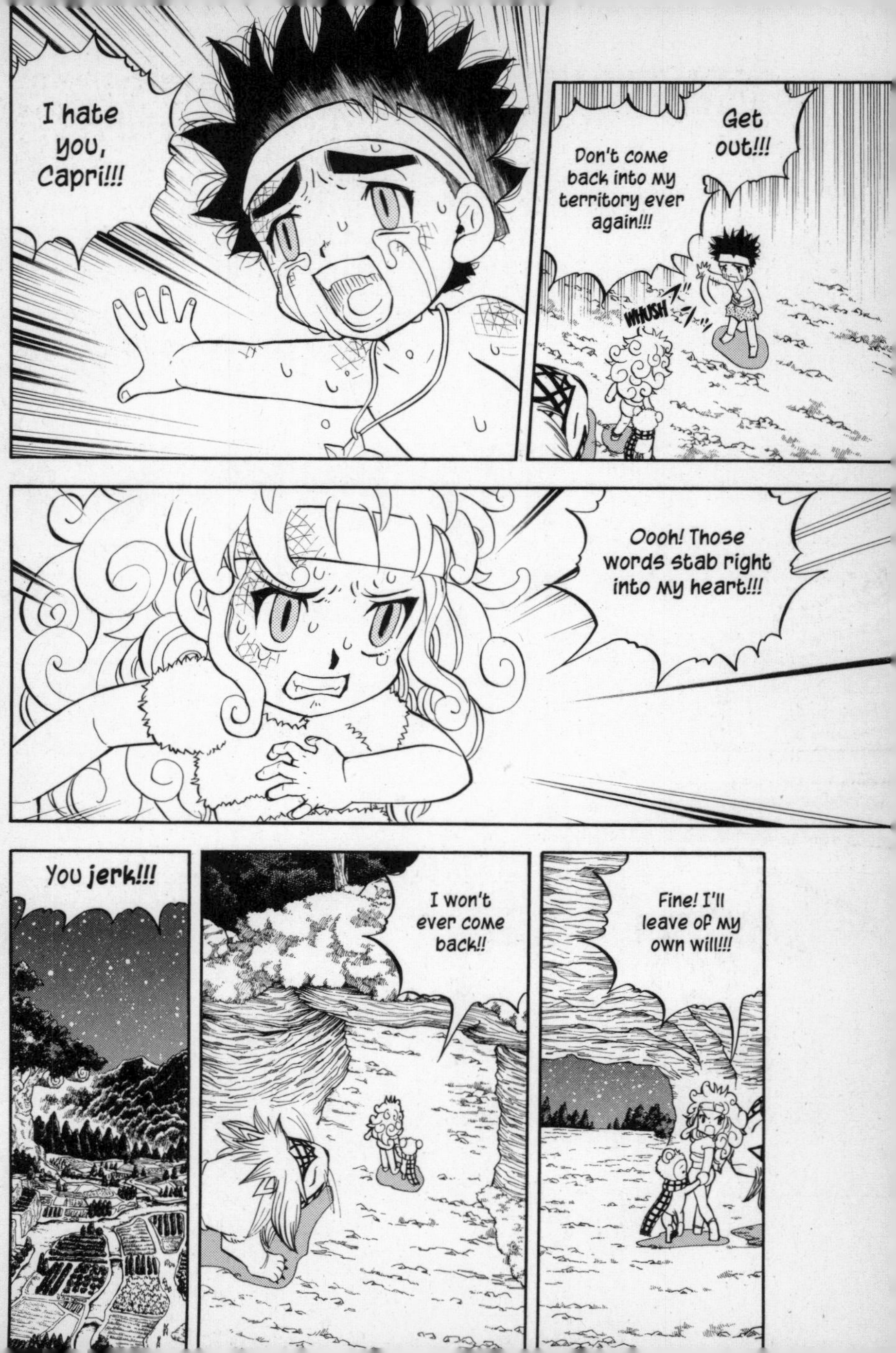
Get out!!!
Don't come back into my territory ever again!!!
WHUSH
I hate you, Capri!!!
Oooh! Those words stab right into my heart!!!
Fine! I'll leave of my own will!!!
I won't ever come back!!
You jerk!!!

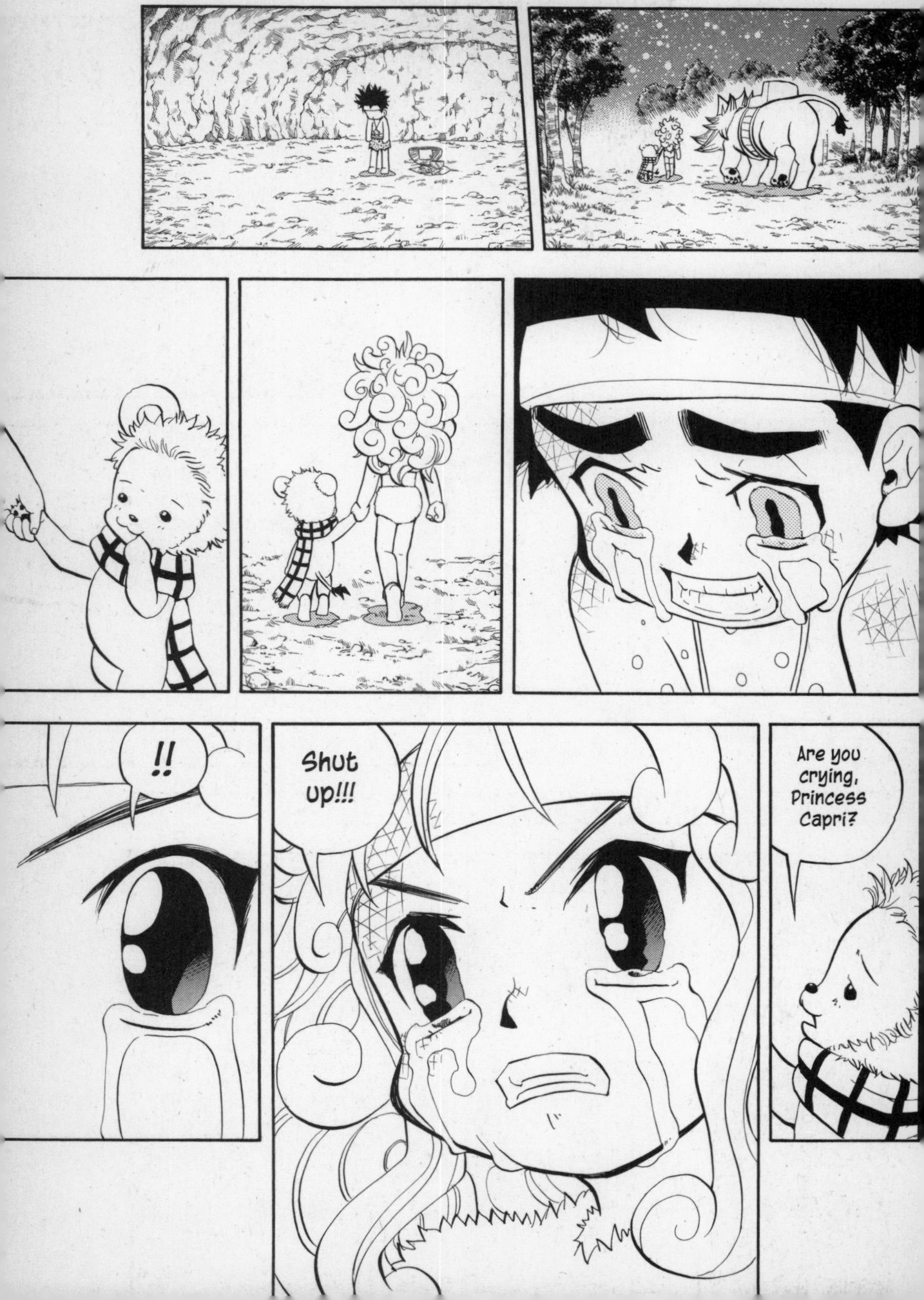
Are you crying, Princess Capri?
Shut up!!!
!!

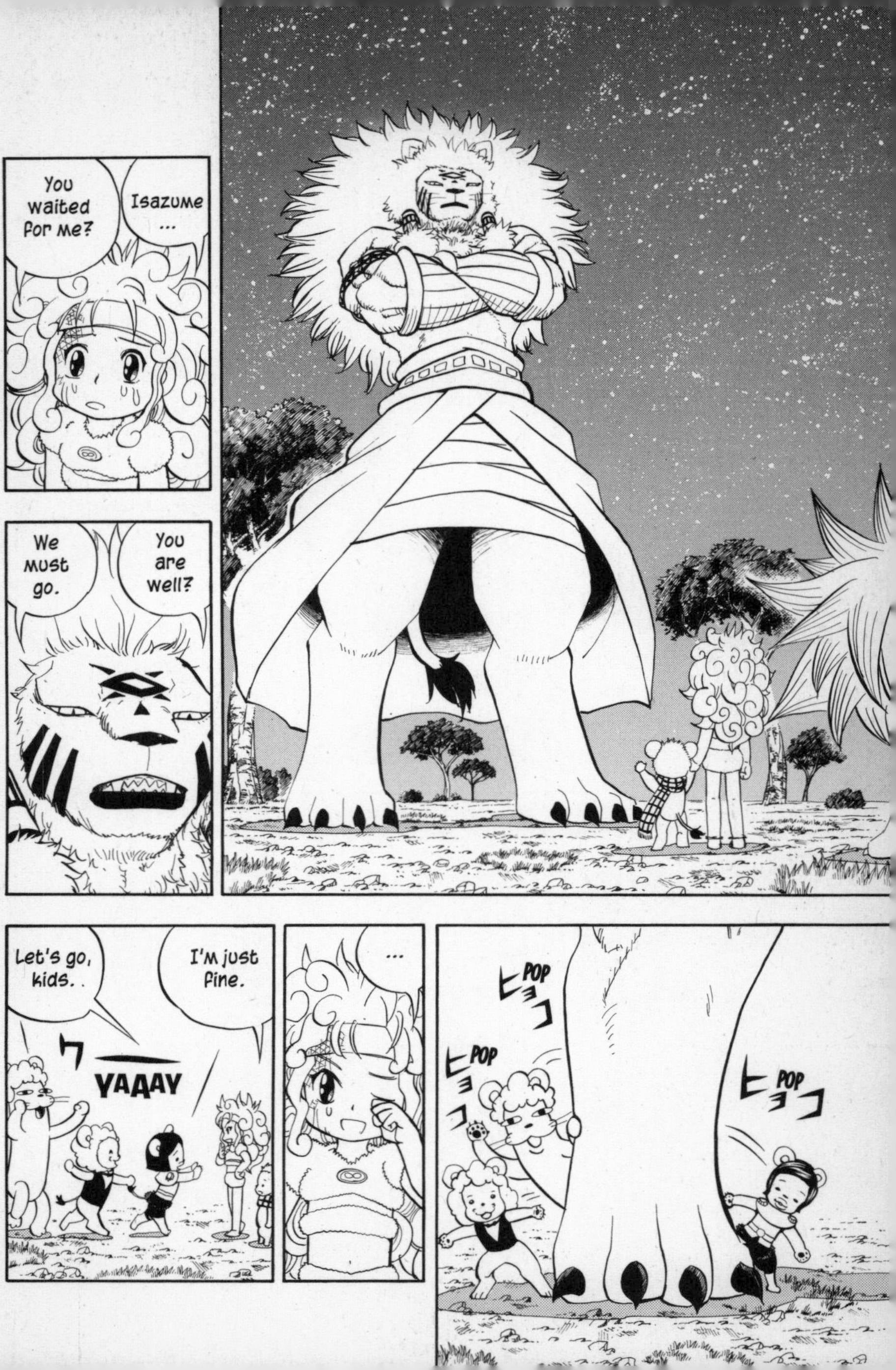
Isazume ...
You waited for me?
You are well?
We must go.
ヒョコ POP
ヒョコ POP
ヒョコ POP
...
I'm just fine.
Let's go, kids..
ワ YAAAY

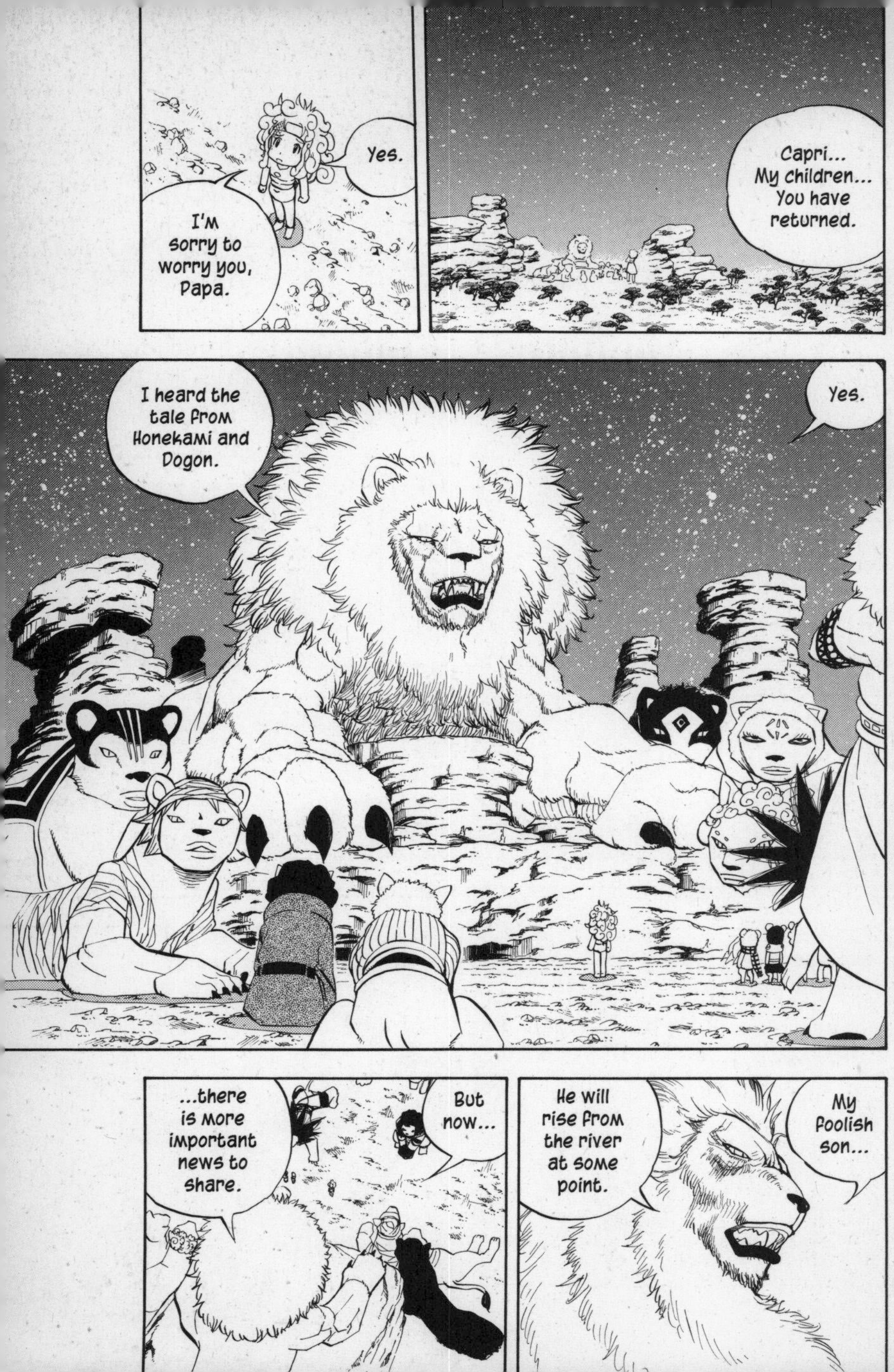
Capri... My children... You have returned.
Yes.
I'm sorry to worry you, Papa.
I heard the tale from Honekami and Dogon.
Yes.
My foolish son...
He will rise from the river at some point.
But now...
...there is more important news to share.

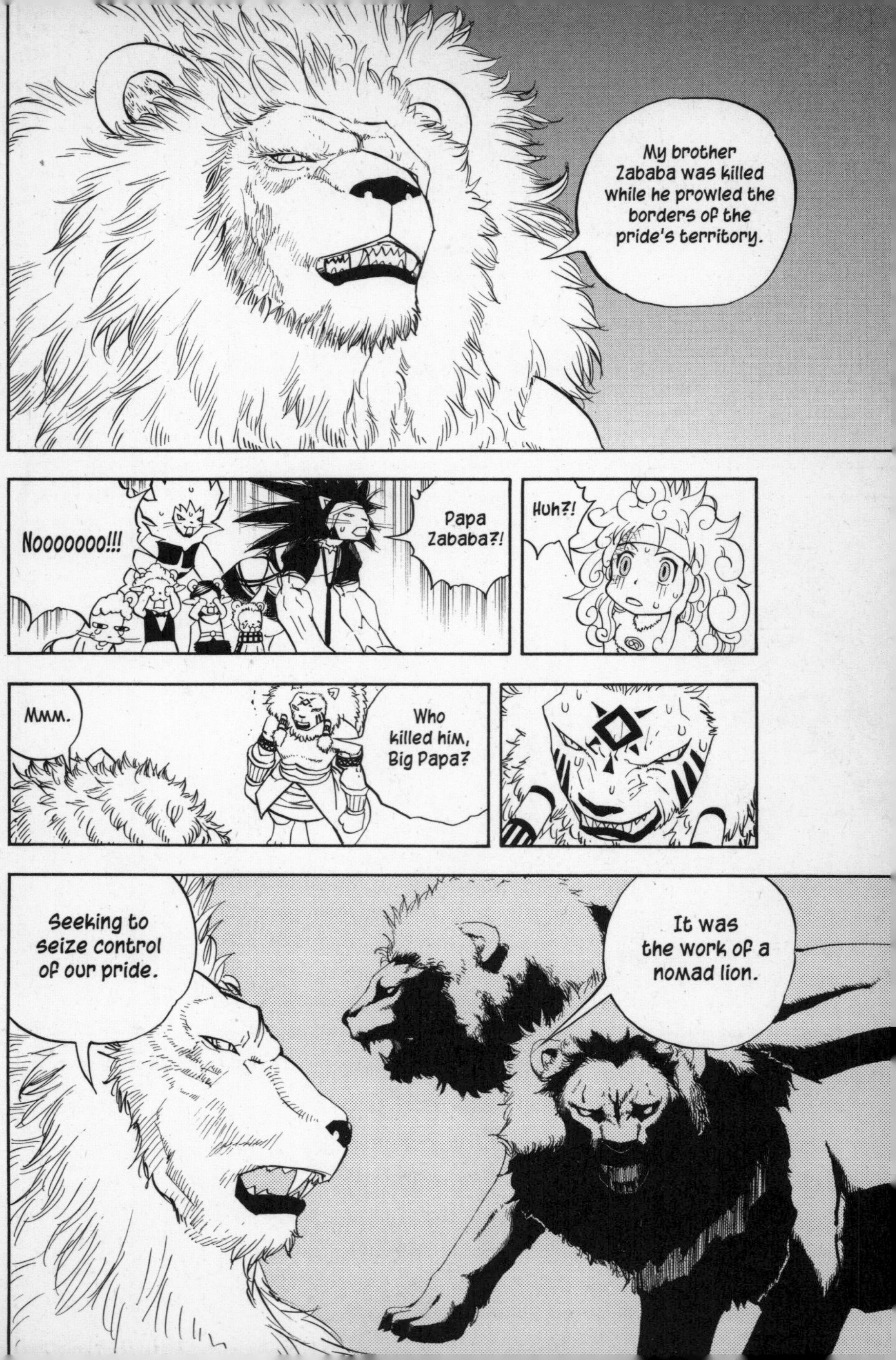
My brother Zababa was killed while he prowled the borders of the pride's territory.
Huh?!
Papa Zababa?!
Nooooooo!!!
Who killed him, Big Papa?
Mmm.
It was the work of a nomad lion.
Seeking to seize control of our pride.

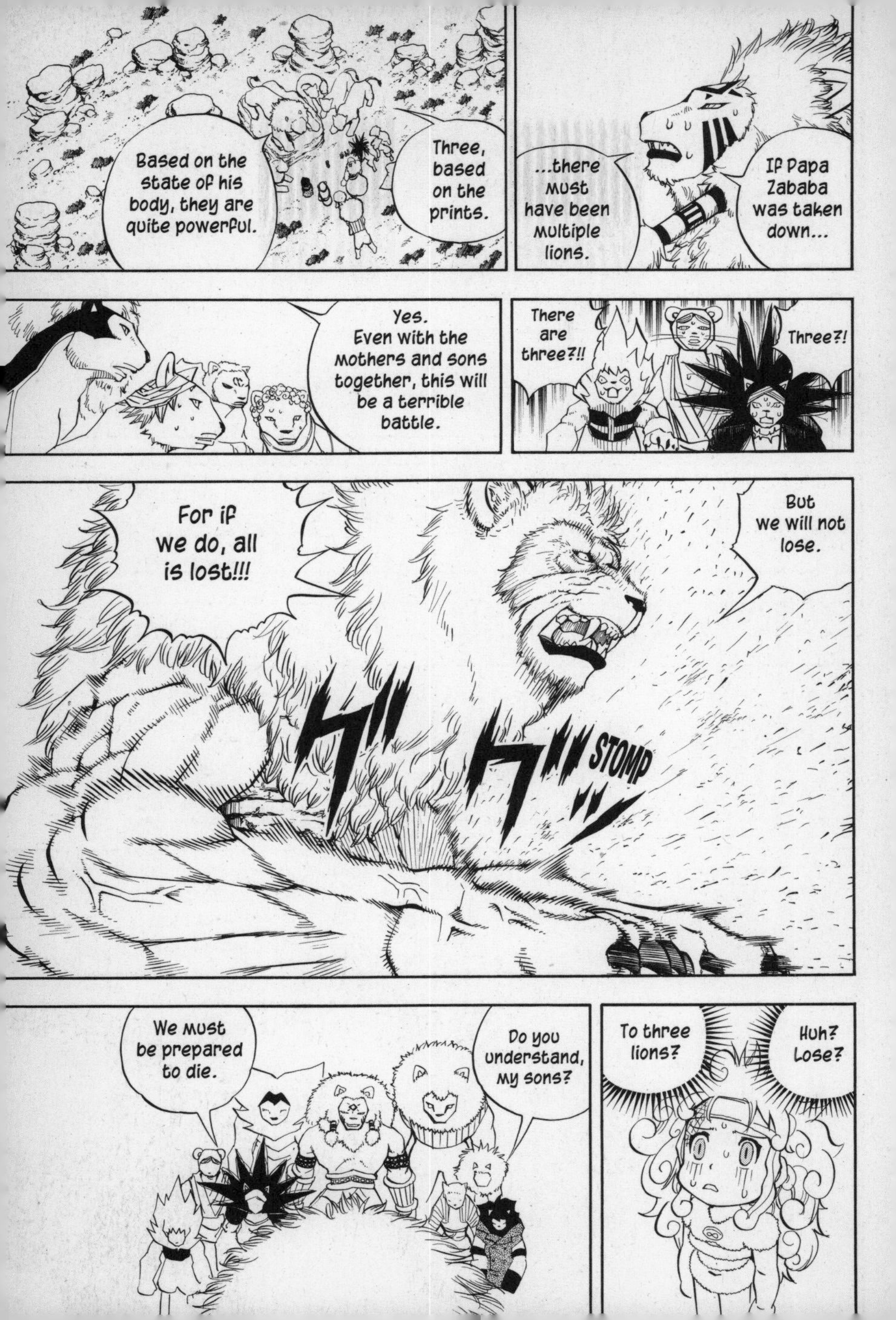
If Papa Zababa was taken down...
...there must have been multiple lions.
Three, based on the prints.
Based on the state of his body, they are quite powerful.
Three?!
There are three?!!
Yes. Even with the mothers and sons together, this will be a terrible battle.
But we will not lose.
For if we do, all is lost!!!
STOMP
Huh? Lose?
To three lions?
Do you understand, my sons?
We must be prepared to die.

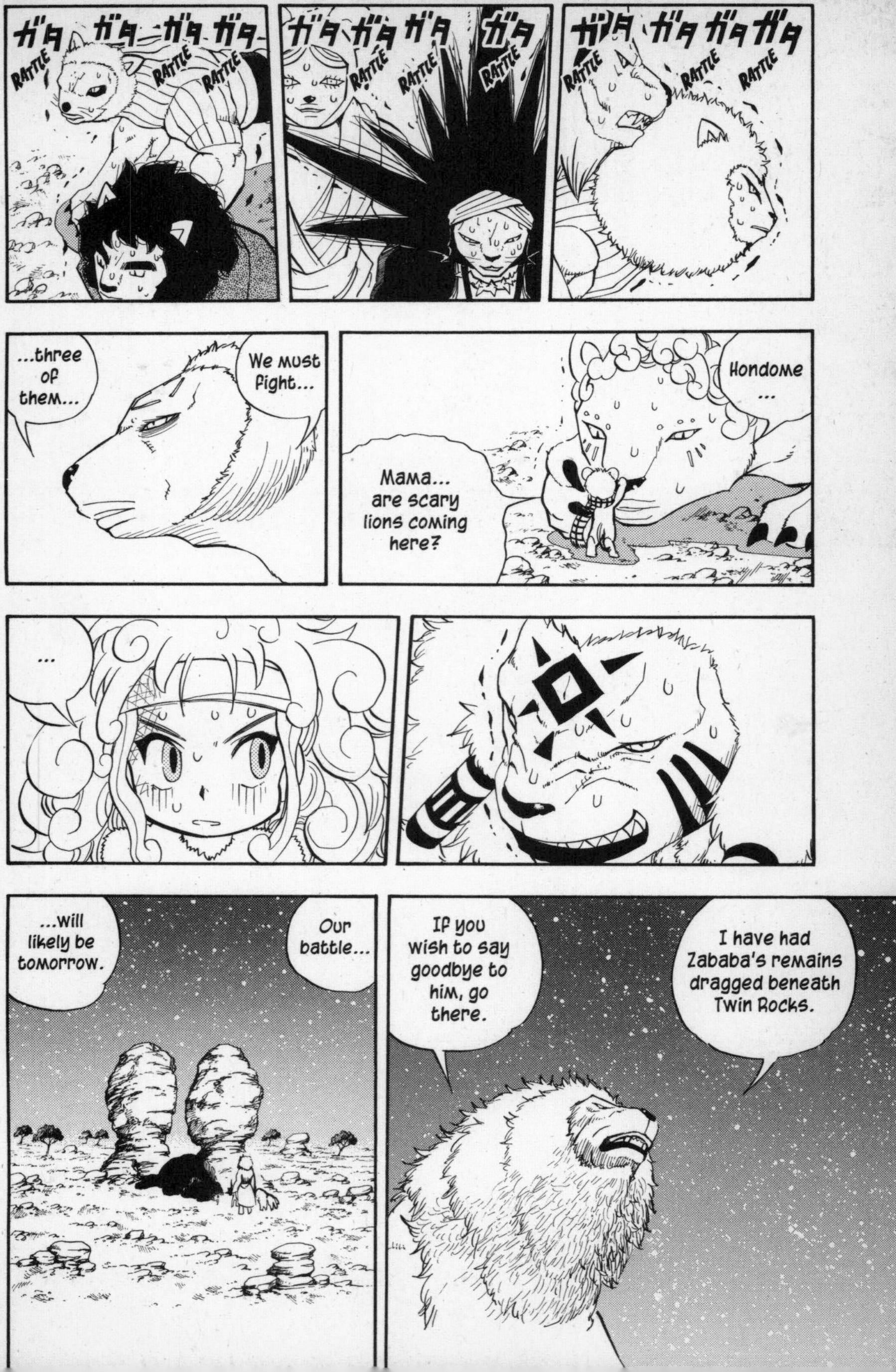
ガタ ガタ ガタ ガタ
RATTLE RATTLE RATTLE
ガタ ガタ ガタ ガタ
RATTLE RATTLE RATTLE
ガタ ガタ ガタ ガタ
RATTLE RATTLE RATTLE
Hondome ...
Mama... are scary lions coming here?
We must fight...
...three of them...
...
I have had Zababa's remains dragged beneath Twin Rocks.
If you wish to say goodbye to him, go there.
Our battle...
...will likely be tomorrow.

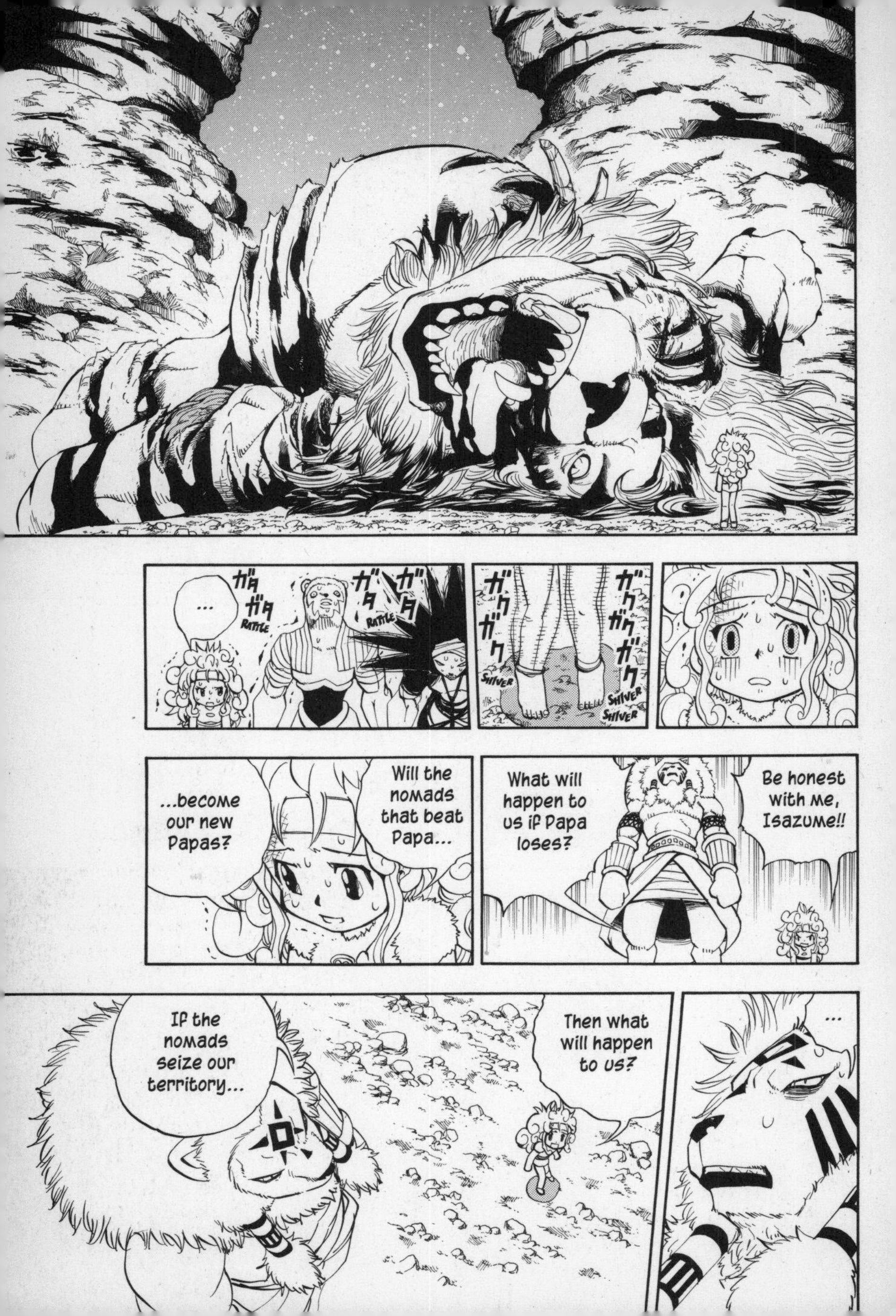

ガクガクガク
SHIVER
SHIVER
ガク
ガク
ガク
SHIVER
ガタ
ガタ
RATTLE
...
ガタ
ガタ
RATTLE
Be honest with me, Isazume!!
What will happen to us if Papa loses?
Will the nomads that beat Papa...
...become our new Papas?
...
Then what will happen to us?
If the nomads seize our territory...

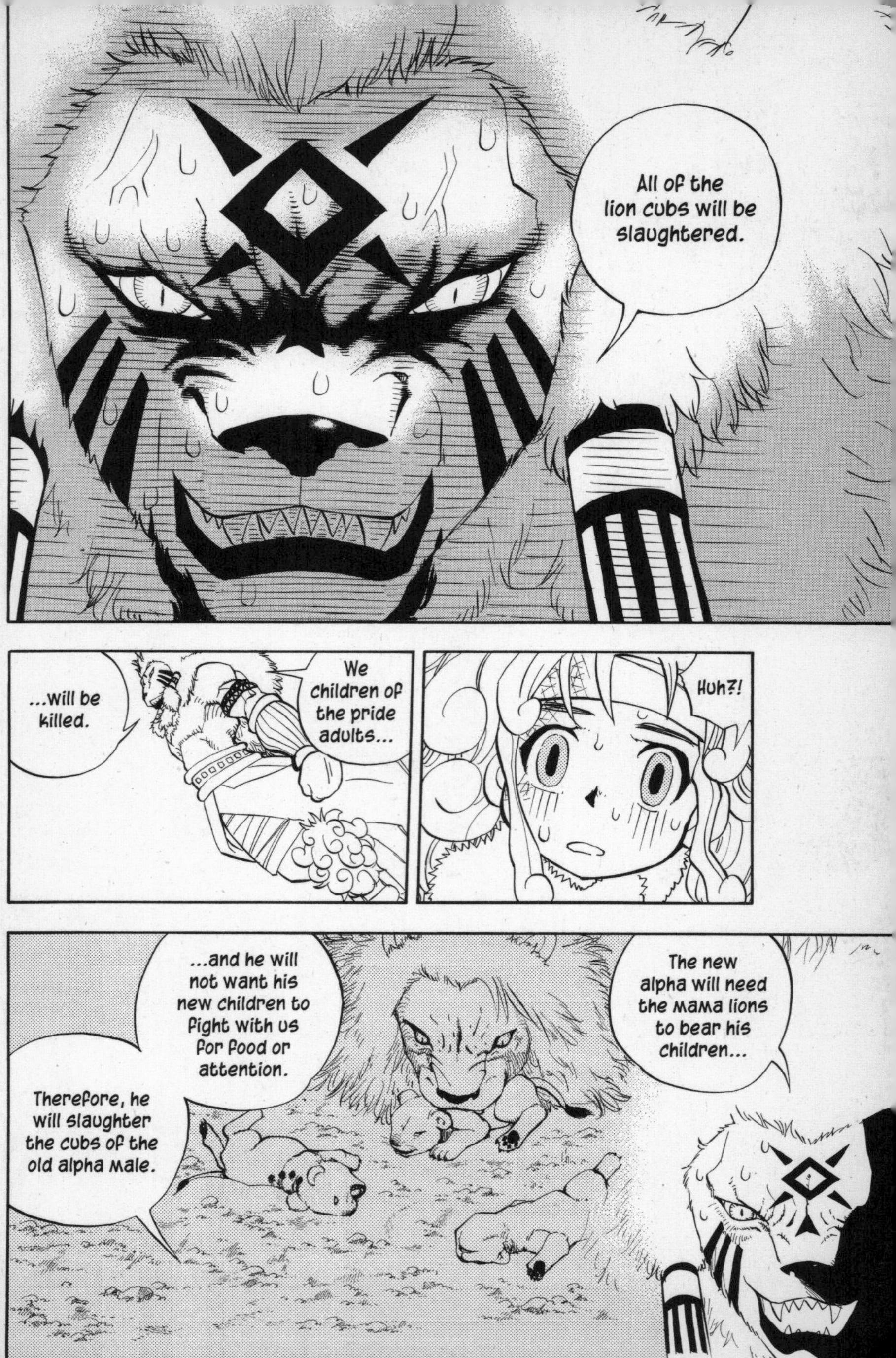
All of the lion cubs will be slaughtered.
Huh?!
We children of the pride adults...
...will be killed.
The new alpha will need the mama lions to bear his children...
...and he will not want his new children to fight with us for food or attention.
Therefore, he will slaughter the cubs of the old alpha male.

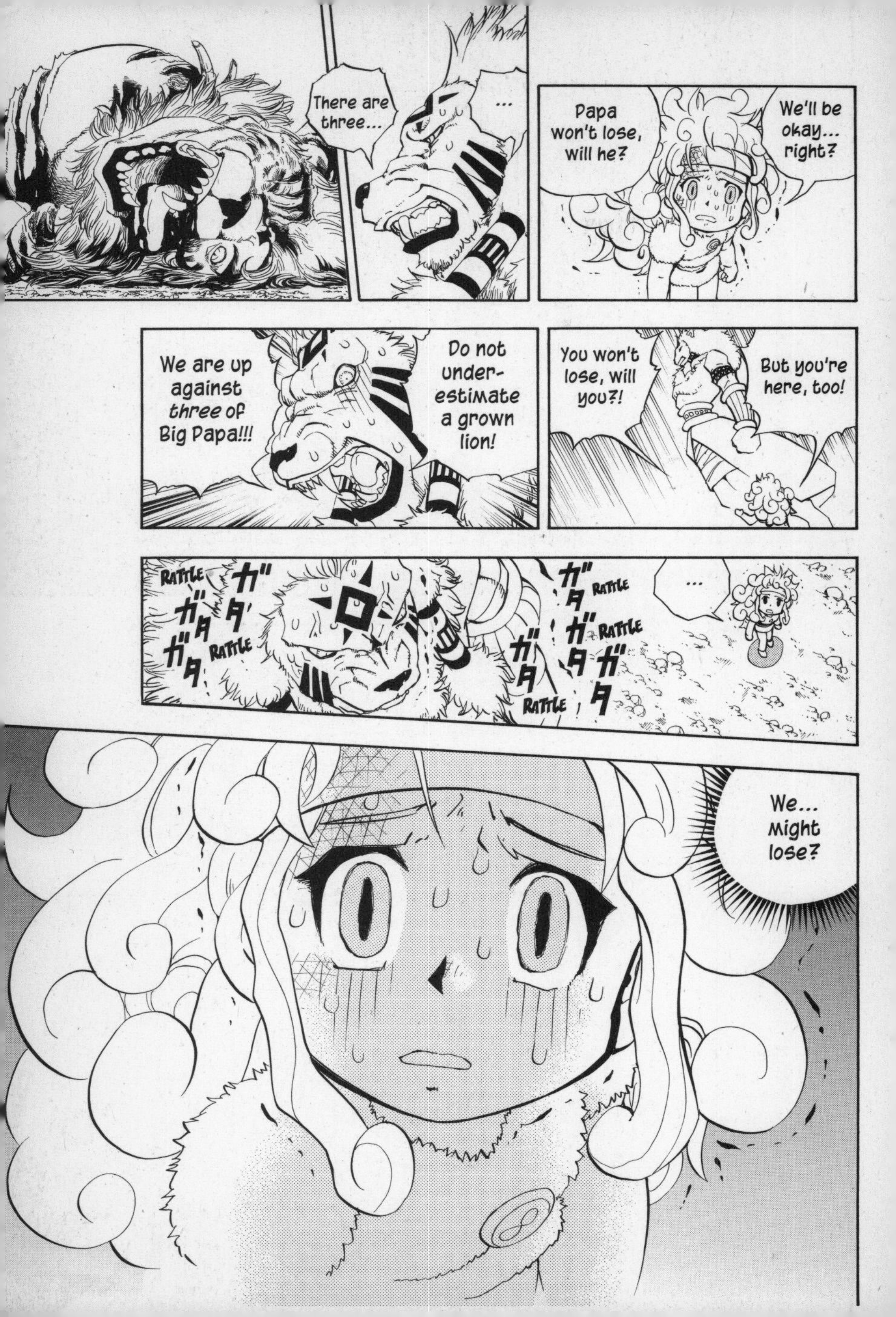
We'll be okay... right?
Papa won't lose, will he?
...
There are three...
But you're here, too!
You won't lose, will you?!
Do not under-estimate a grown lion!
We are up against three of Big Papa!!!
...
ガタ RATTLE
ガタ RATTLE
ガタ ガタ
ガタ RATTLE
ガタ RATTLE
ガタ ガタ ガタ RATTLE
RATTLE
We... Might lose?

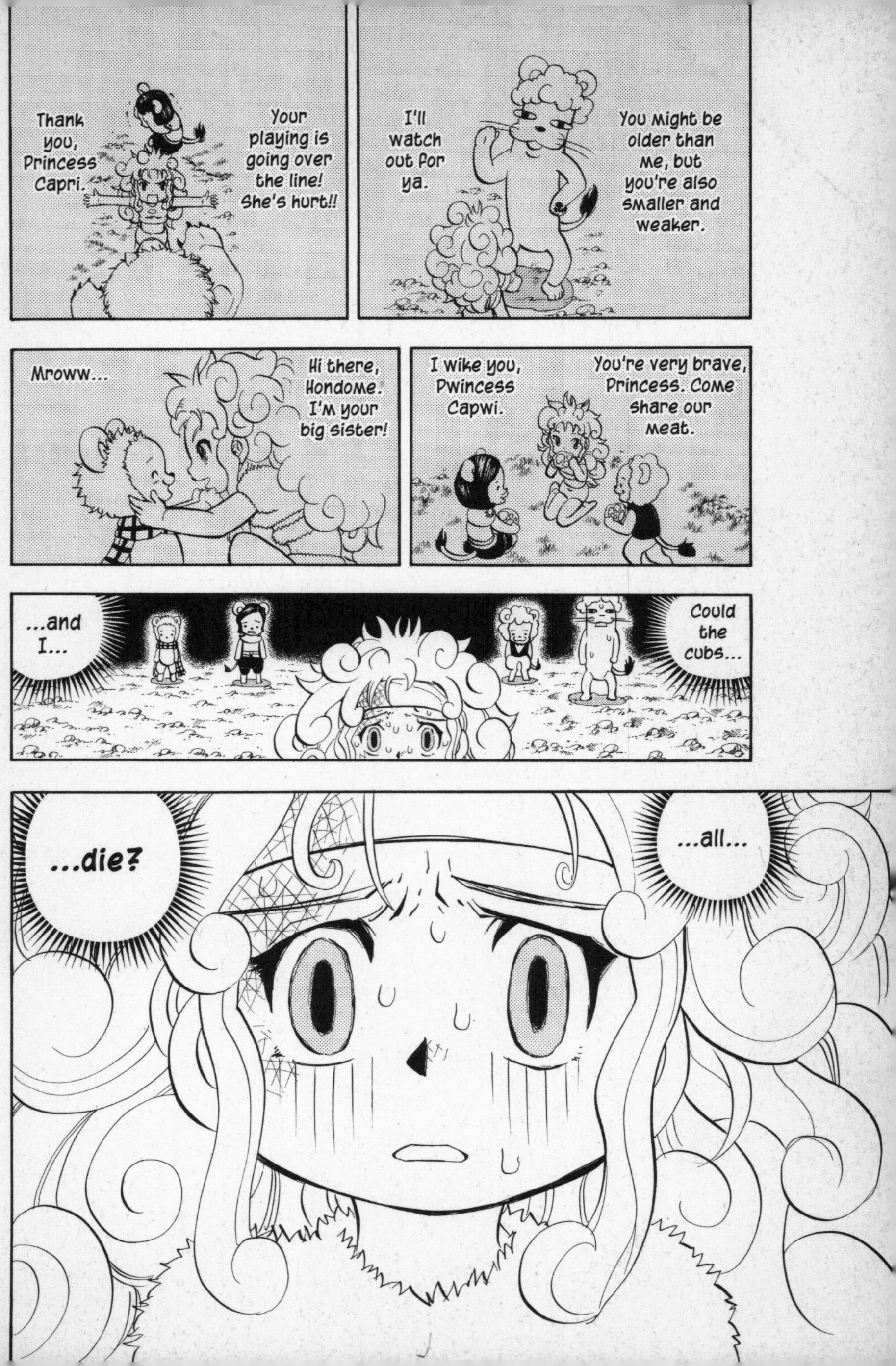
You might be older than me, but you're also smaller and weaker.
I'll watch out for ya.
Your playing is going over the line! She's hurt!!
Thank you, Princess Capri.
You're very brave, Princess. Come share our meat.
I wike you, Pwincess Capwi.
Hi there, Hondome. I'm your big sister!
Mroww...
Could the cubs...
...and I...
...all...
...die?

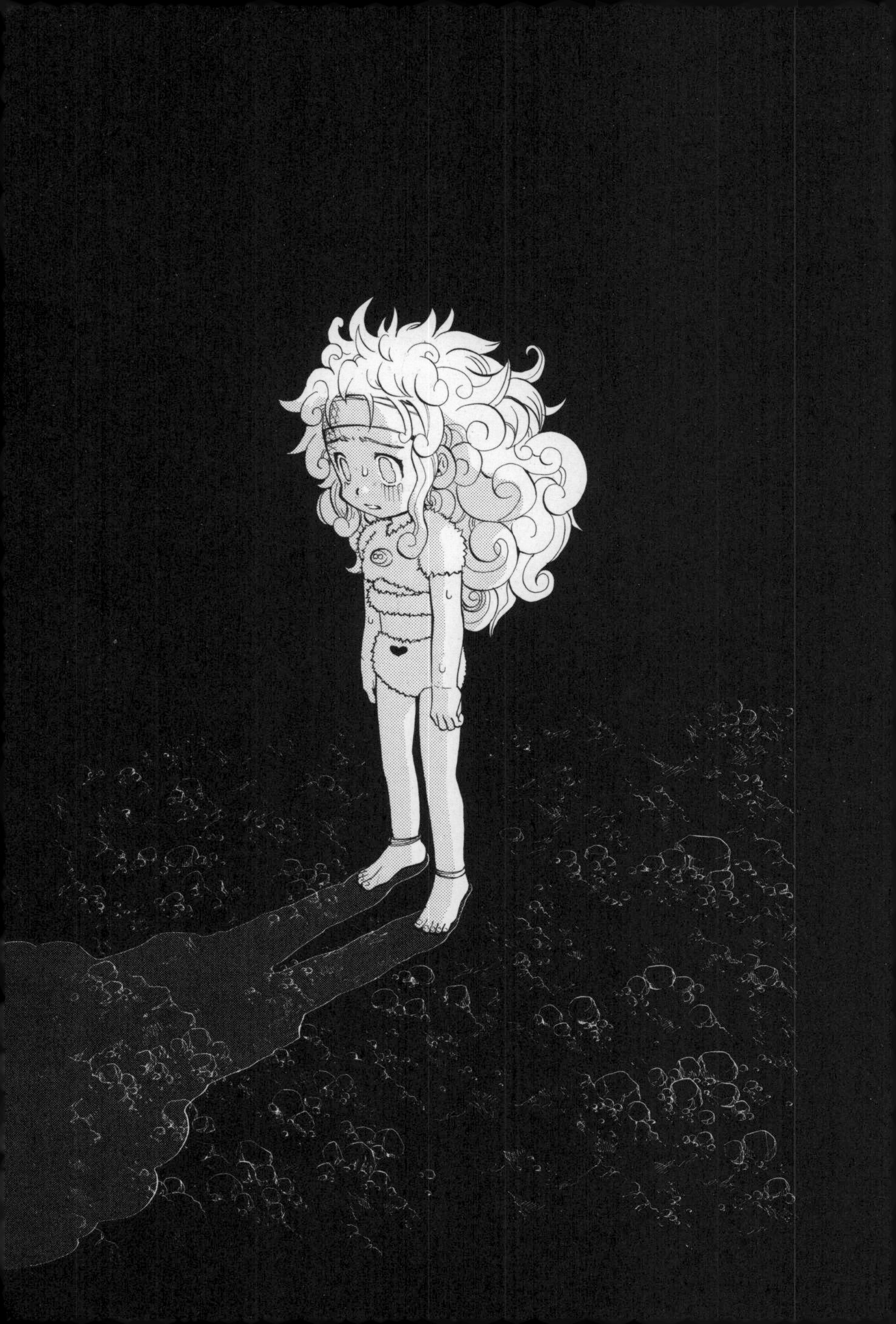

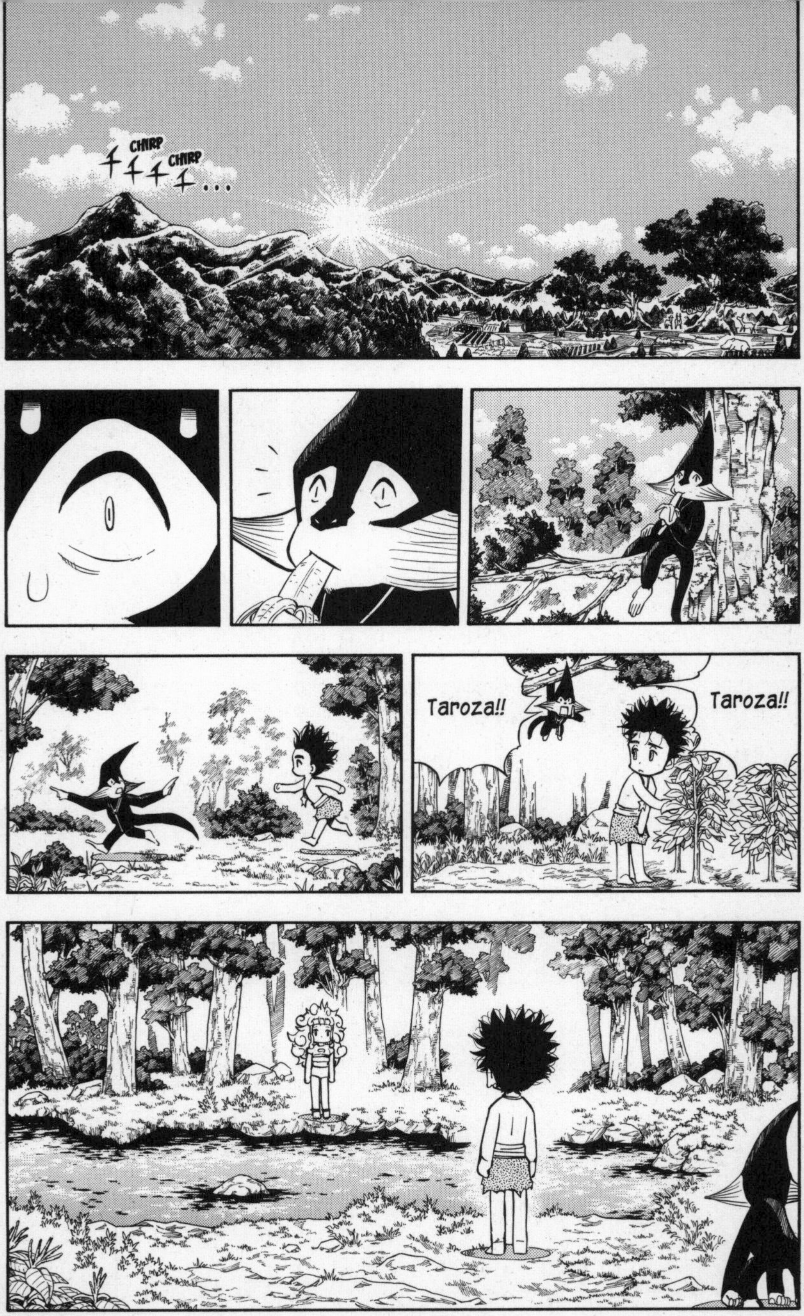

CHIRP
CHIRP
チチチチ...
Taroza!!
Taroza!!

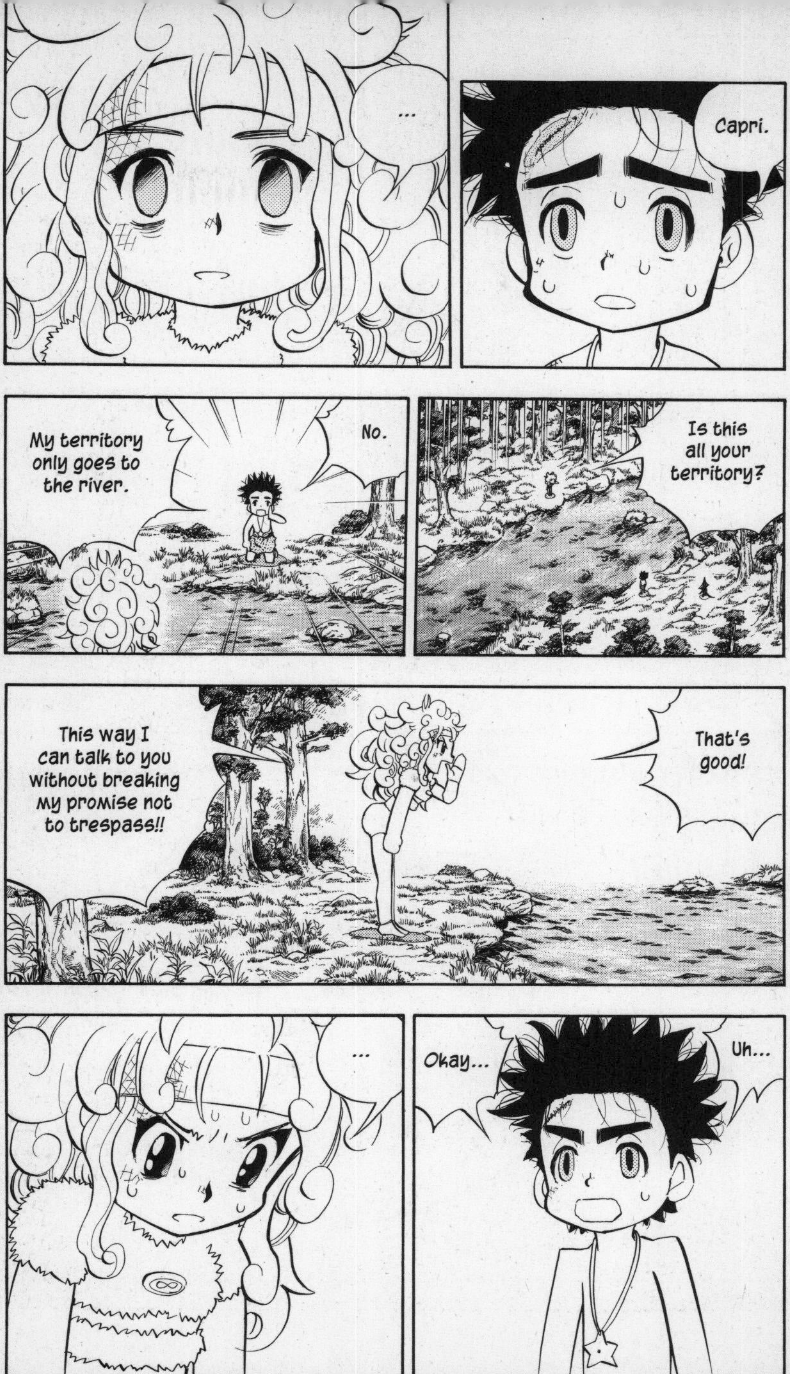
Capri.
...
Is this all your territory?
No.
My territory only goes to the river.
That's good!
This way I can talk to you without breaking my promise not to trespass!!
Uh...
Okay...
...

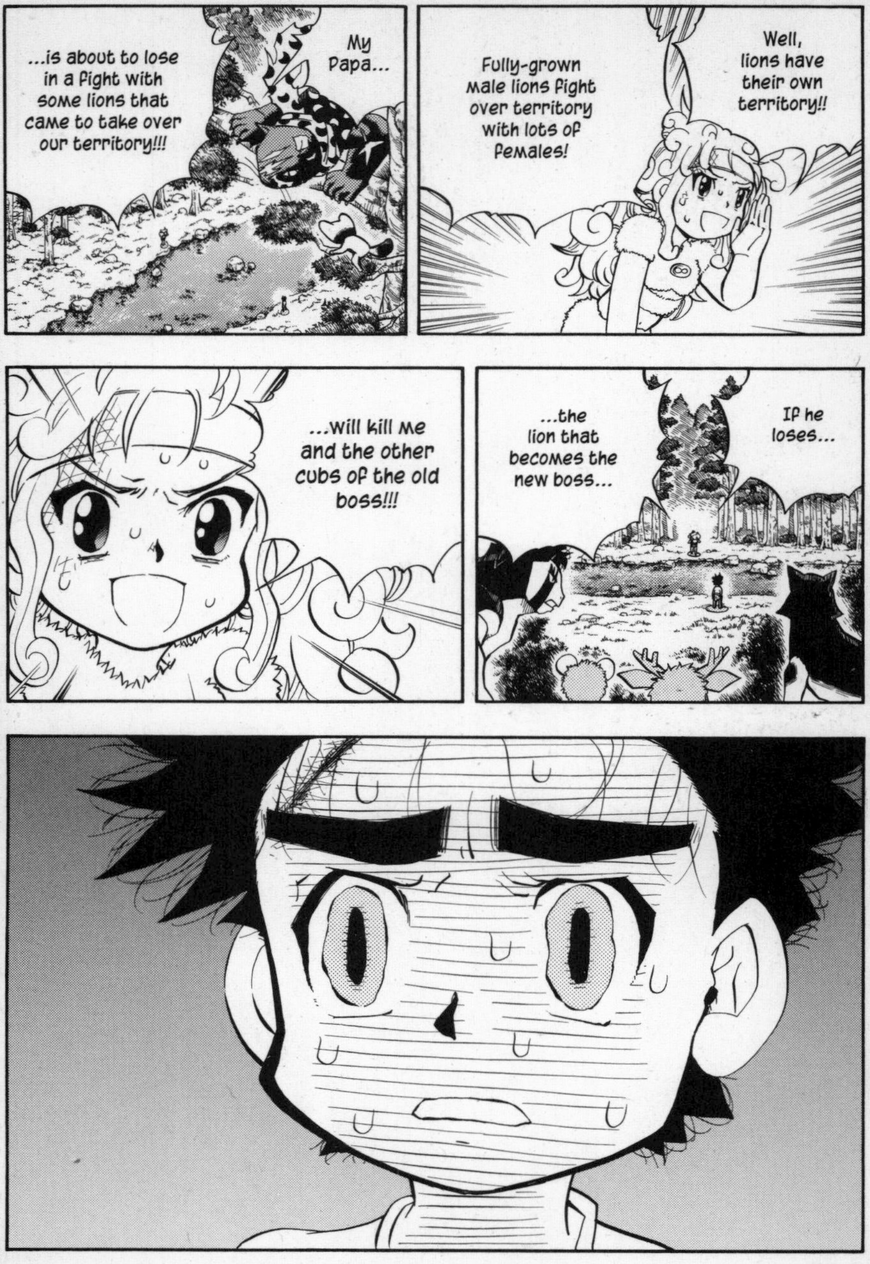
Well, lions have their own territory!!
Fully-grown male lions fight over territory with lots of females!
My Papa...
...is about to lose in a fight with some lions that came to take over our territory!!!
If he loses...
...the lion that becomes the new boss...
...will kill me and the other cubs of the old boss!!!

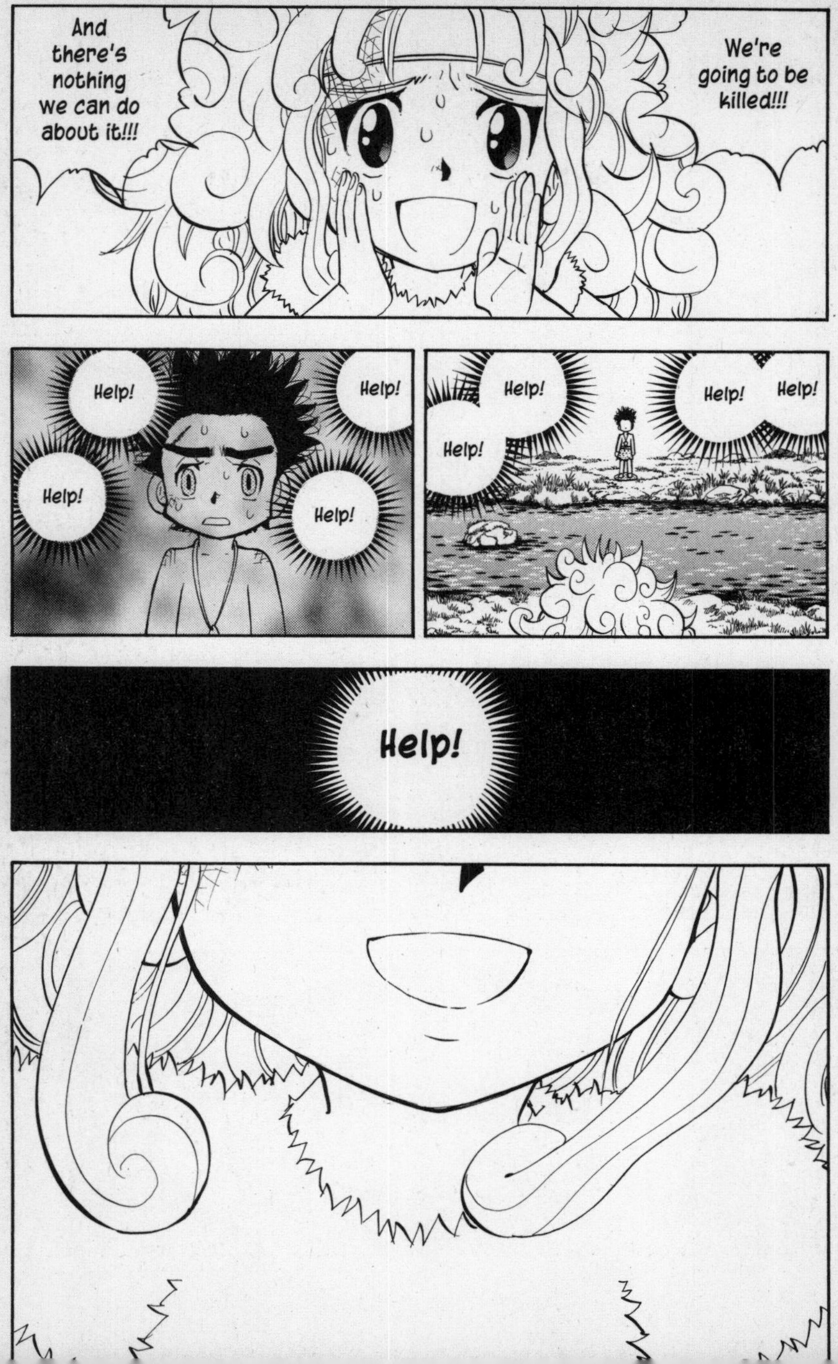
We're going to be killed!!!
And there's nothing we can do about it!!!
Help!
Help!
Help!
Help!
Help!
Help!
Help!
Help!
Help!

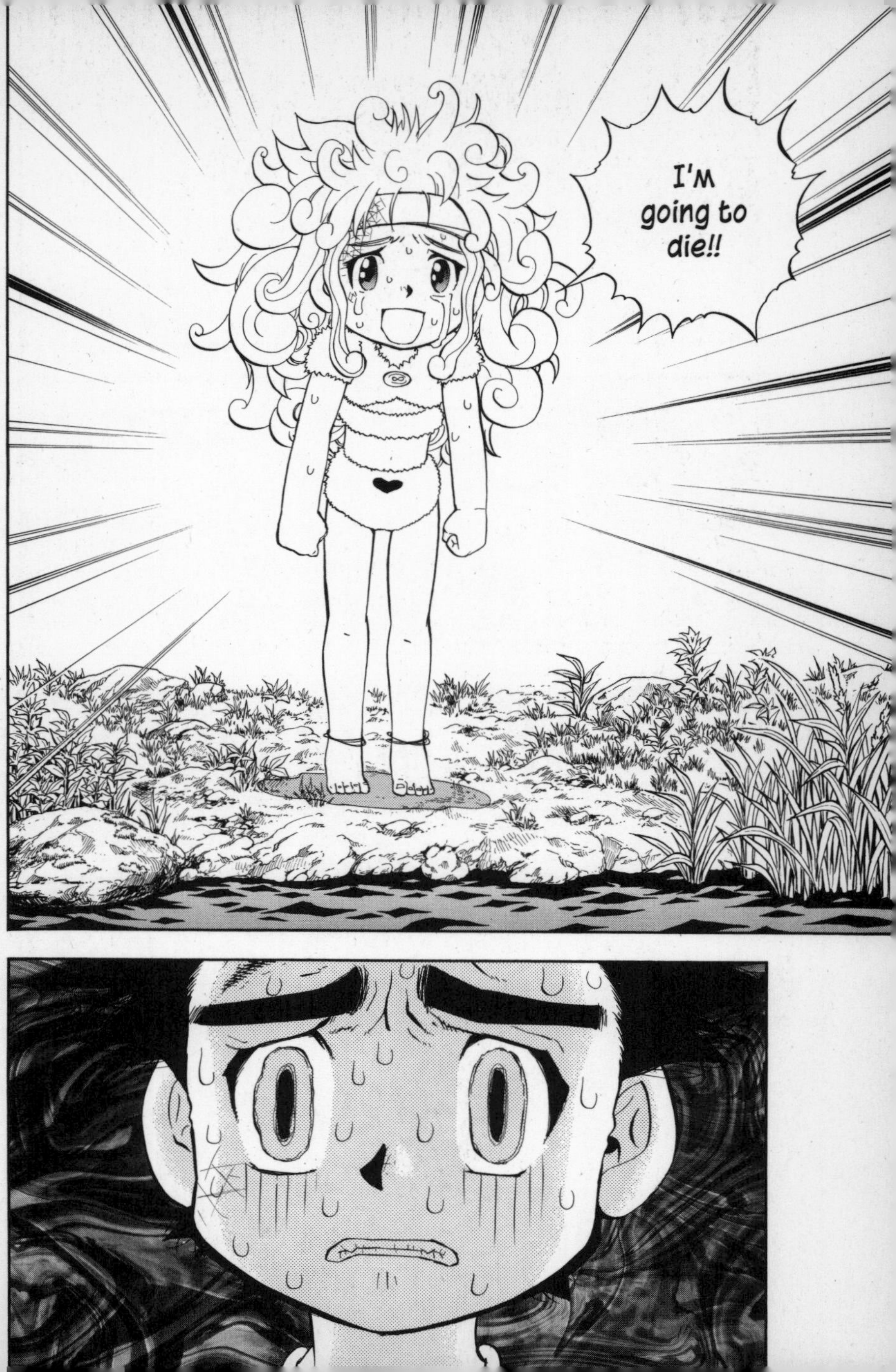
I'M going to die!!

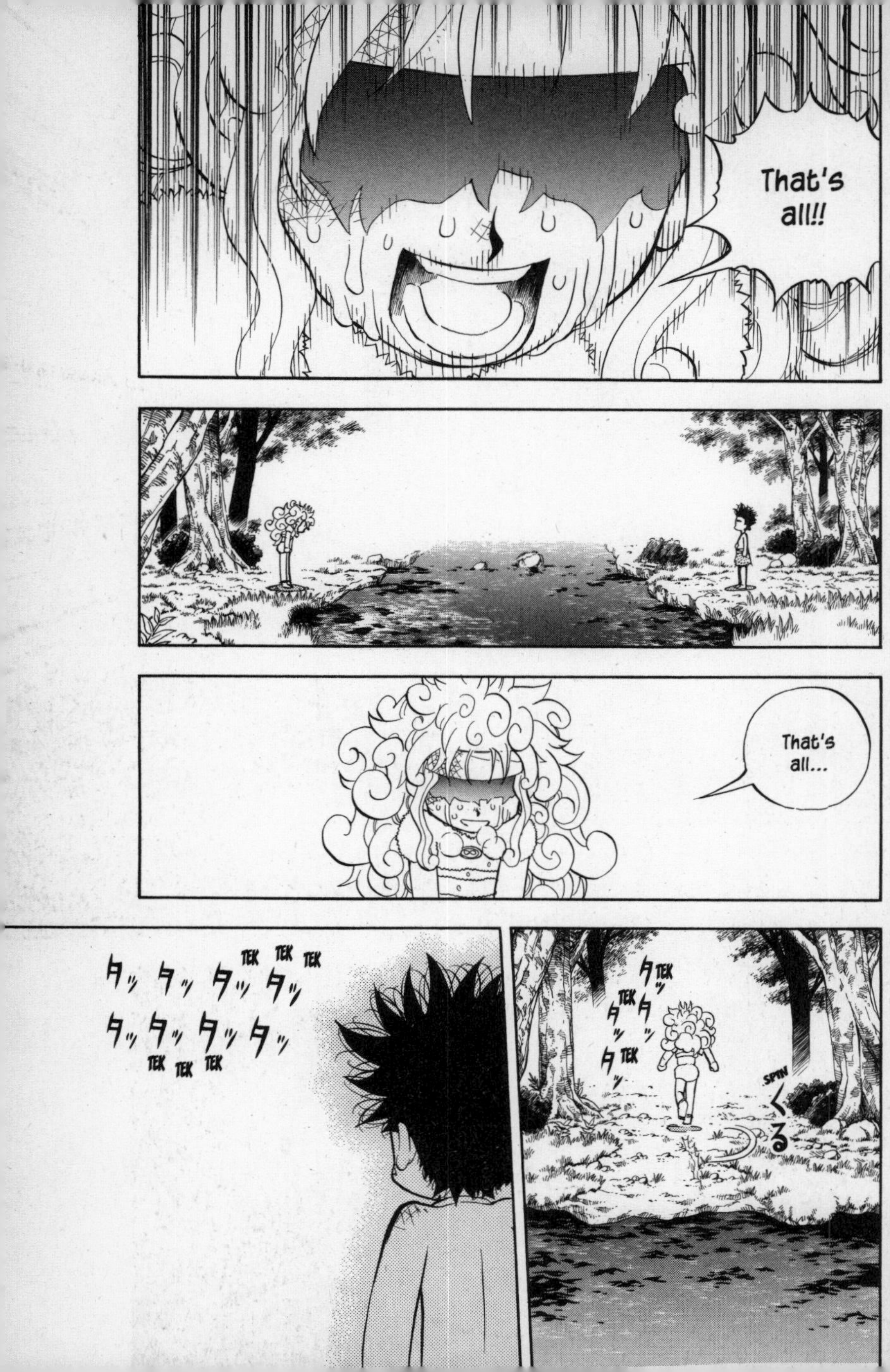
That's all!!
That's all...
タッ TEK
タッ TEK
タッ TEK
SPIN くる
タッ タッ タッ タッ
TEK TEK TEK
タッ タッ タッ タッ
TEK TEK TEK

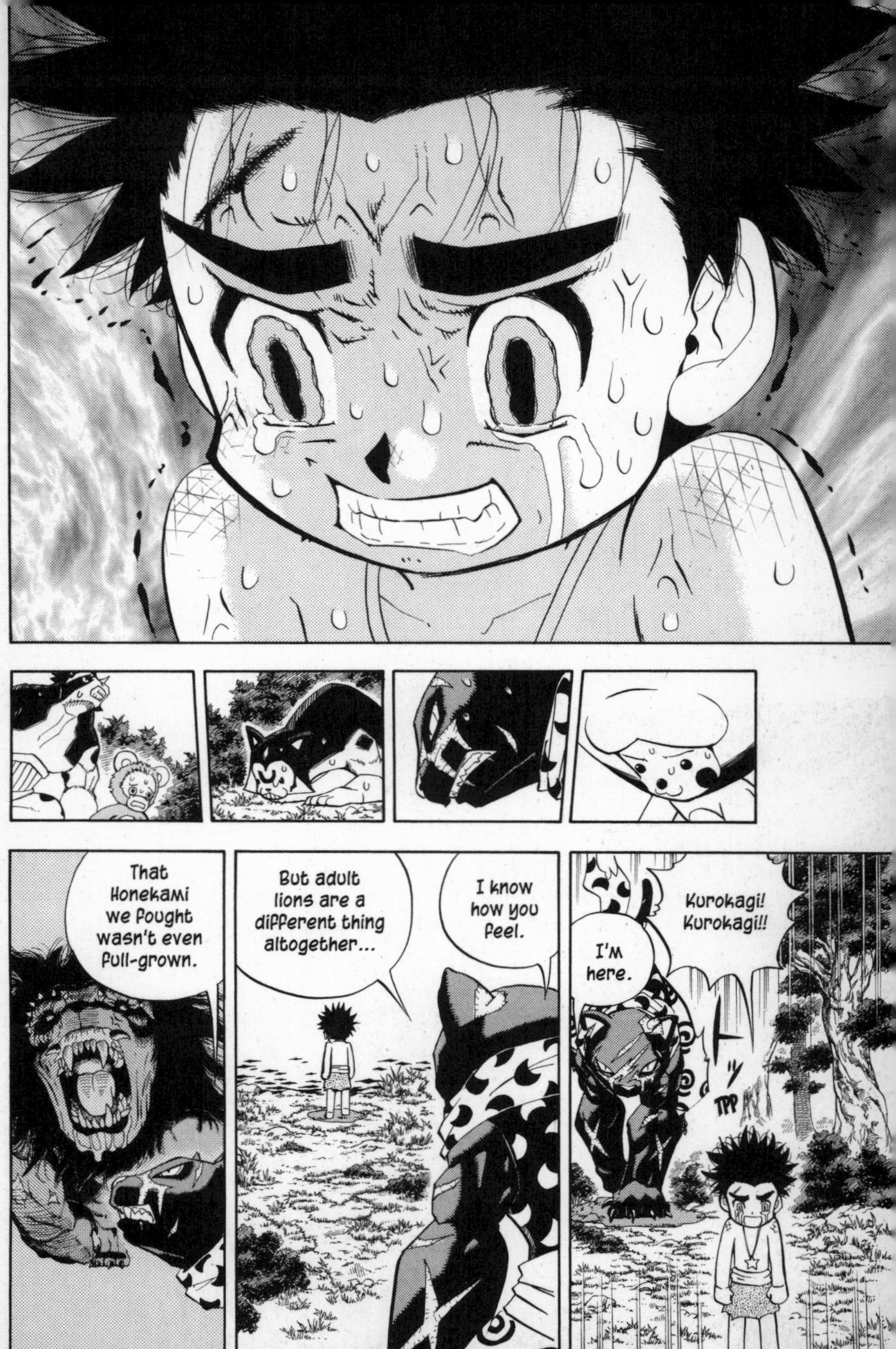
Kurokagi! Kurokagi!!
I'm here.
TPP
I know how you feel.
But adult lions are a different thing altogether...
That Honekami we fought wasn't even full-grown.

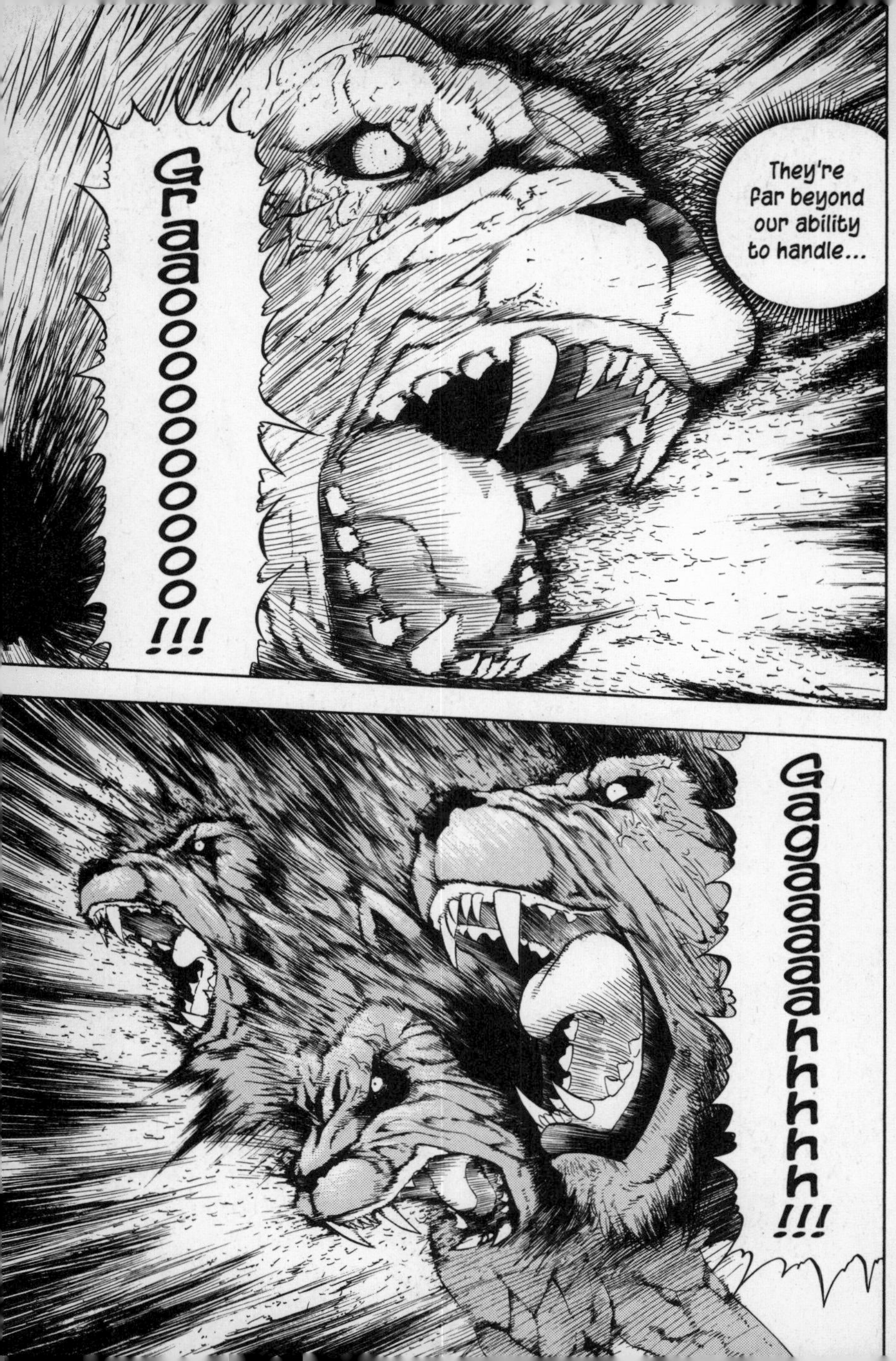
They're far beyond our ability to handle...
Graaooooooooooo!!!
Gaaaaaaahhhhh!!!

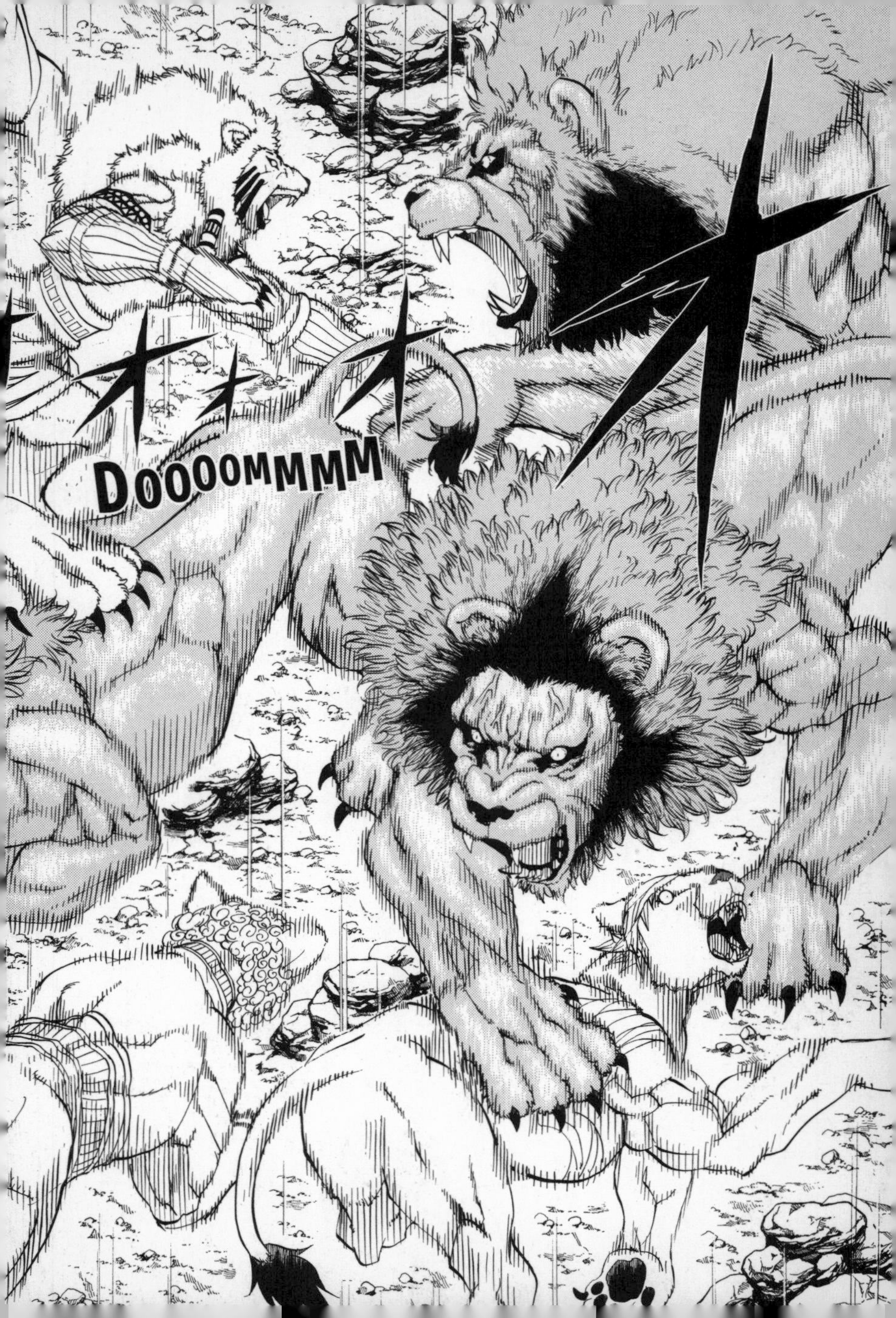
オ
オオオ
DOOOOMMMM

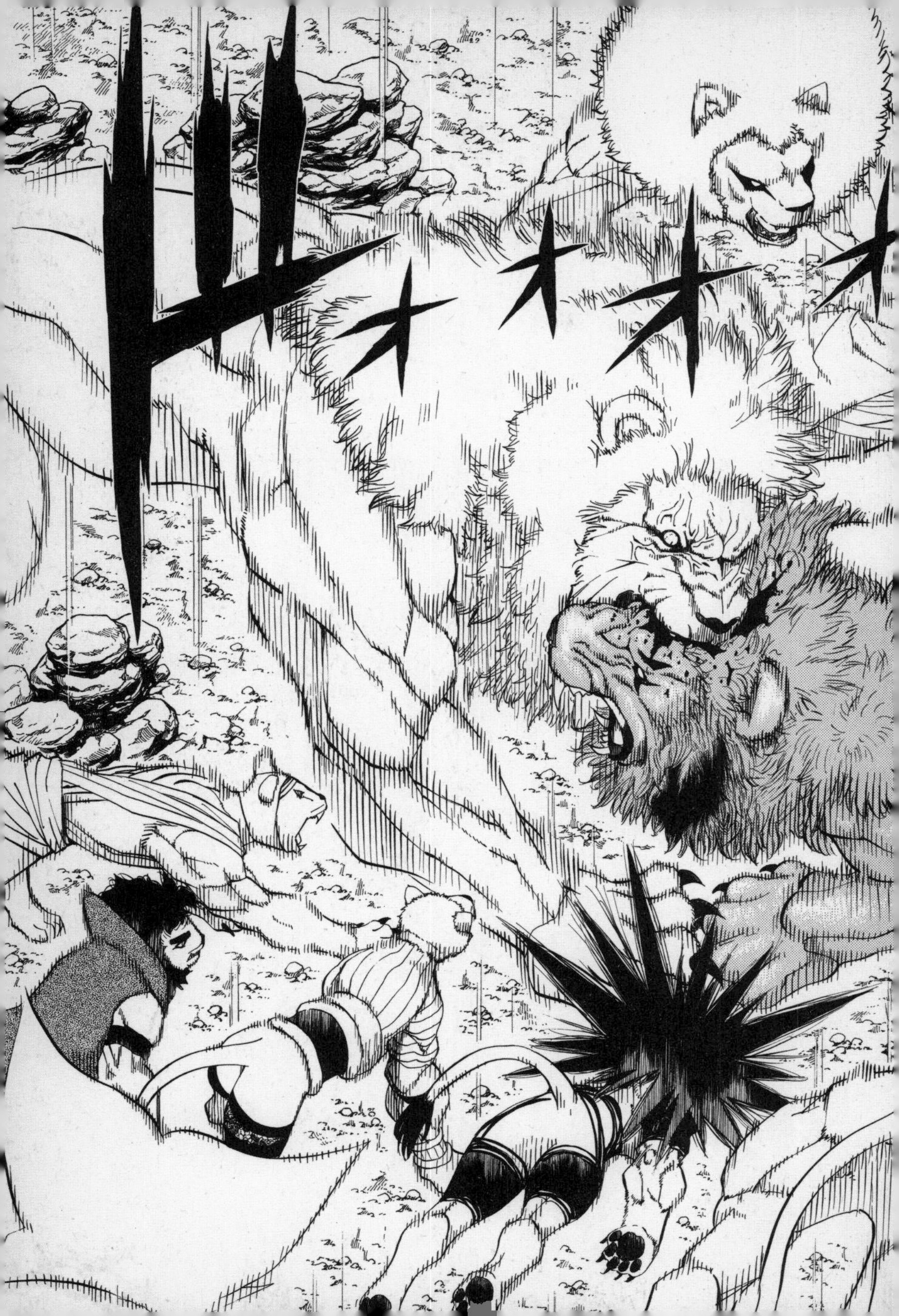
ドォォォォ

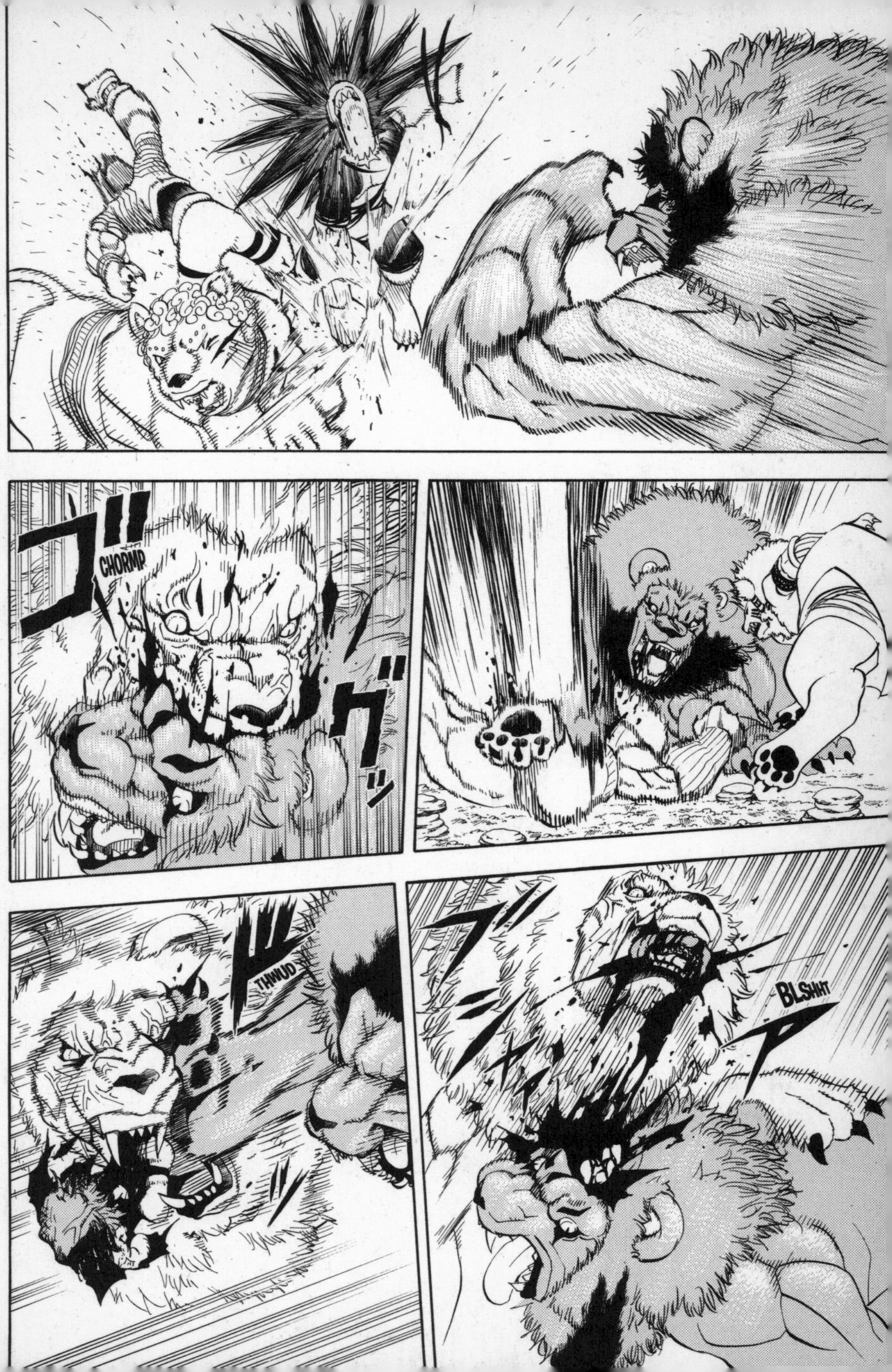
CHORMP
BLSHT
THWUD

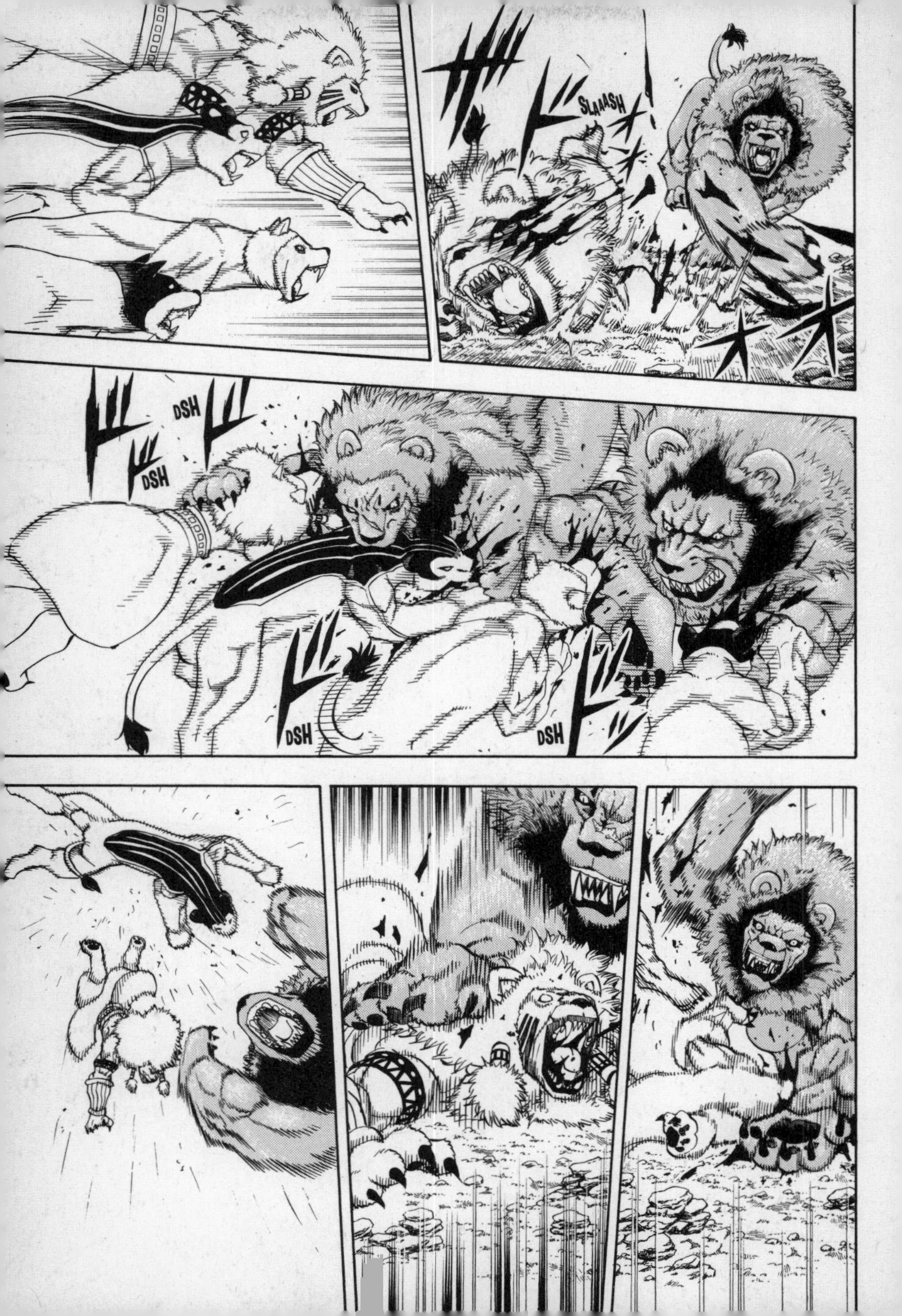
SLAAASH
DSH
DSH
DSH
DSH

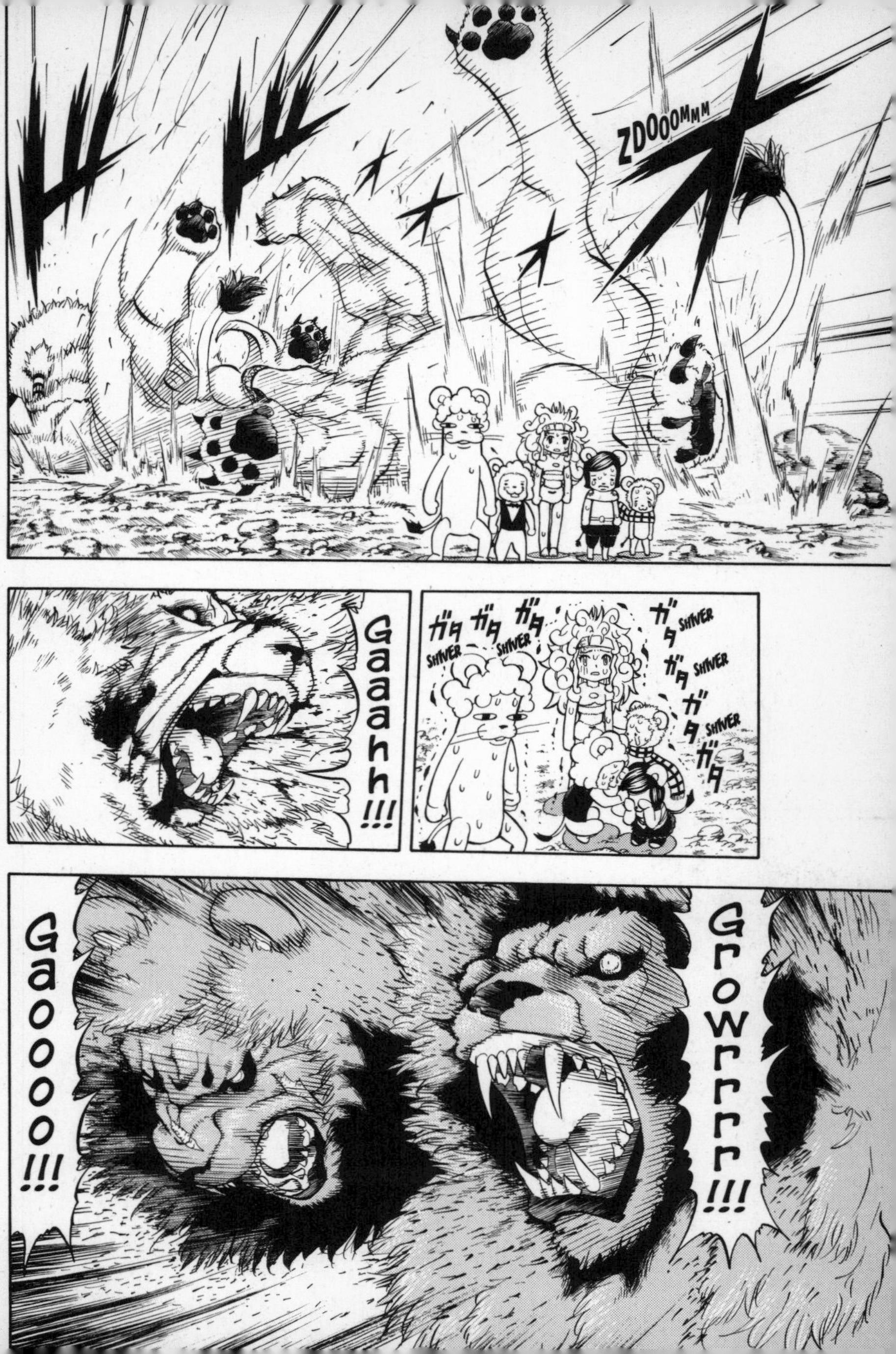
ZDOOOMMM
ガタ
SHIVER
ガタ
SHIVER
ガタ
ガタ
SHIVER
ガタ
SHIVER
ガタ
SHIVER
ガタ
Gaaaahh!!!
Growrrrr!!!
Gaoooooo!!!

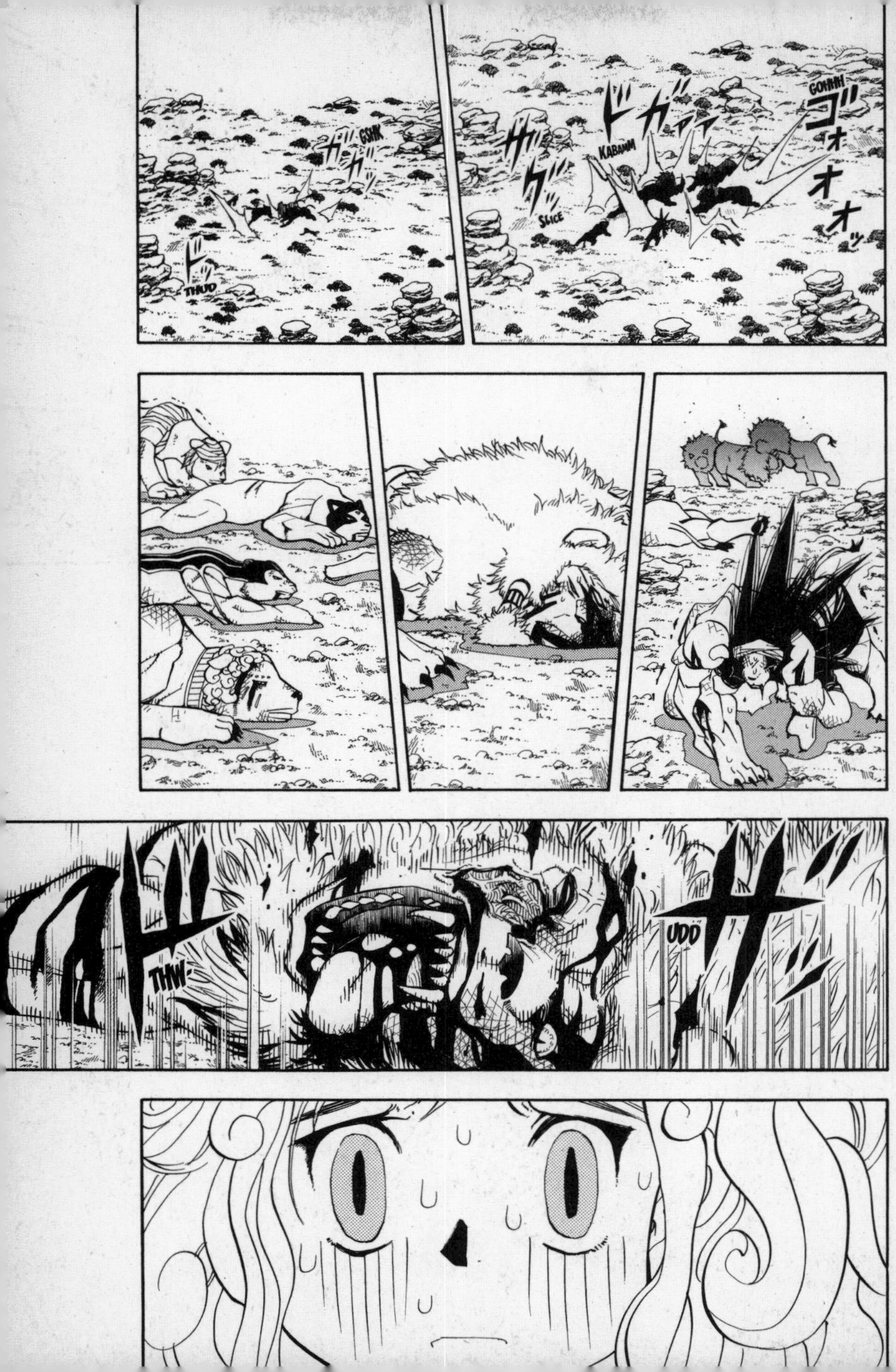
GOHHH
KABAMM
SLICE
GSHK
THUD
UDO
THW-

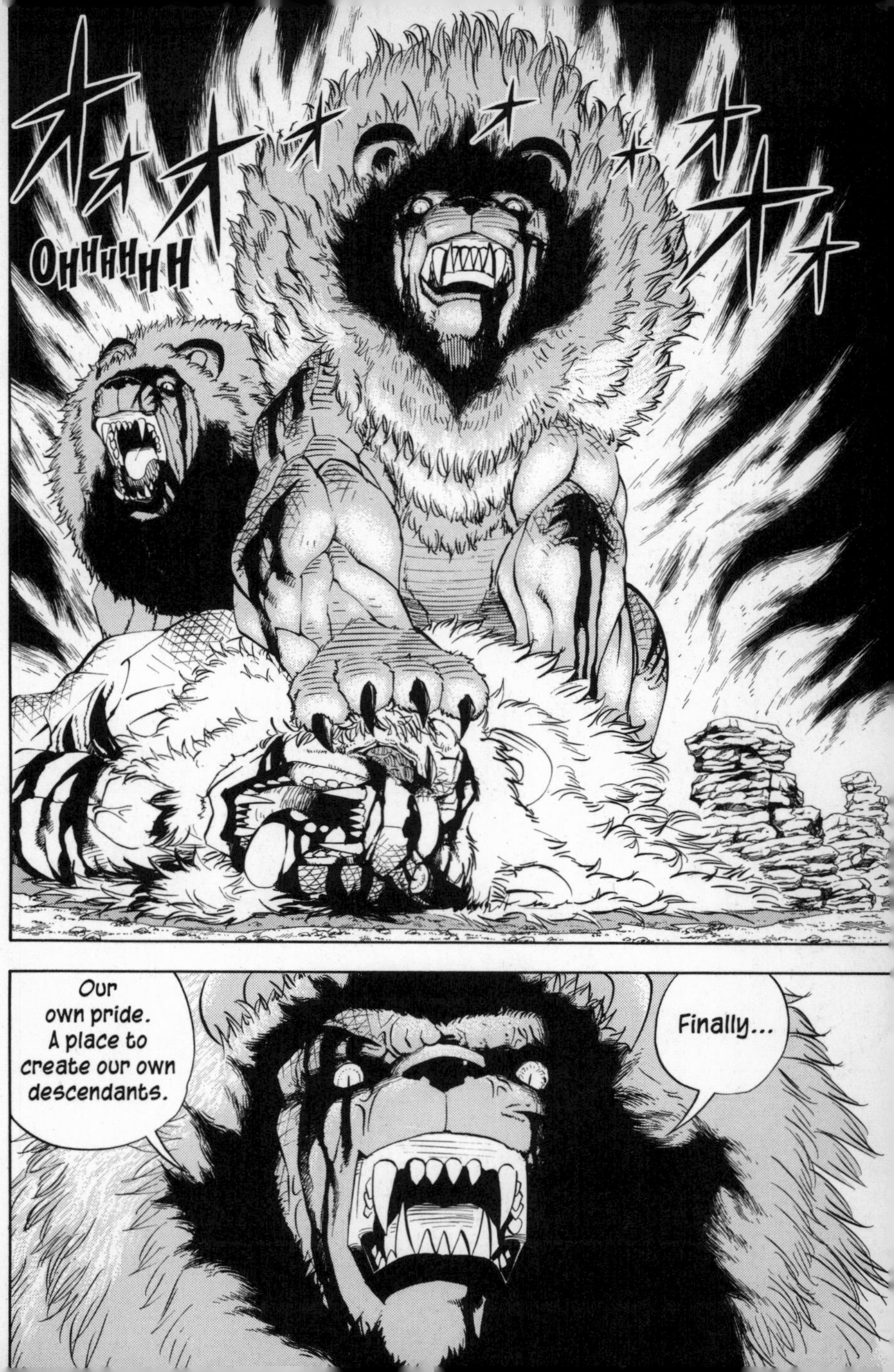
OHHHHHH
Finally...
Our own pride. A place to create our own descendants.

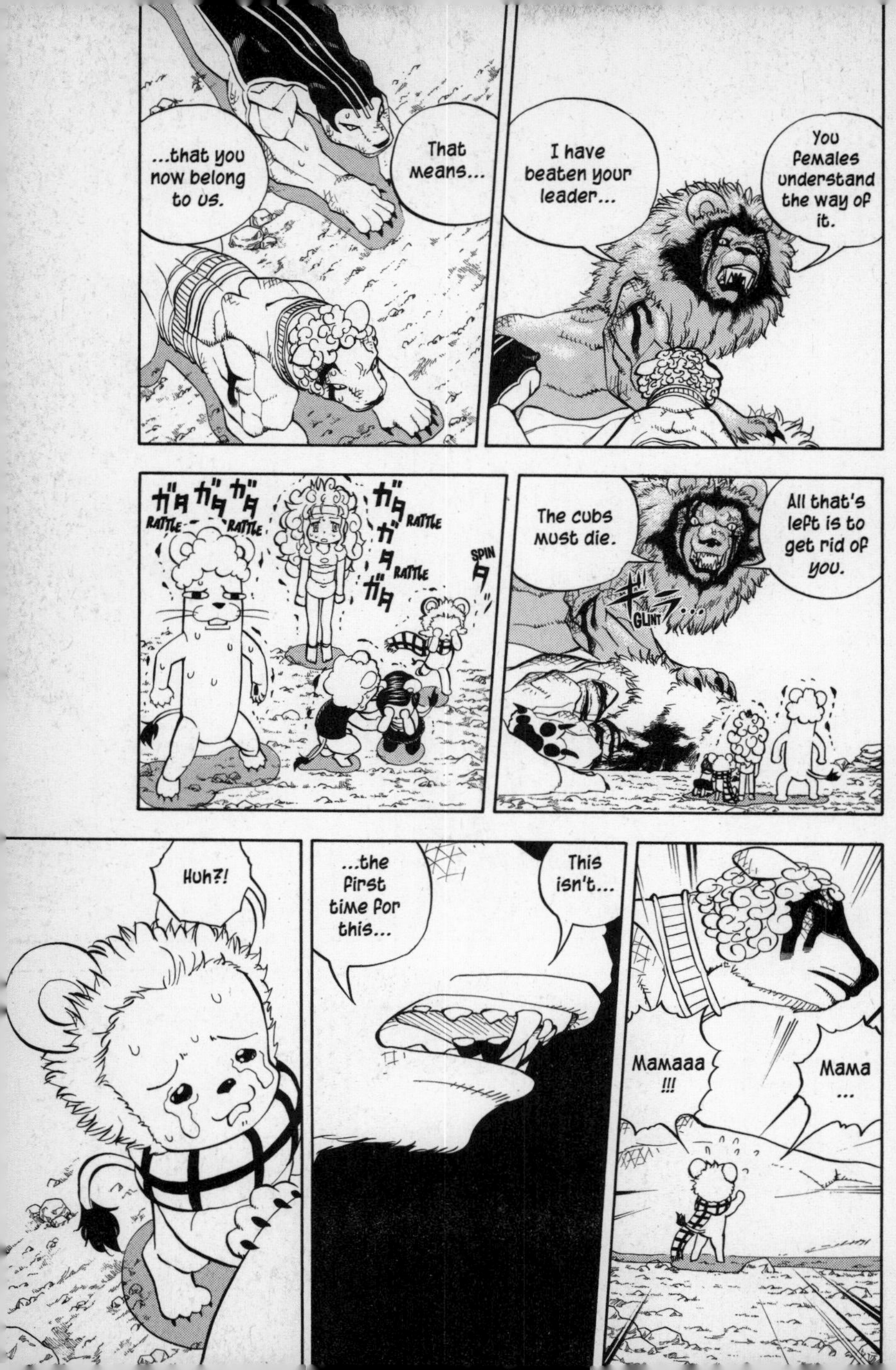
You females understand the way of it.
I have beaten your leader...
That means...
...that you now belong to us.
All that's left is to get rid of you.
The cubs must die.
ギラ GLINT
ガタ RATTLE
ガタ RATTLE
ガタ RATTLE
ガタ RATTLE
タ SPIN
Mama ...
Mamaaa !!!
This isn't...
...the first time for this...
Huh?!

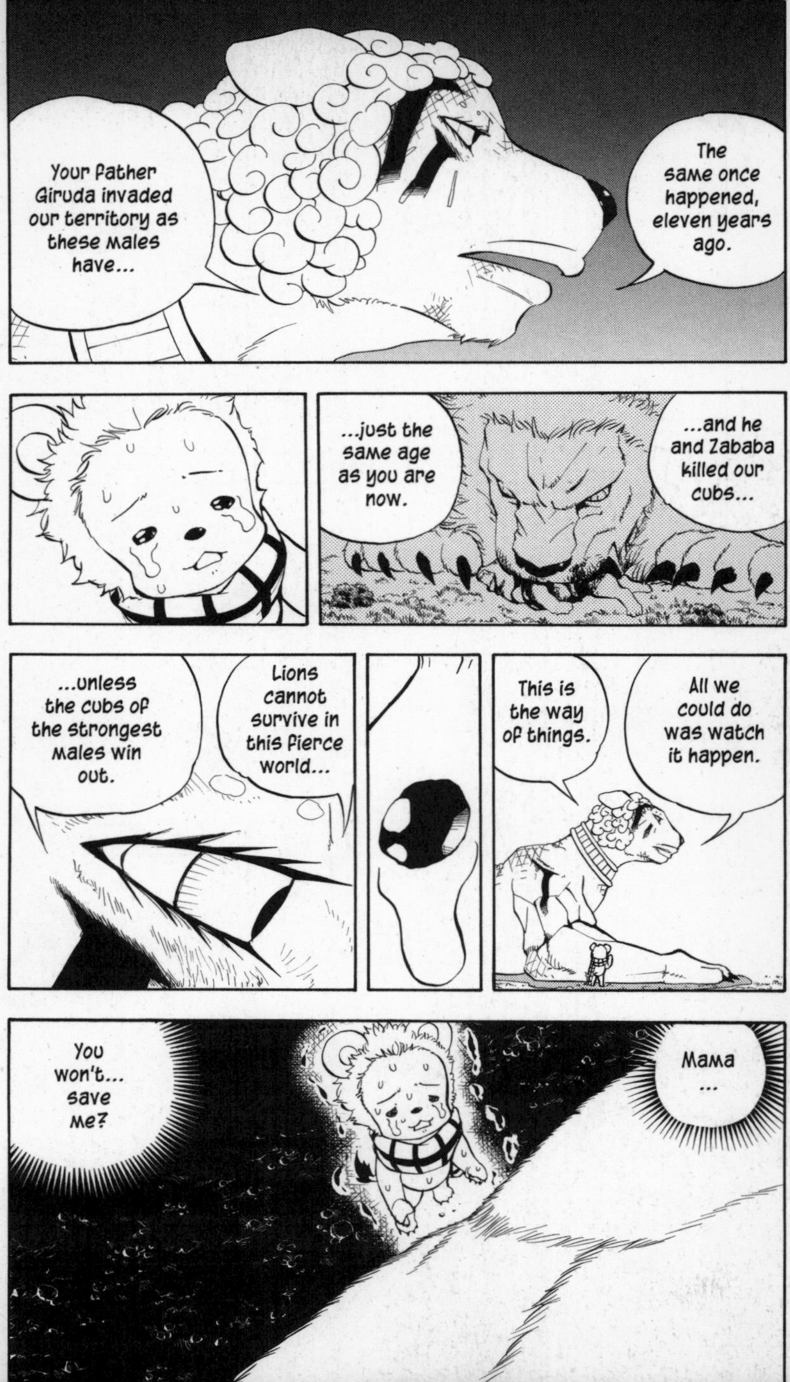
The same once happened, eleven years ago.
Your father Giruda invaded our territory as these males have...
...and he and Zababa killed our cubs...
...just the same age as you are now.
All we could do was watch it happen.
This is the way of things.
Lions cannot survive in this fierce world...
...unless the cubs of the strongest males win out.
Mama ...
You won't... save me?

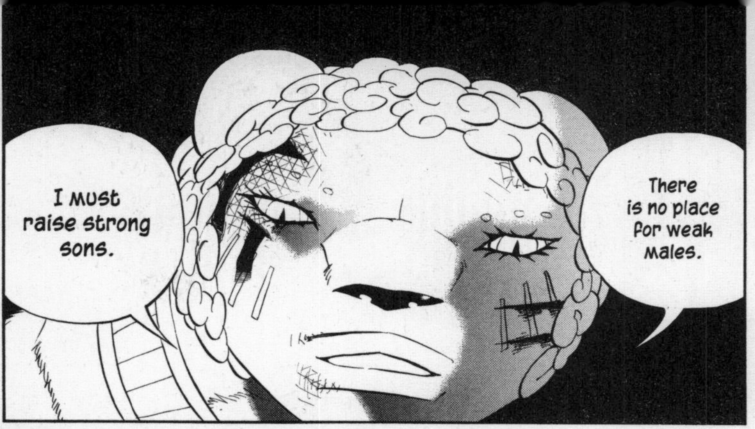
There is no place for weak males.
I must raise strong sons.
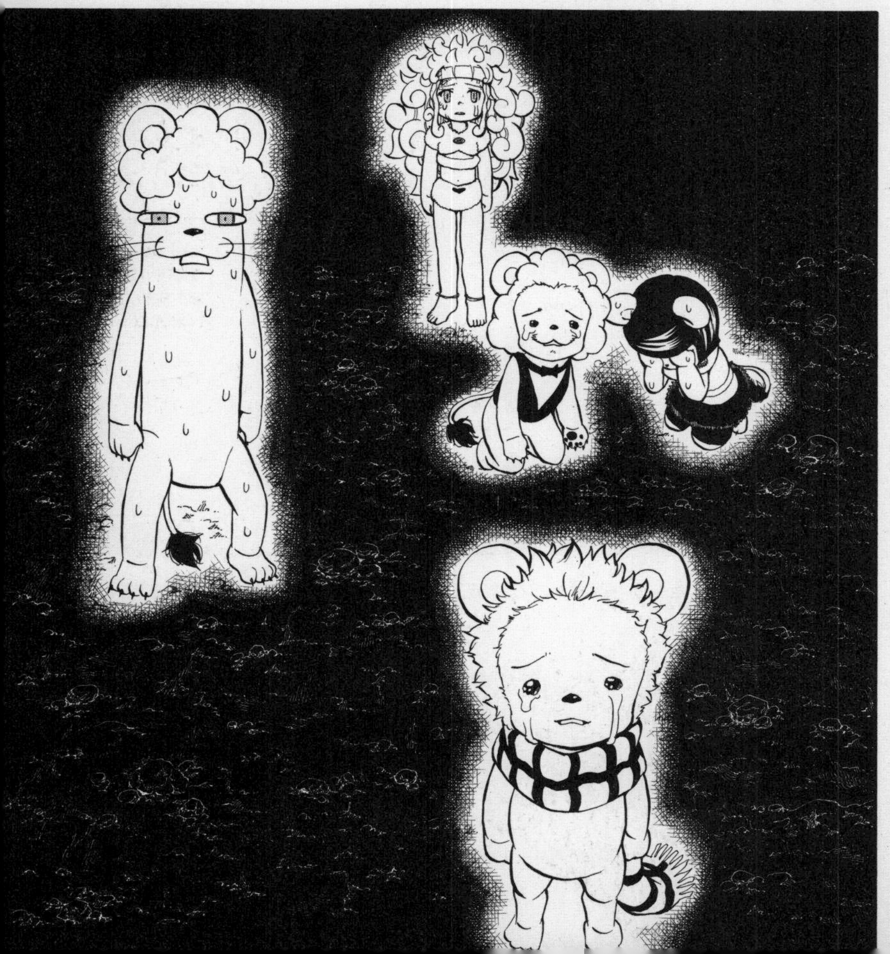

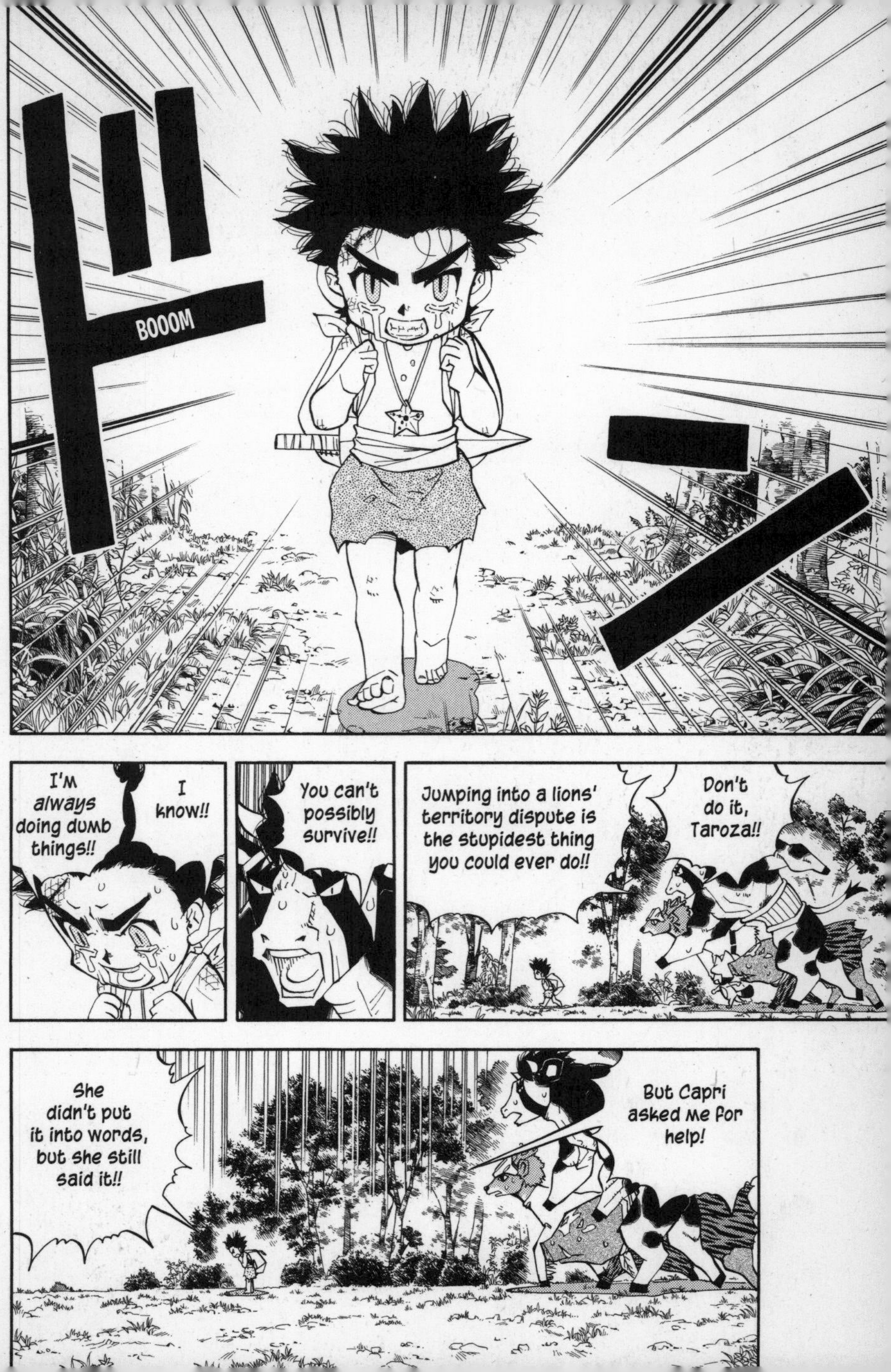
BOOOM
Don't do it, Taroza!!
Jumping into a lions' territory dispute is the stupidest thing you could ever do!!
You can't possibly survive!!
I know!!
I'm always doing dumb things!!
But Capri asked me for help!
She didn't put it into words, but she still said it!!

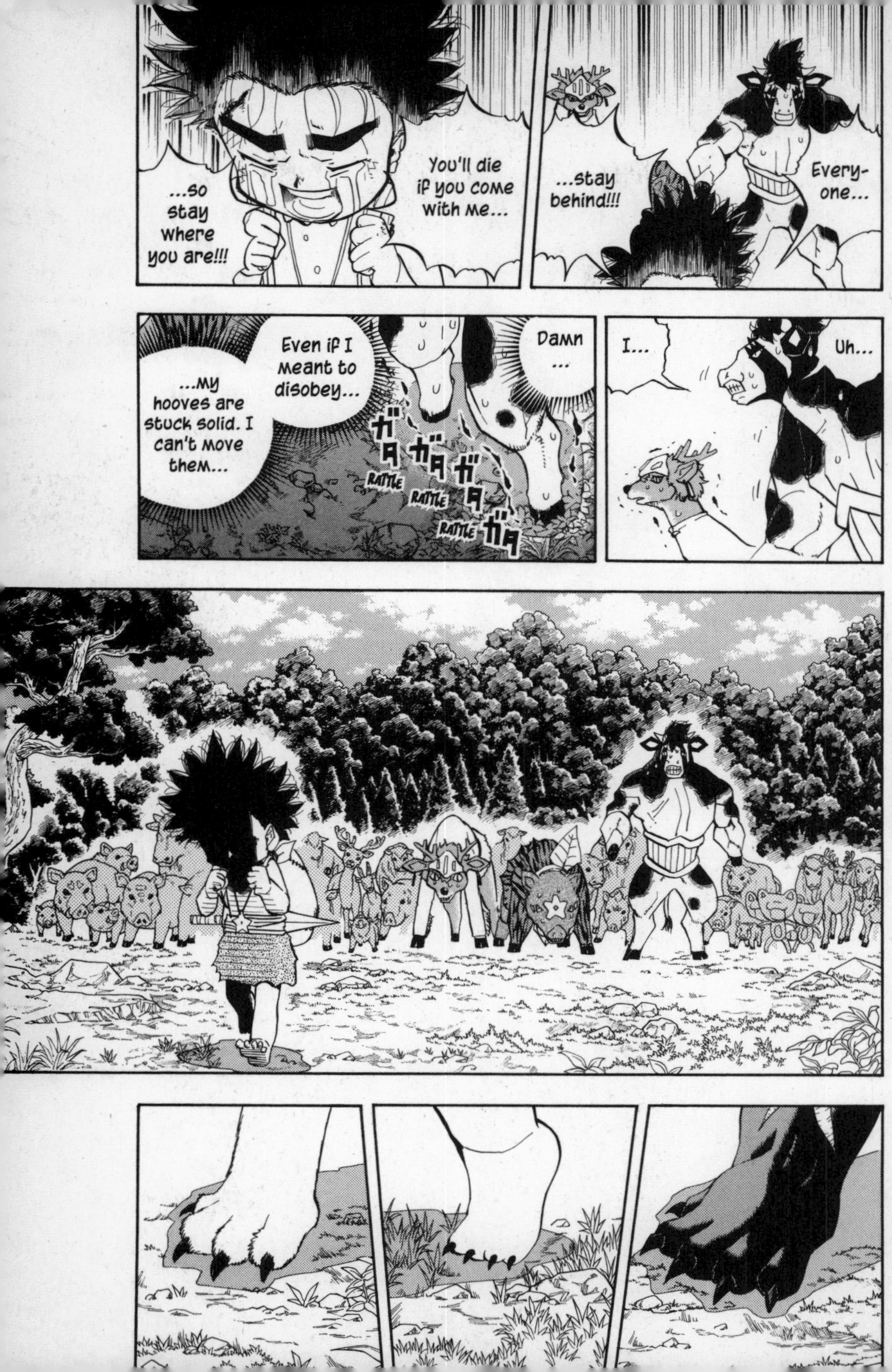
Every-one...
...stay behind!!!
You'll die if you come with me...
...so stay where you are!!!
Uh...
I...
Damn...
Even if I meant to disobey...
...my hooves are stuck solid. I can't move them...
ガタ
RATTLE
ガタ
RATTLE
ガタ
RATTLE
ガタ

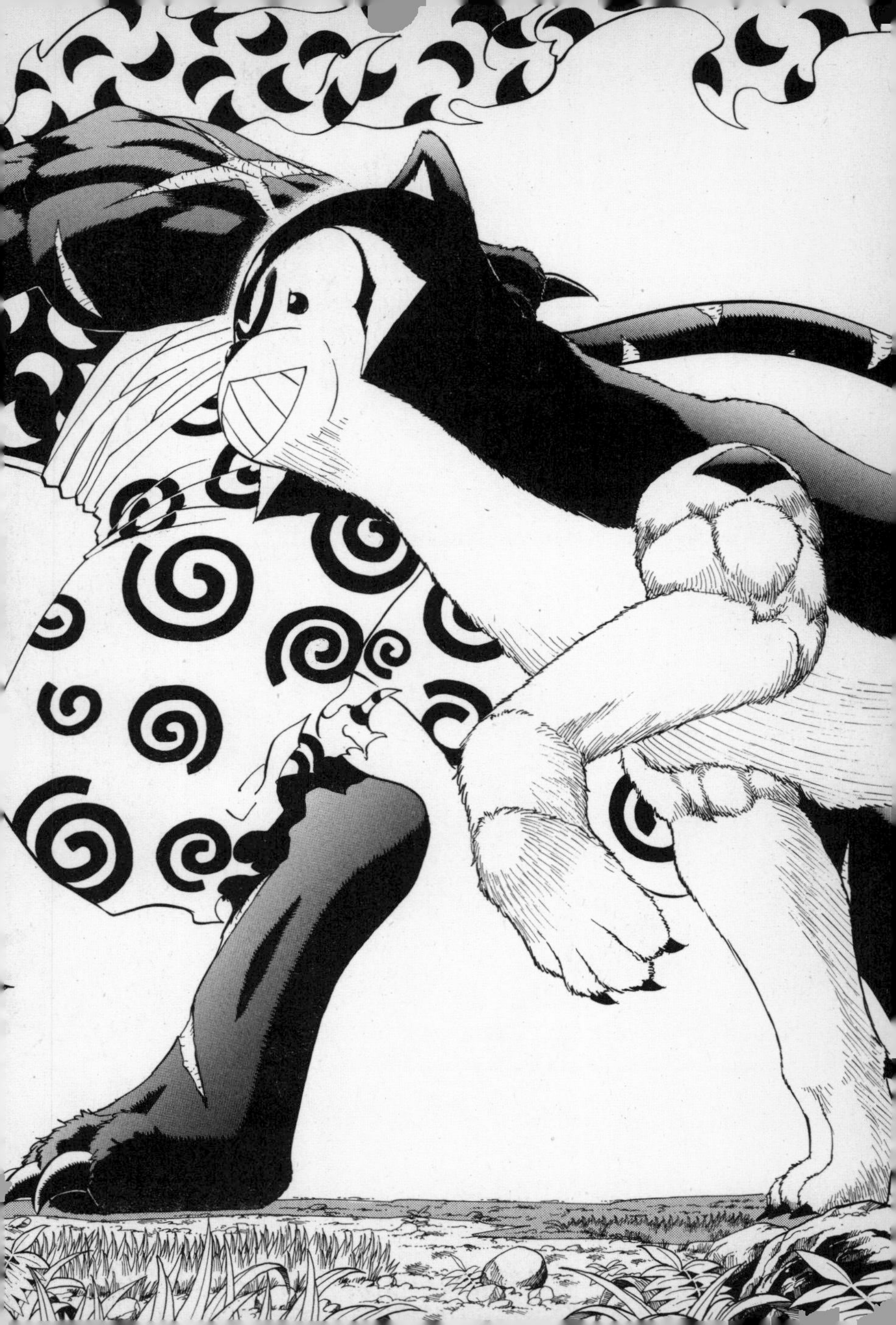

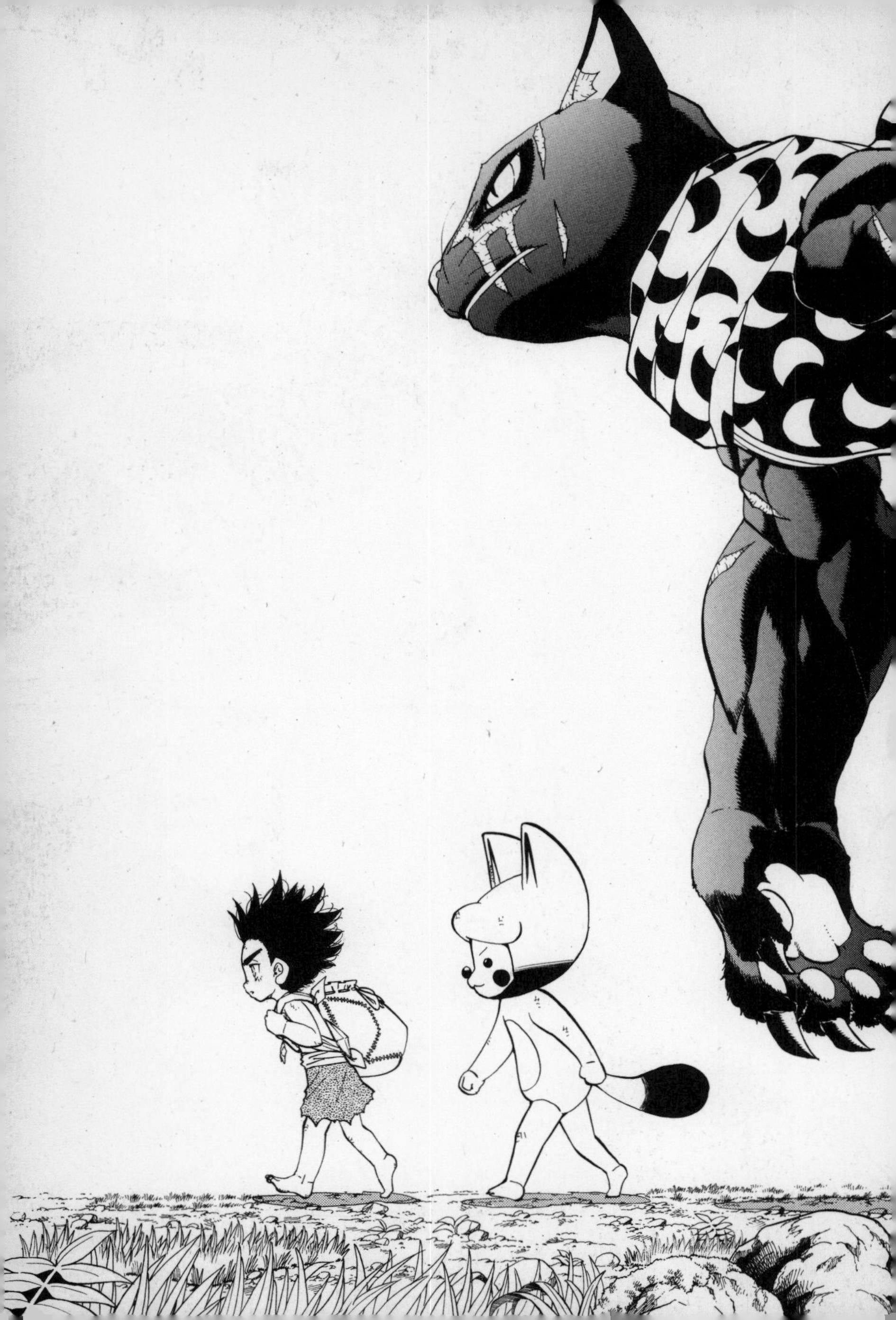

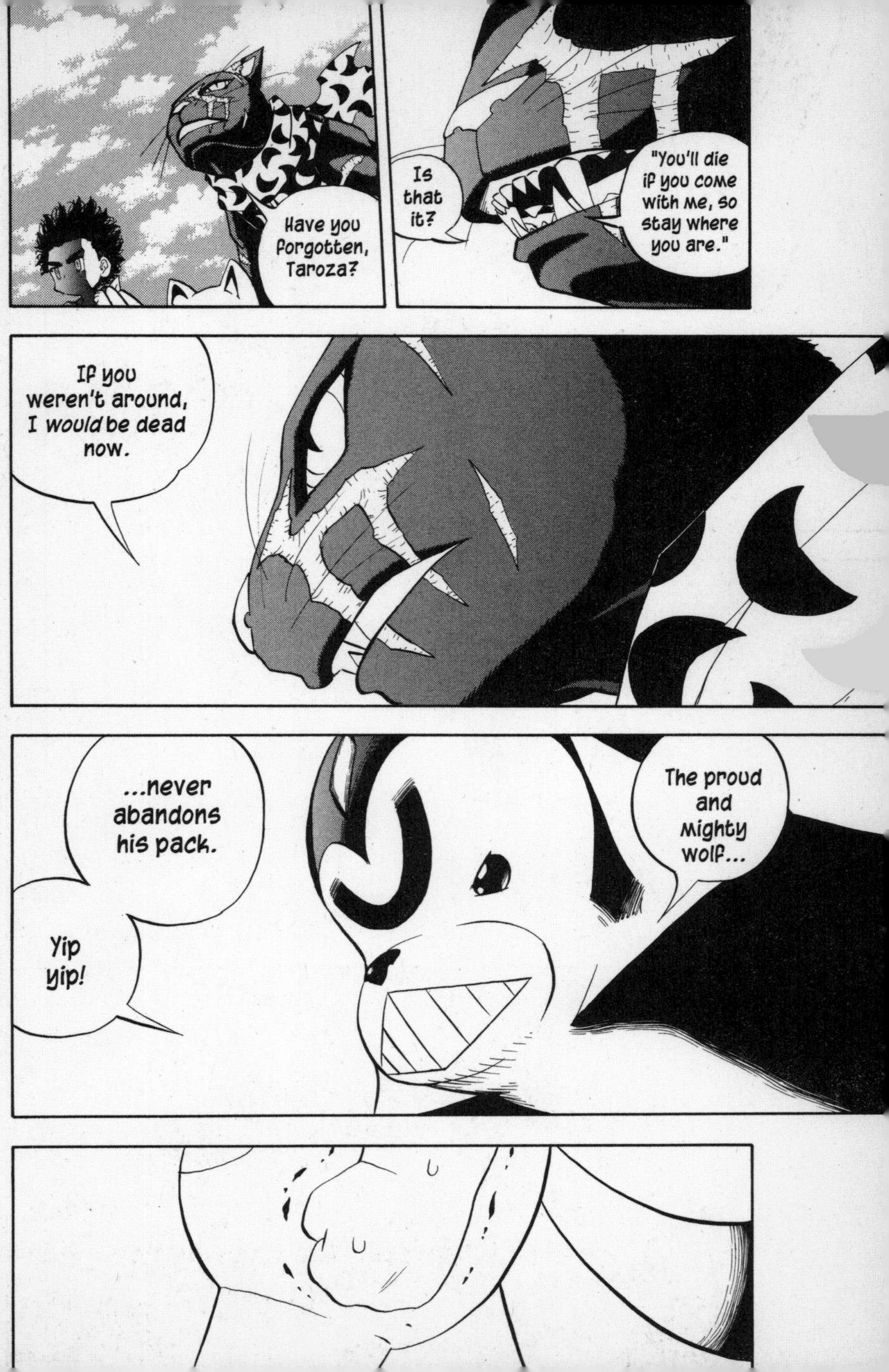
"You'll die if you come with me, so stay where you are."
Is that it?
Have you forgotten, Taroza?
If you weren't around, I *would* be dead now.
The proud and mighty wolf...
...never abandons his pack.
Yip yip!

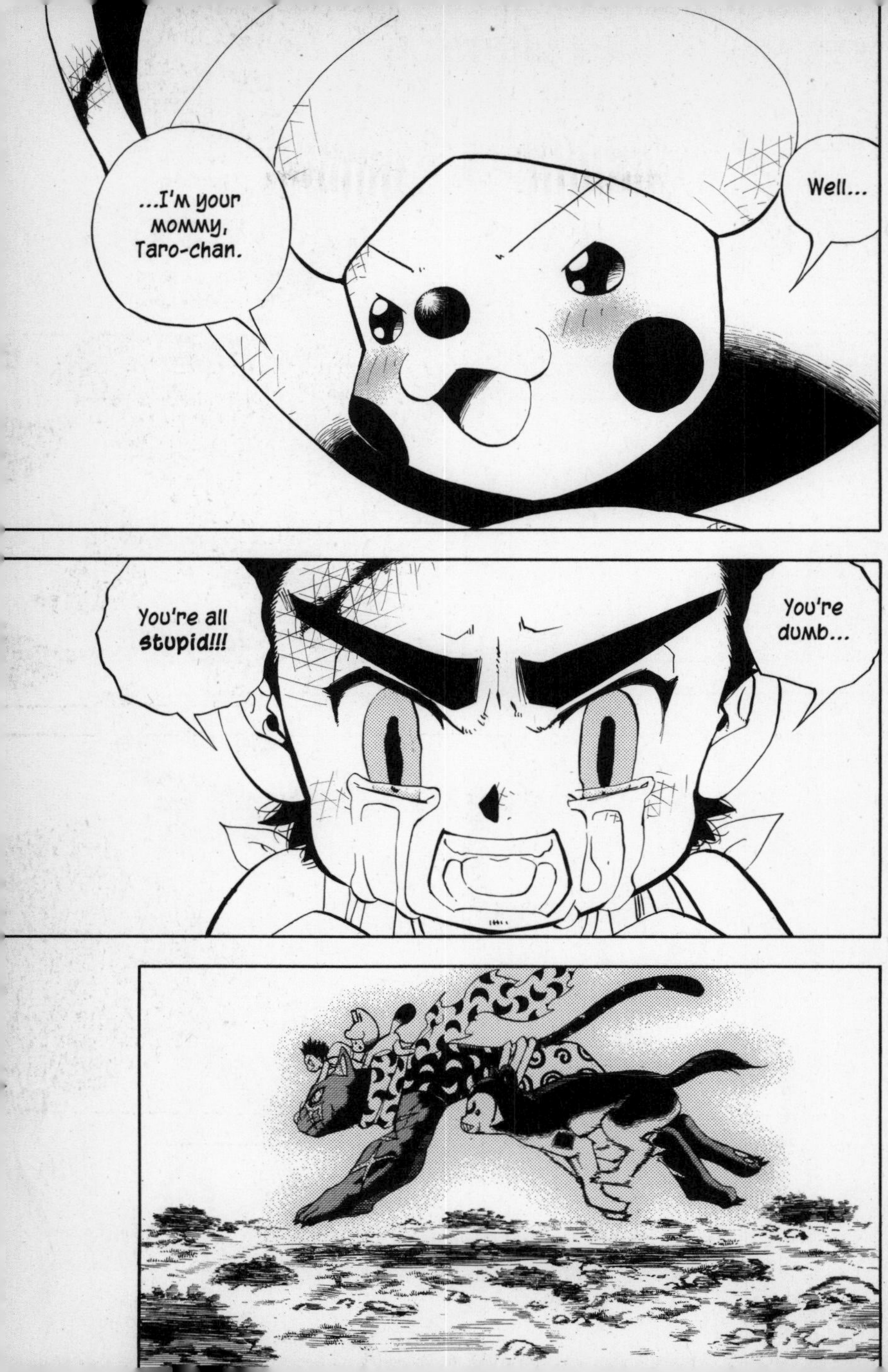
Well...
...I'm your mommy, Taro-chan.
You're dumb...
You're all stupid!!!

Bonus Page 1

Akiko Llama

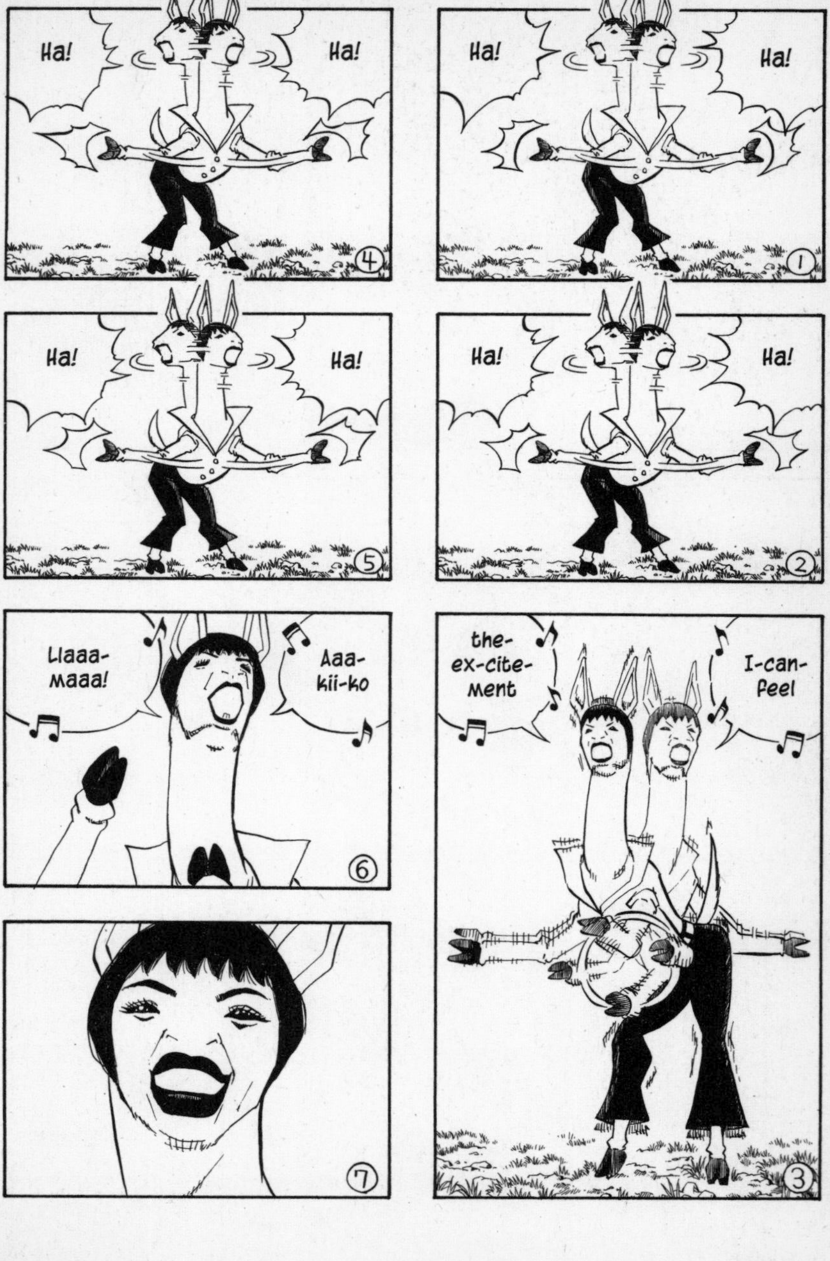
Ha!
Ha!
Ha!
Ha!
I-can-feel
the-ex-cite-ment
Ha!
Ha!
Ha!
Ha!
Aaa-kii-ko
Llaaa-maaa!

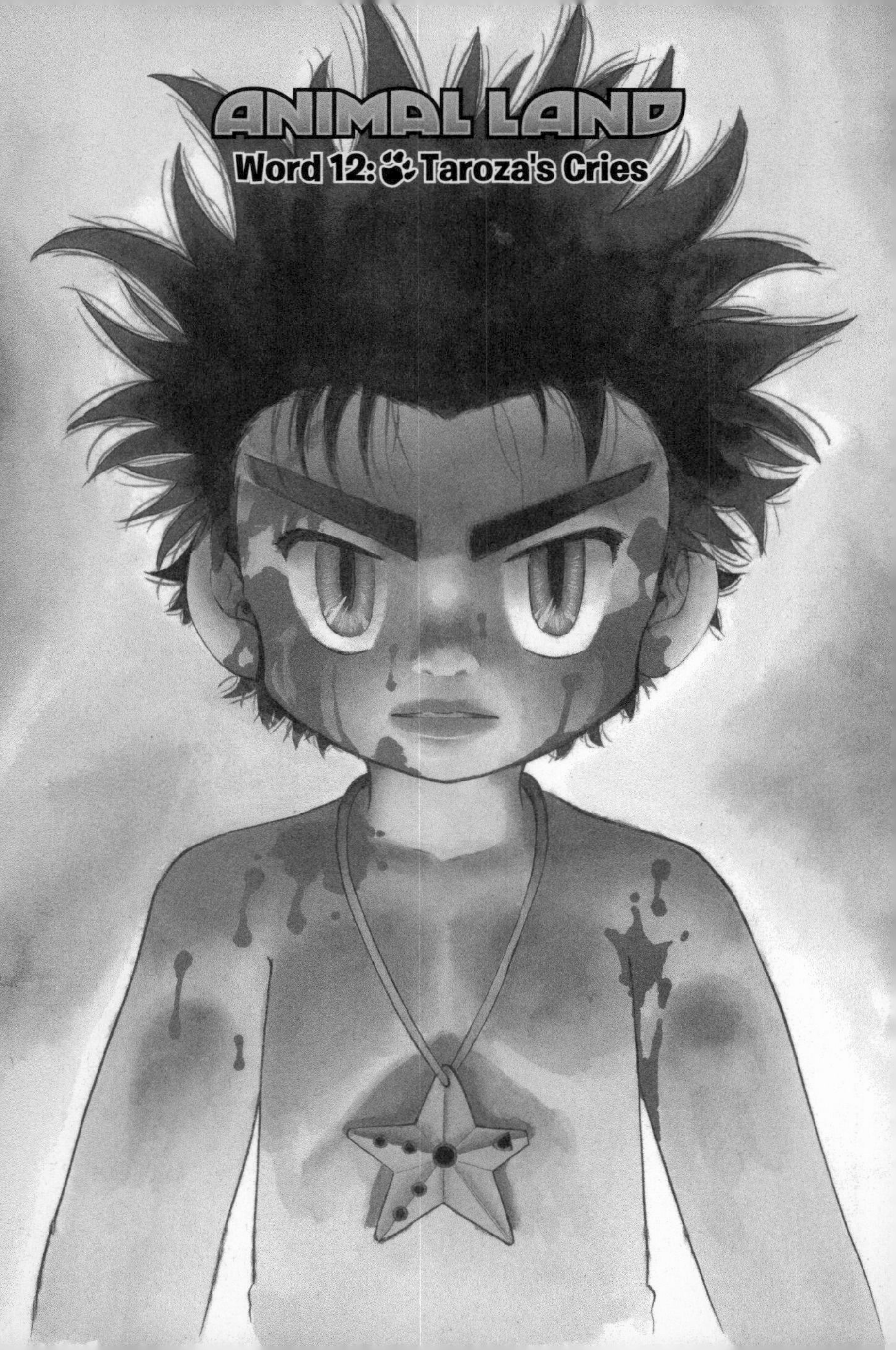
ANIMAL LAND
Word 12: Taroza's Cries

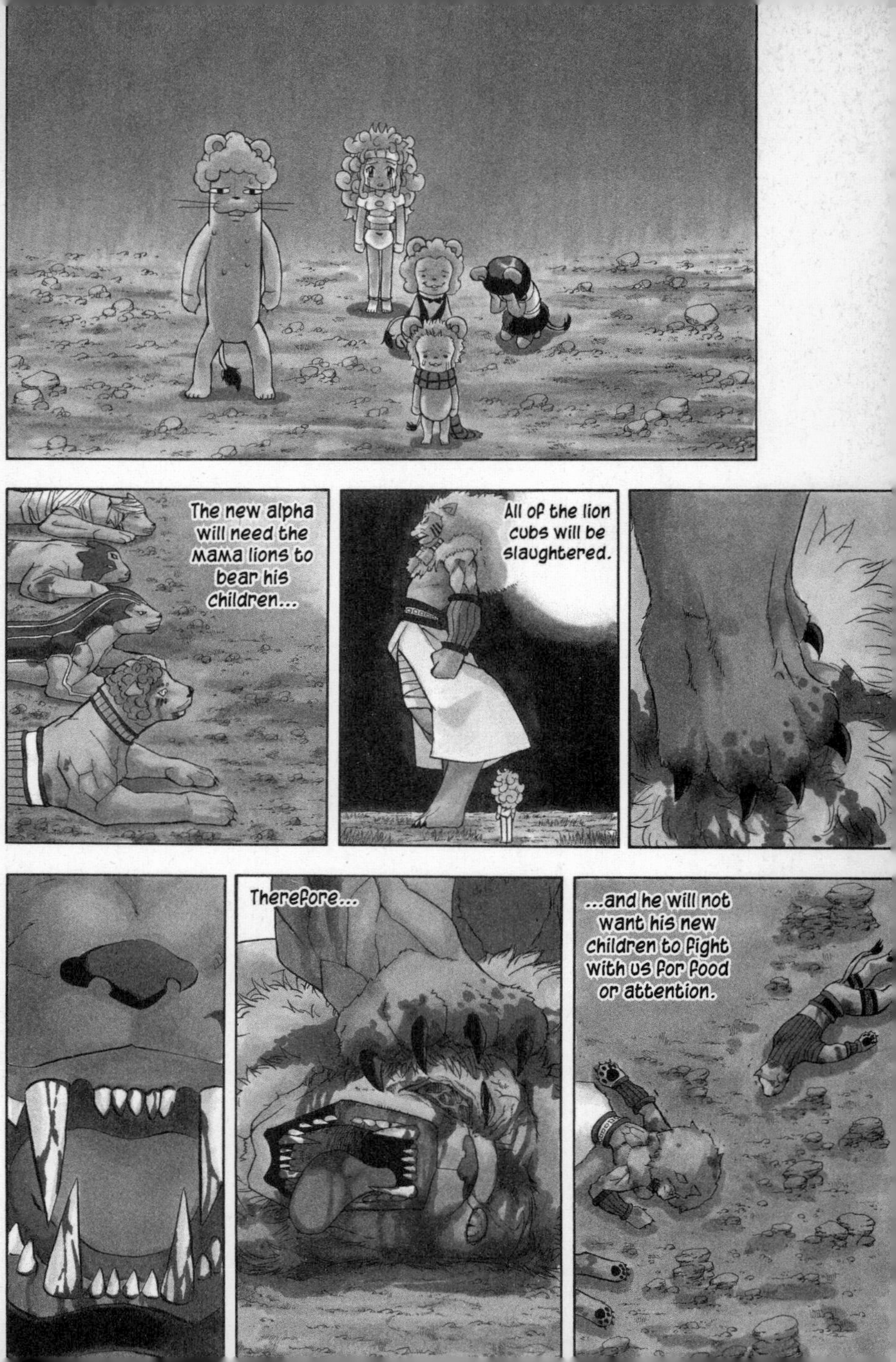
All of the lion cubs will be slaughtered.
The new alpha will need the mama lions to bear his children...
...and he will not want his new children to fight with us for food or attention.
Therefore...

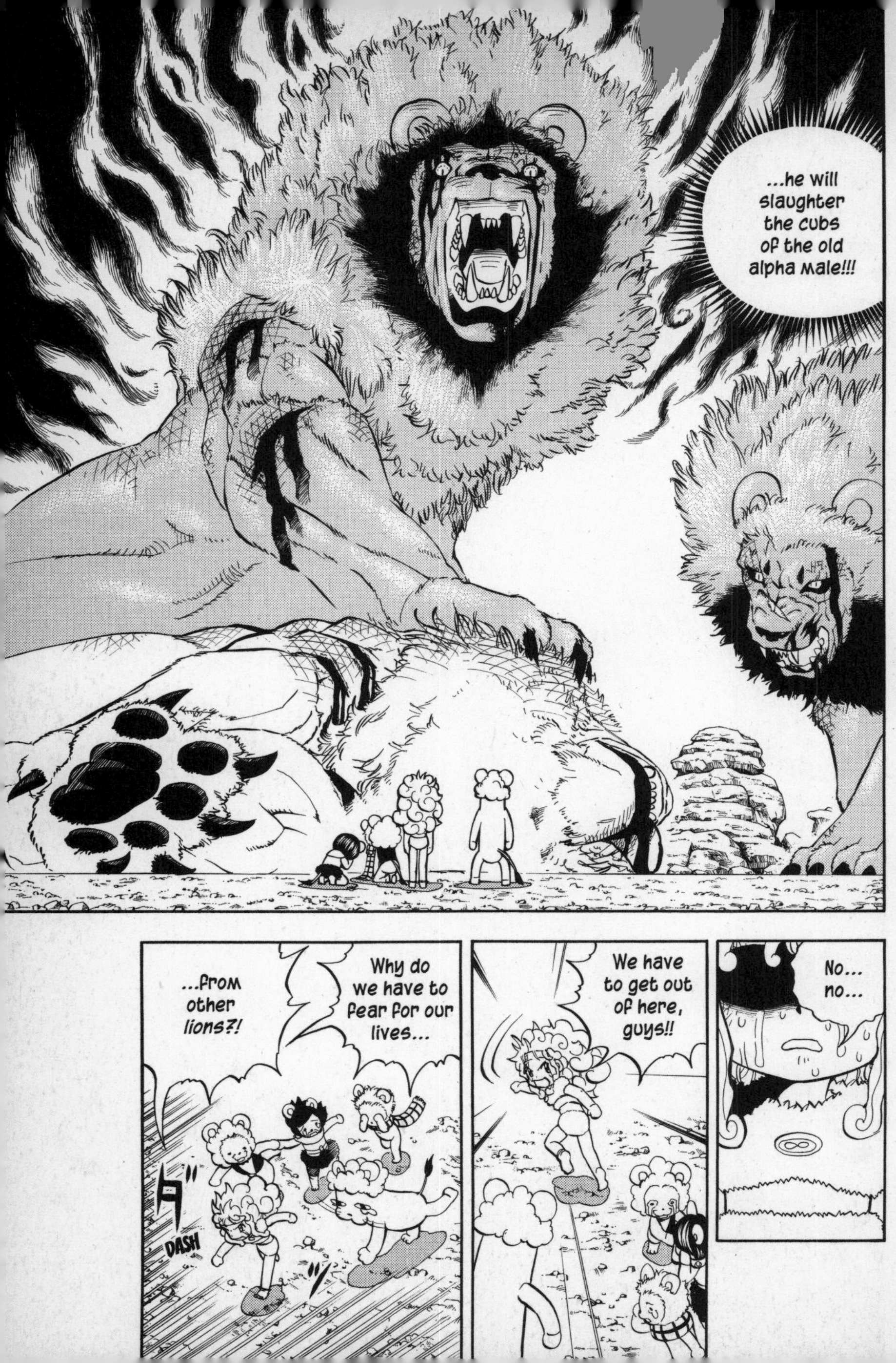
...he will slaughter the cubs of the old alpha male!!!
No... no...
We have to get out of here, guys!!
Why do we have to fear for our lives...
...from other lions?!
DASH

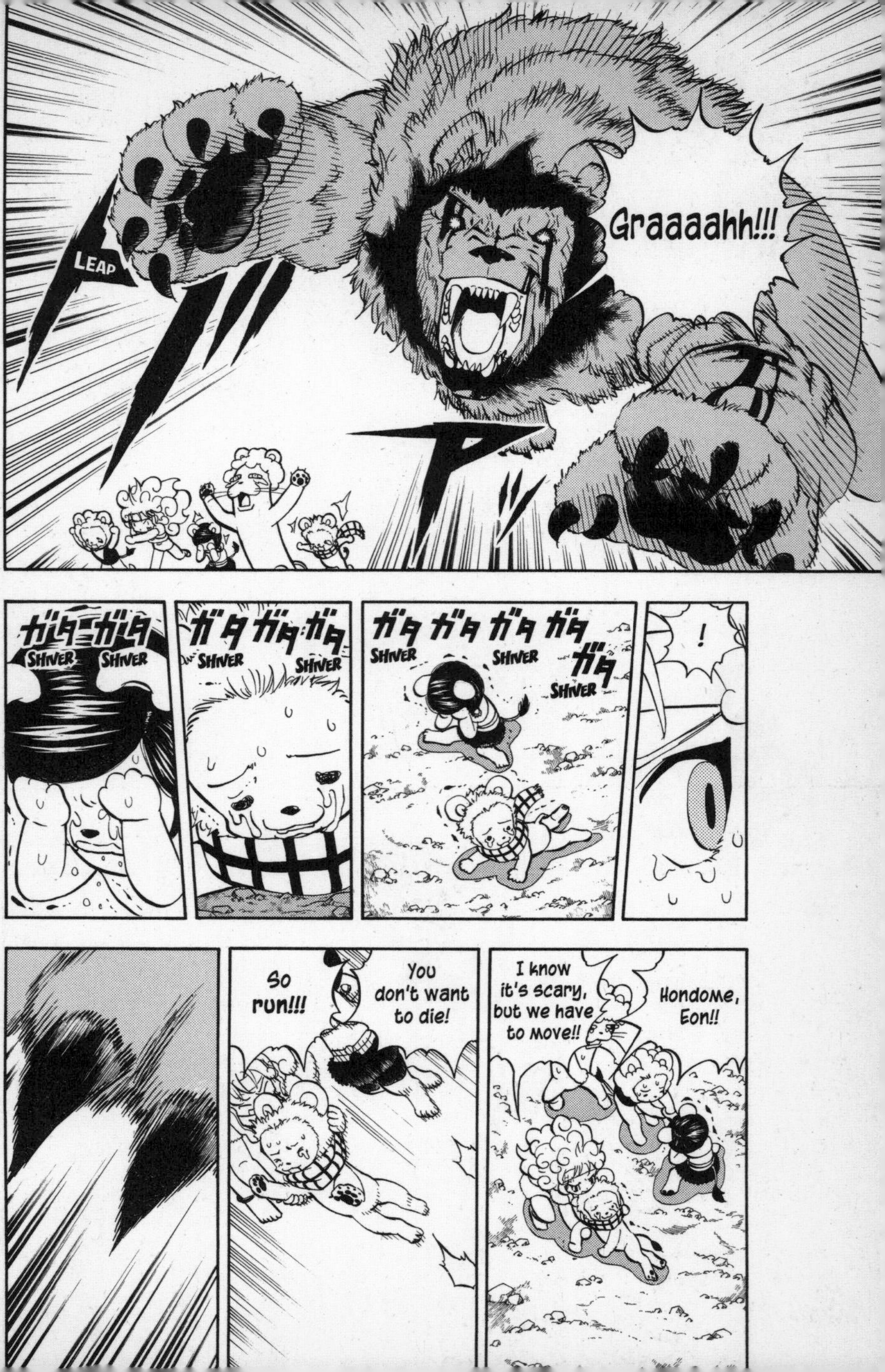
Graaaahh!!!
LEAP
!
ガタ ガタ ガタ ガタ ガタ
SHIVER SHIVER SHIVER
ガタ ガタ ガタ
SHIVER SHIVER
ガタ ガタ
SHIVER SHIVER
Hondome, Eon!!
I know it's scary, but we have to move!!
You don't want to die!
So run!!!

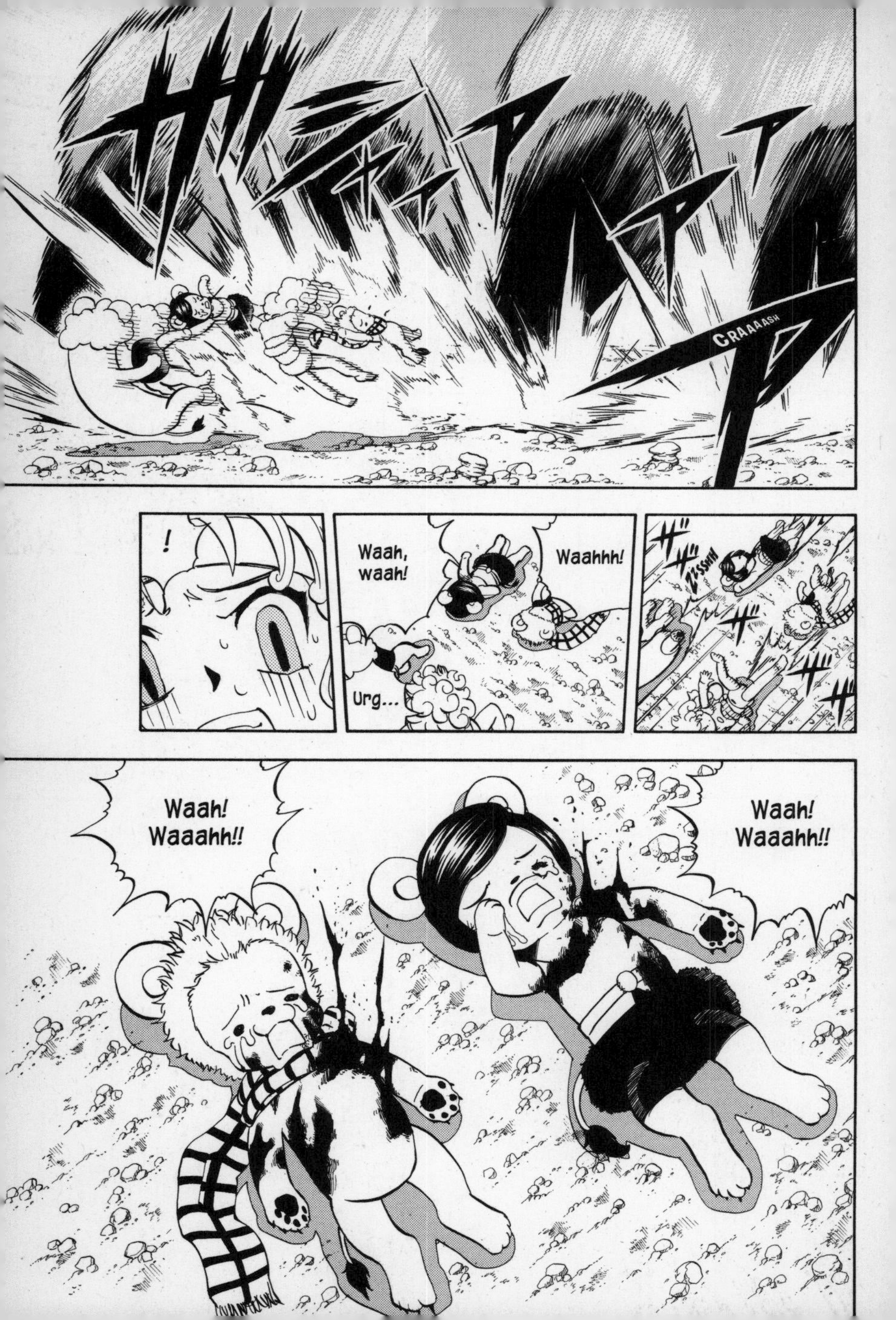
CRAAAASH
ZZSSHH
Waahhh!
Waah, waah!
Urg...
!
Waah! Waaahh!!
Waah! Waaahh!!

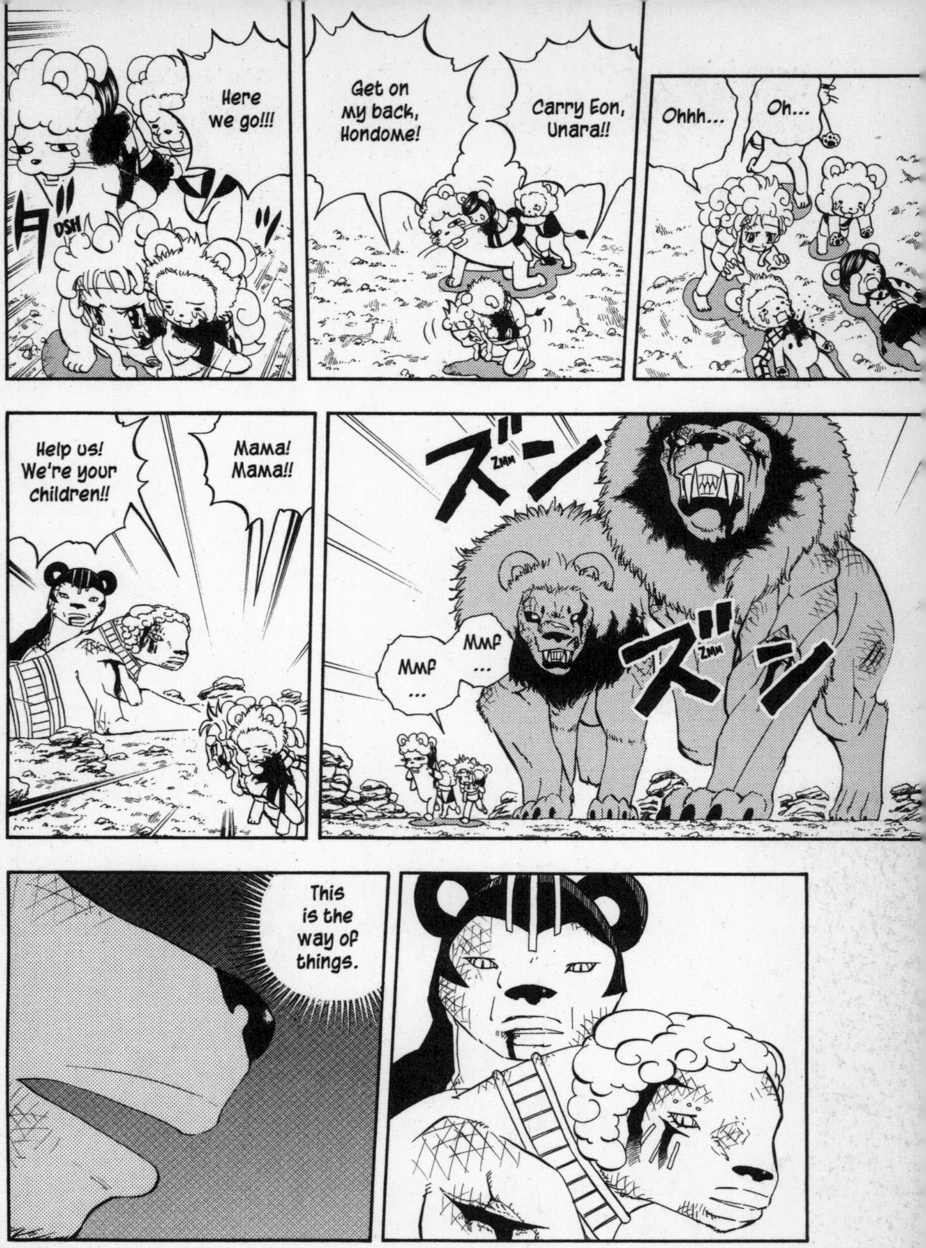
Oh...
Ohhh...
Carry Eon, Unara!!
Get on my back, Hondome!
Here we go!!!
DSH
ZMM
ZMM
Mmf ...
Mmf ...
Mama! Mama!!
Help us! We're your children!!
This is the way of things.

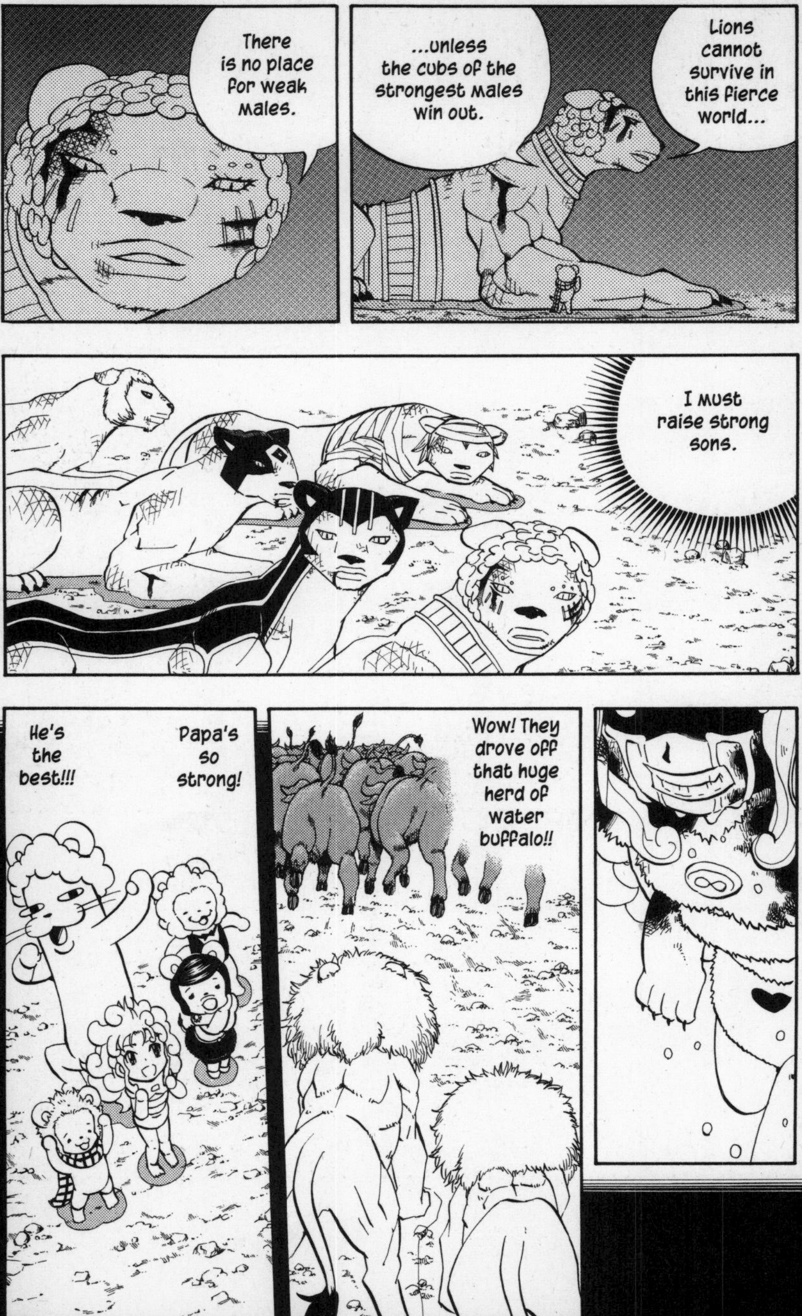
Lions cannot survive in this fierce world...
...unless the cubs of the strongest males win out.
There is no place for weak males.
I must raise strong sons.
Wow! They drove off that huge herd of water buffalo!!
Papa's so strong!
He's the best!!!

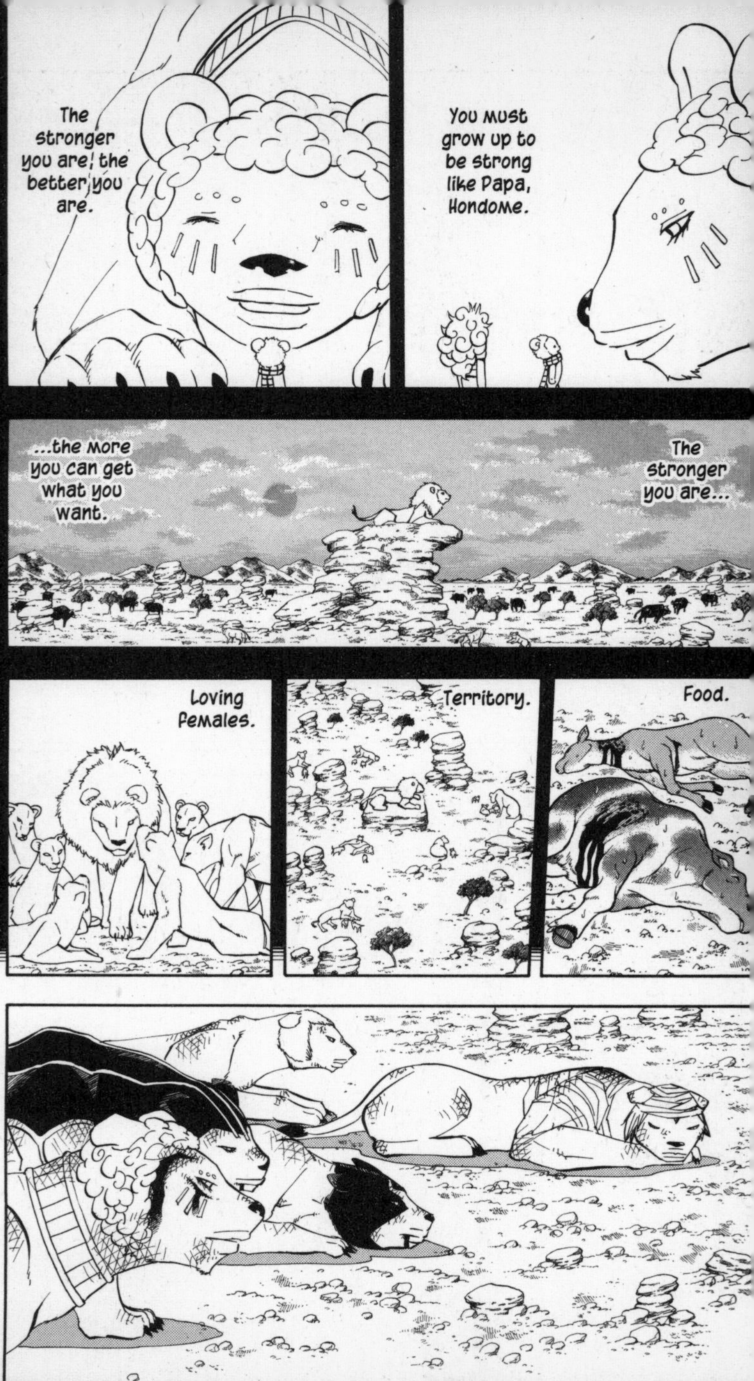
You must grow up to be strong like Papa, Hondome.
The stronger you are, the better you are.
The stronger you are...
...the more you can get what you want.
Food.
Territory.
Loving females.

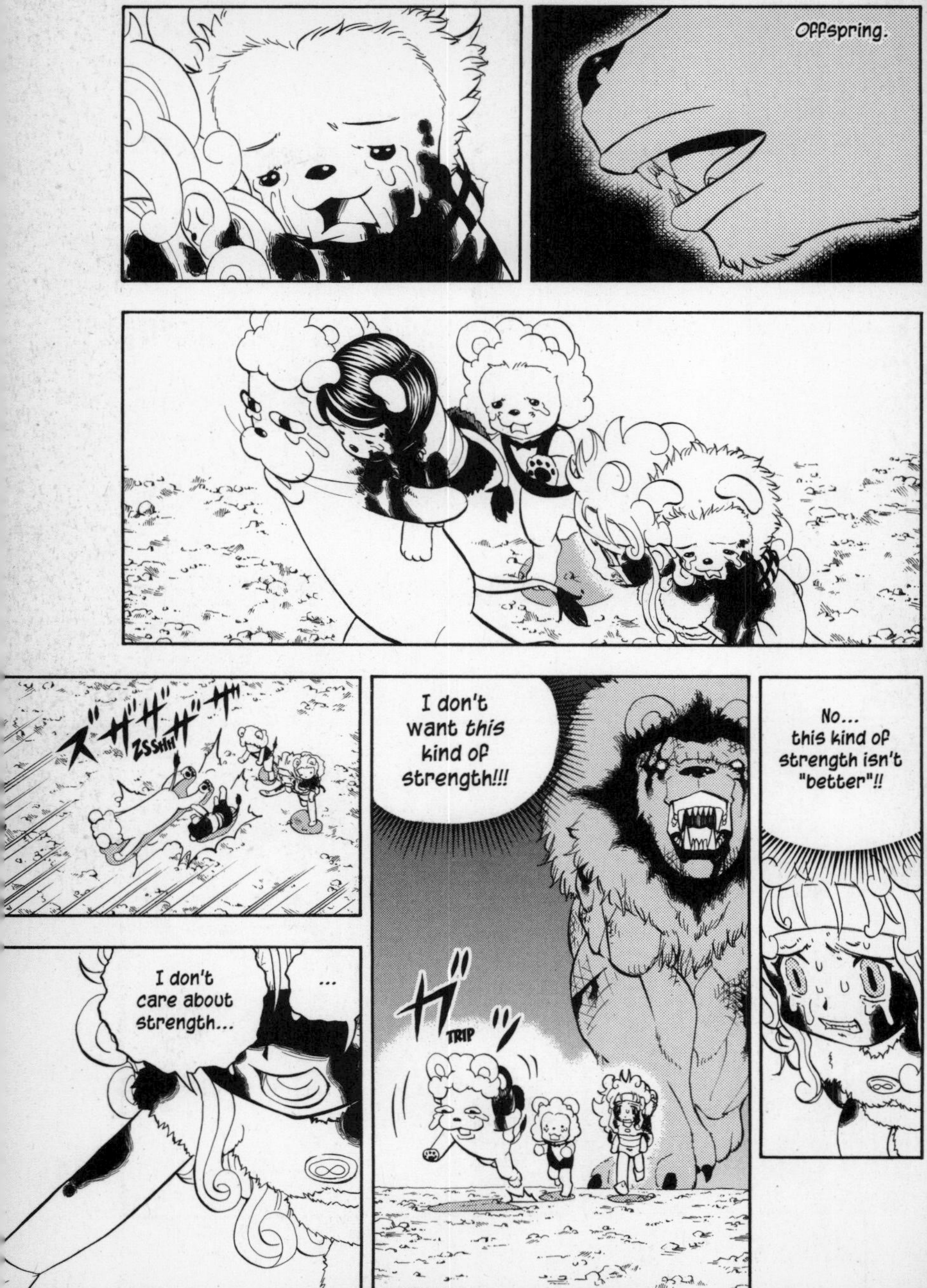
Offspring.
No... this kind of strength isn't "better"!!
I don't want *this* kind of strength!!!
TRIP
ZSSHH
...
I don't care about strength...

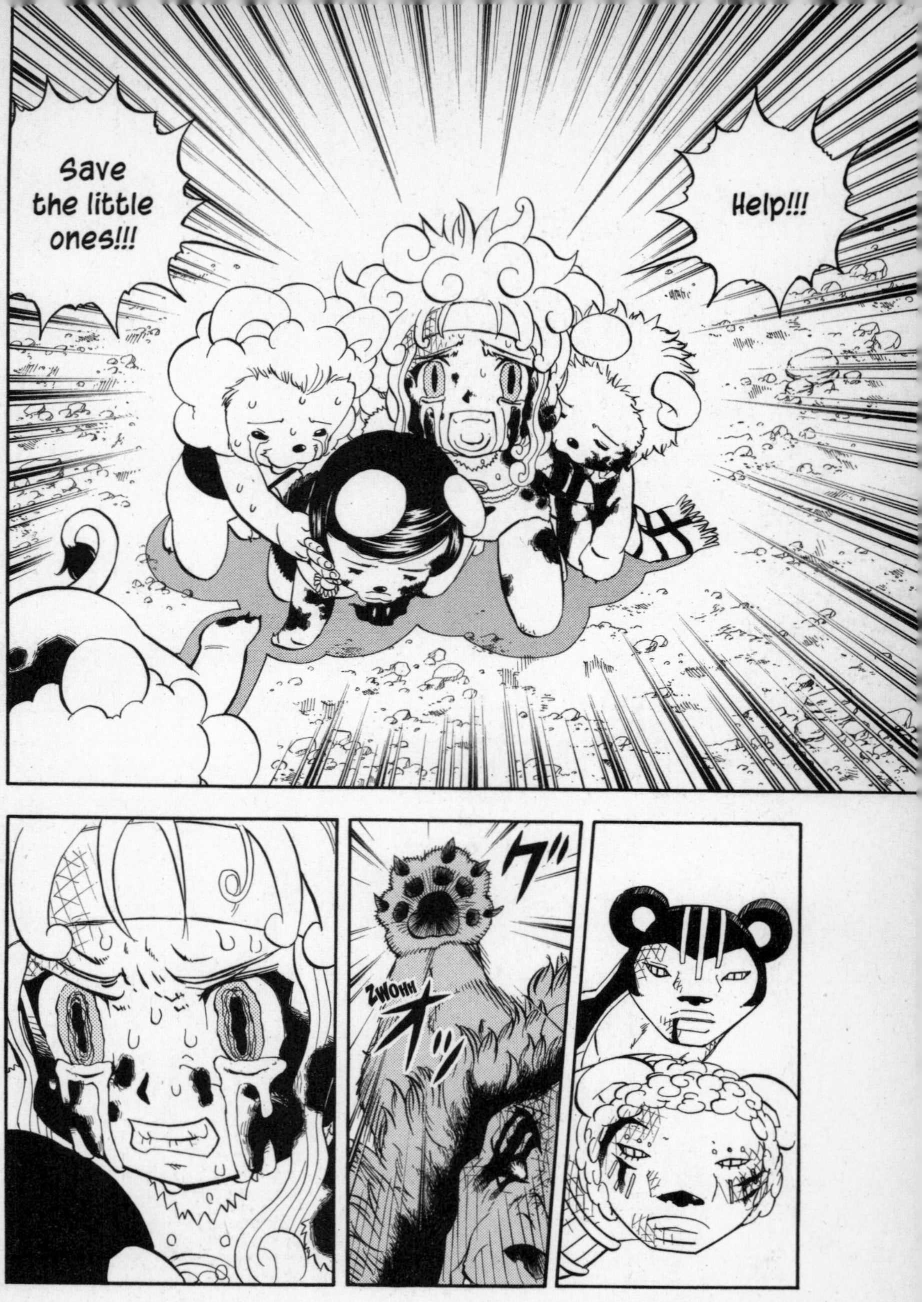
Help!!!
Save the little ones!!!
ZWOHH

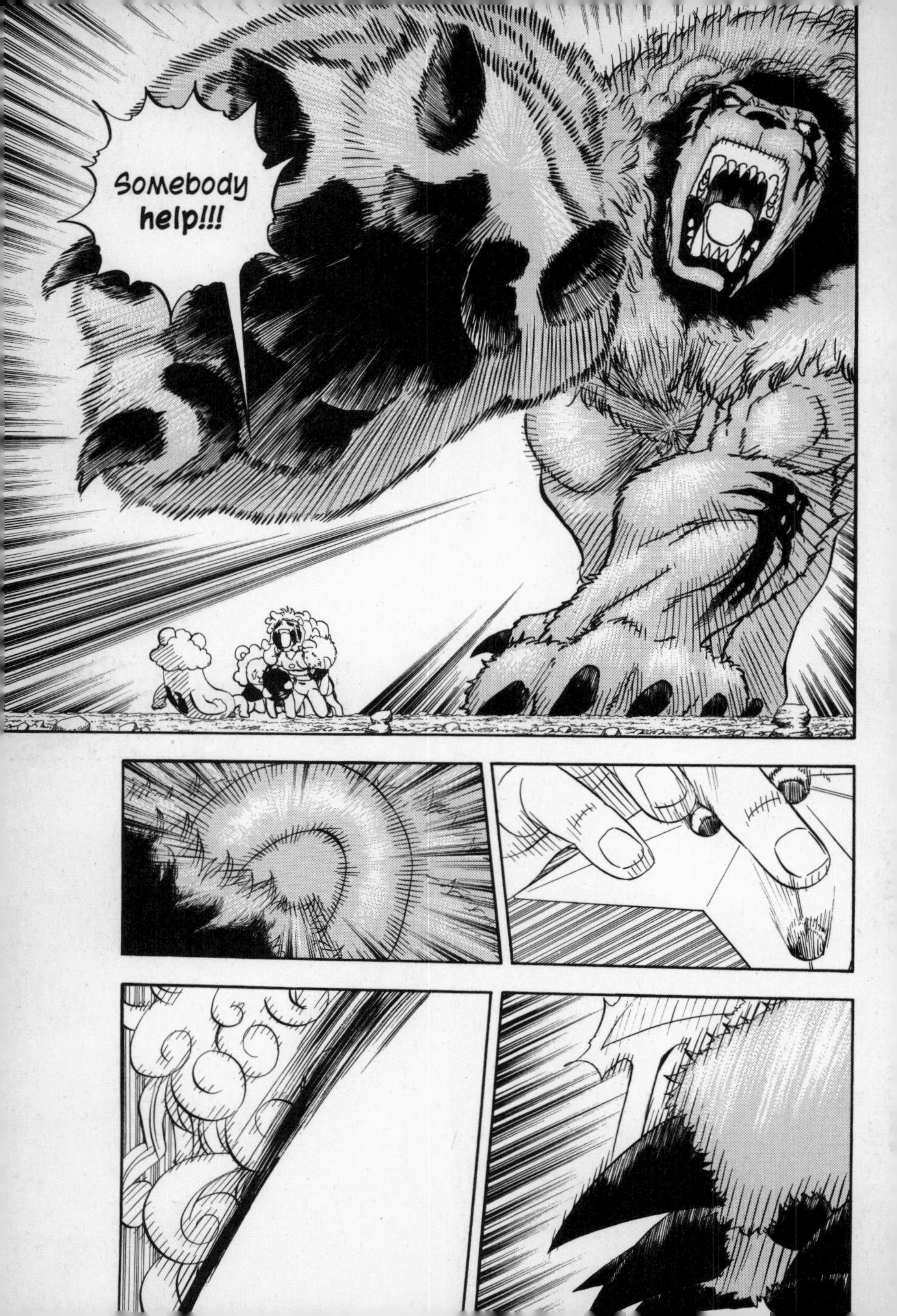
Somebody help!!!

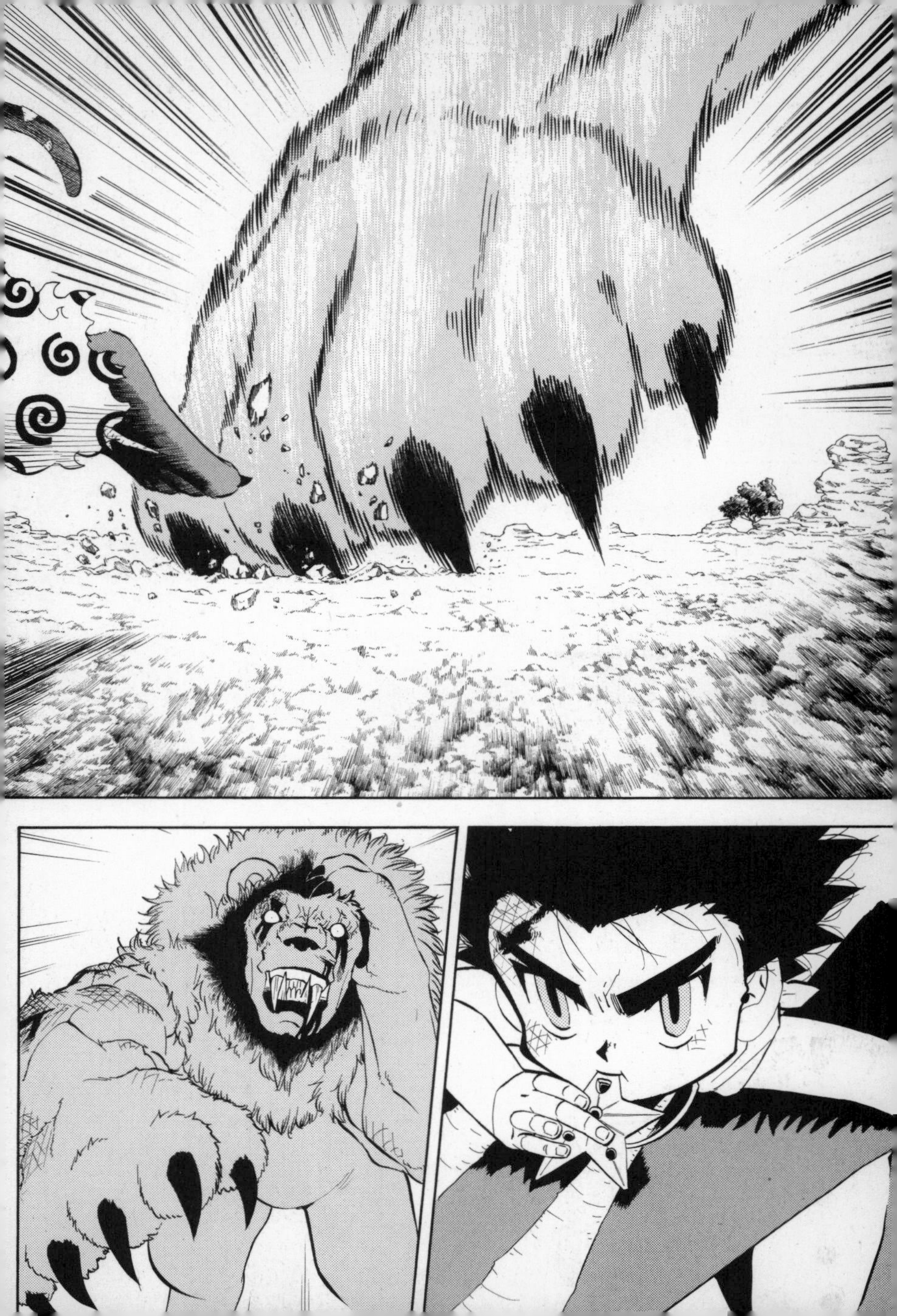

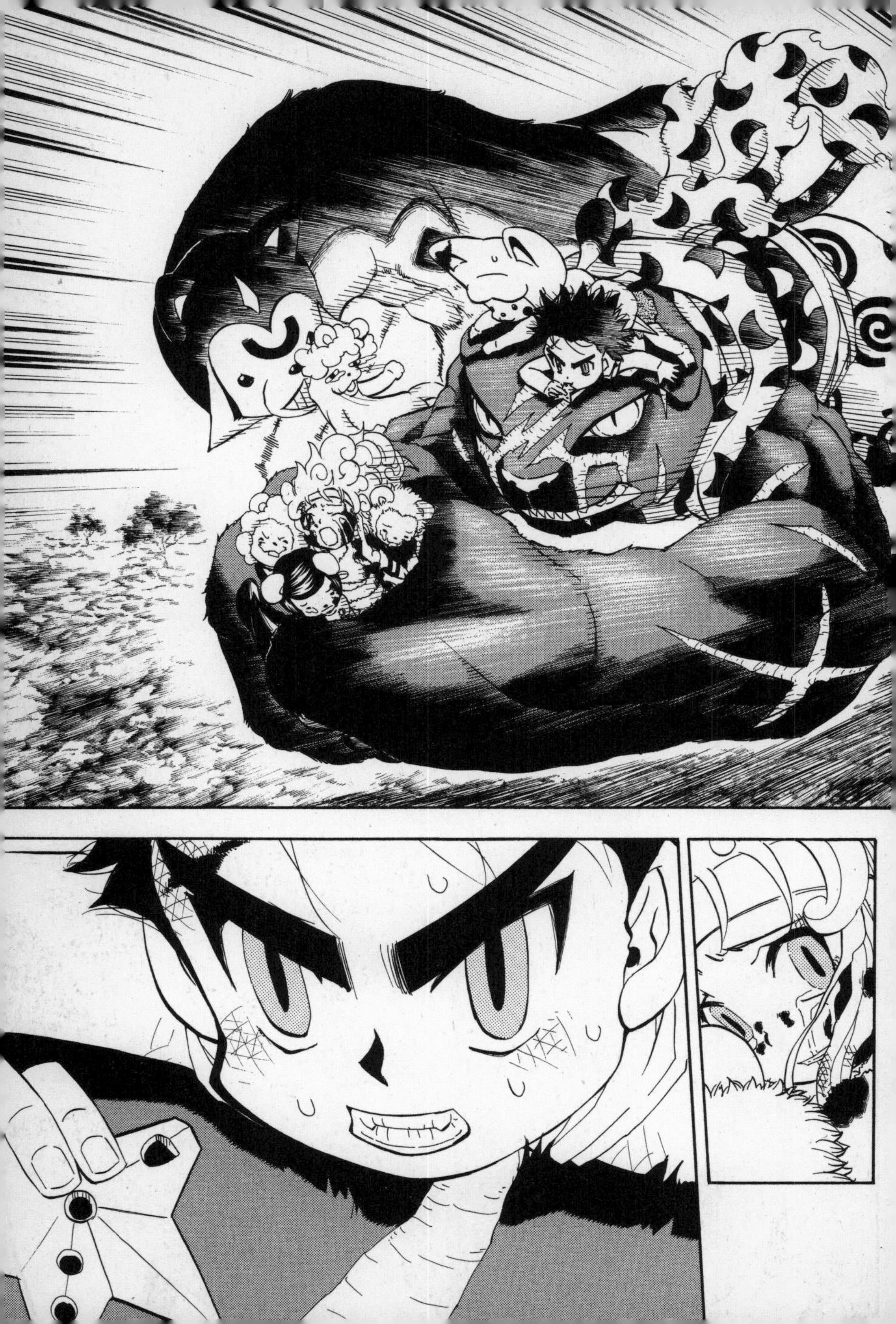

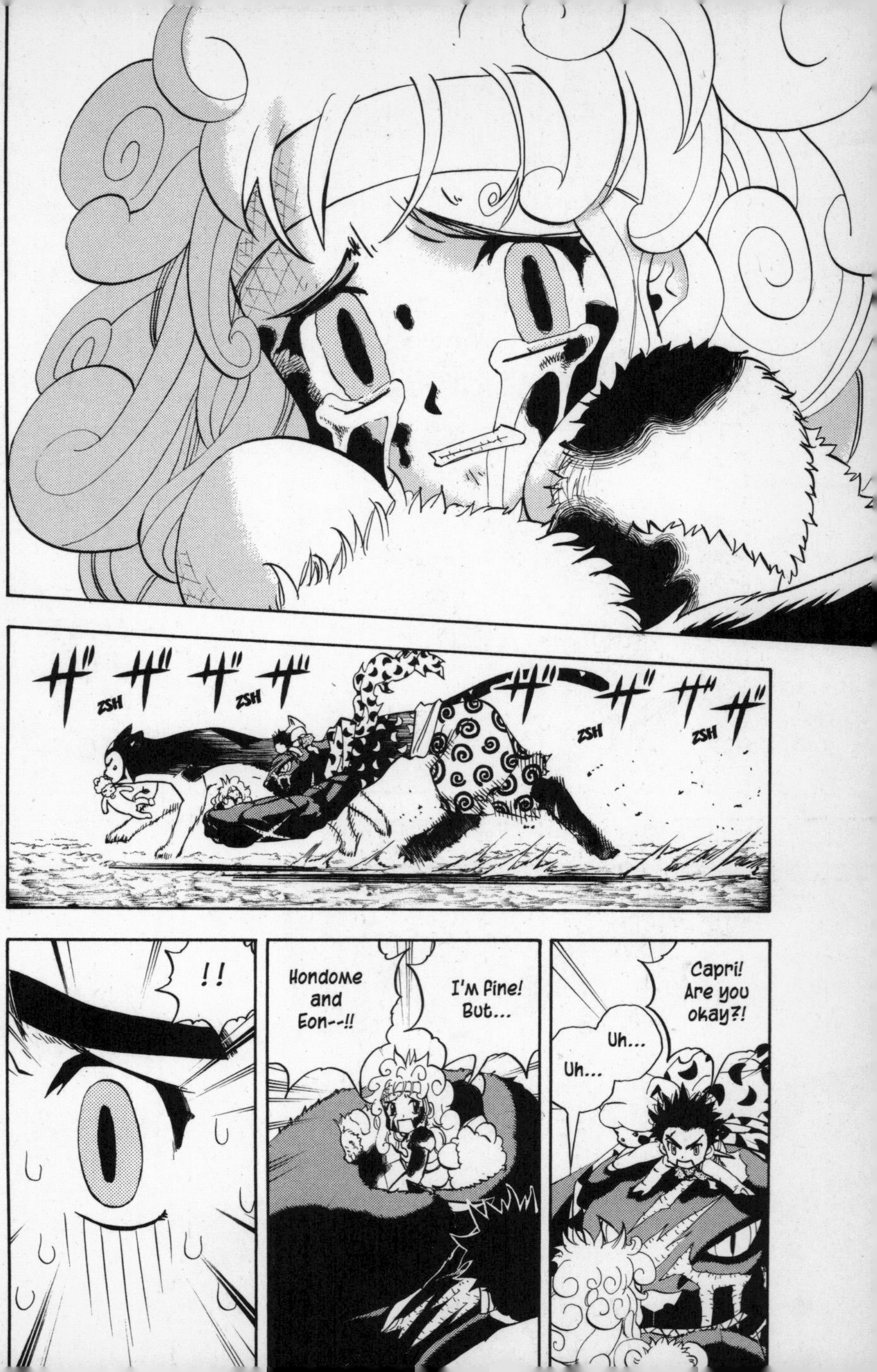
ザ ザ ザ ザ
ZSH
ZSH
ザ ザ ザ ザ
ZSH
ZSH
Capri! Are you okay?!
Uh...
Uh...
I'm fine! But...
Hondome and Eon--!!
!!

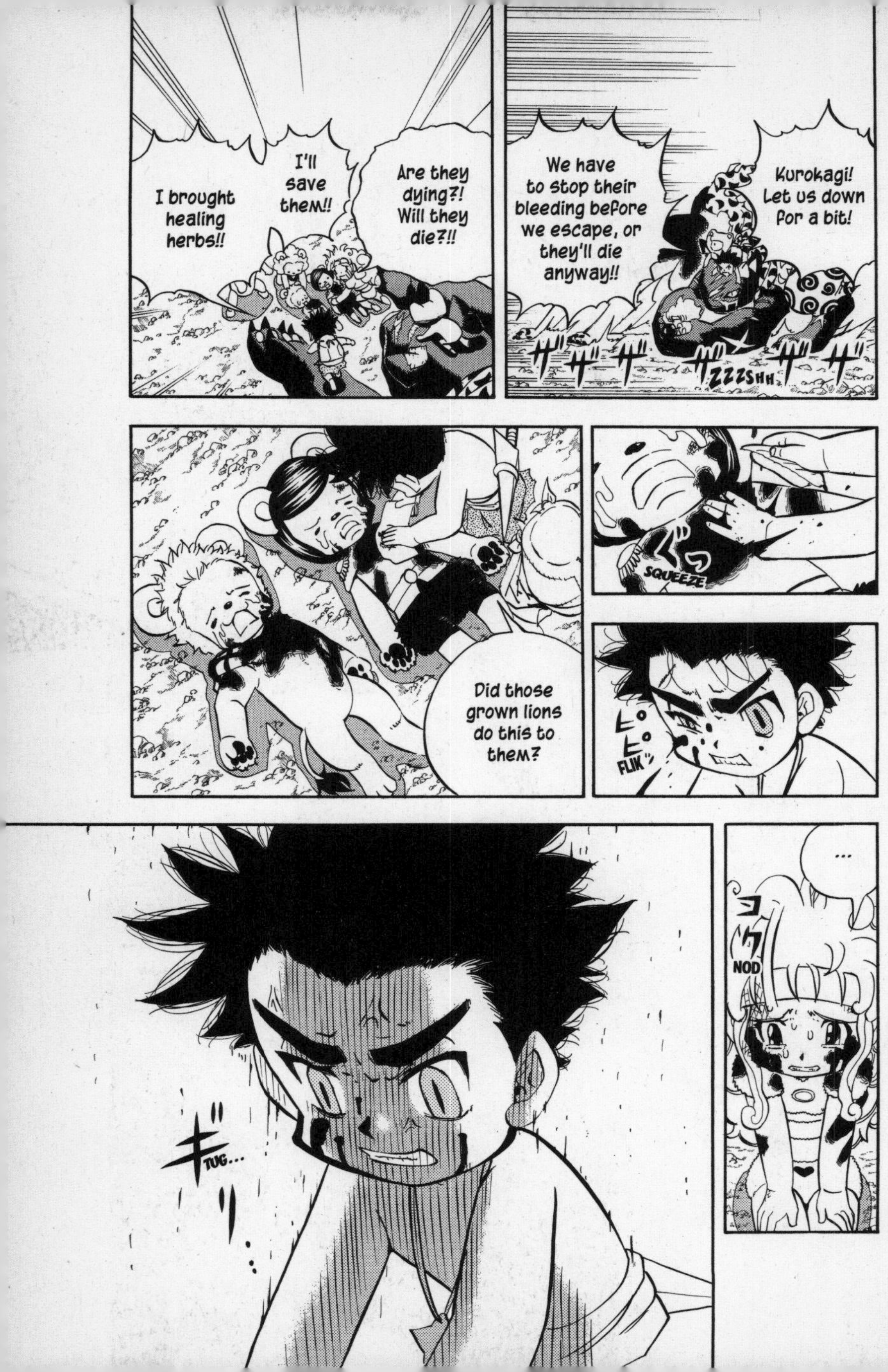

Kurokagi! Let us down for a bit!
We have to stop their bleeding before we escape, or they'll die anyway!!
ZZZSHH
Are they dying?! Will they die?!!
I'll save them!!
I brought healing herbs!!
SQUEEZE
FLIK
Did those grown lions do this to them?
...
NOD
TUG...

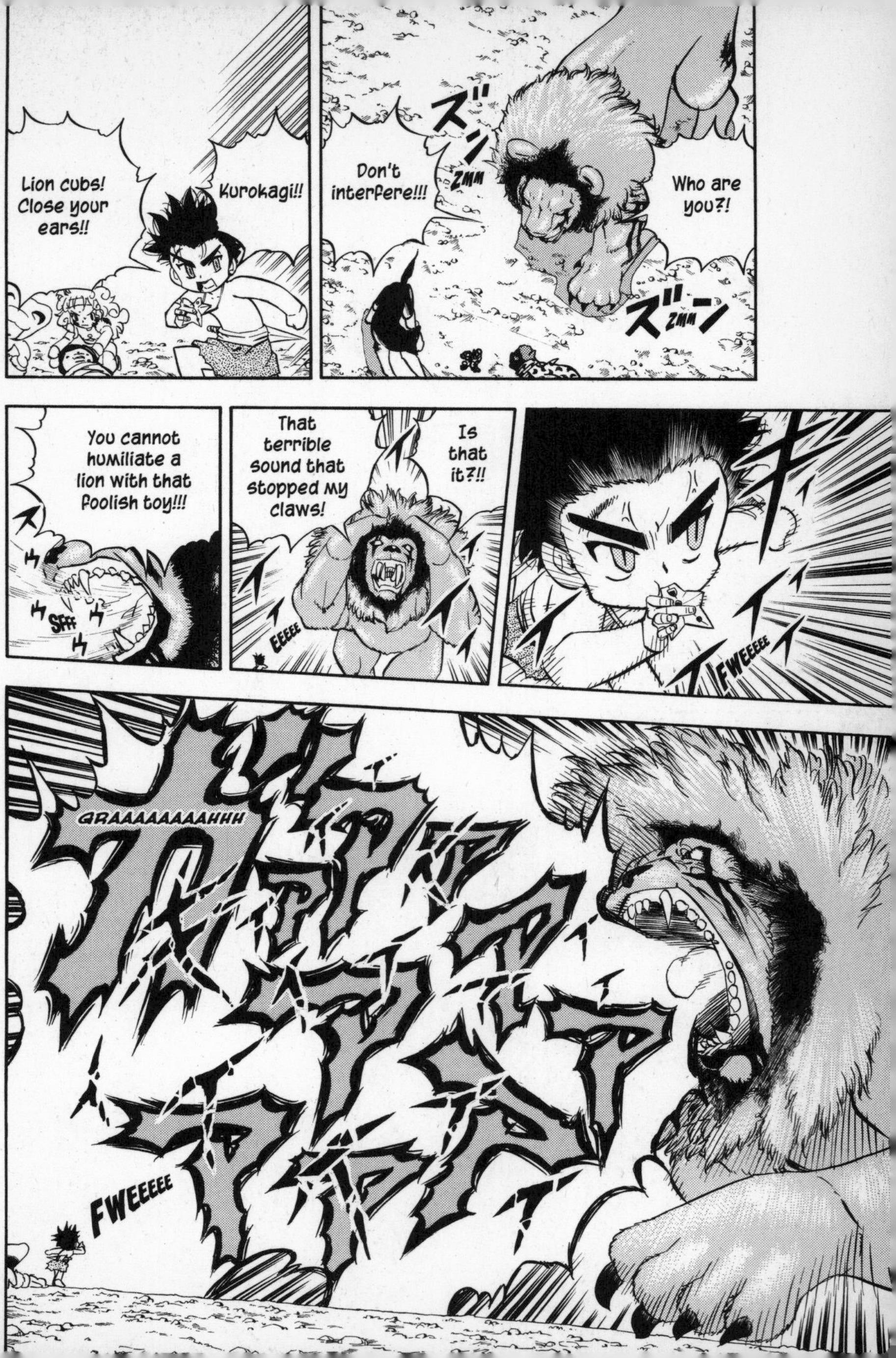
Who are you?!
ズン
ZMM
Don't interfere!!!
ズーン
ZMM
Kurokagi!!
Lion cubs! Close your ears!!
FWEEEEE
Is that it?!!
That terrible sound that stopped my claws!
EEEEE
You cannot humiliate a lion with that foolish toy!!!
SFFF
GRAAAAAAAAAHHH
FWEEEEE

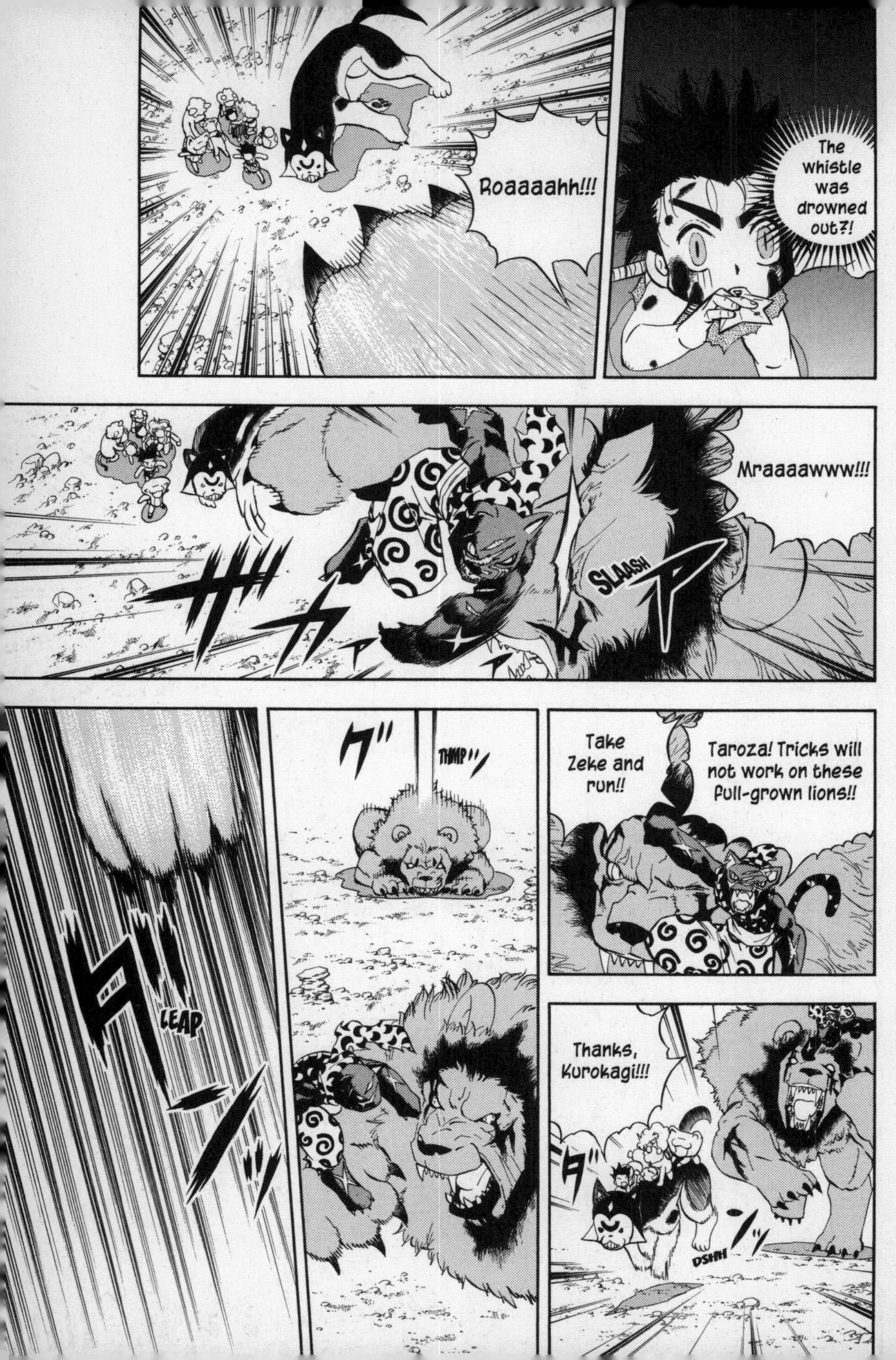
The whistle was drowned out?!
Roaaaaahh!!!
Mraaaawww!!!
SLAASH
Taroza! Tricks will not work on these full-grown lions!!
Take Zeke and run!!
Thanks, Kurokagi!!!
DSHH
THMP
LEAP

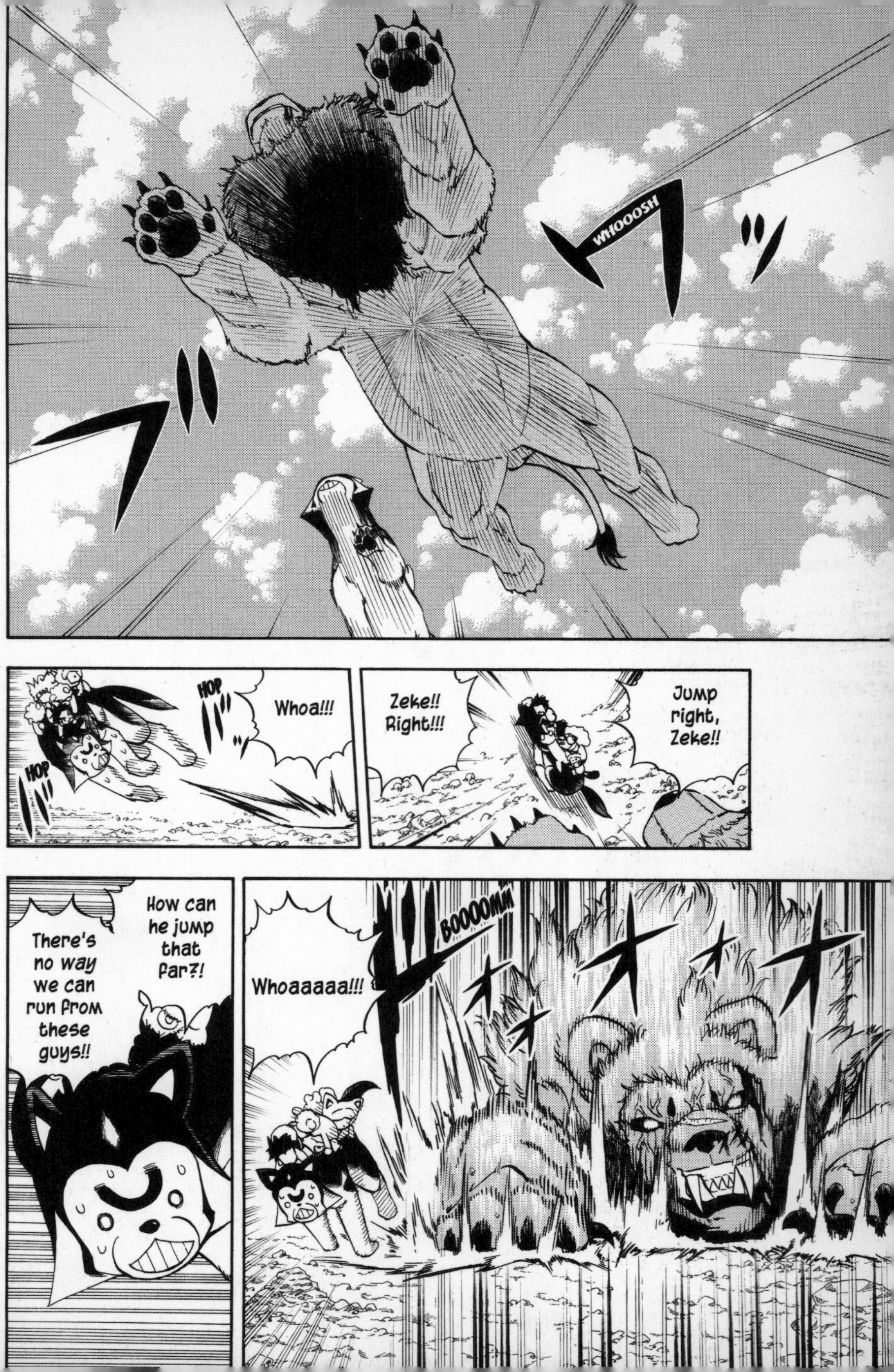
WHOOOSH
Jump right, Zeke!!
Zeke!! Right!!!
HOP
Whoa!!!
HOP
BOOOOMM
Whoaaaaa!!!
How can he jump that far?!
There's no way we can run from these guys!!

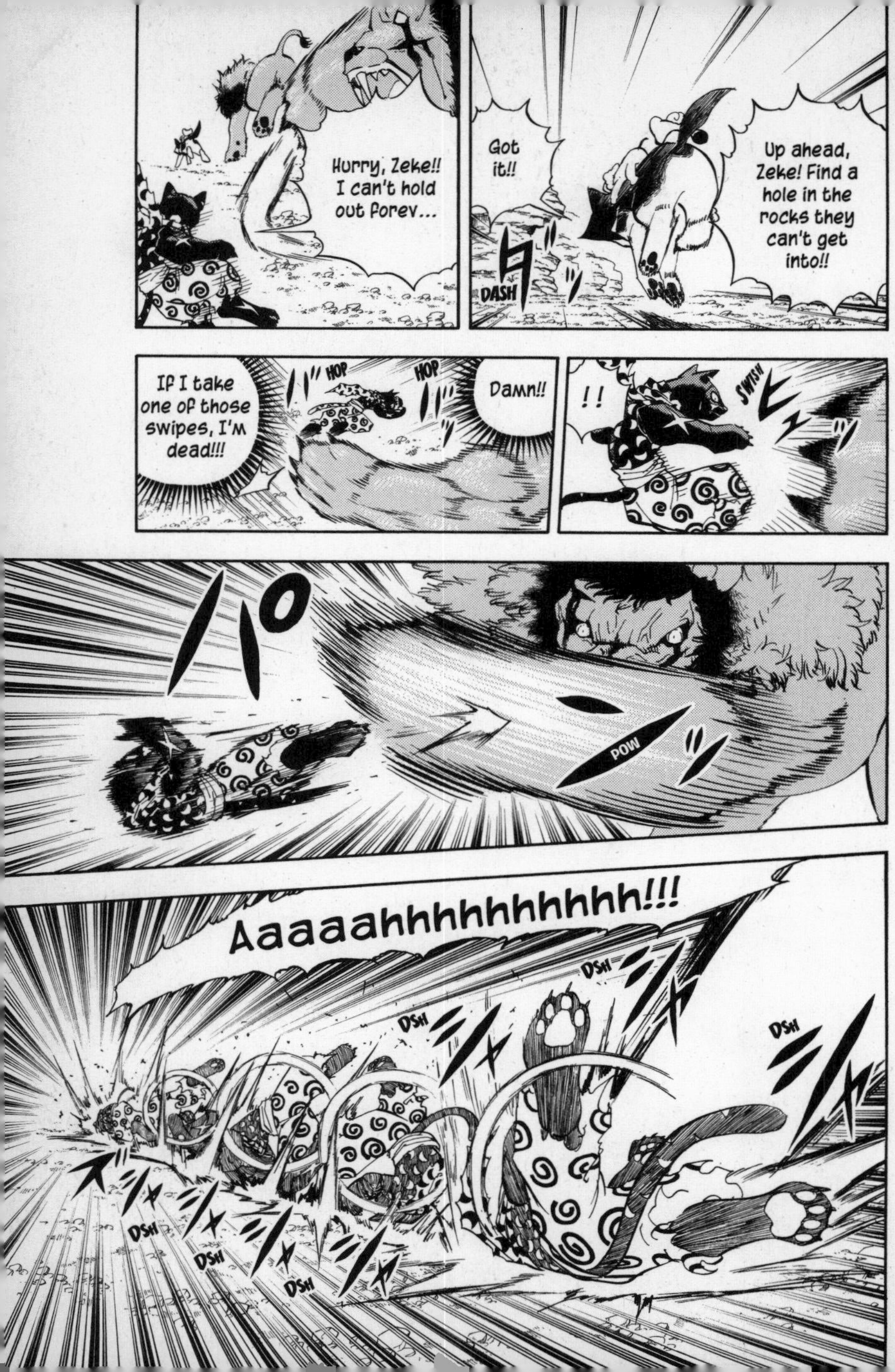
Up ahead, Zeke! Find a hole in the rocks they can't get into!!
Got it!!
DASH
Hurry, Zeke!! I can't hold out forev...
SWISH
!!
Damn!!
HOP
HOP
If I take one of those swipes, I'm dead!!!
POW
Aaaaahhhhhhhhhh!!!
DSH
DSH
DSH
DSH
DSH
DSH

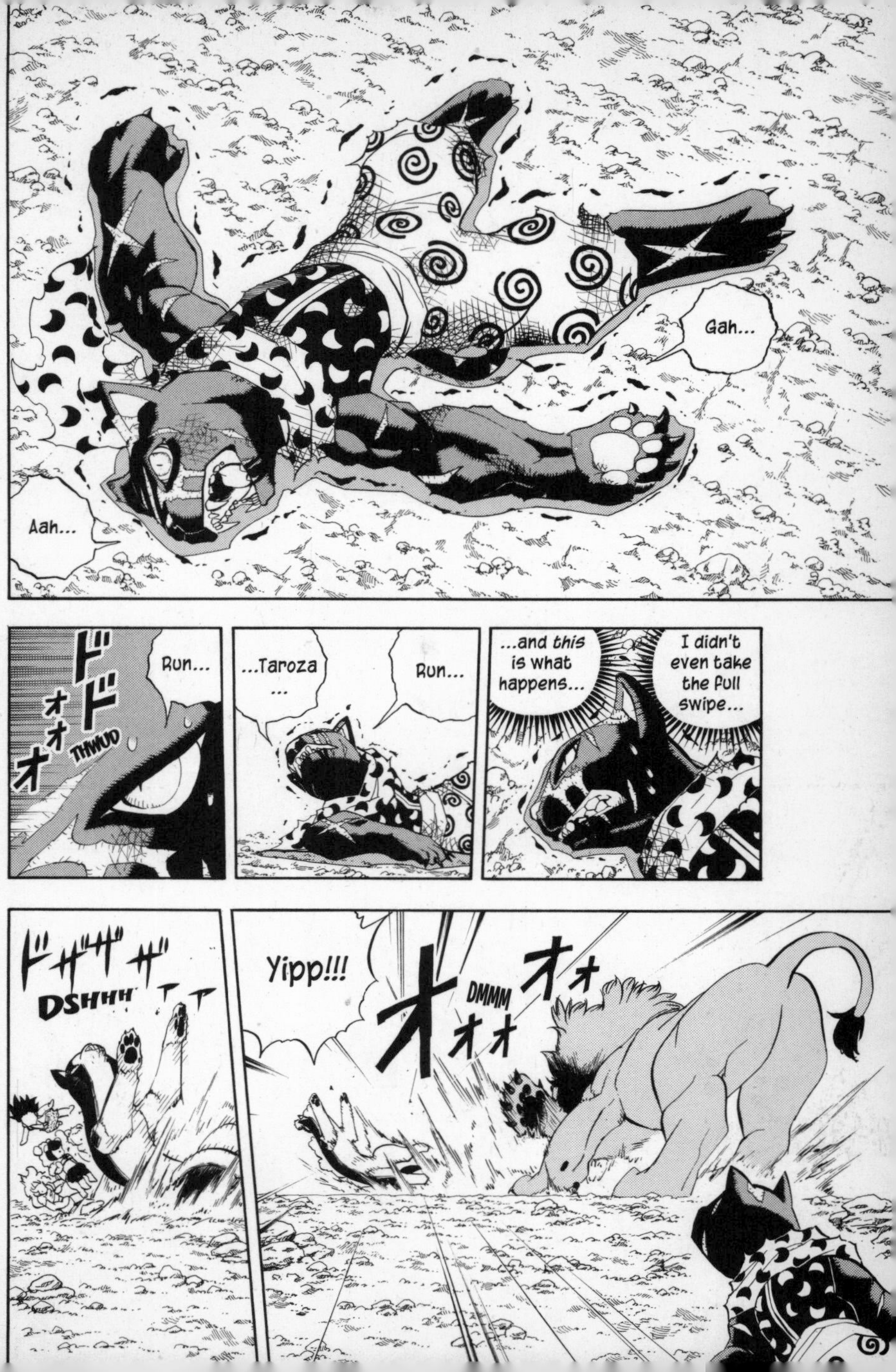

Gah...
Aah...
I didn't even take the full swipe...
...and this is what happens...
Run...
...Taroza ...
Run...
ドドオオオ
THWUD
Yipp!!!
オオオオオ
DMMM
ドザザザァァ
DSHHH

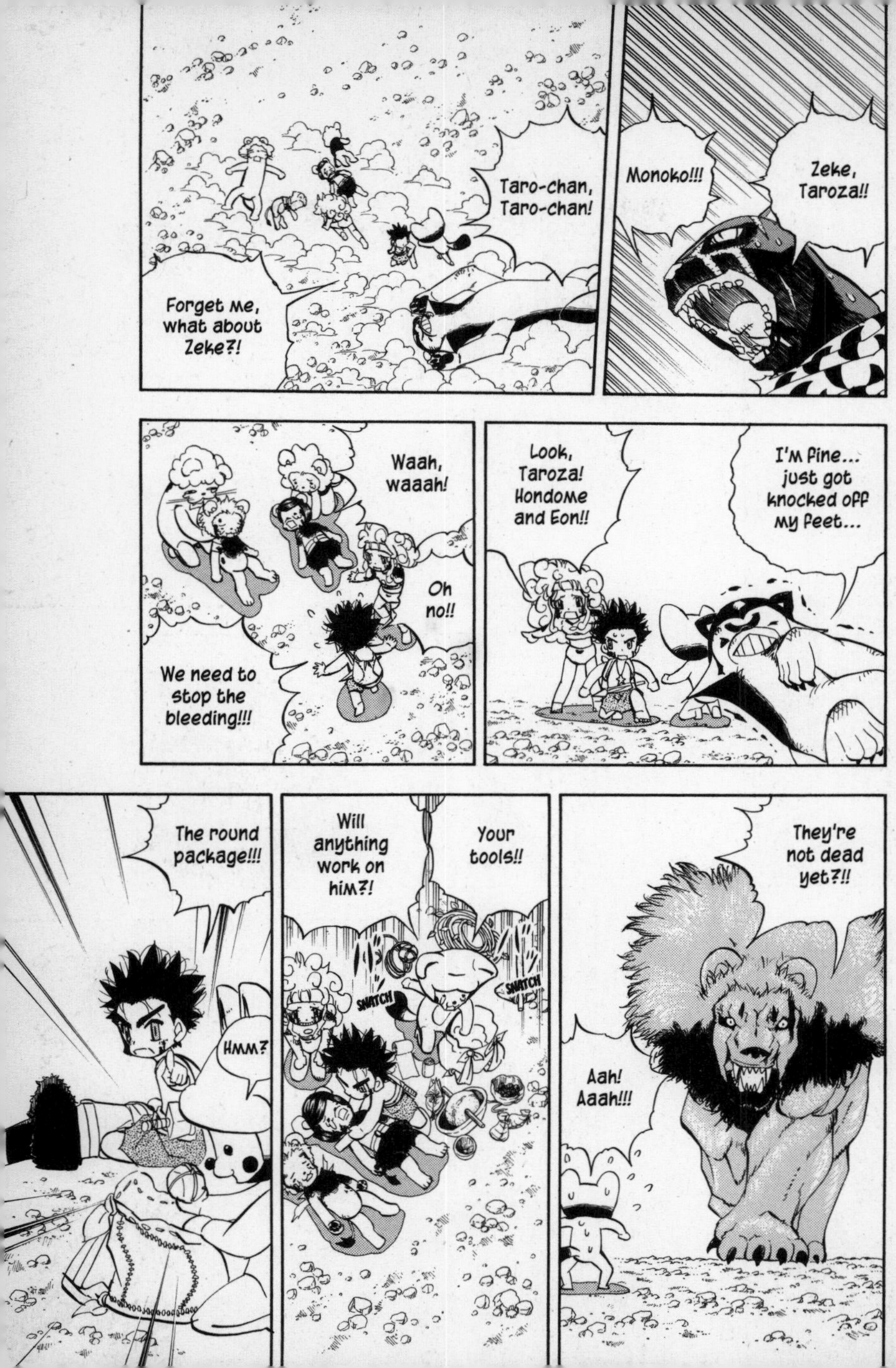
Zeke, Taroza!!
Monoko!!!
Taro-chan, Taro-chan!
Forget me, what about Zeke?!
I'm fine... just got knocked off my feet...
Look, Taroza! Hondome and Eon!!
Waah, waaah!
Oh no!!
We need to stop the bleeding!!!
They're not dead yet?!!
Aah! Aaah!!!
Your tools!!
Will anything work on him?!
SNATCH
SNATCH
The round package!!!
Hmm?

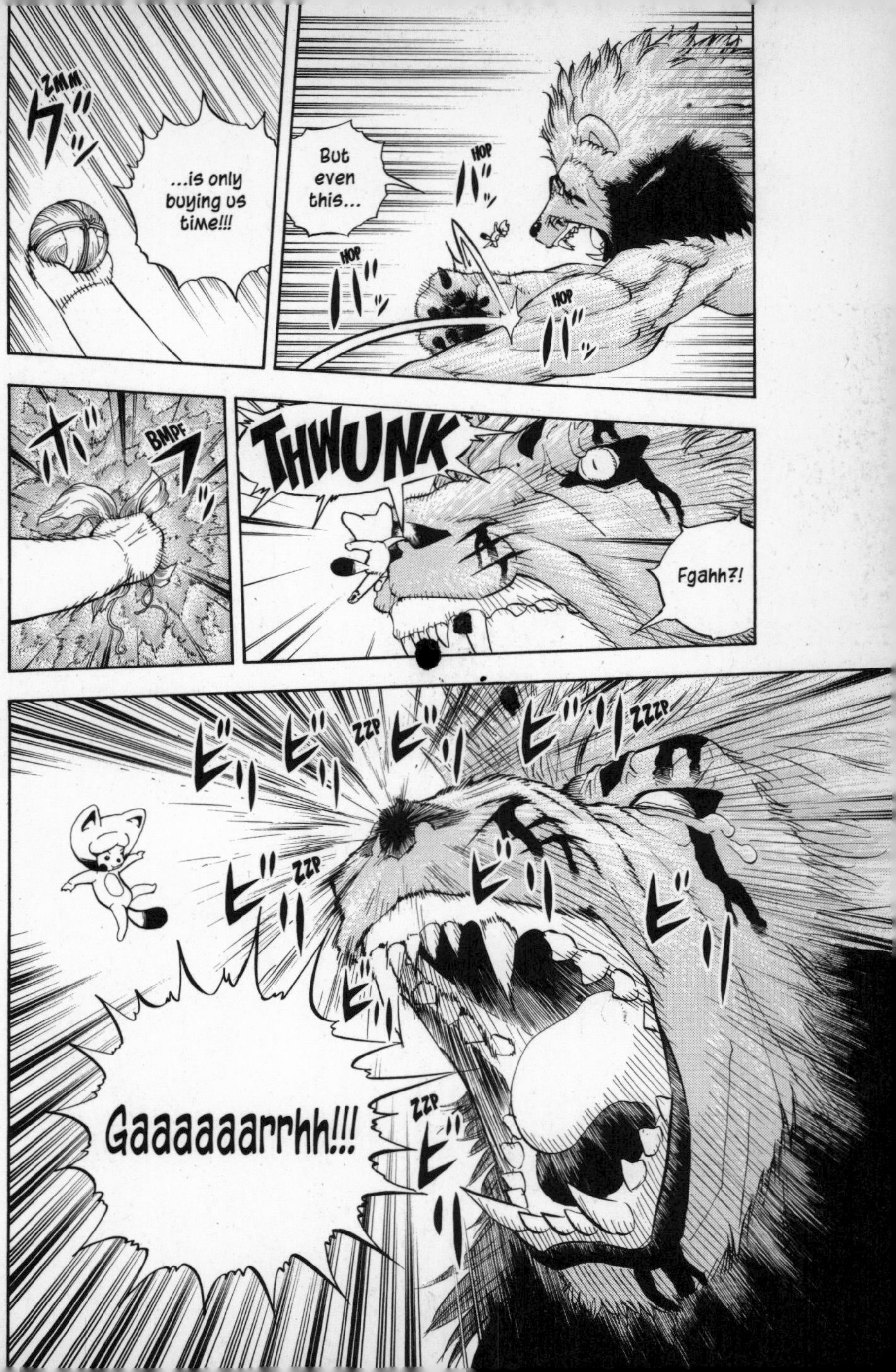
But even this...
HOP
HOP
HOP
ZMM
...is only buying us time!!!
THWUNK
Fgahh?!
BMPF
ZZZP
ZZP
ZZP
ZZP
Gaaaaaarrhh!!!

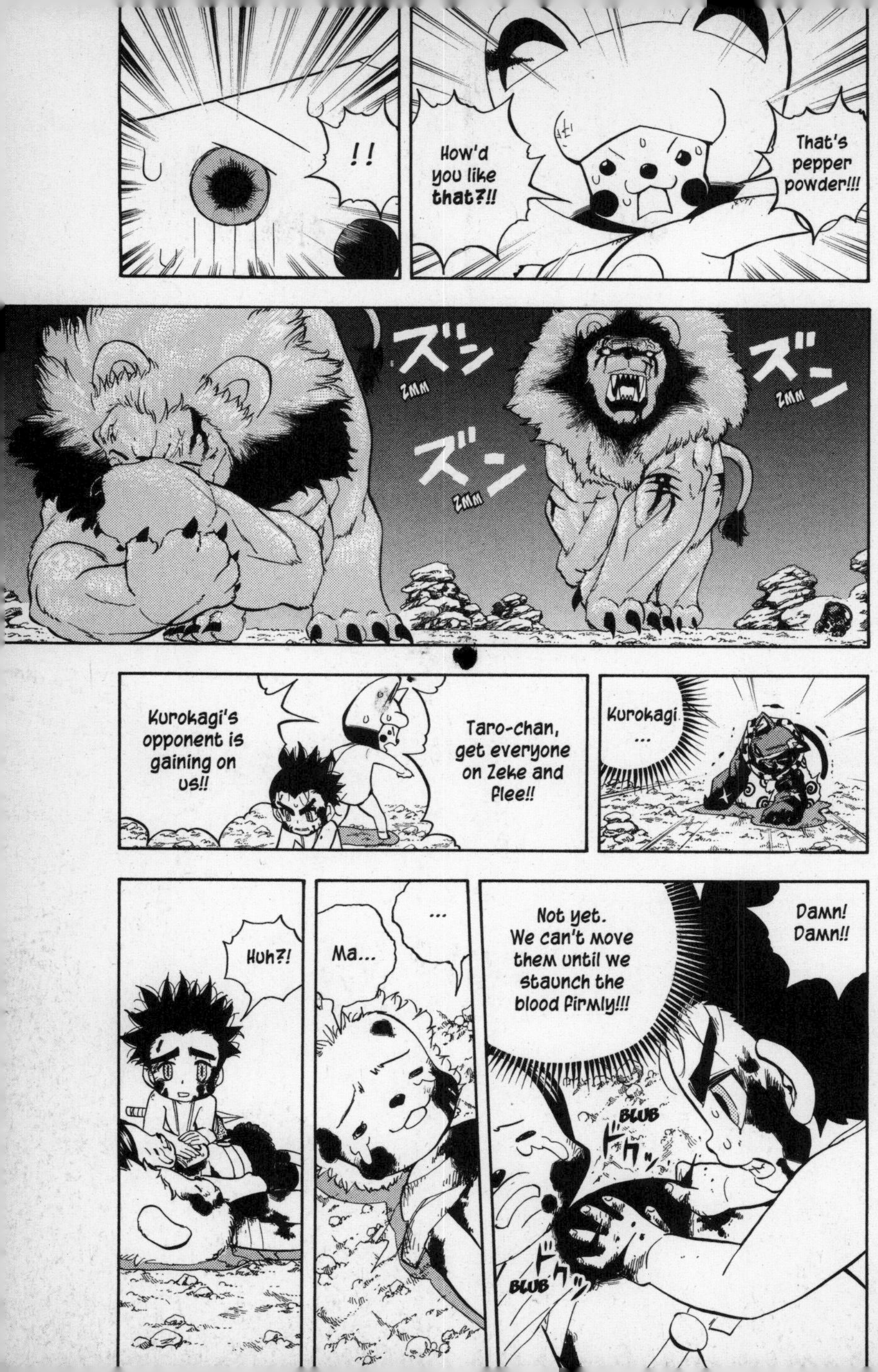
That's pepper powder!!!
How'd you like that?!!
!!
ズン
ZMM
ズシン
ZMM
ズン
ZMM
Kurokagi ...
Taro-chan, get everyone on Zeke and flee!!
Kurokagi's opponent is gaining on us!!
Damn! Damn!!
Not yet. We can't move them until we staunch the blood firmly!!!
BLUB
ドクン
BLUB
ドクン
...
Ma...
Huh?!

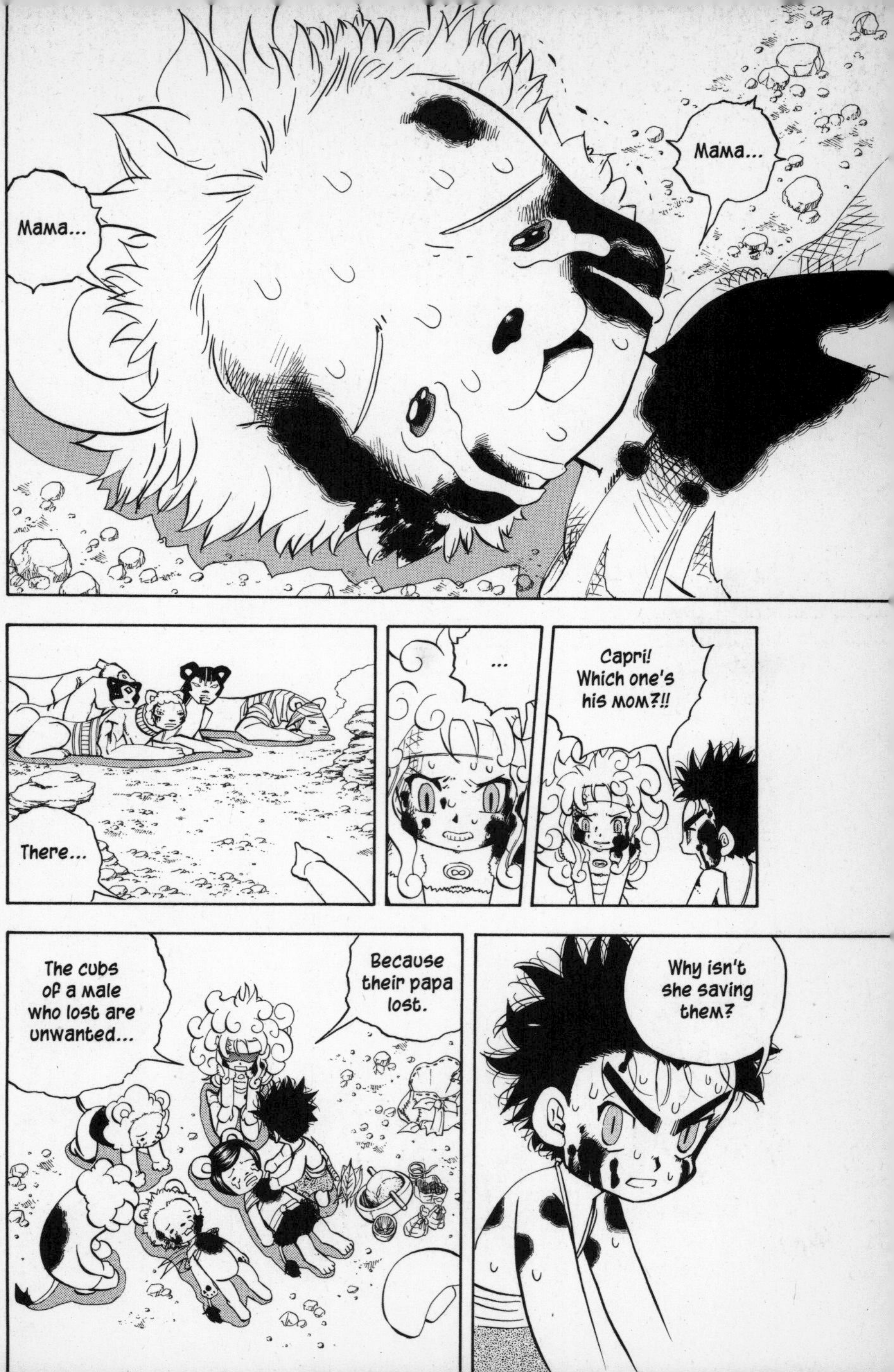
Mama...
Mama...
Capri! Which one's his mom?!!
...
There...
Why isn't she saving them?
Because their papa lost.
The cubs of a male who lost are unwanted...

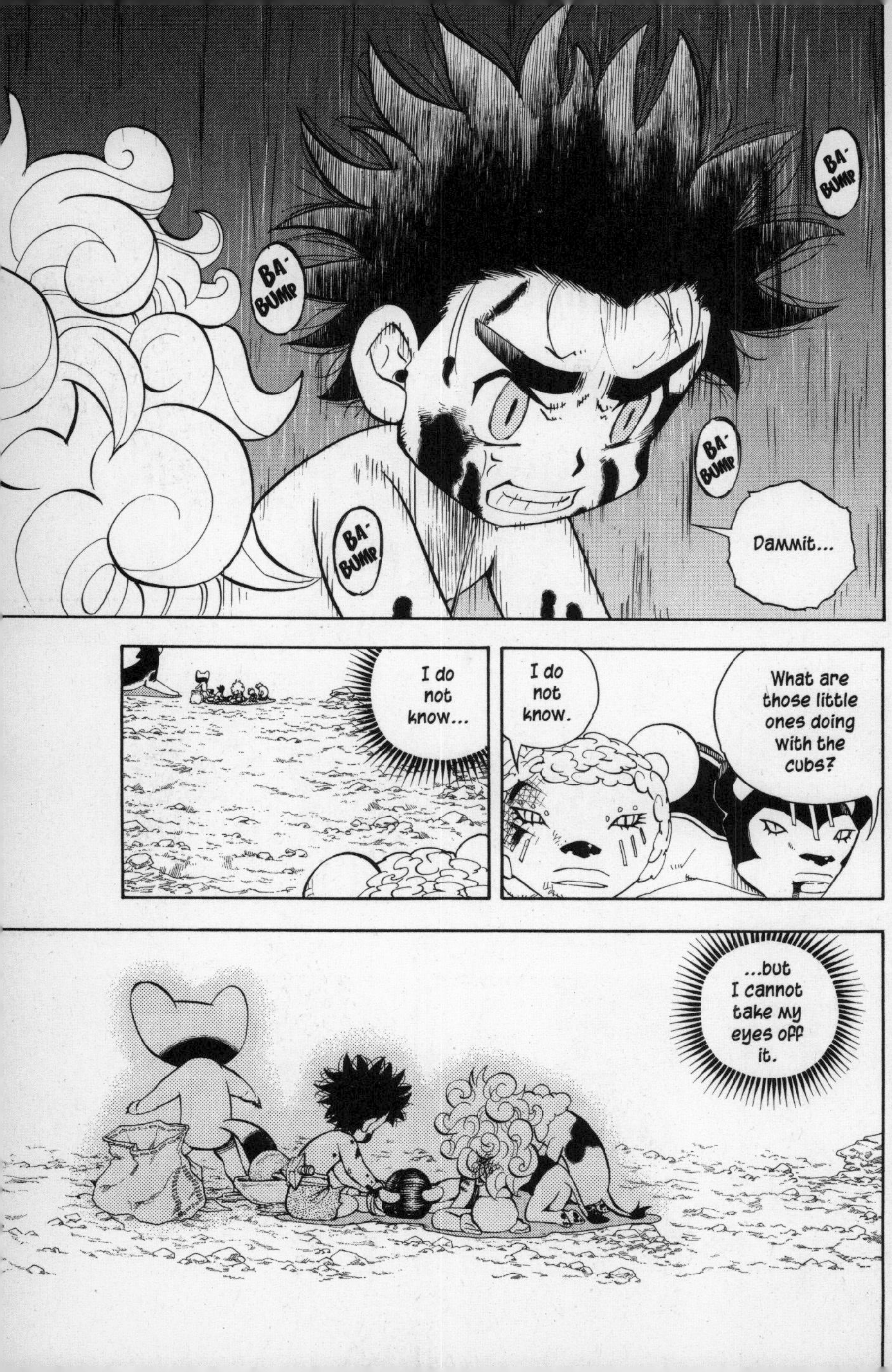
BA-BUMP
BA-BUMP
Dammit...
BA-BUMP
BA-BUMP
What are those little ones doing with the cubs?
I do not know.
I do not know...
...but I cannot take my eyes off it.

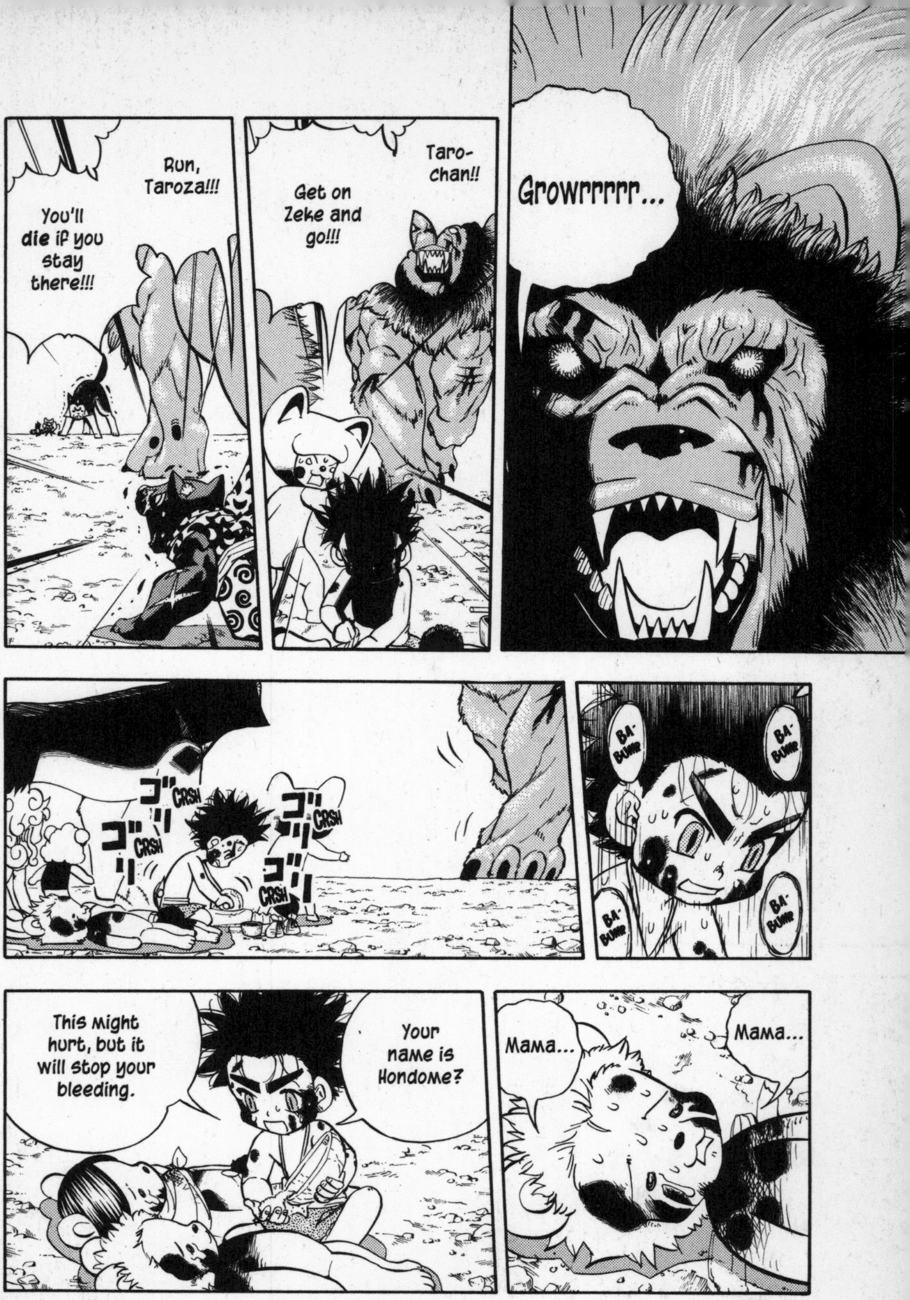
Growrrrrr...
Taro-chan!!
Get on Zeke and go!!!
Run, Taroza!!!
You'll die if you stay there!!!
BA-BUMP
BA-BUMP
BA-BUMP
BA-BUMP
ゴリ CRSH
ゴリ CRSH
ゴリ CRSH
ゴリ CRSH
Mama...
Mama...
Your name is Hondome?
This might hurt, but it will stop your bleeding.

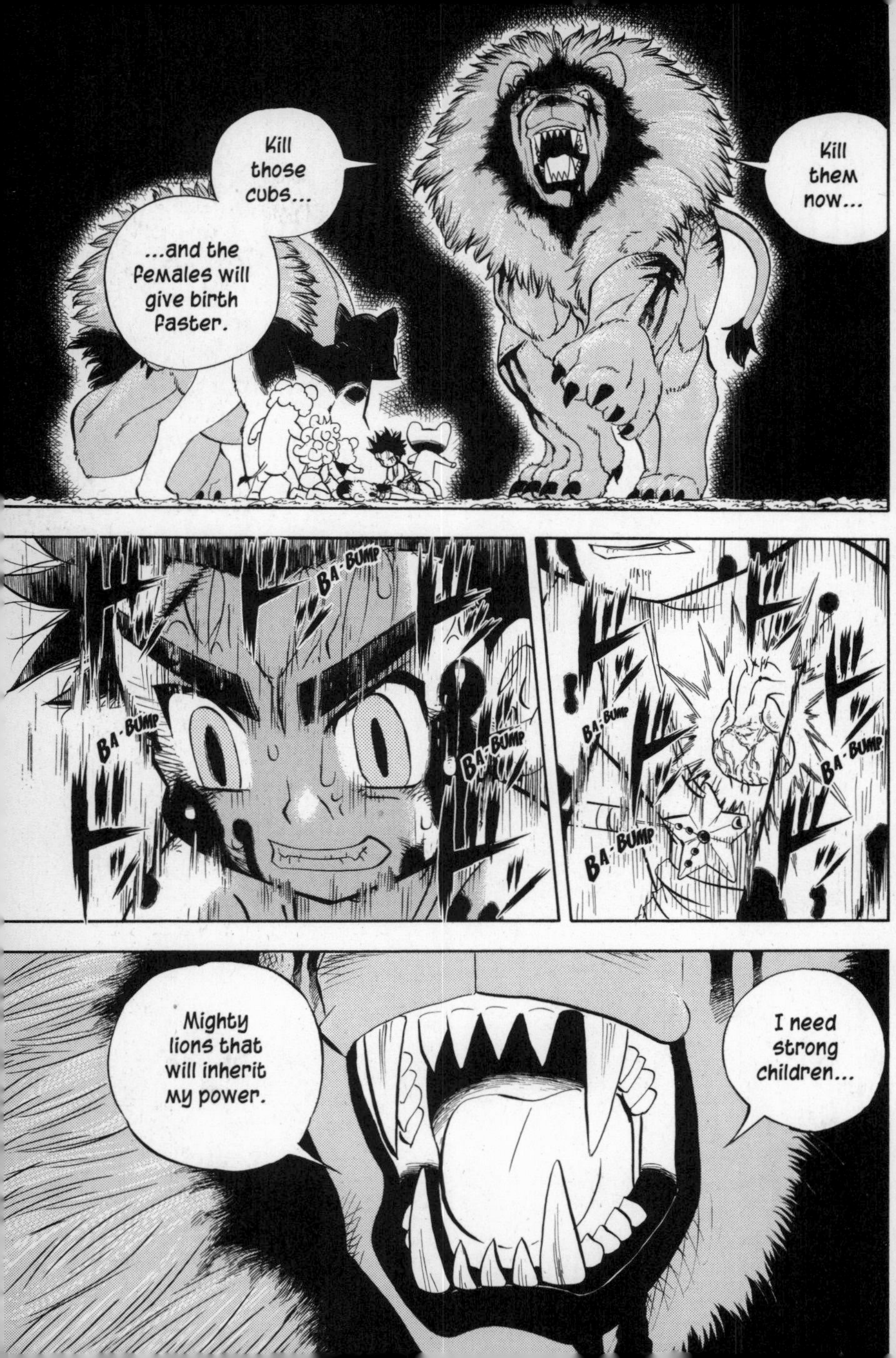
Kill them now...
Kill those cubs...
...and the females will give birth faster.
BA-BUMP
BA-BUMP
BA-BUMP
BA-BUMP
BA-BUMP
BA-BUMP
I need strong children...
Mighty lions that will inherit my power.

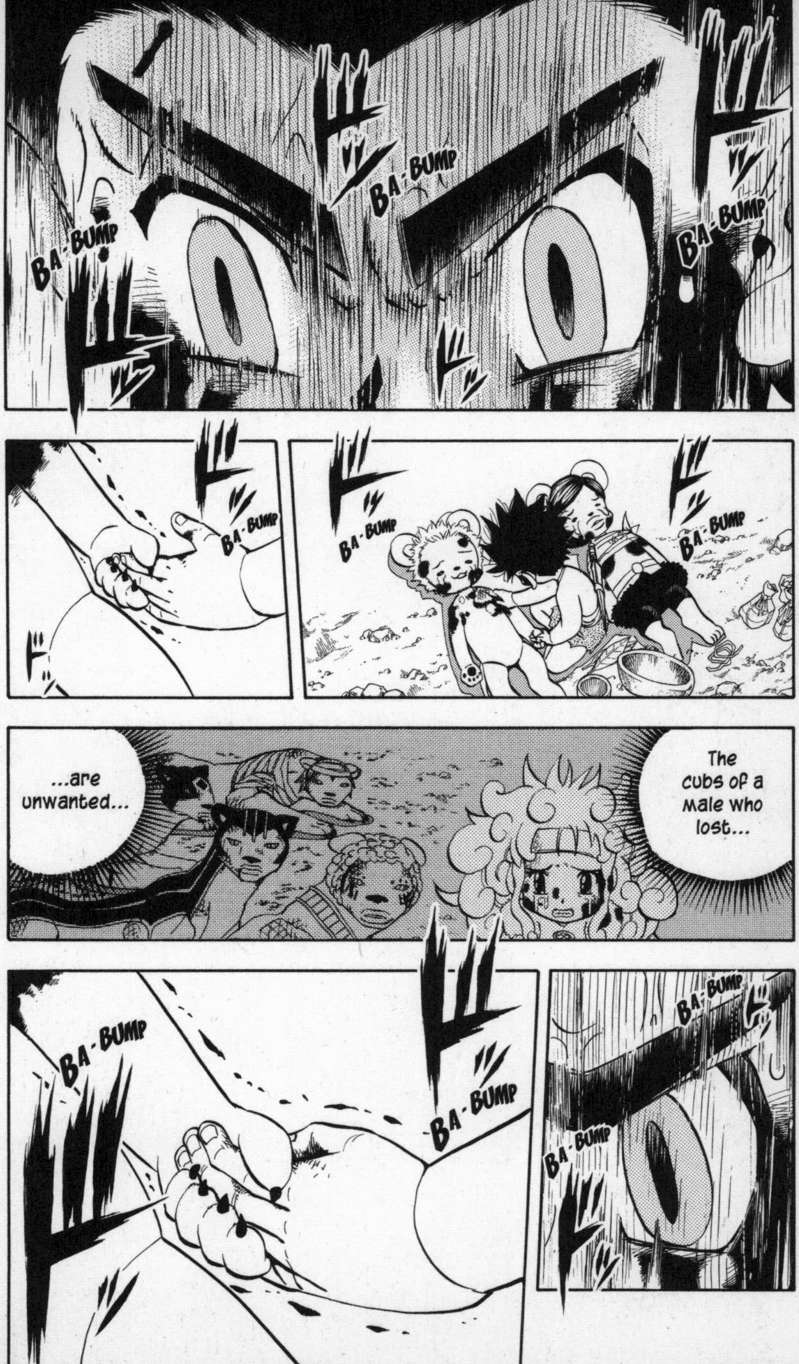
BA-BUMP
BA-BUMP
BA-BUMP
BA-BUMP
BA-BUMP
BA-BUMP
The cubs of a male who lost...
...are unwanted...
BA-BUMP
BA-BUMP
BA-BUMP
BA-BUMP

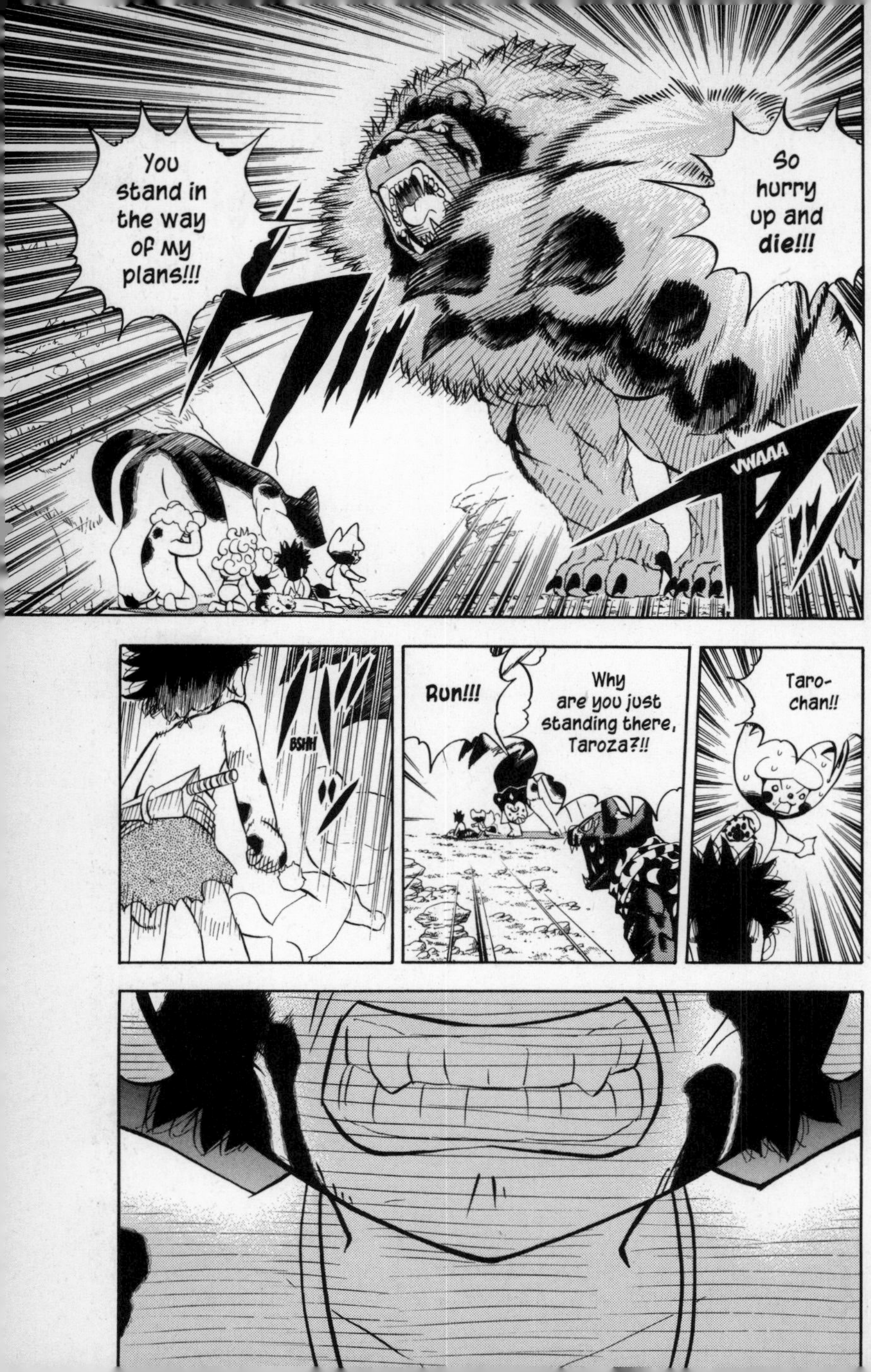
You stand in the way of my plans!!!
So hurry up and die!!!
VWAAA
Taro-chan!!
Why are you just standing there, Taroza?!!
Run!!!
BSHH

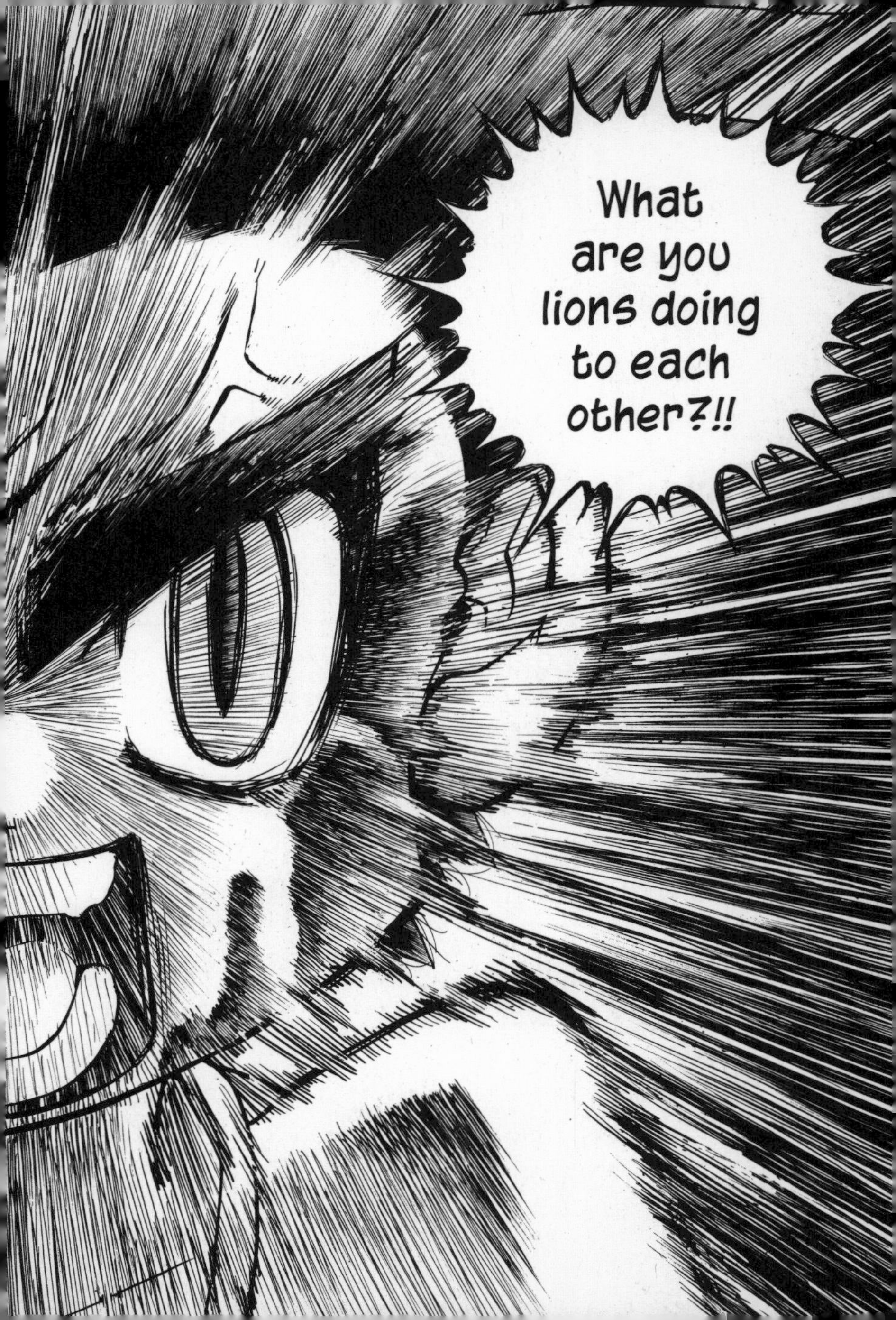
What are you lions doing to each other?!!

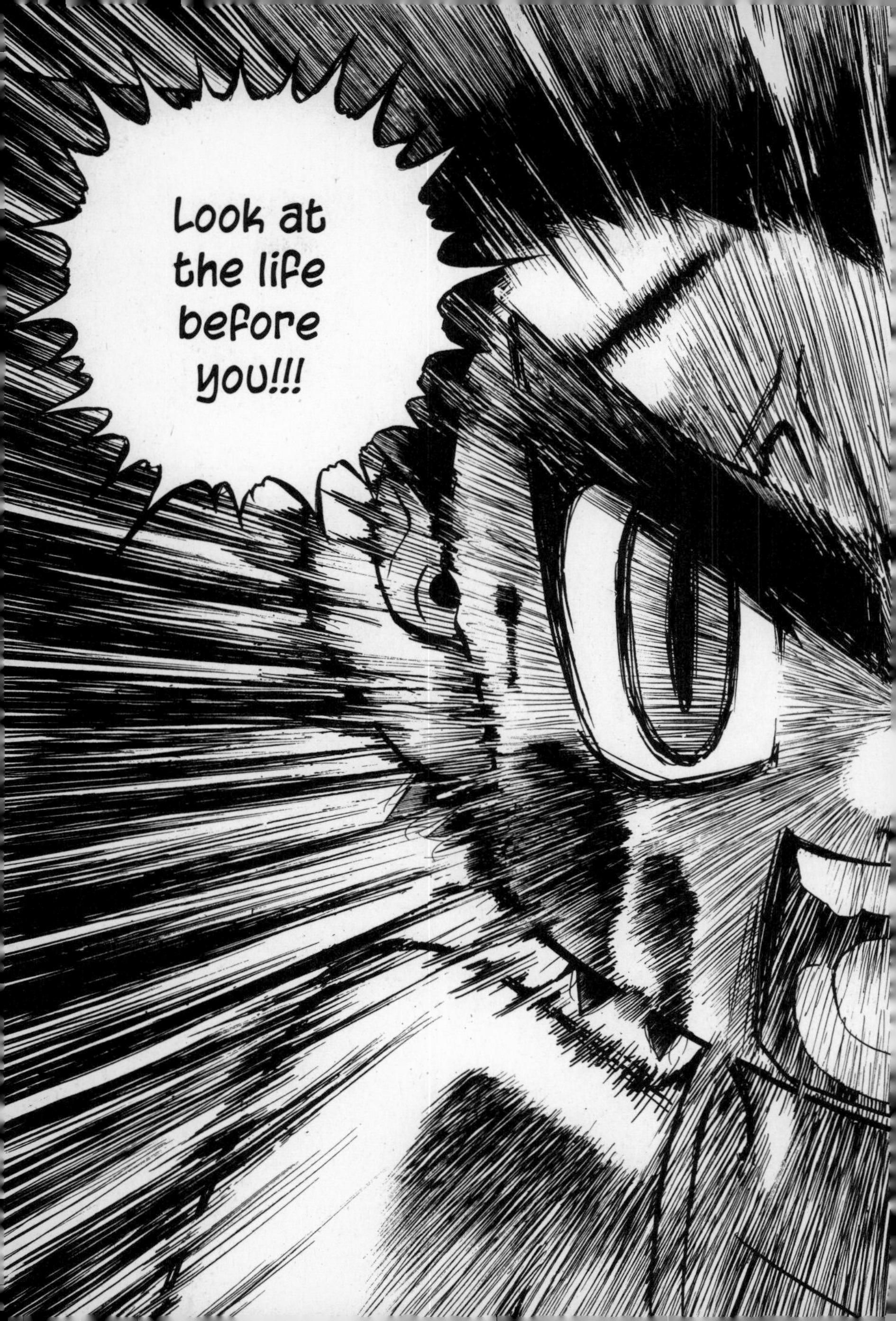
Look at the life before you!!!

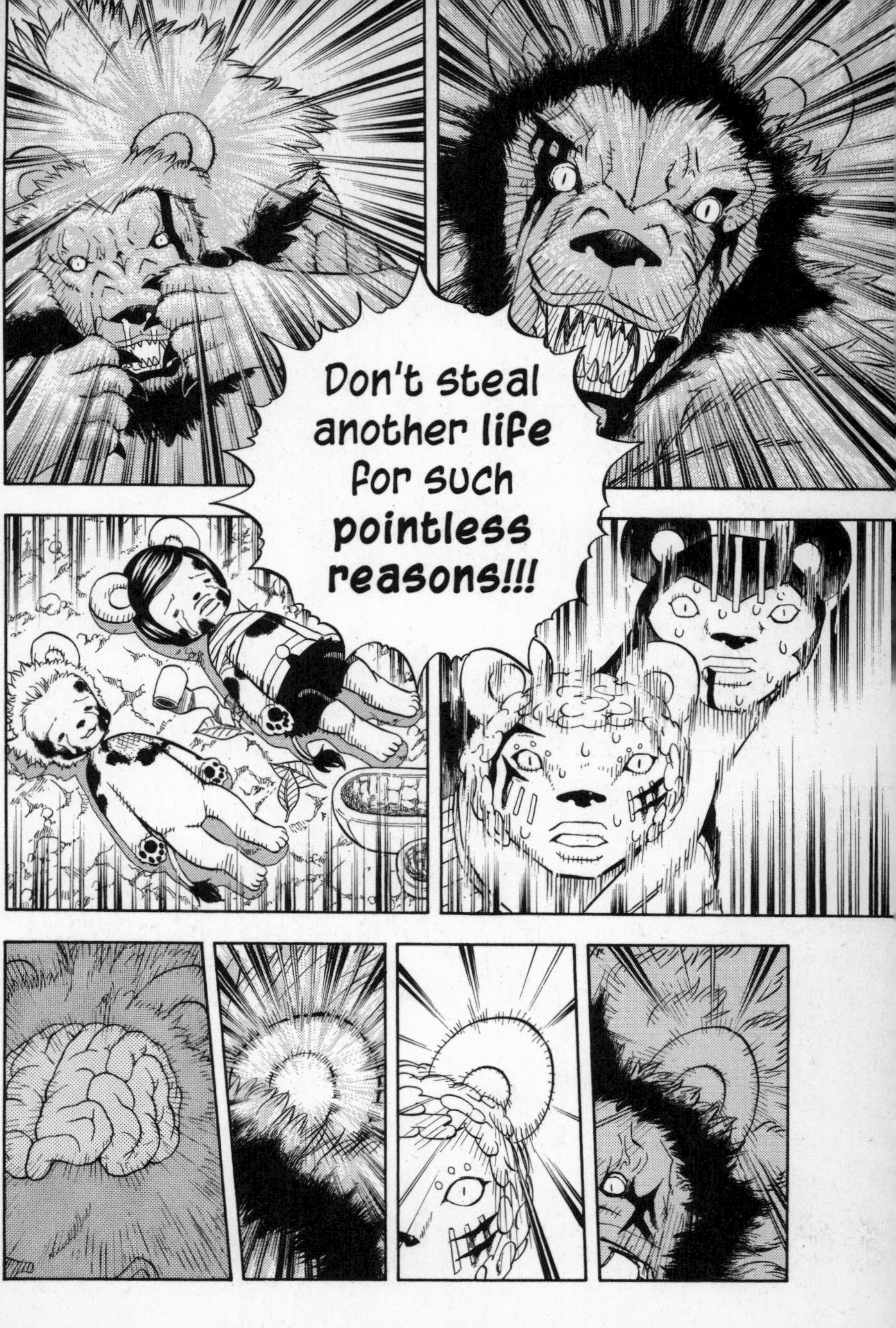
Don't steal another life for such pointless reasons!!!

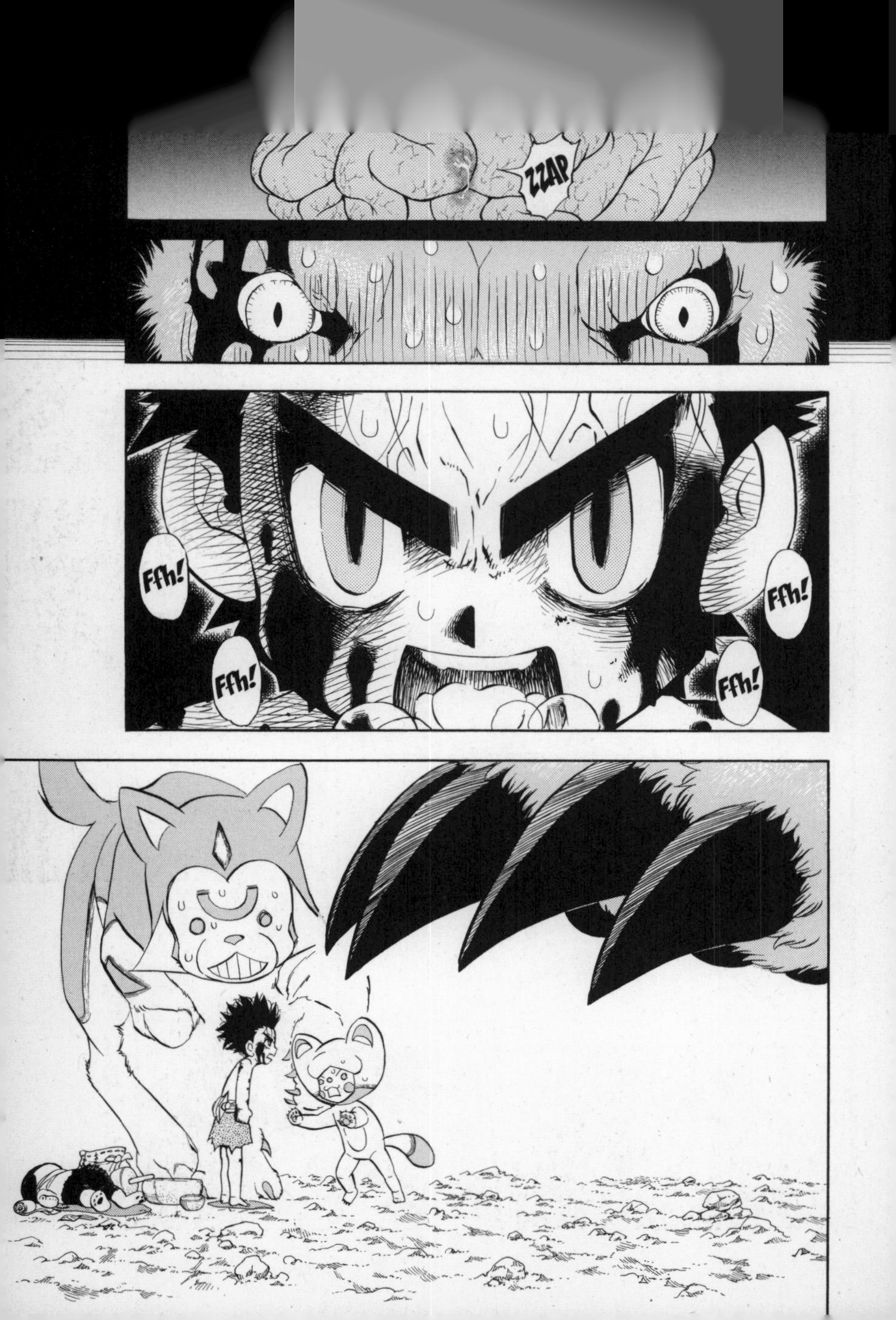
ZZAP
Ffh!
F-fh!
Ffh!
Ffh!

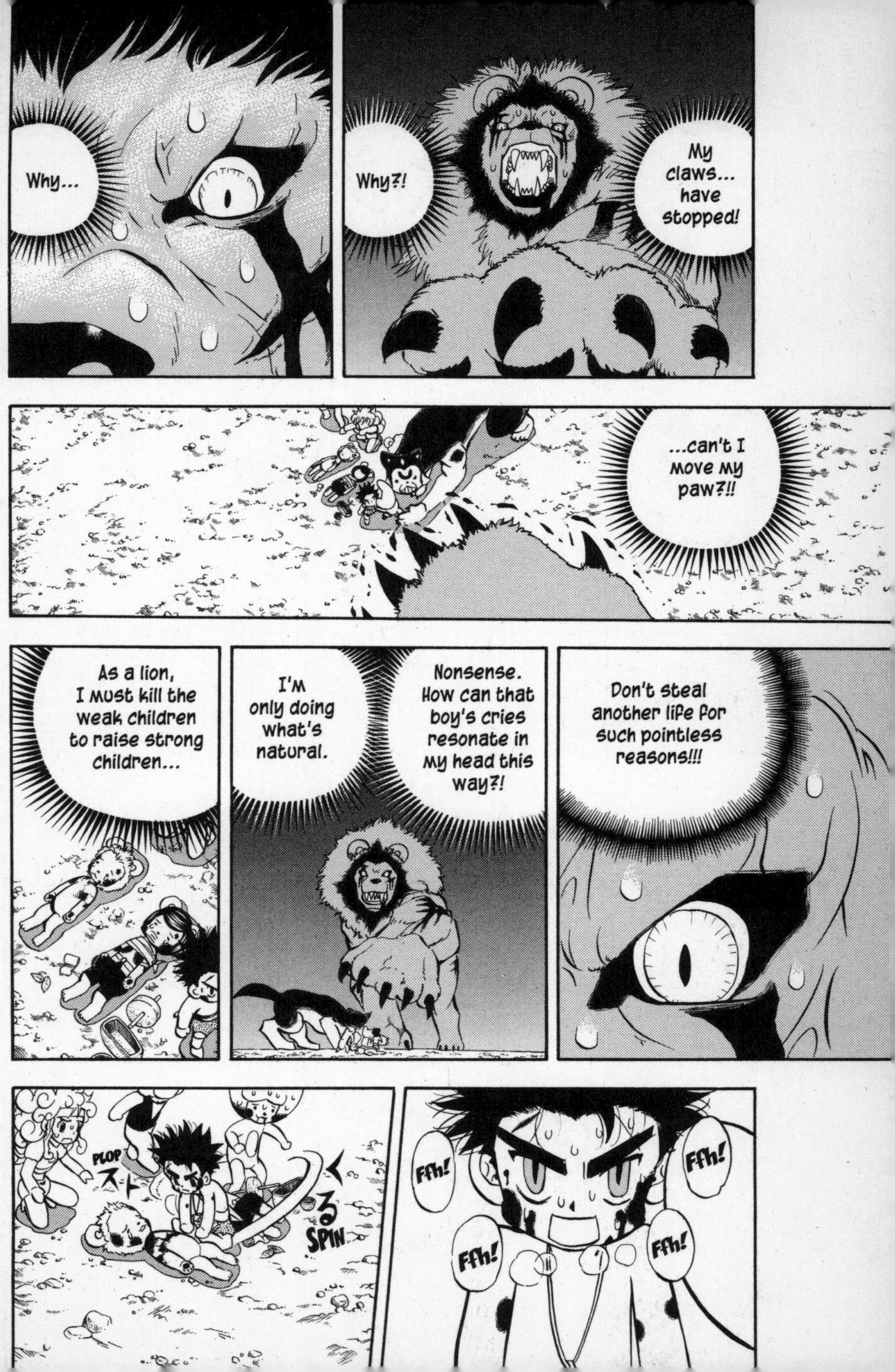
My claws... have stopped!
Why?!
Why...
...can't I move my paw?!!
Don't steal another life for such pointless reasons!!!
Nonsense. How can that boy's cries resonate in my head this way?!
I'm only doing what's natural.
As a lion, I must kill the weak children to raise strong children...
Ffh!
Ffh!
Ffh!
Ffh!
SPIN
PLOP

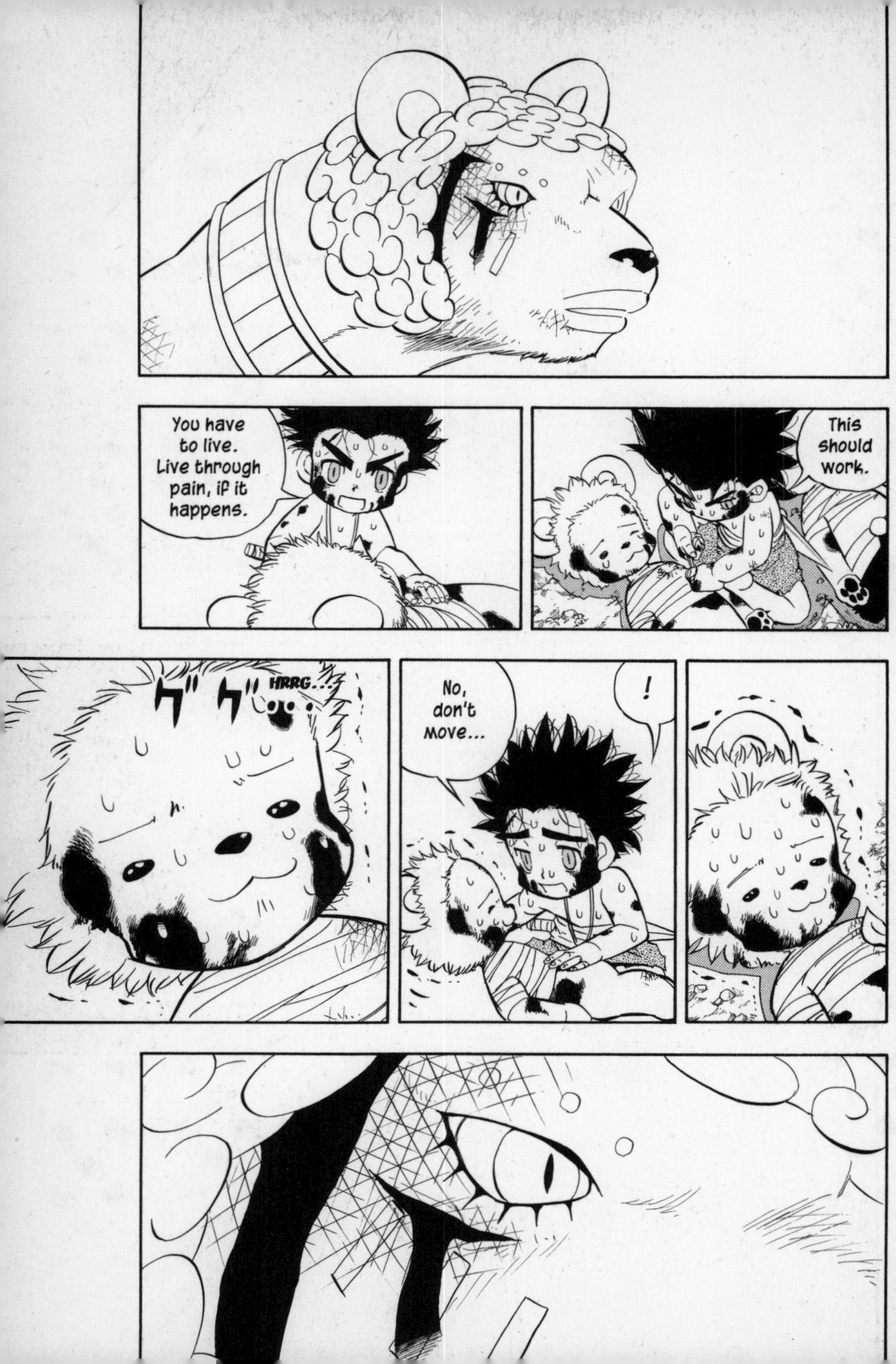
This should work.
You have to live. Live through pain, if it happens.
!
No, don't move...
HRRG...

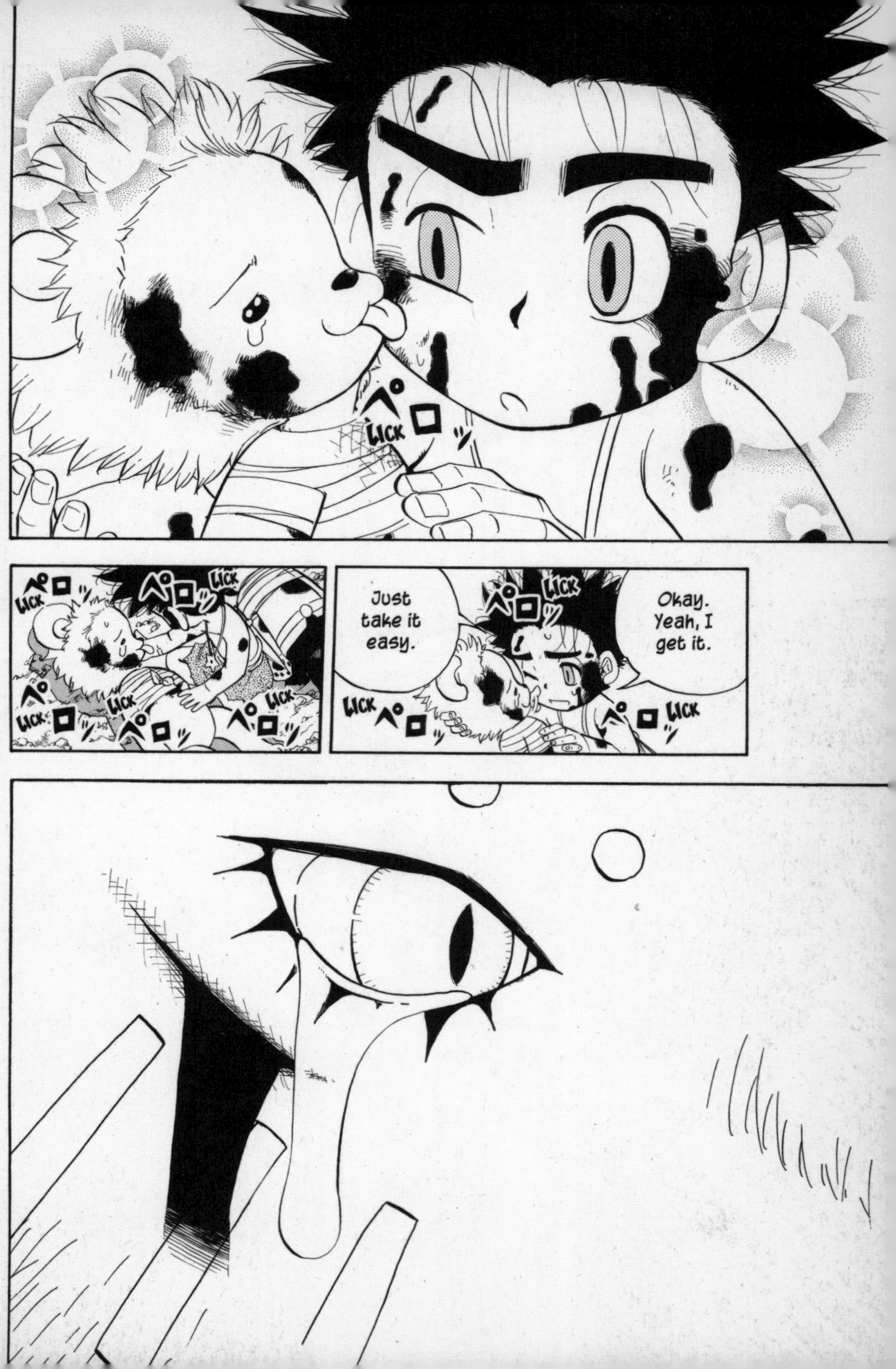
ペロッ
LICK
ペロッ
LICK
ペロッ
LICK
Okay. Yeah, I get it.
Just take it easy.
ペロッ
LICK
ペロッ
LICK

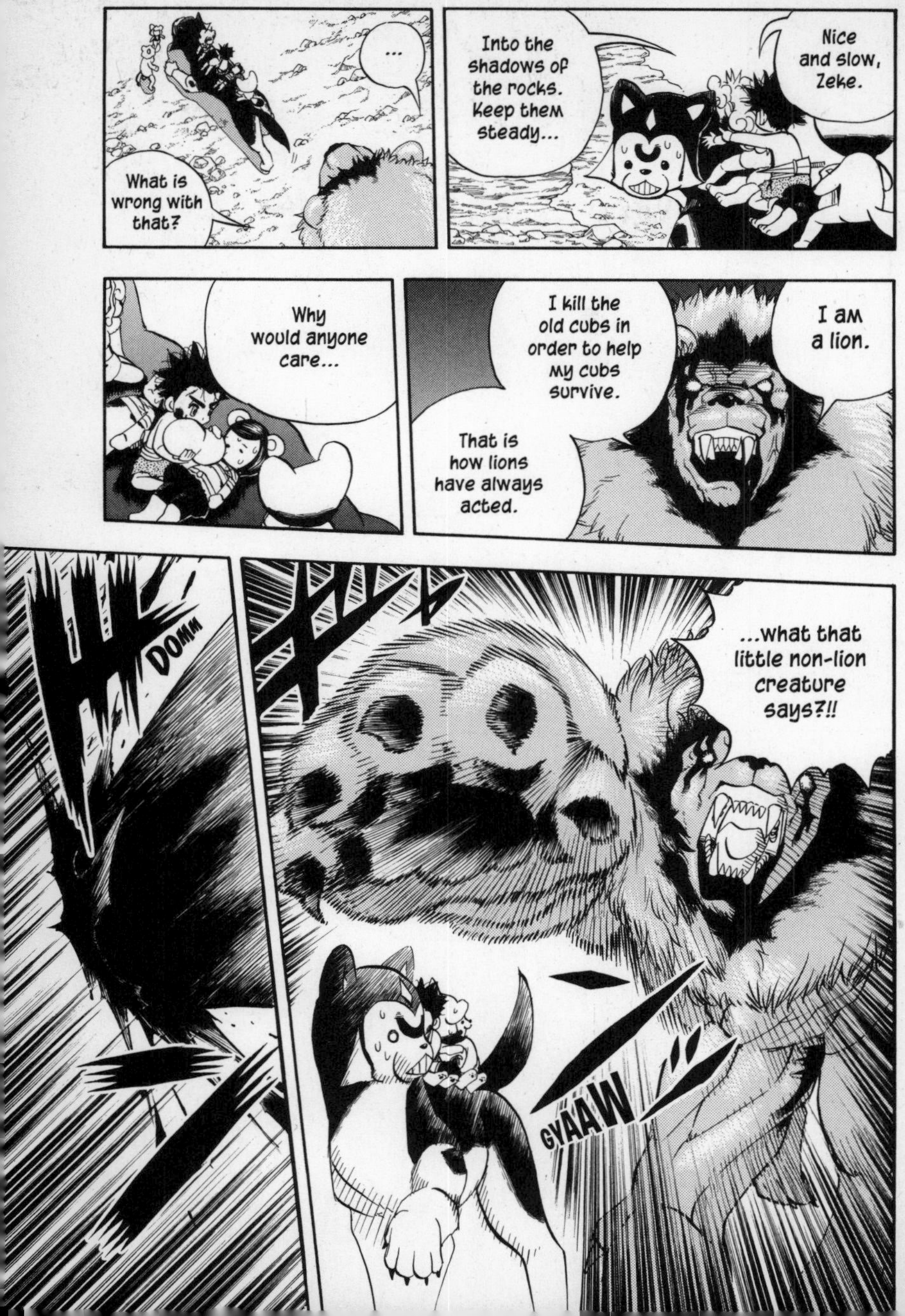
Nice and slow, Zeke.
Into the shadows of the rocks. Keep them steady...
...
What is wrong with that?
I am a lion.
I kill the old cubs in order to help my cubs survive.
That is how lions have always acted.
Why would anyone care...
...what that little non-lion creature says?!!
GYAAW
DOMM

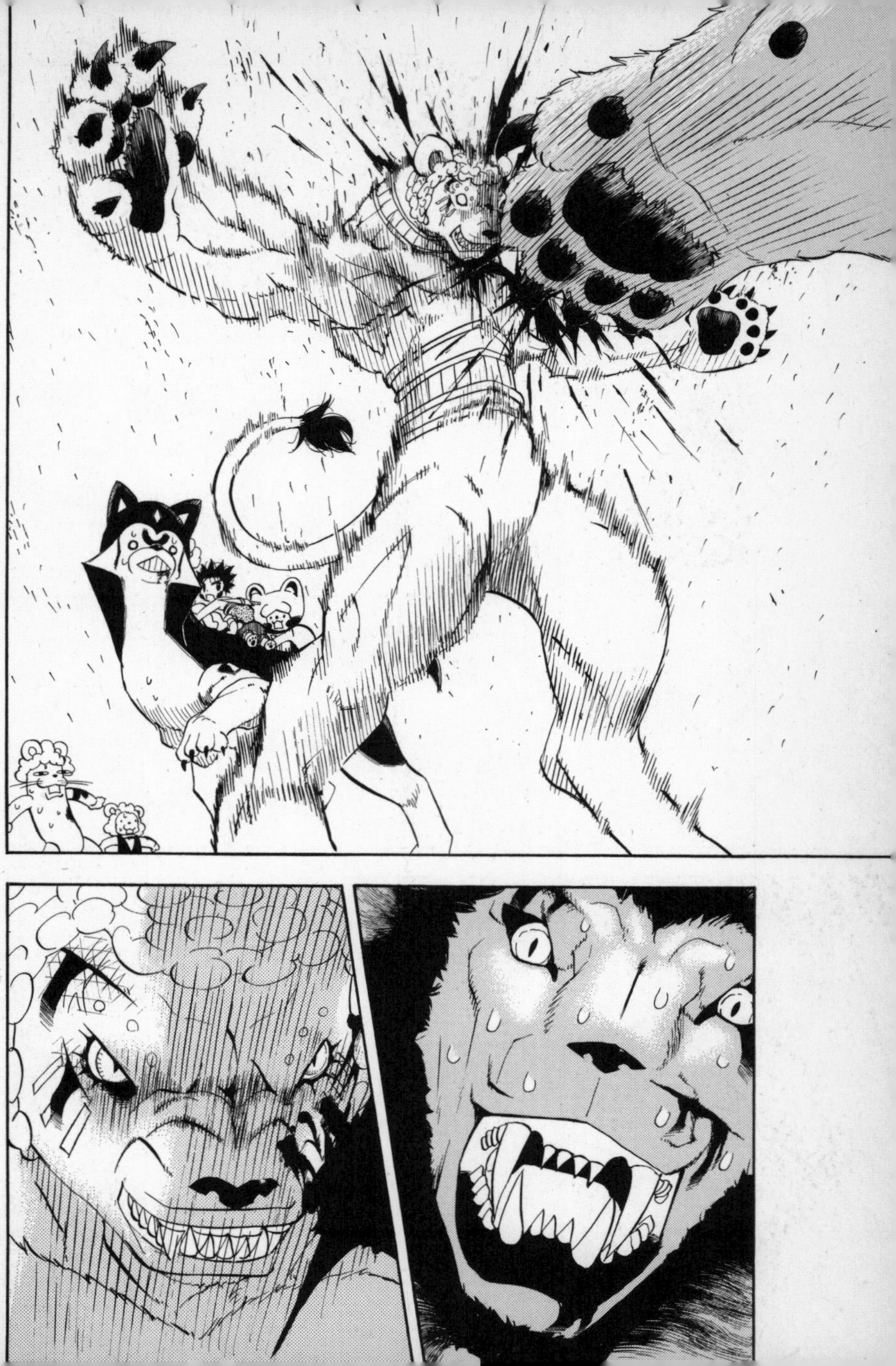

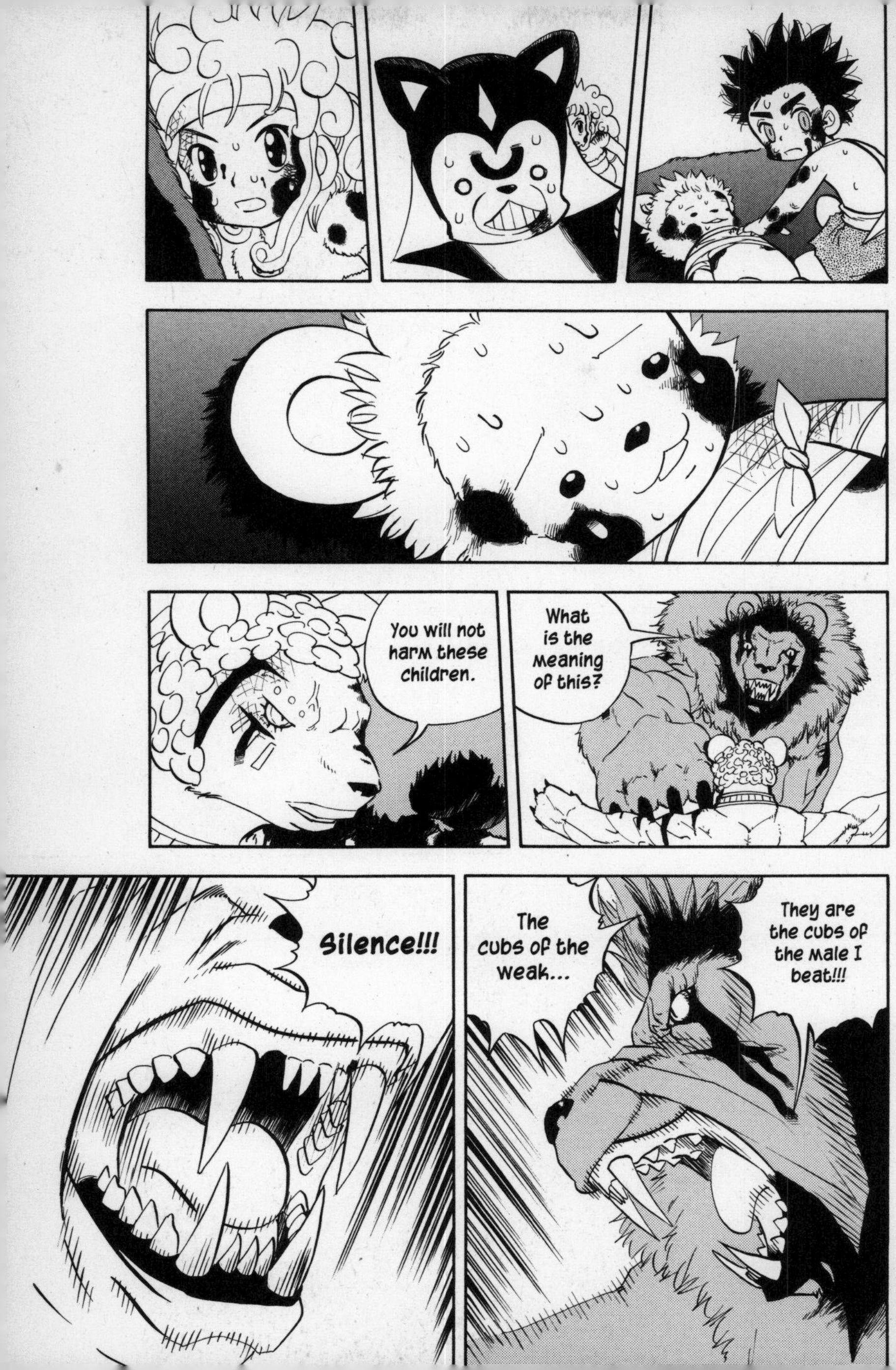
What is the meaning of this?
You will not harm these children.
They are the cubs of the male I beat!!!
The cubs of the weak...
Silence!!!

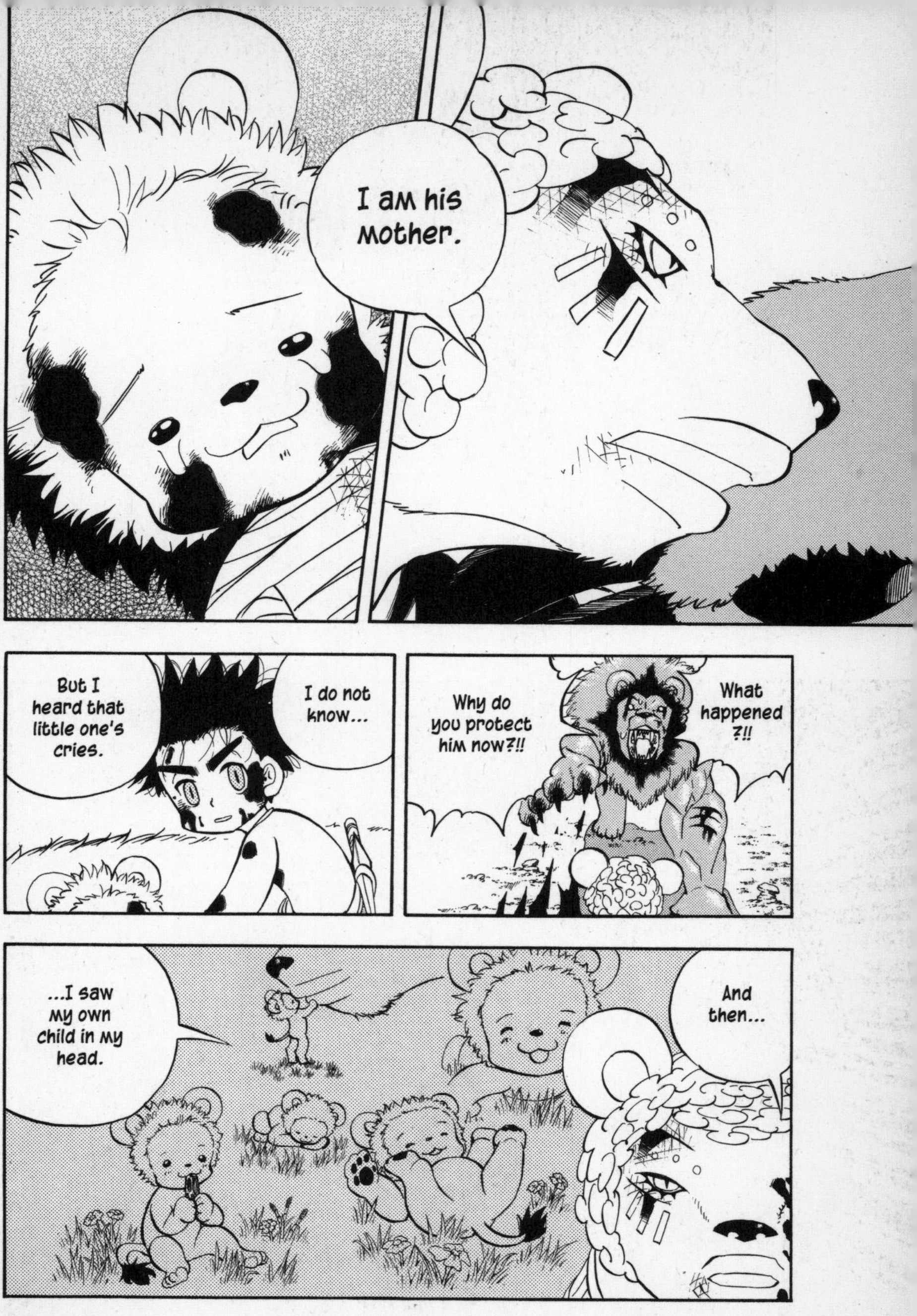

I am his mother.
What happened ?!!
Why do you protect him now?!!
I do not know...
But I heard that little one's cries.
And then...
...I saw my own child in my head.

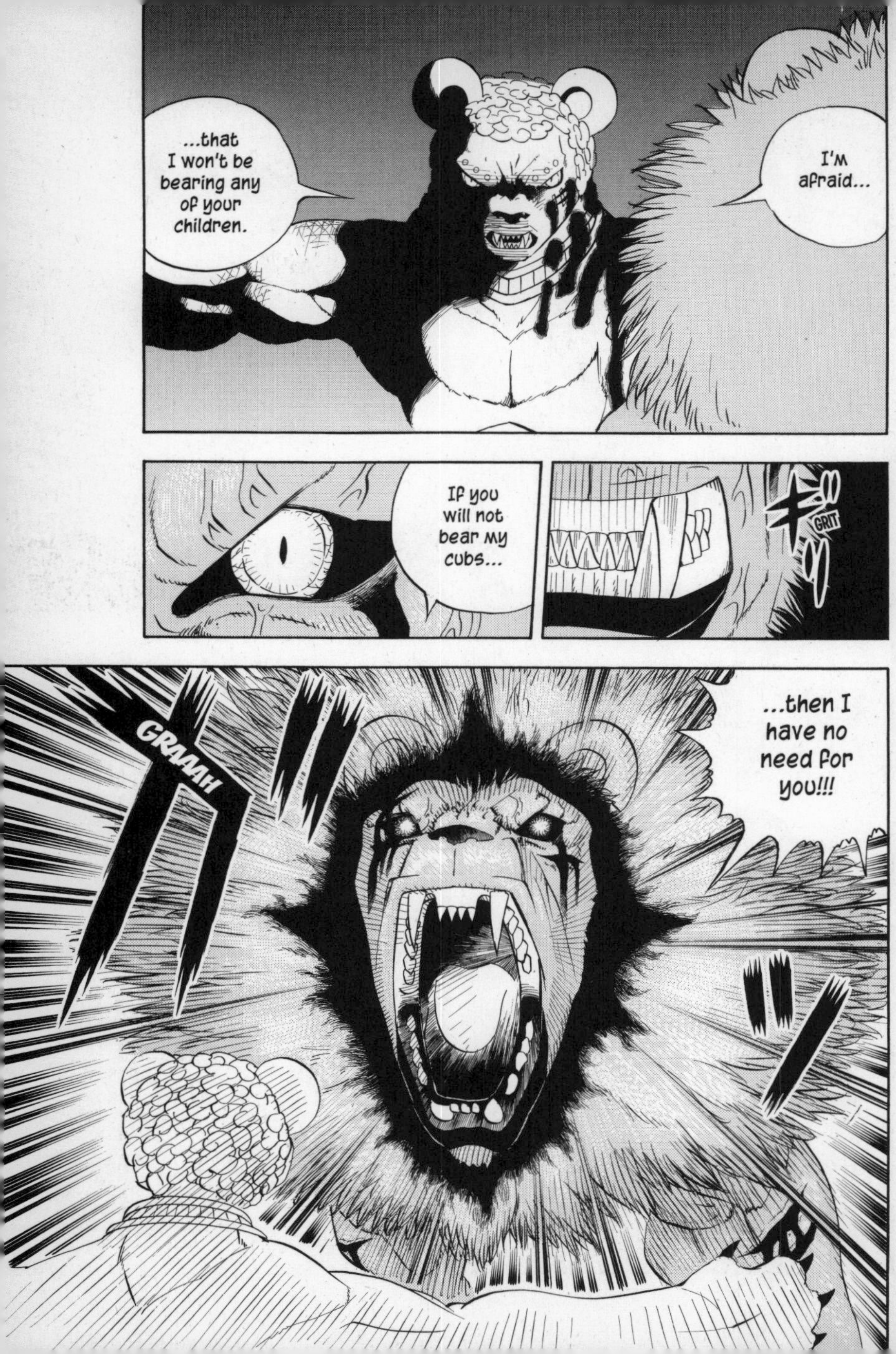
I'm afraid...
...that I won't be bearing any of your children.
GRIT
If you will not bear my cubs...
...then I have no need for you!!!
GRAAAH

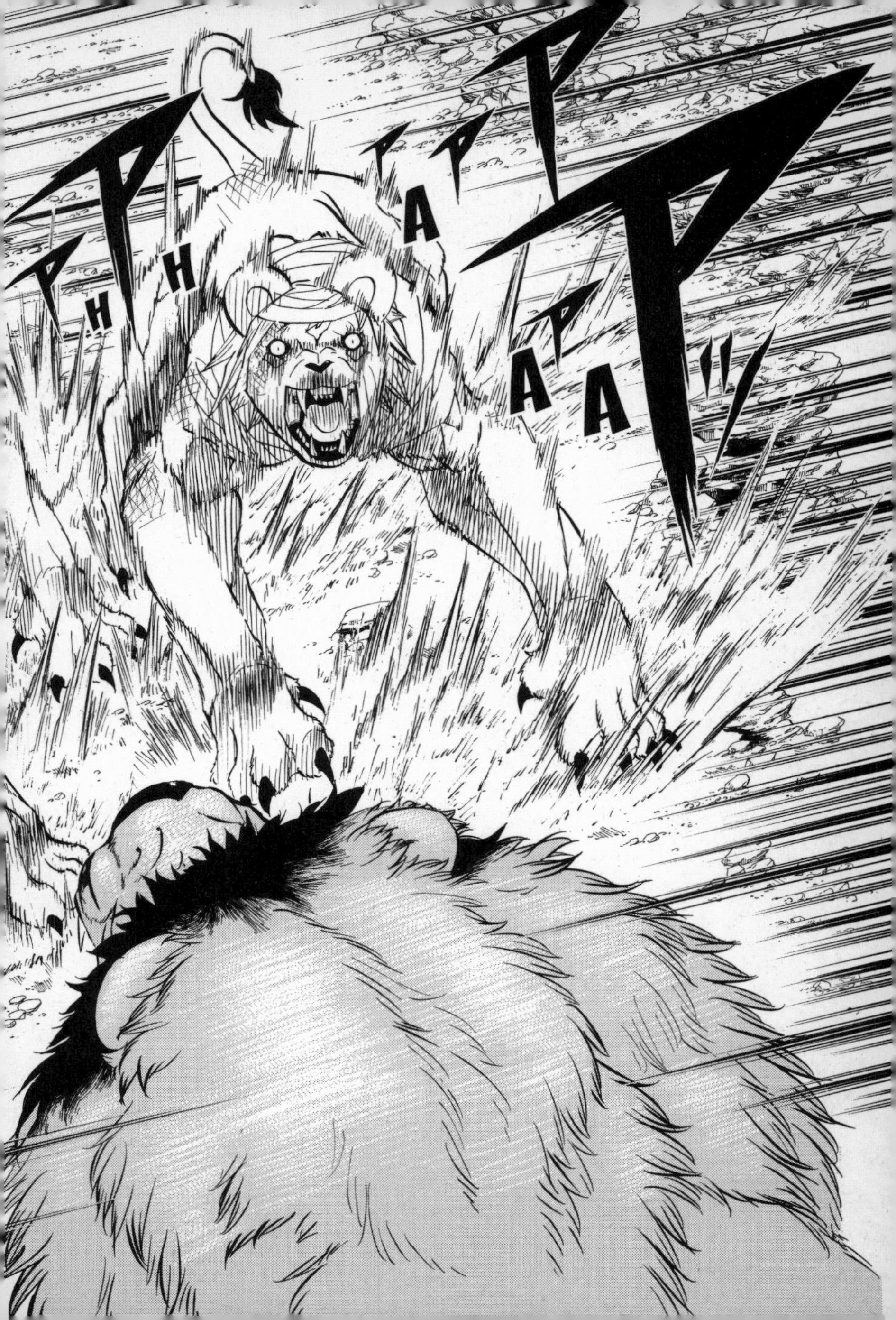
AHH
AAA!!

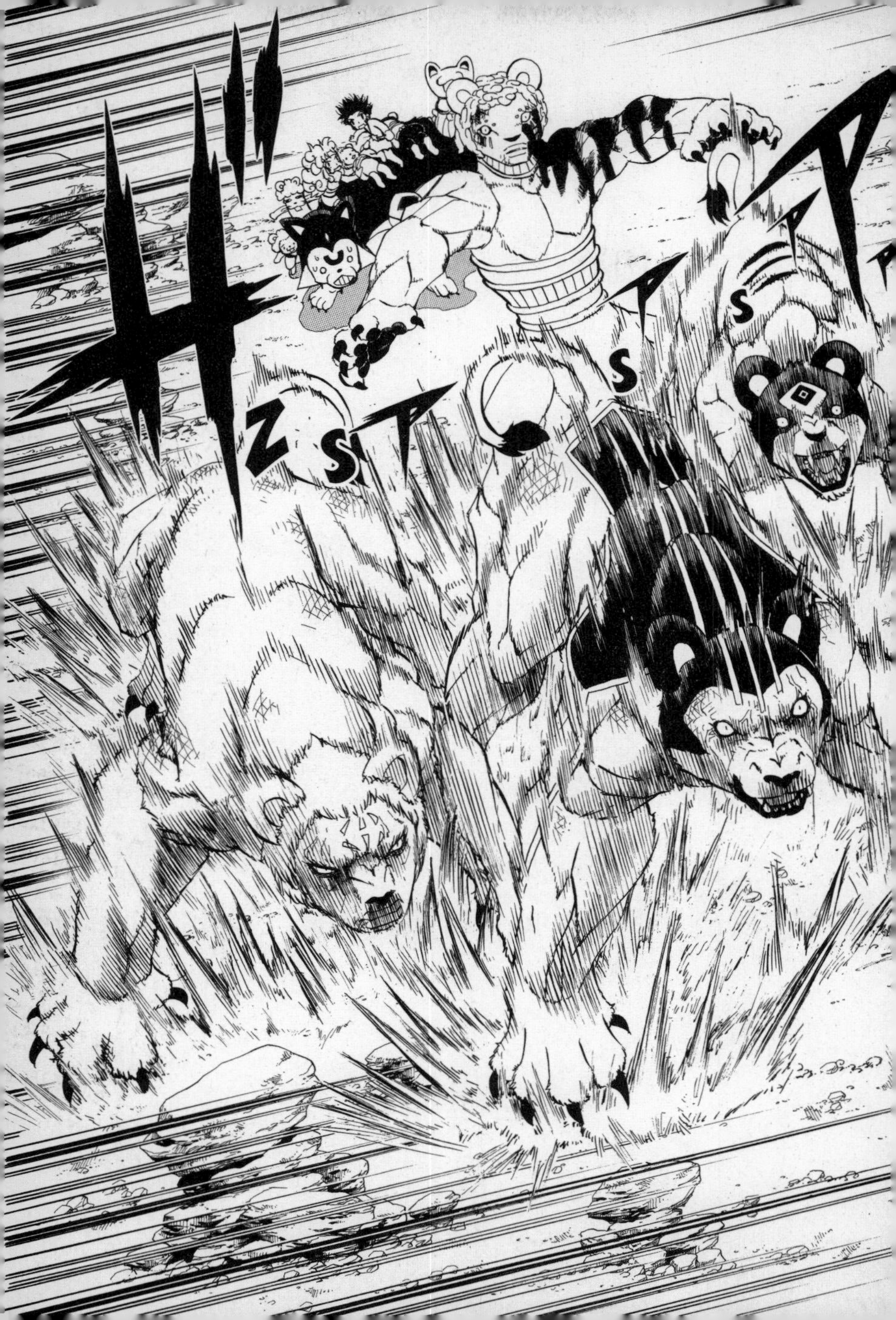
H!!
ZSP

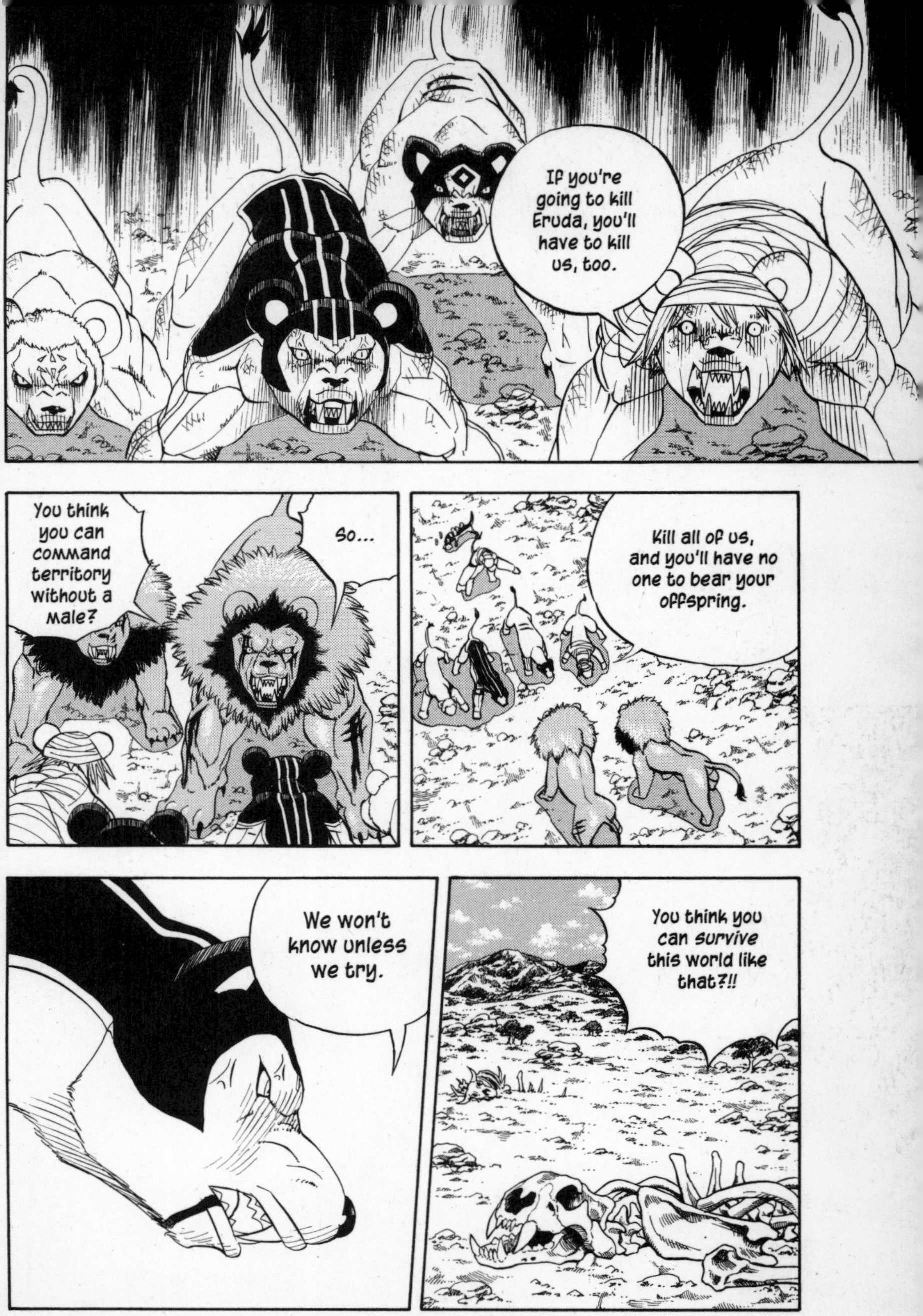
If you're going to kill Eruda, you'll have to kill us, too.
Kill all of us, and you'll have no one to bear your offspring.
So...
You think you can command territory without a male?
You think you can survive this world like that?!!
We won't know unless we try.

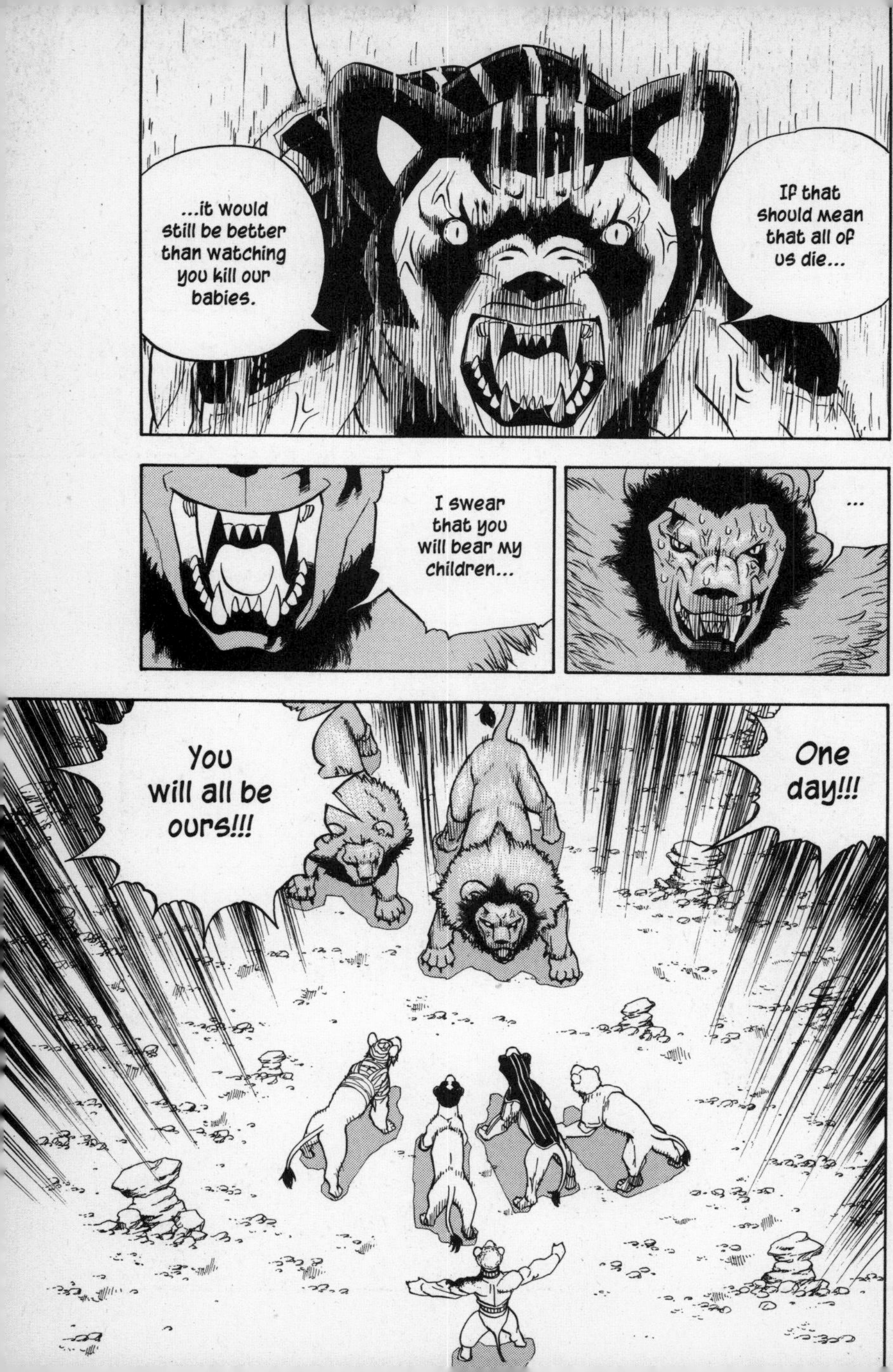
If that should mean that all of us die...
...it would still be better than watching you kill our babies.
...
I swear that you will bear my children...
One day!!!
You will all be ours!!!

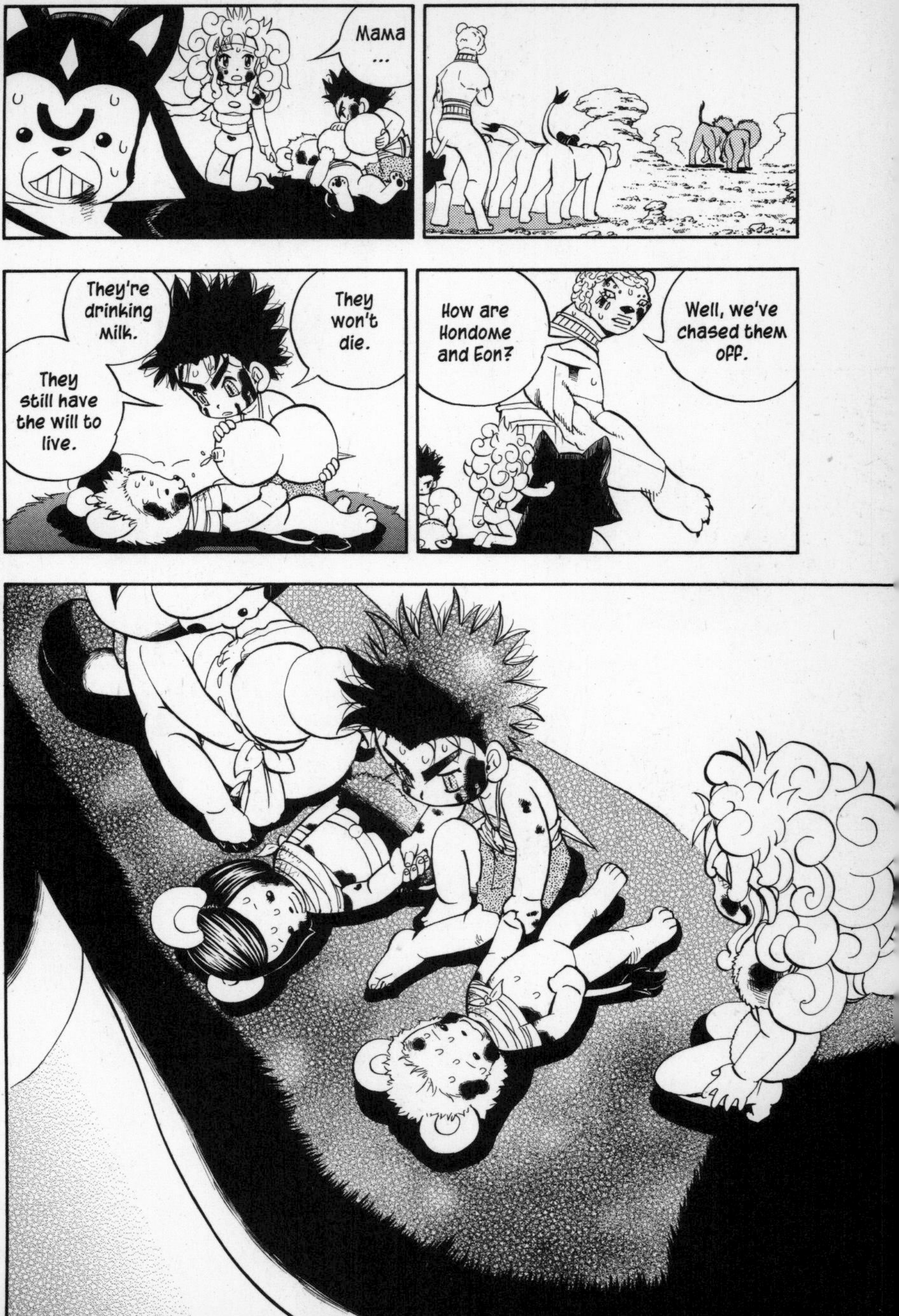
Mama ...
Well, we've chased them off.
How are Hondome and Eon?
They won't die.
They're drinking milk.
They still have the will to live.

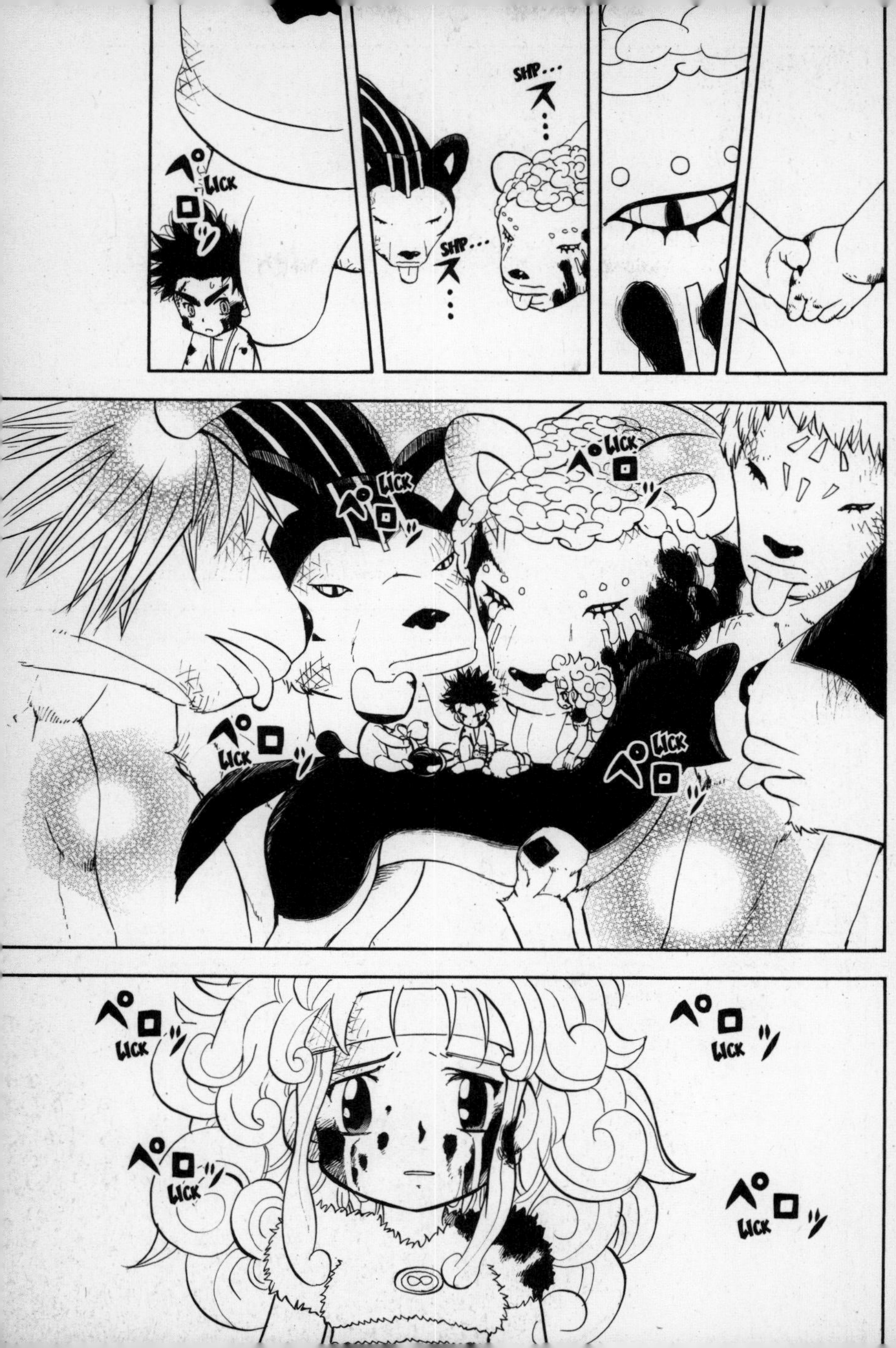
SHP…
ス…
SHP…
ス…
ペロッ
LICK
ペロッ
LICK
ペロッ
LICK
ペロッ
LICK
ペロッ
LICK
ペロッ
LICK
ペロッ
LICK
ペロッ
LICK
ペロッ
LICK

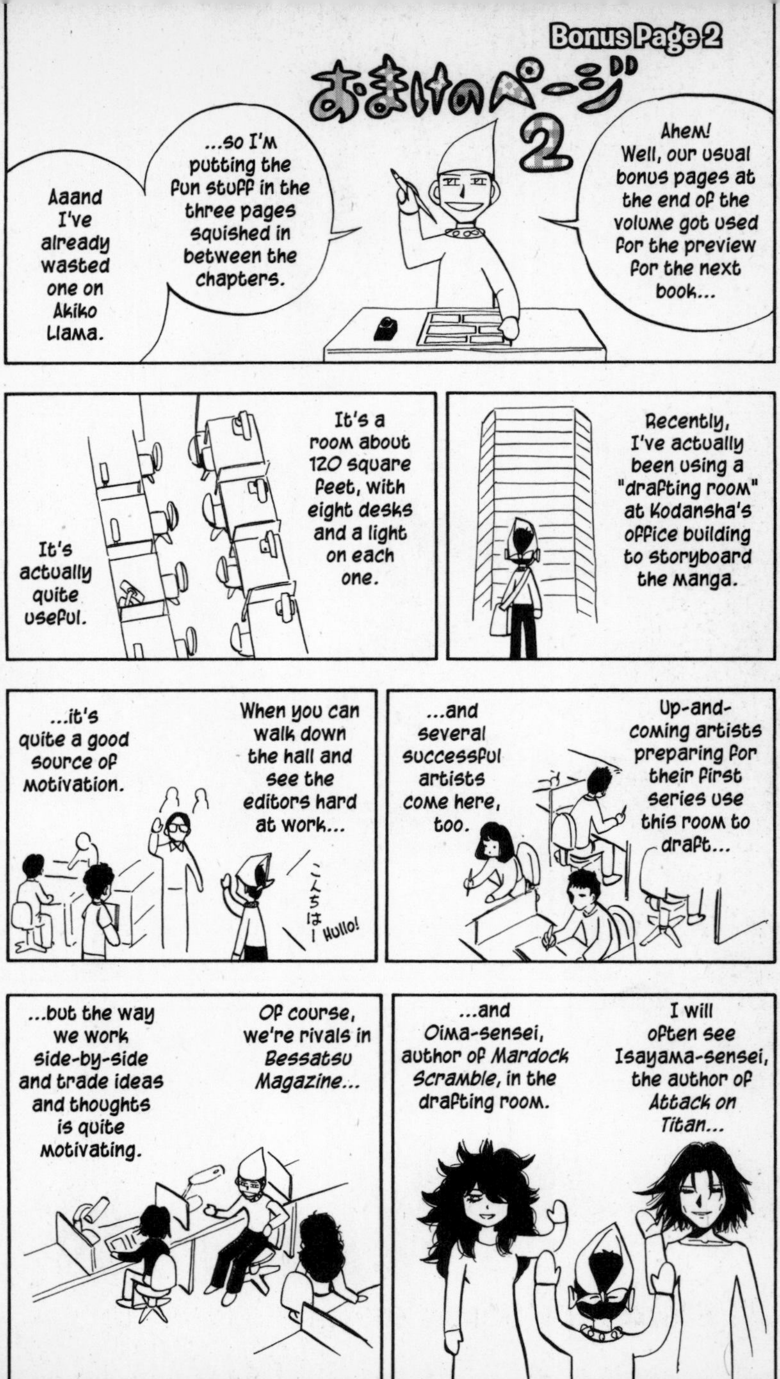
Bonus Page 2
おまけのページ 2
Ahem! Well, our usual bonus pages at the end of the volume got used for the preview for the next book...
...so I'm putting the fun stuff in the three pages squished in between the chapters.
Aaand I've already wasted one on Akiko Llama.
Recently, I've actually been using a "drafting room" at Kodansha's office building to storyboard the manga.
It's a room about 120 square feet, with eight desks and a light on each one.
It's actually quite useful.
Up-and-coming artists preparing for their first series use this room to draft...
...and several successful artists come here, too.
When you can walk down the hall and see the editors hard at work...
...it's quite a good source of motivation.
こんちは！ Hullo!
I will often see Isayama-sensei, the author of *Attack on Titan*...
...and Oima-sensei, author of *Mardock Scramble*, in the drafting room.
Of course, we're rivals in *Bessatsu Magazine*...
...but the way we work side-by-side and trade ideas and thoughts is quite motivating.

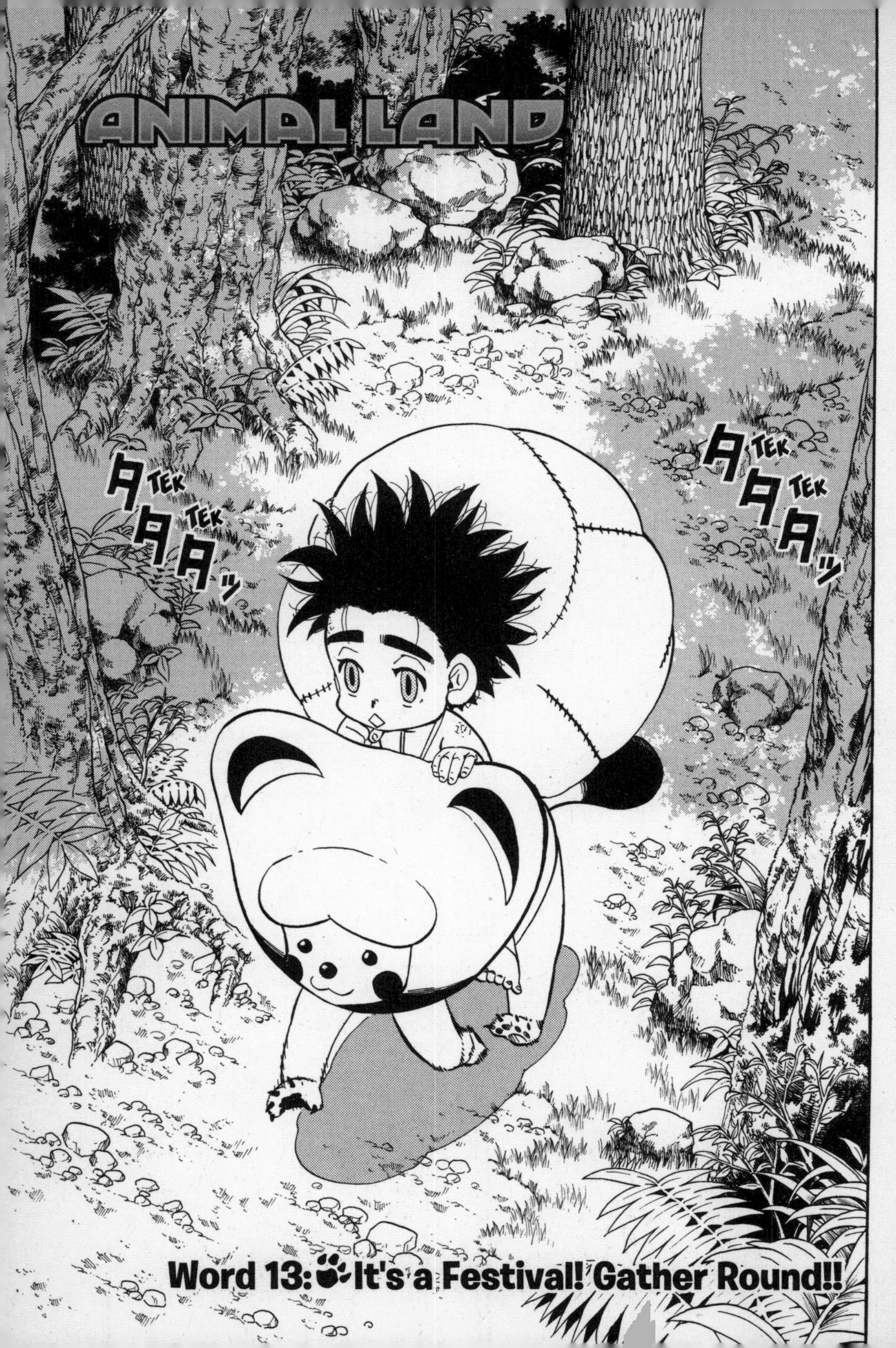
ANIMAL LAND
タタタッ
TEK TEK
タタタッ
TEK TEK
Word 13: It's a Festival! Gather Round!!

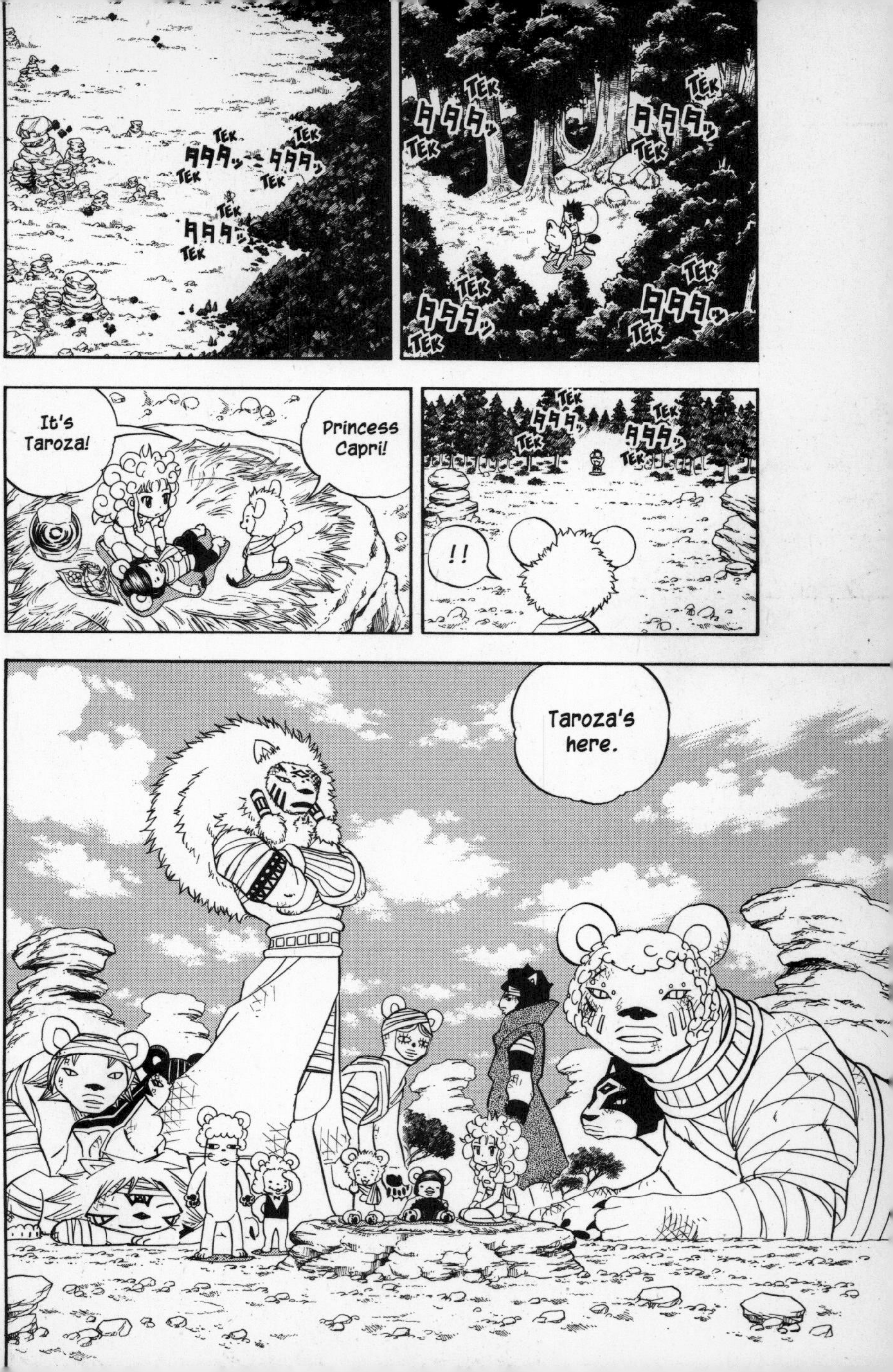
TEK
タタタッ
TEK
TEK
タタタッ
TEK
TEK
タタタッ
TEK
TEK
タタタッ
TEK
TEK
タタタッ
TEK
TEK
タタタッ
TEK
TEK
タタタッ
TEK
TEK
タタタッ
TEK
TEK
タタタッ
TEK
!!
Princess Capri!
It's Taroza!
Taroza's here.

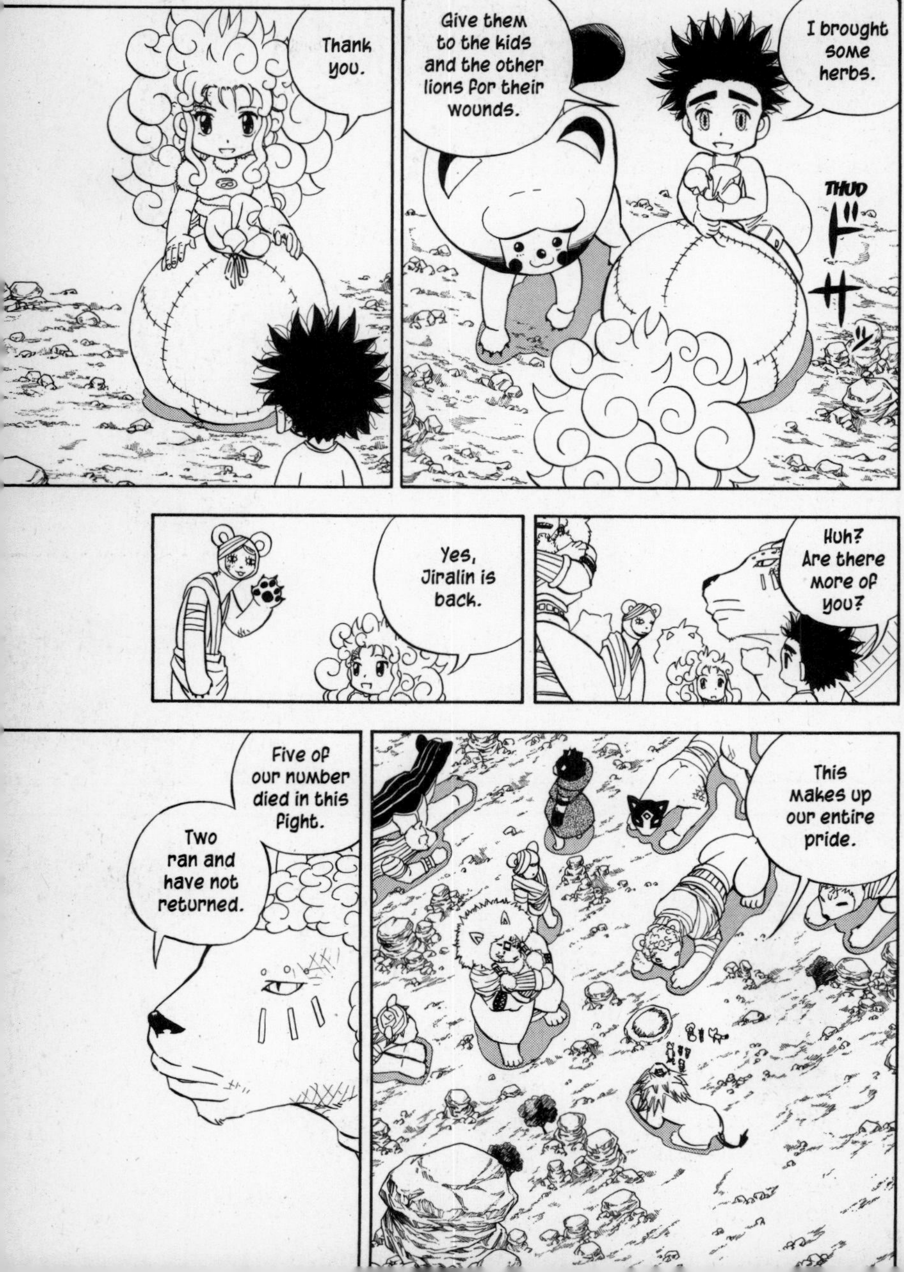
I brought some herbs.
THUD
ドサッ
Give them to the kids and the other lions for their wounds.
Thank you.
Huh? Are there more of you?
Yes, Jiralin is back.
This makes up our entire pride.
Five of our number died in this fight.
Two ran and have not returned.

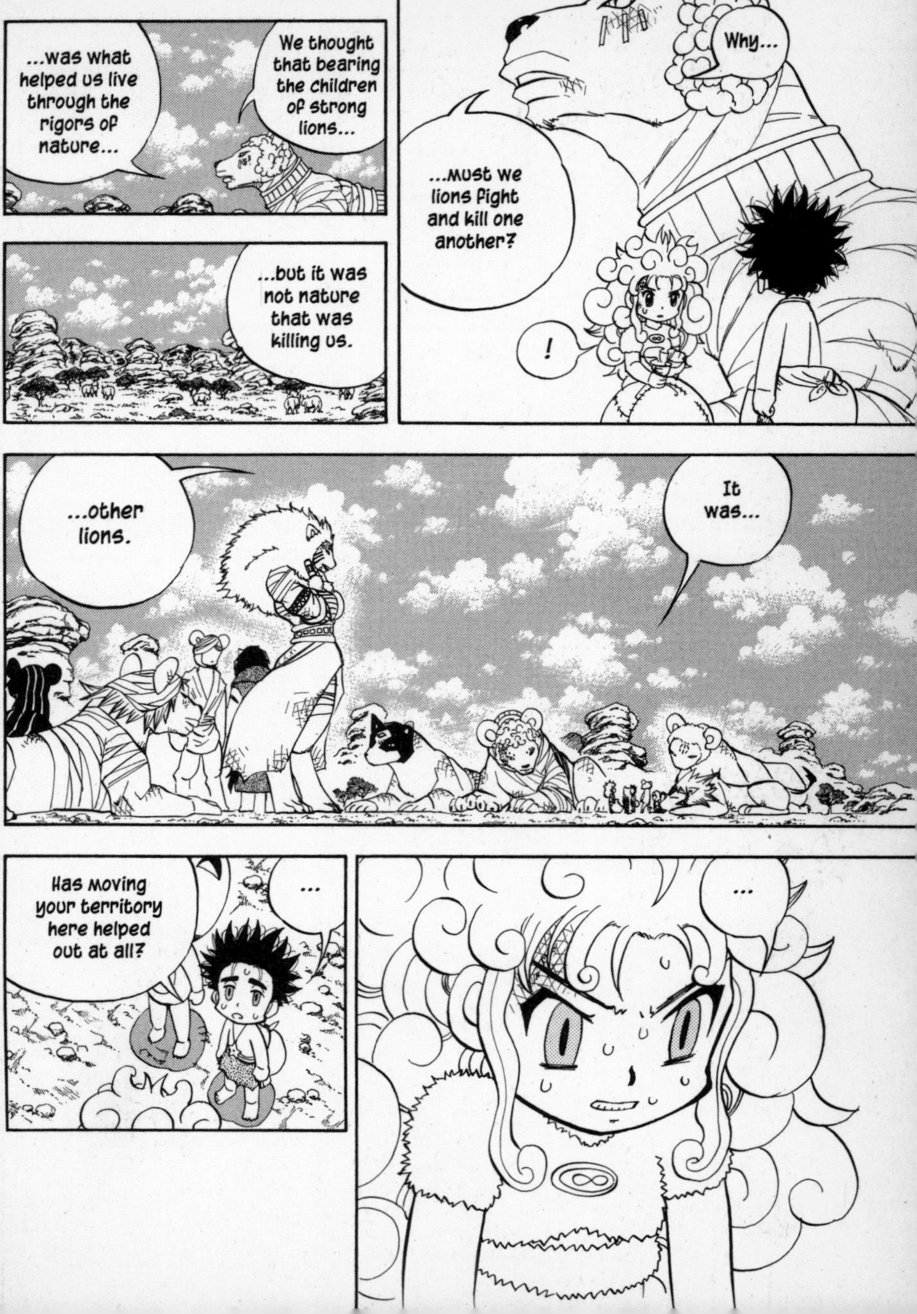
Why...
...must we lions fight and kill one another?
!
We thought that bearing the children of strong lions...
...was what helped us live through the rigors of nature...
...but it was not nature that was killing us.
It was...
...other lions.
...
...
Has moving your territory here helped out at all?

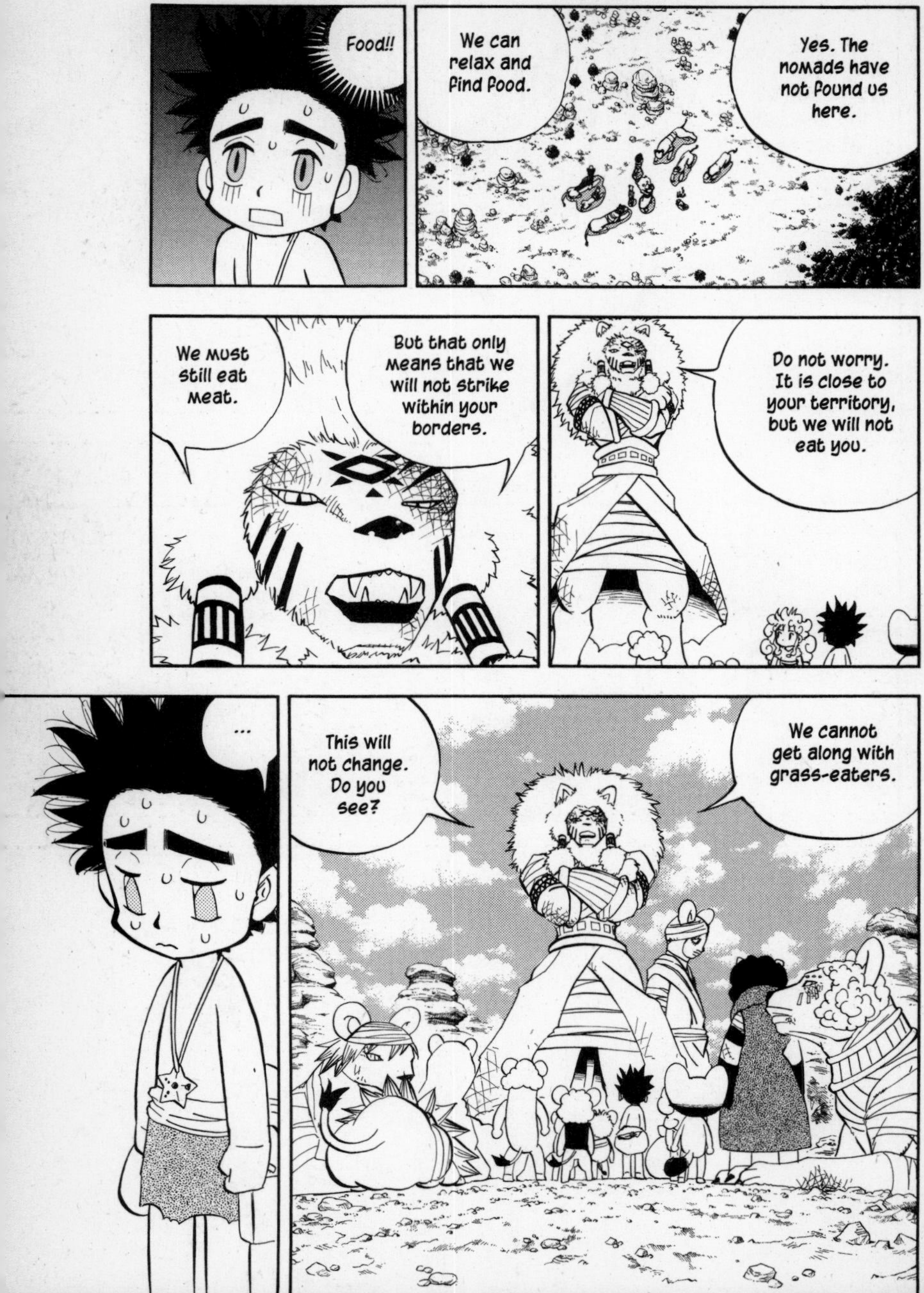
Yes. The nomads have not found us here.
We can relax and find food.
Food!!
Do not worry. It is close to your territory, but we will not eat you.
But that only means that we will not strike within your borders.
We must still eat meat.
We cannot get along with grass-eaters.
This will not change. Do you see?
...

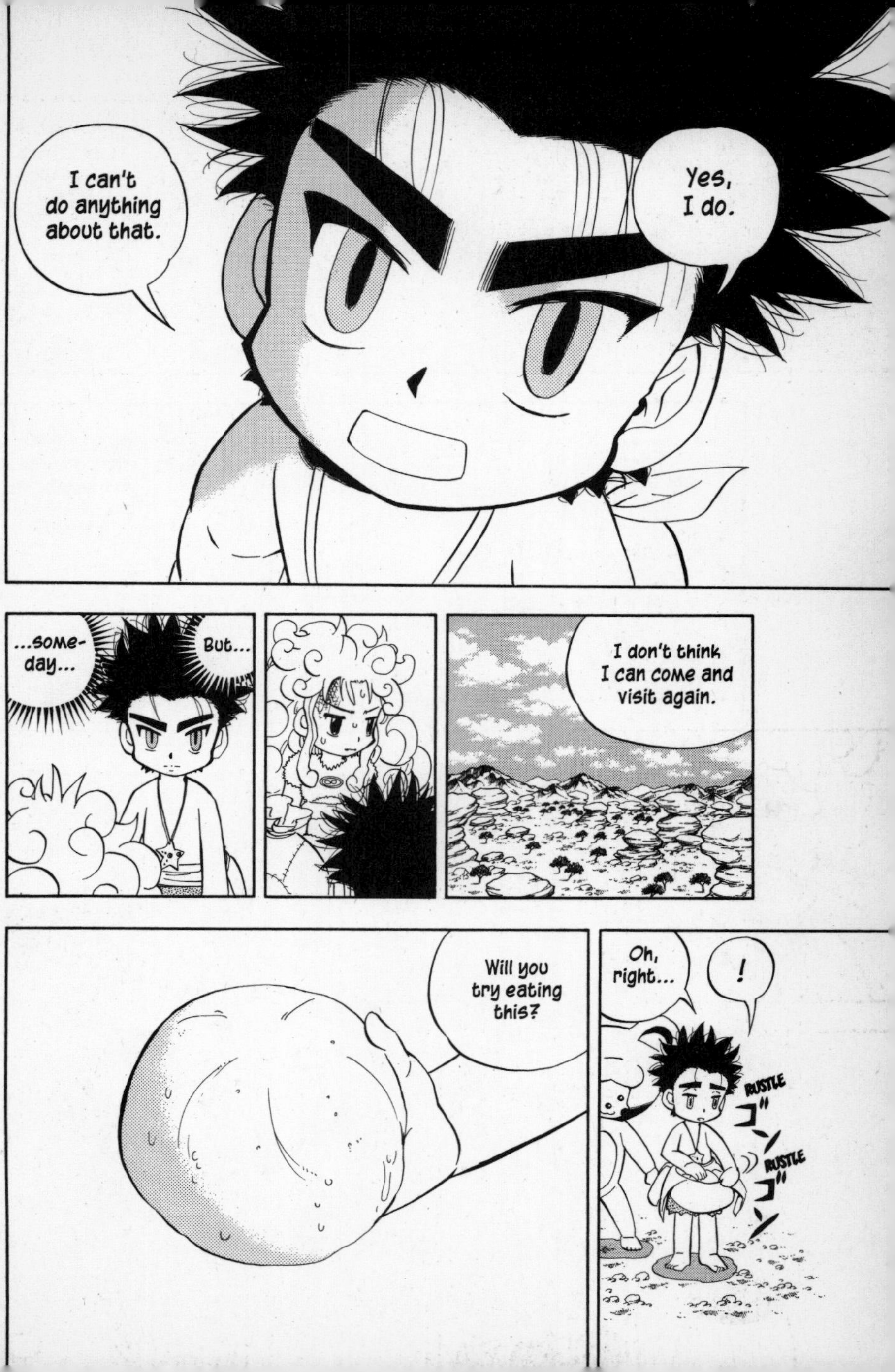
Yes, I do.
I can't do anything about that.
I don't think I can come and visit again.
But...
...some-day...
!
Oh, right...
RUSTLE
ゴソ
RUSTLE
ゴソ
Will you try eating this?

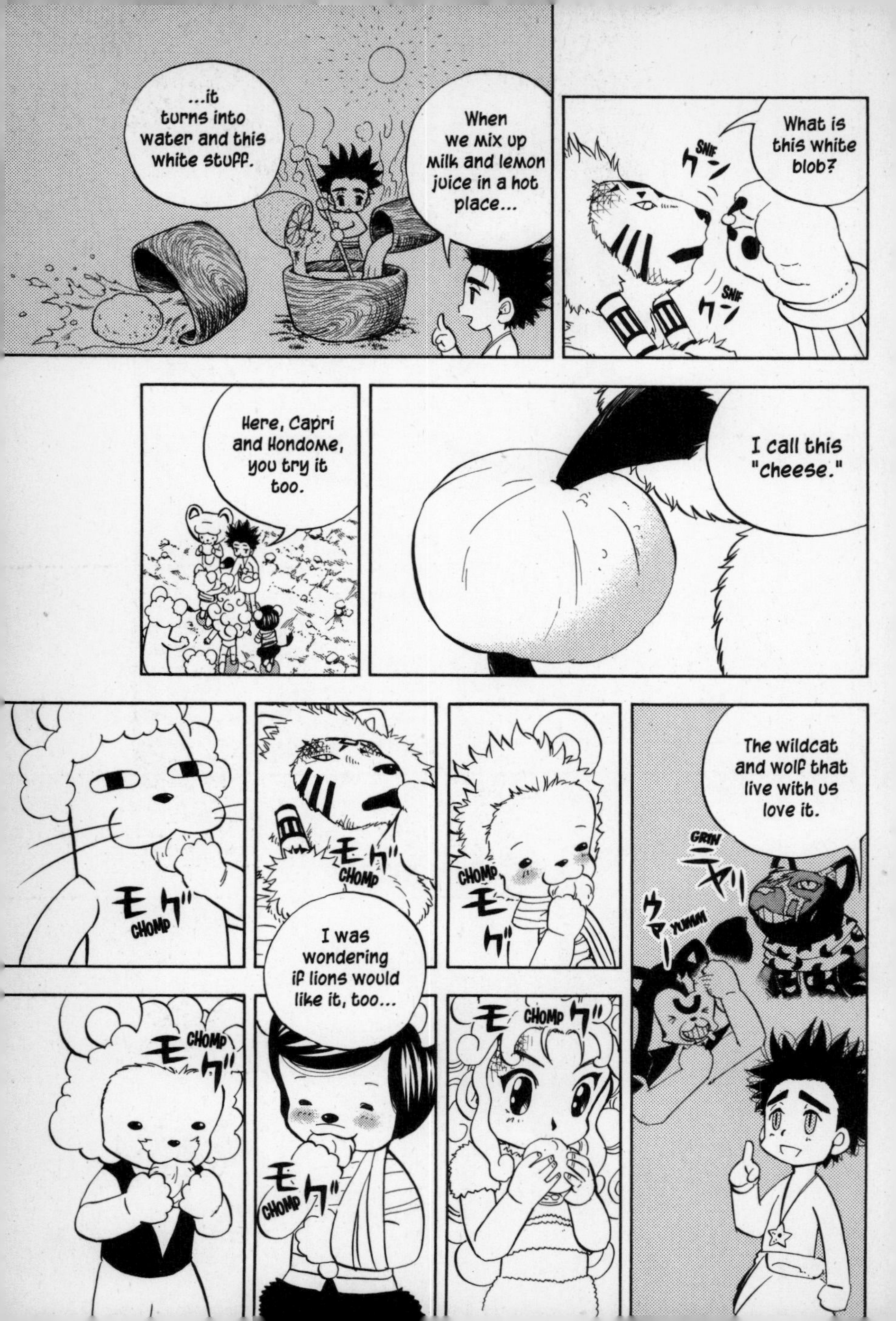

What is this white blob?
SNIF
SNIF
When we mix up milk and lemon juice in a hot place...
...it turns into water and this white stuff.
I call this "cheese."
Here, Capri and Hondome, you try it too.
The wildcat and wolf that live with us love it.
GRIN
YUMMM
CHOMP
CHOMP
CHOMP
CHOMP
I was wondering if lions would like it, too...
CHOMP
CHOMP

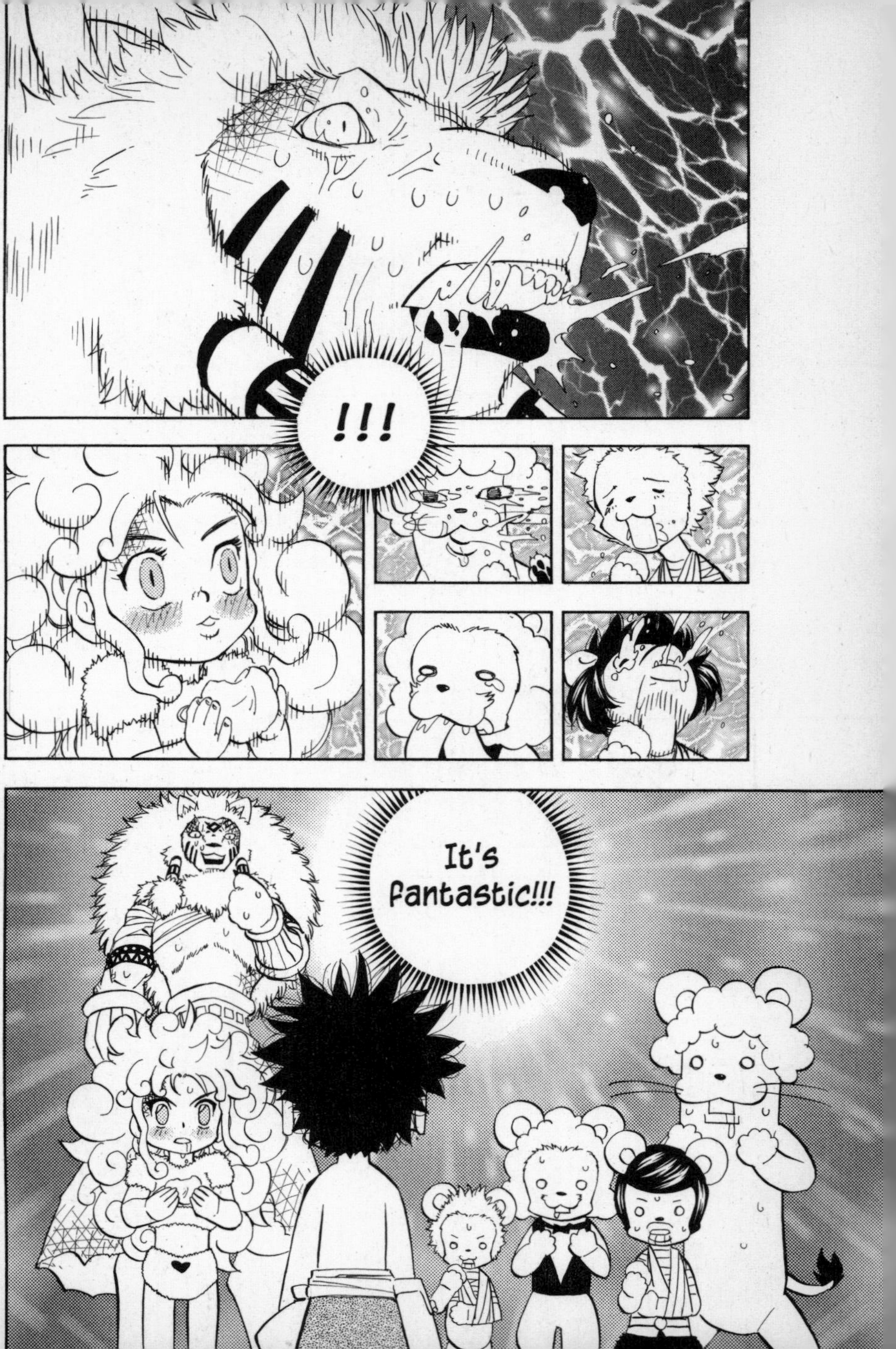
!!!
It's fantastic!!!

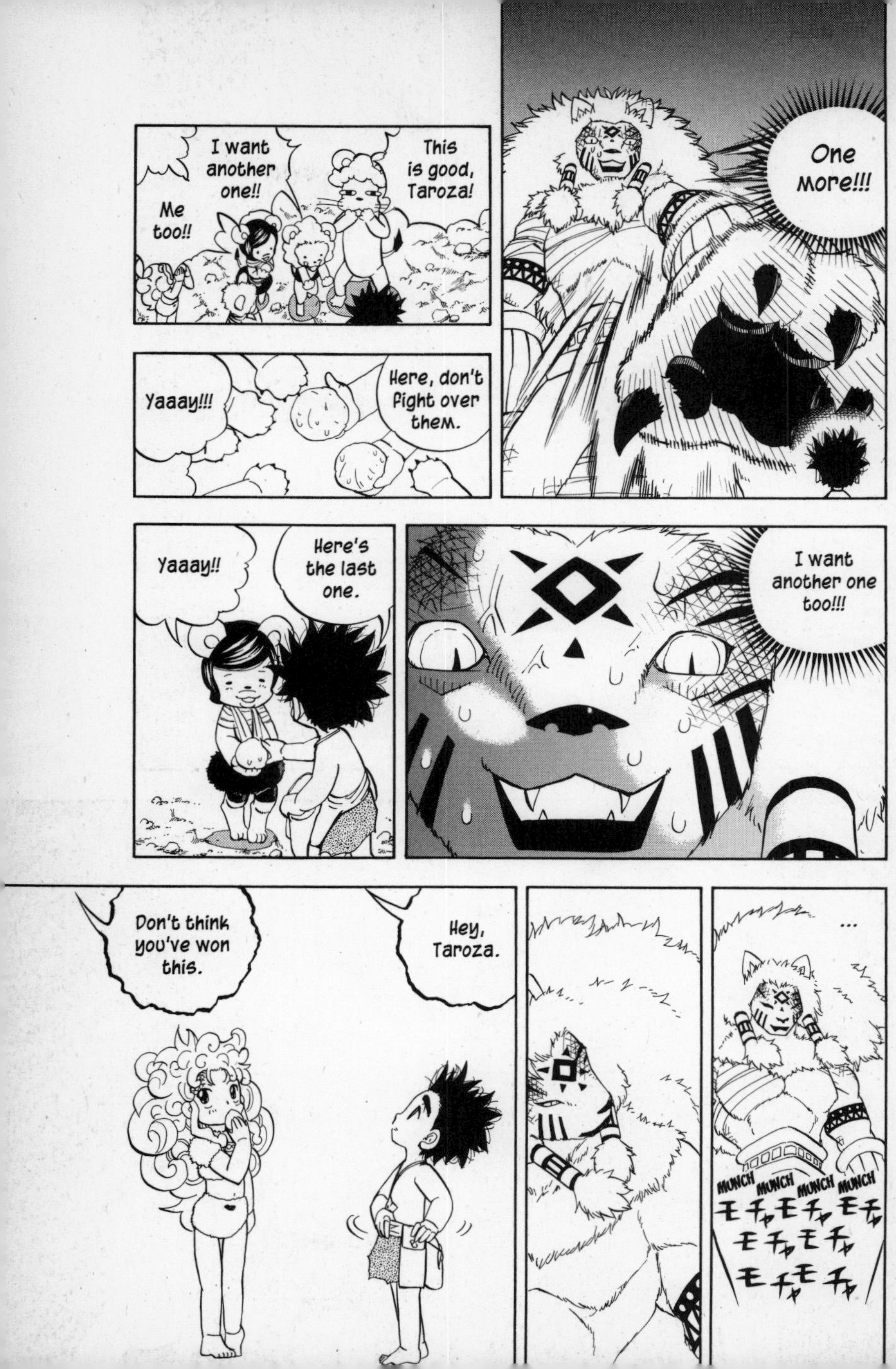
One more!!!
This is good, Taroza!
I want another one!!
Me too!!
Here, don't fight over them.
Yaaay!!!
I want another one too!!!
Here's the last one.
Yaaay!!
...
MUNCH MUNCH MUNCH MUNCH
モチャモチャモチャ
モチャモチャ
モチャモチャ
Hey, Taroza.
Don't think you've won this.

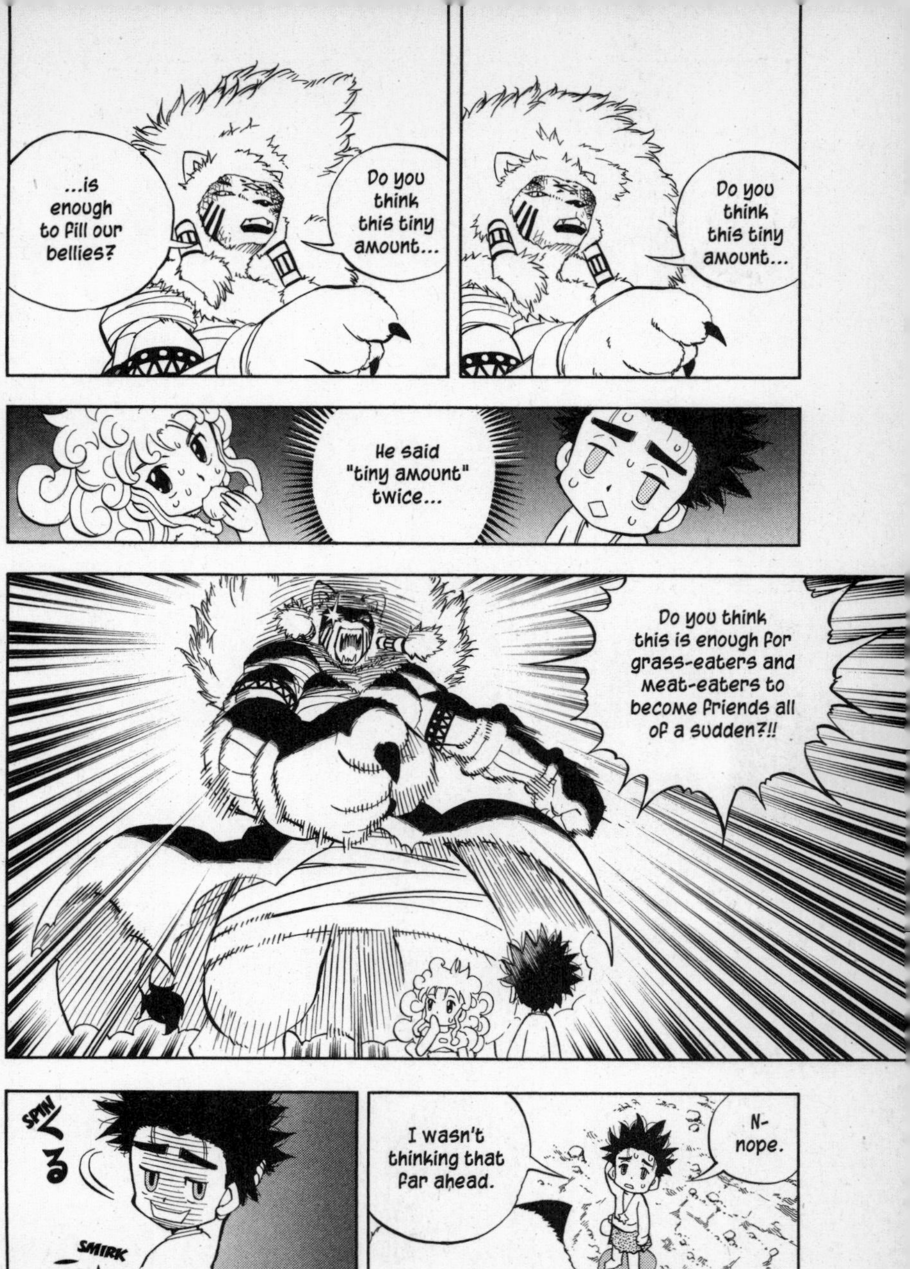
Do you think this tiny amount...
Do you think this tiny amount...
...is enough to fill our bellies?
He said "tiny amount" twice...
Do you think this is enough for grass-eaters and meat-eaters to become friends all of a sudden?!!
N-nope.
I wasn't thinking that far ahead.
SPIN くる
SMIRK ニヤリ

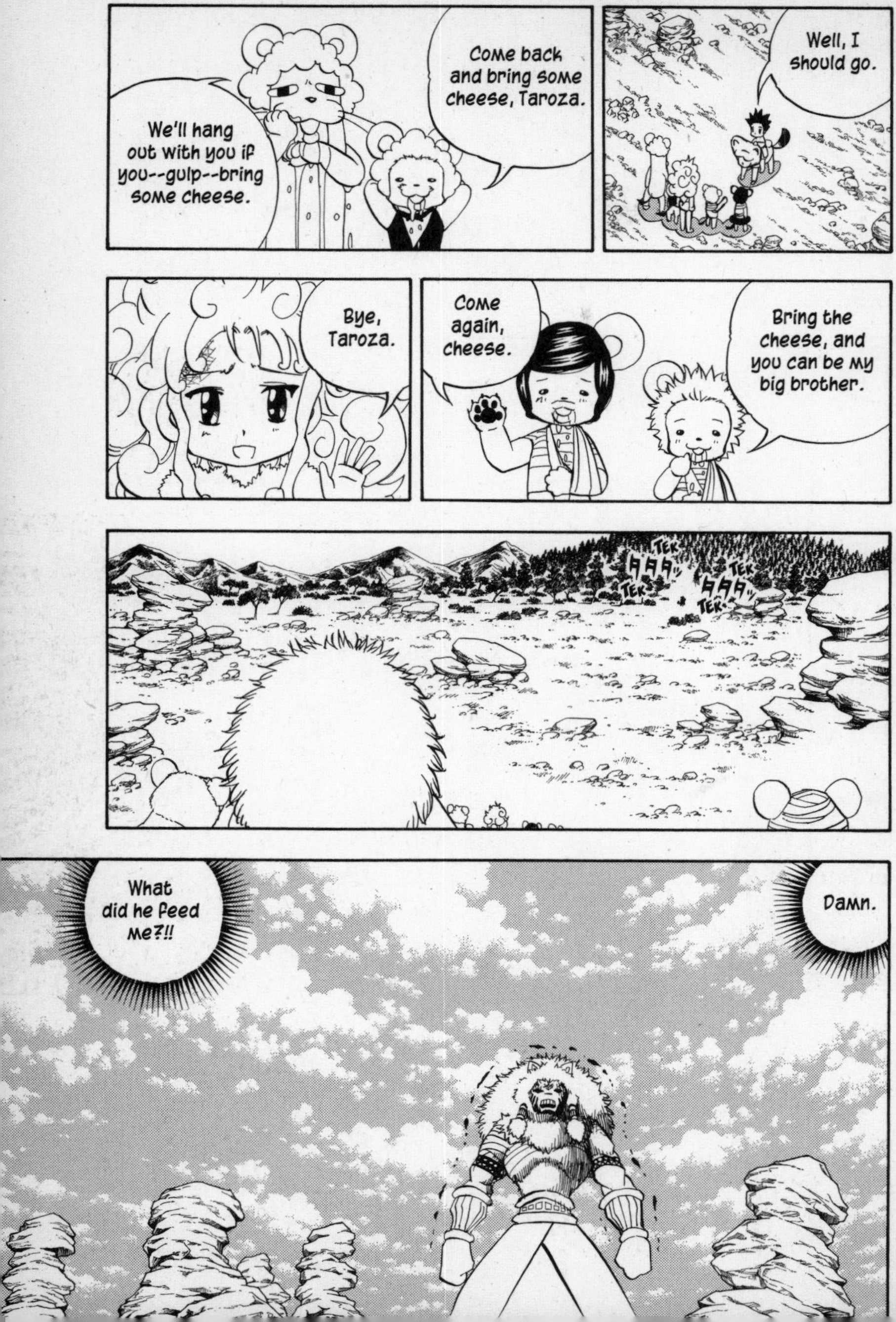
Well, I should go.
Come back and bring some cheese, Taroza.
We'll hang out with you if you--gulp--bring some cheese.
Bring the cheese, and you can be my big brother.
Come again, cheese.
Bye, Taroza.
TEK タタタッ TEK
TEK タタタッ TEK
Damn.
What did he feed me?!!

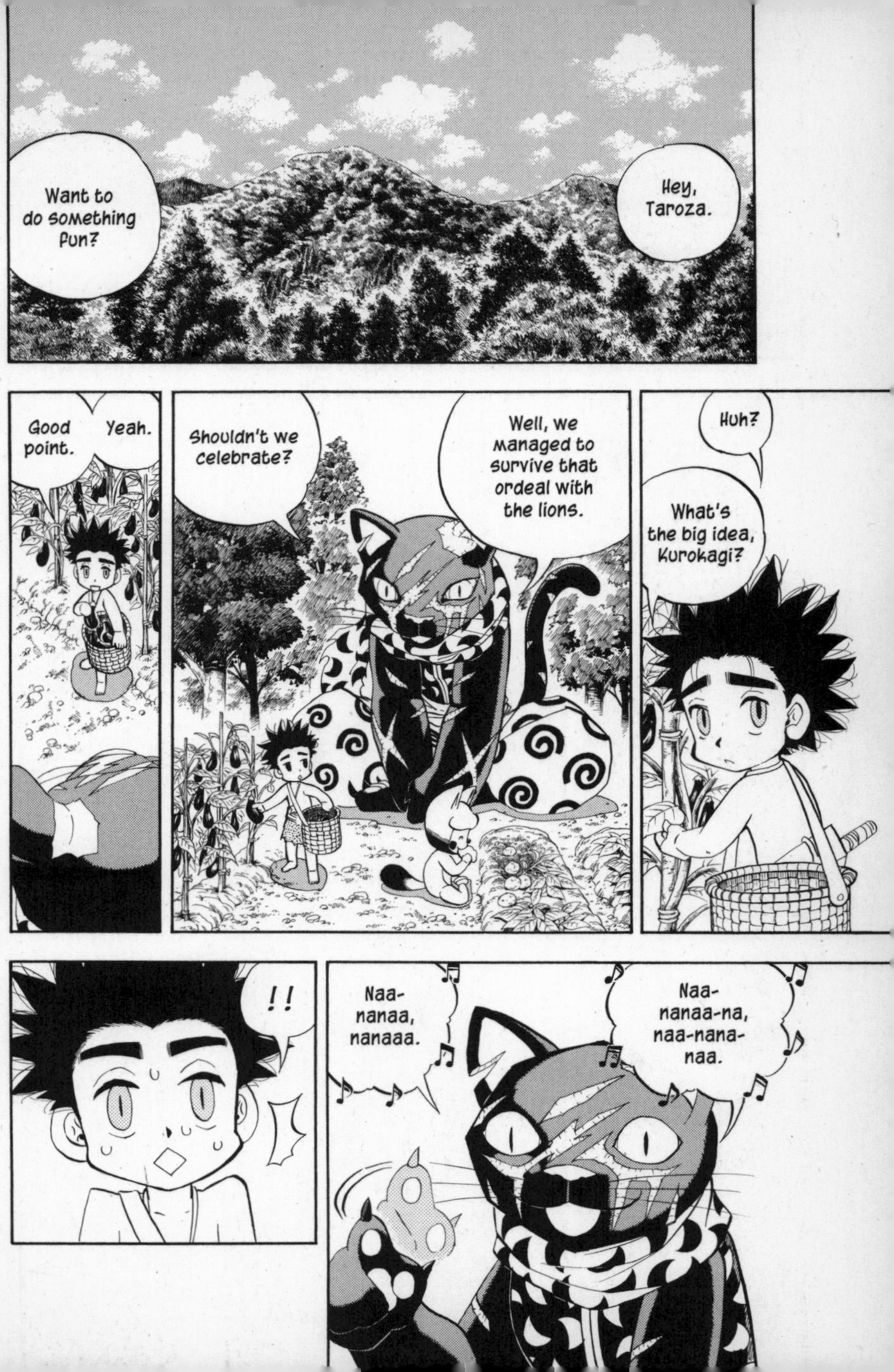
Hey, Taroza.
Want to do something fun?
Huh?
What's the big idea, Kurokagi?
Well, we managed to survive that ordeal with the lions.
Shouldn't we celebrate?
Yeah.
Good point.
Naa-nanaa-na, naa-nana-naa.
Naa-nanaa, nanaaa.
!!

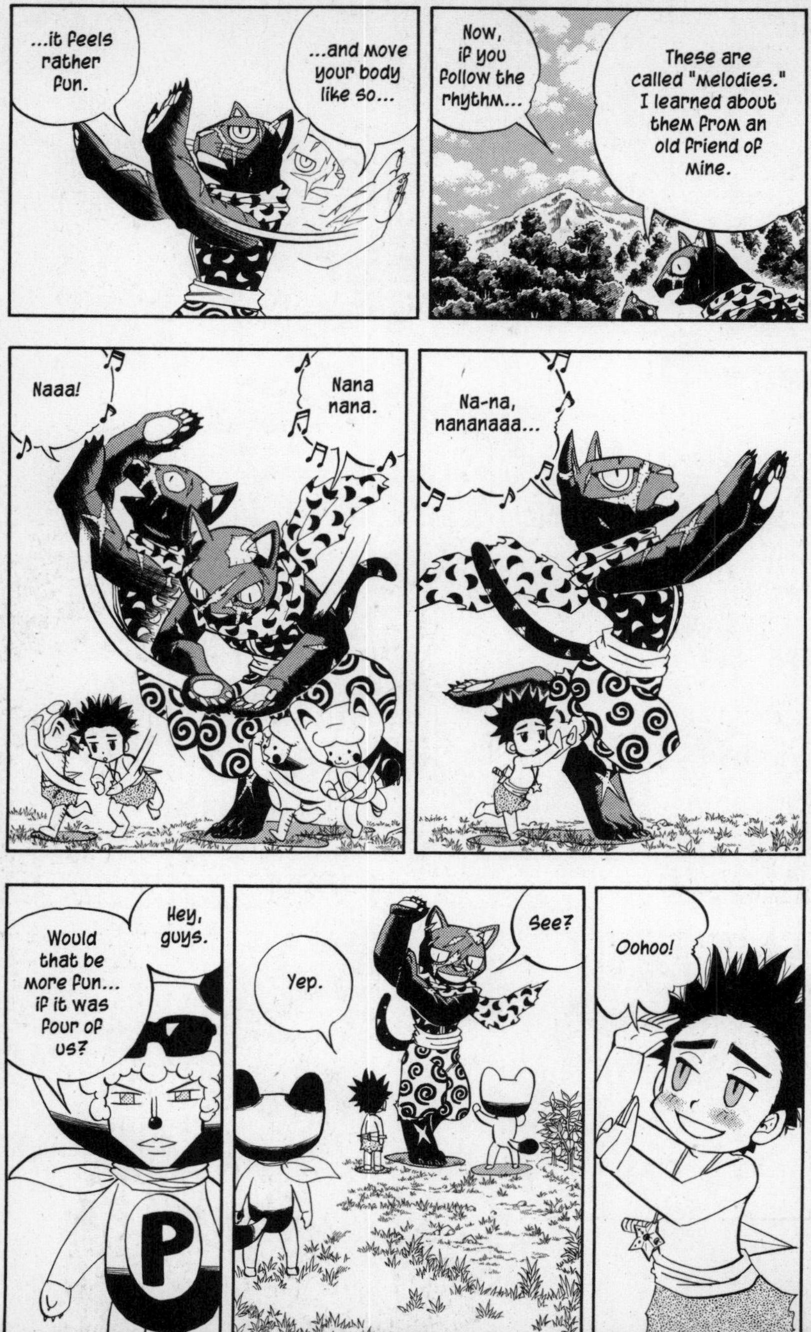

These are called "Melodies." I learned about them from an old friend of mine.
Now, if you follow the rhythm...
...and move your body like so...
...it feels rather fun.
Na-na, nananaaa...
Nana nana.
Naaa!
Oohoo!
See?
Yep.
Hey, guys.
Would that be more fun... if it was four of us?

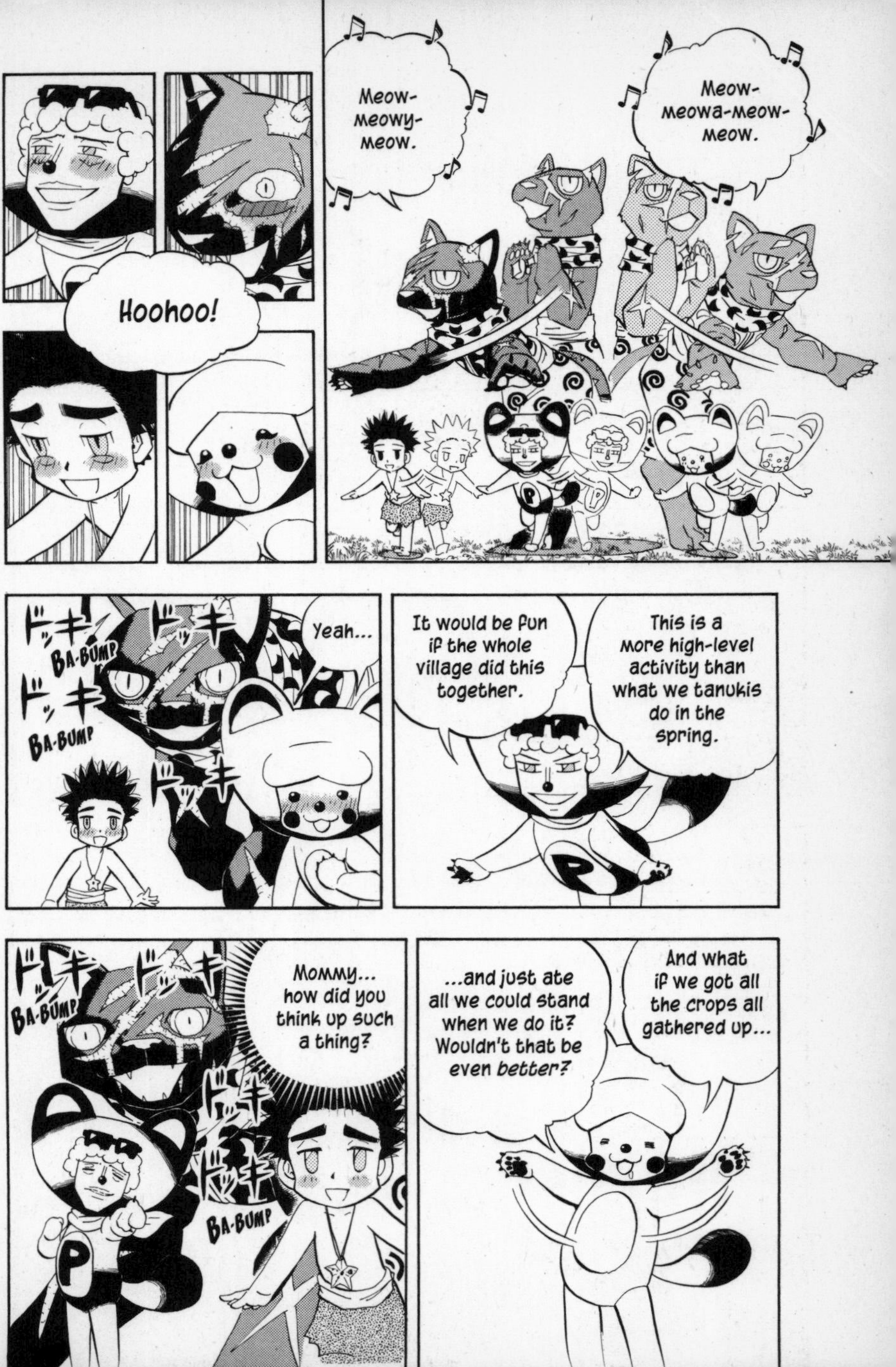
Meow-
meowa-meow-
meow.
Meow-
meowy-
meow.
Hoohoo!
This is a more high-level activity than what we tanukis do in the spring.
It would be fun if the whole village did this together.
Yeah...
ドッキ ドッキ
BA-BUMP
ドッキ
BA-BUMP
ドッキ
And what if we got all the crops all gathered up...
...and just ate all we could stand when we do it? Wouldn't that be even *better*?
Mommy... how did you think up such a thing?
ドキ ドッキ
BA-BUMP
ドッキ
ドッキ
BA-BUMP

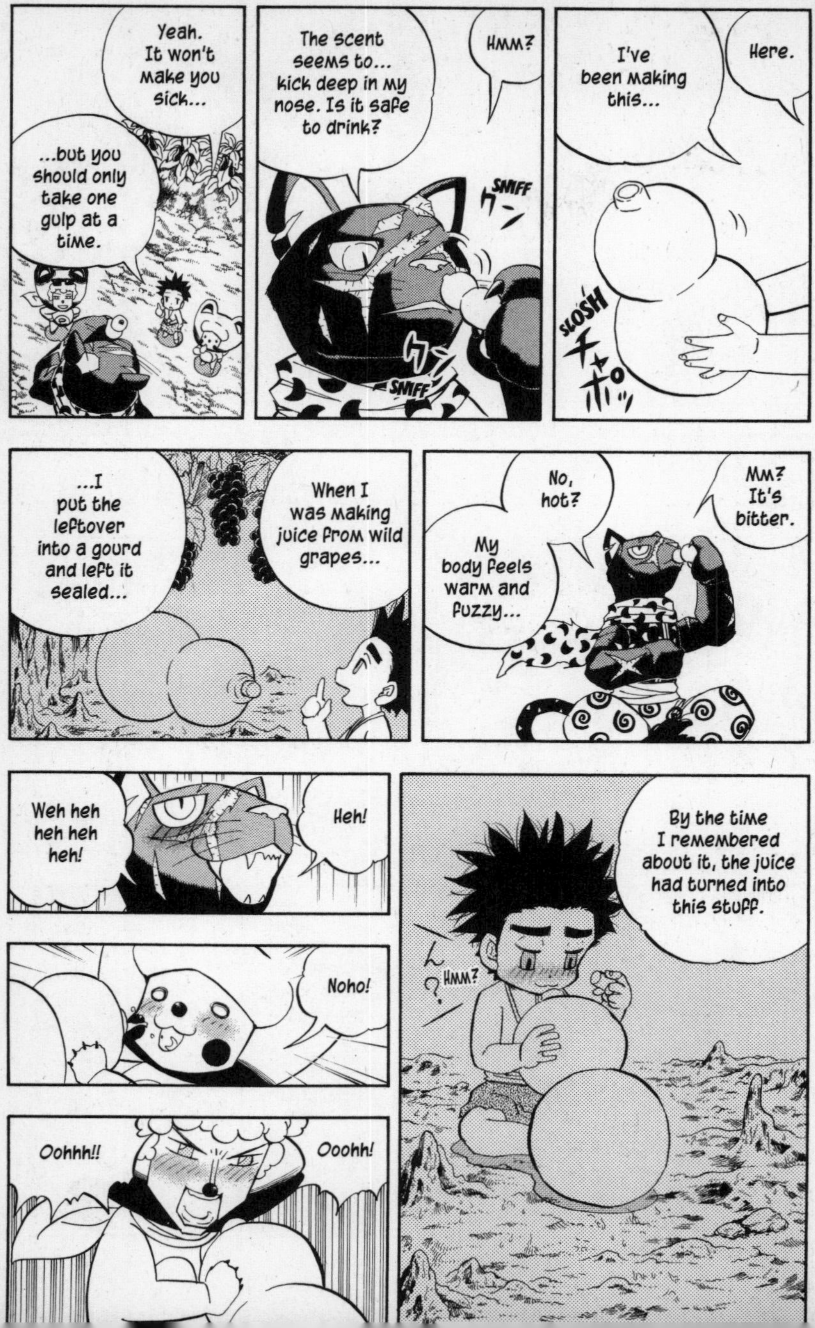
Here.
I've been making this...
SLOSH
HMM?
The scent seems to... kick deep in my nose. Is it safe to drink?
SNIFF
SNIFF
Yeah. It won't make you sick...
...but you should only take one gulp at a time.
Mm? It's bitter.
No, hot?
My body feels warm and fuzzy...
When I was making juice from wild grapes...
...I put the leftover into a gourd and left it sealed...
By the time I remembered about it, the juice had turned into this stuff.
HMM?
Heh!
Weh heh heh heh heh!
Noho!
Ooohh!
Oohhh!!

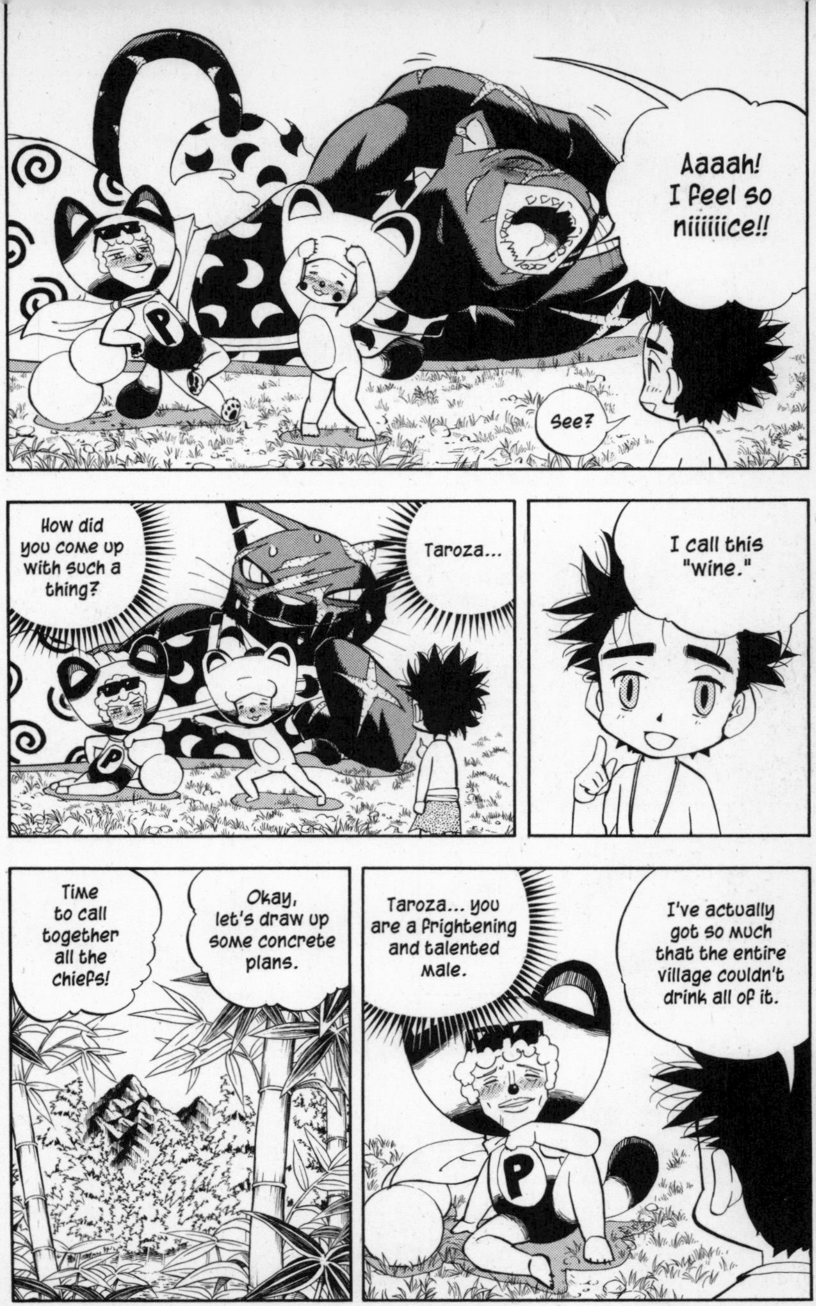
Aaaah! I feel so niiiiiice!!
See?
I call this "wine."
Taroza...
How did you come up with such a thing?
I've actually got so much that the entire village couldn't drink all of it.
Taroza... you are a frightening and talented male.
Okay, let's draw up some concrete plans.
Time to call together all the chiefs!

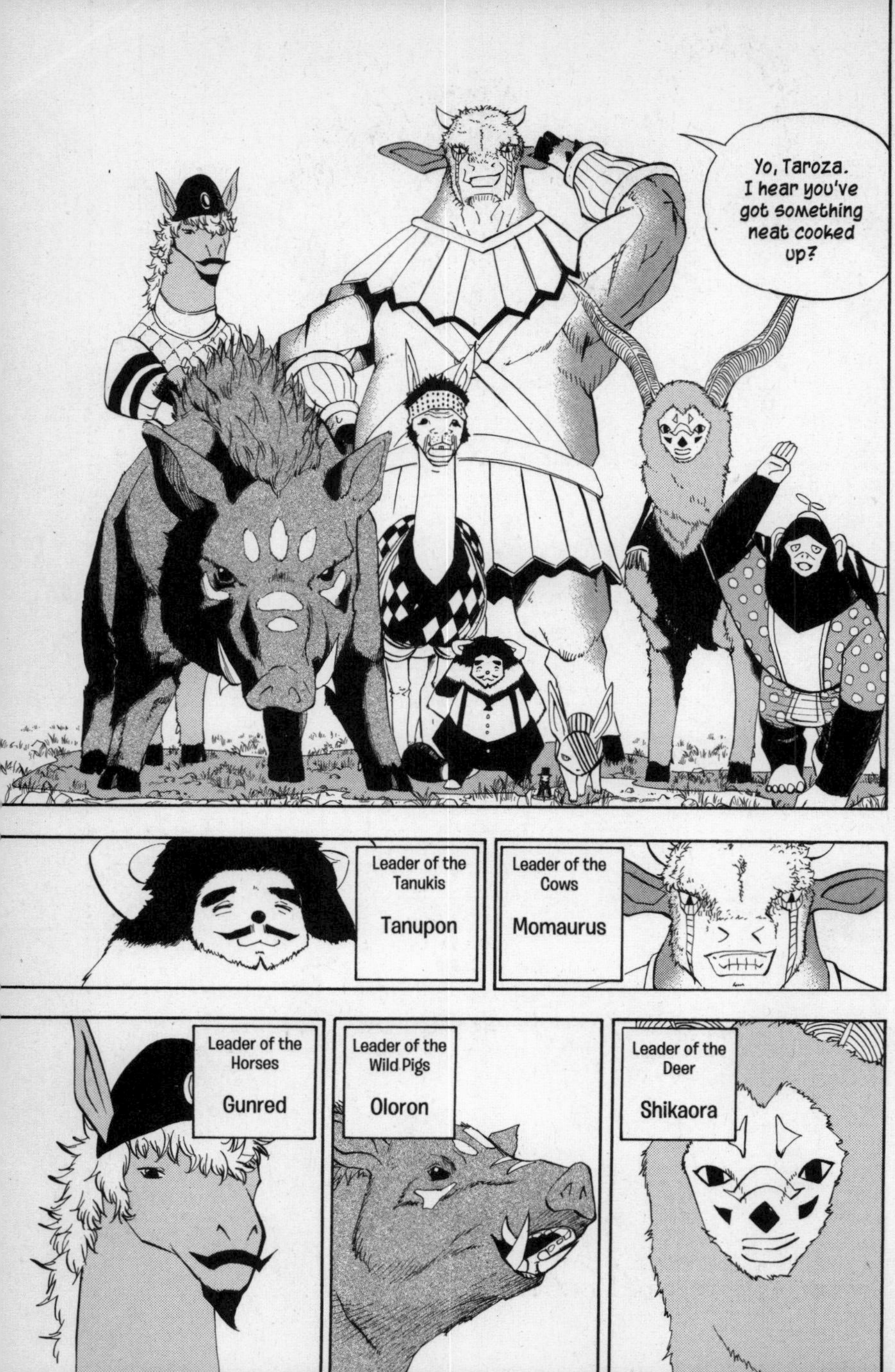

Yo, Taroza. I hear you've got something neat cooked up?
Leader of the Cows
Momaurus
Leader of the Tanukis
Tanupon
Leader of the Deer
Shikaora
Leader of the Wild Pigs
Oloron
Leader of the Horses
Gunred

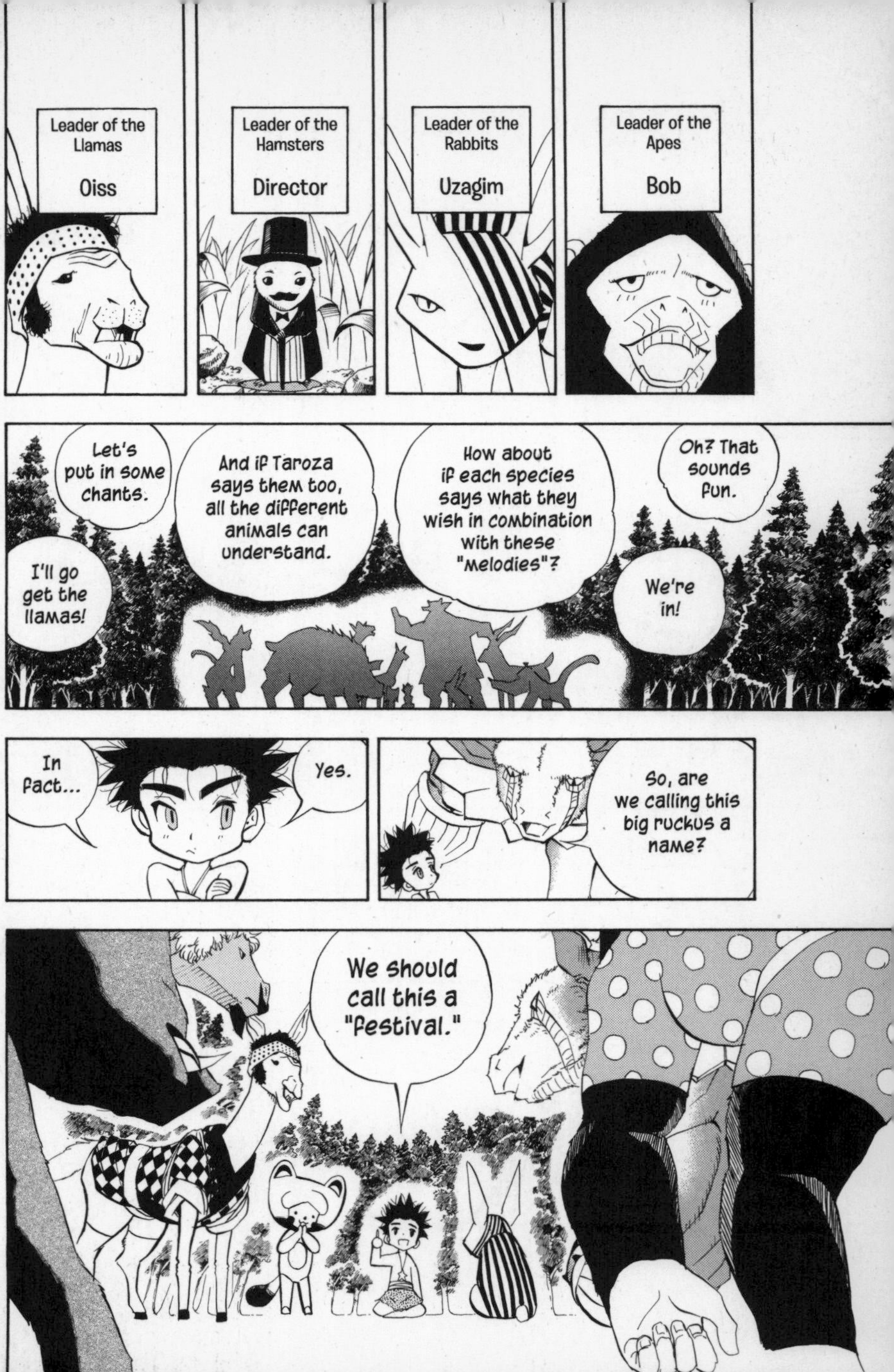
Leader of the Apes
Bob
Leader of the Rabbits
Uzagim
Leader of the Hamsters
Director
Leader of the Llamas
Oiss
Oh? That sounds fun.
We're in!
How about if each species says what they wish in combination with these "melodies"?
And if Taroza says them too, all the different animals can understand.
Let's put in some chants.
I'll go get the llamas!
So, are we calling this big ruckus a name?
Yes.
In fact...
We should call this a "festival."

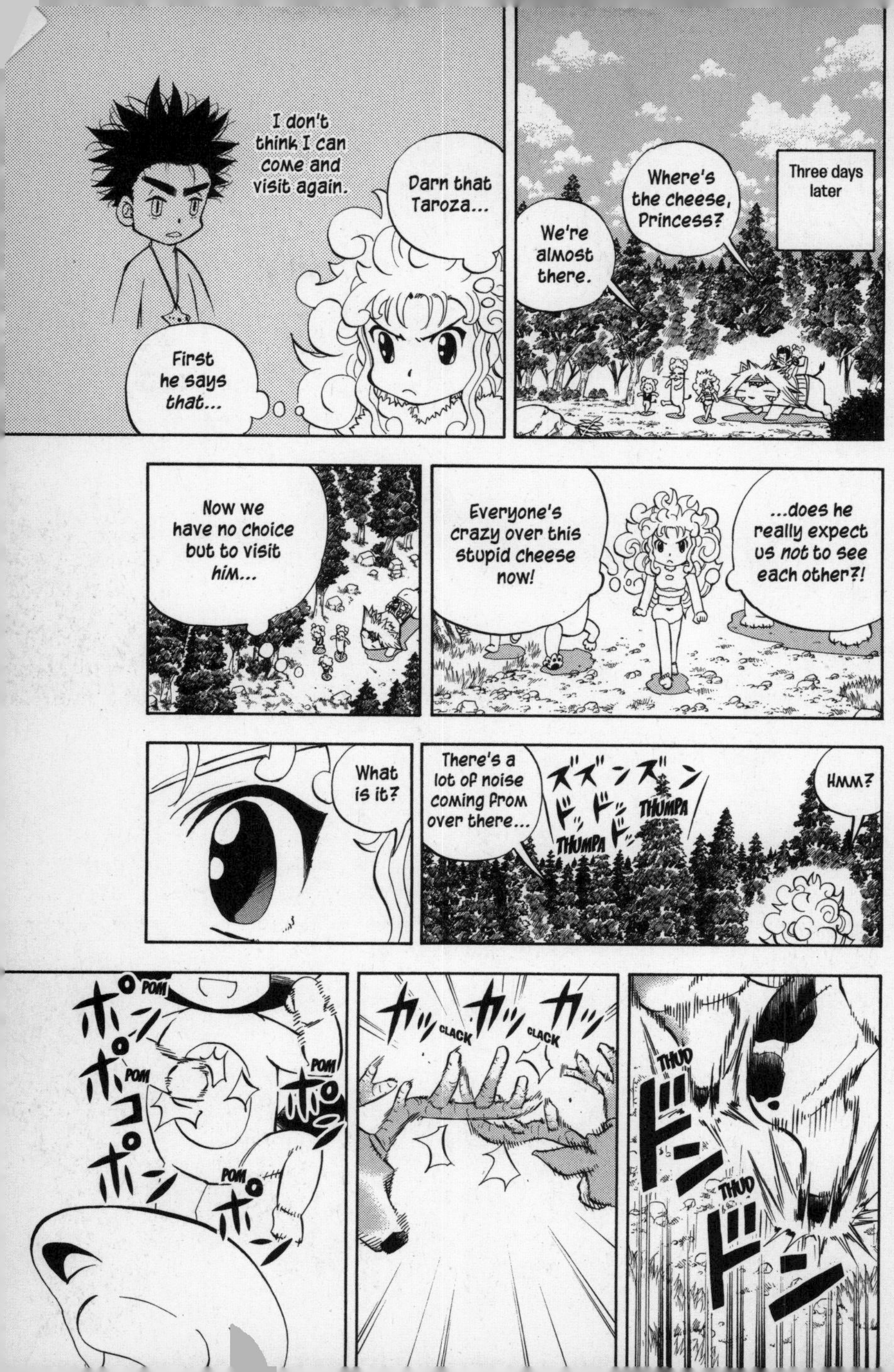
Three days later
Where's the cheese, Princess?
We're almost there.
Darn that Taroza...
I don't think I can come and visit again.
First he says that...
...does he really expect us *not* to see each other?!
Everyone's crazy over this stupid cheese now!
Now we have no choice but to visit *him*...
HMM?
THUMPA
THUMPA
There's a lot of noise coming from over there...
What is it?
THUD
THUD
CLACK
CLACK
POM
POM
POM
POM

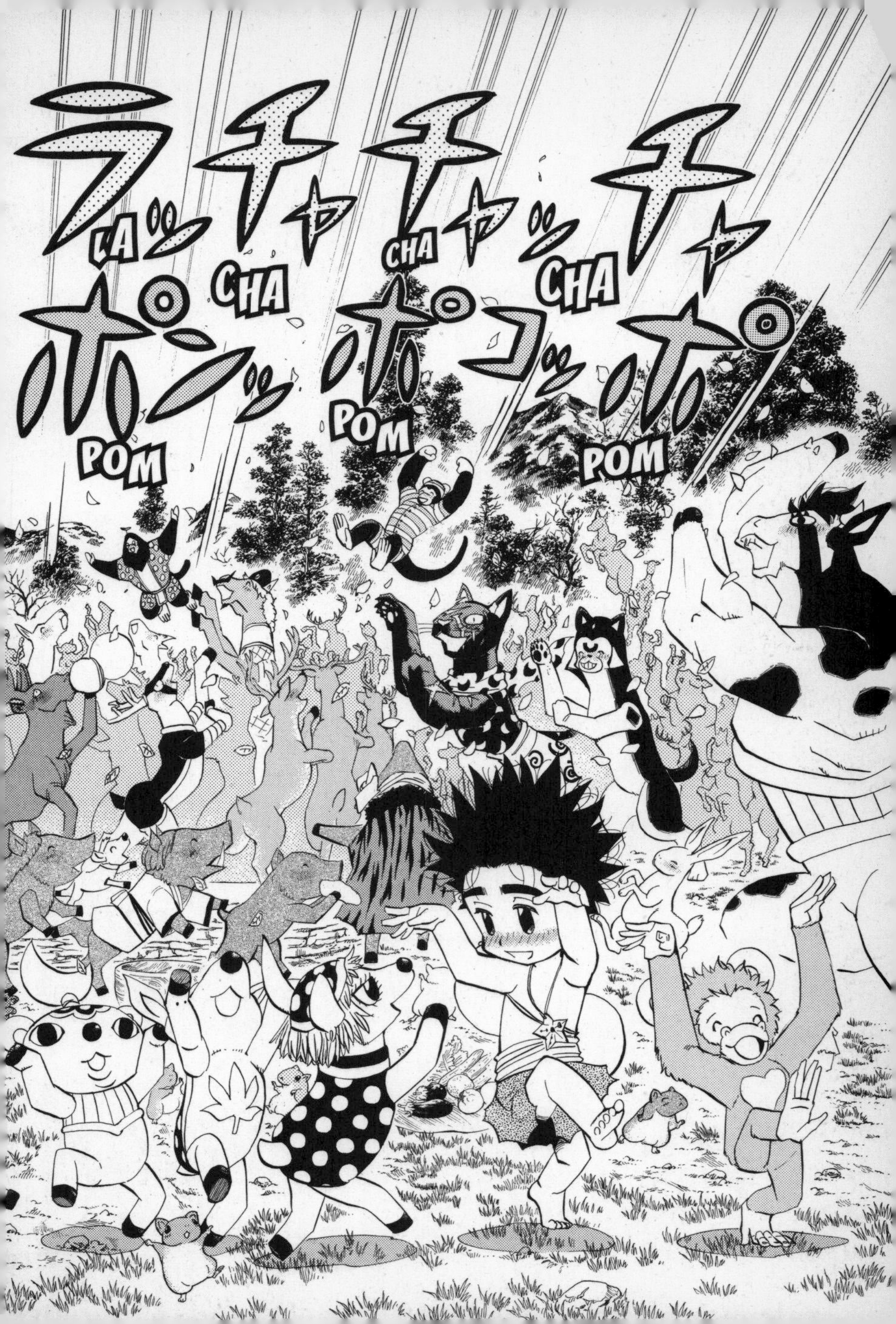
ラッチャチャッチャ
LA CHA CHA CHA
ポンッポコッポ
POM POM POM

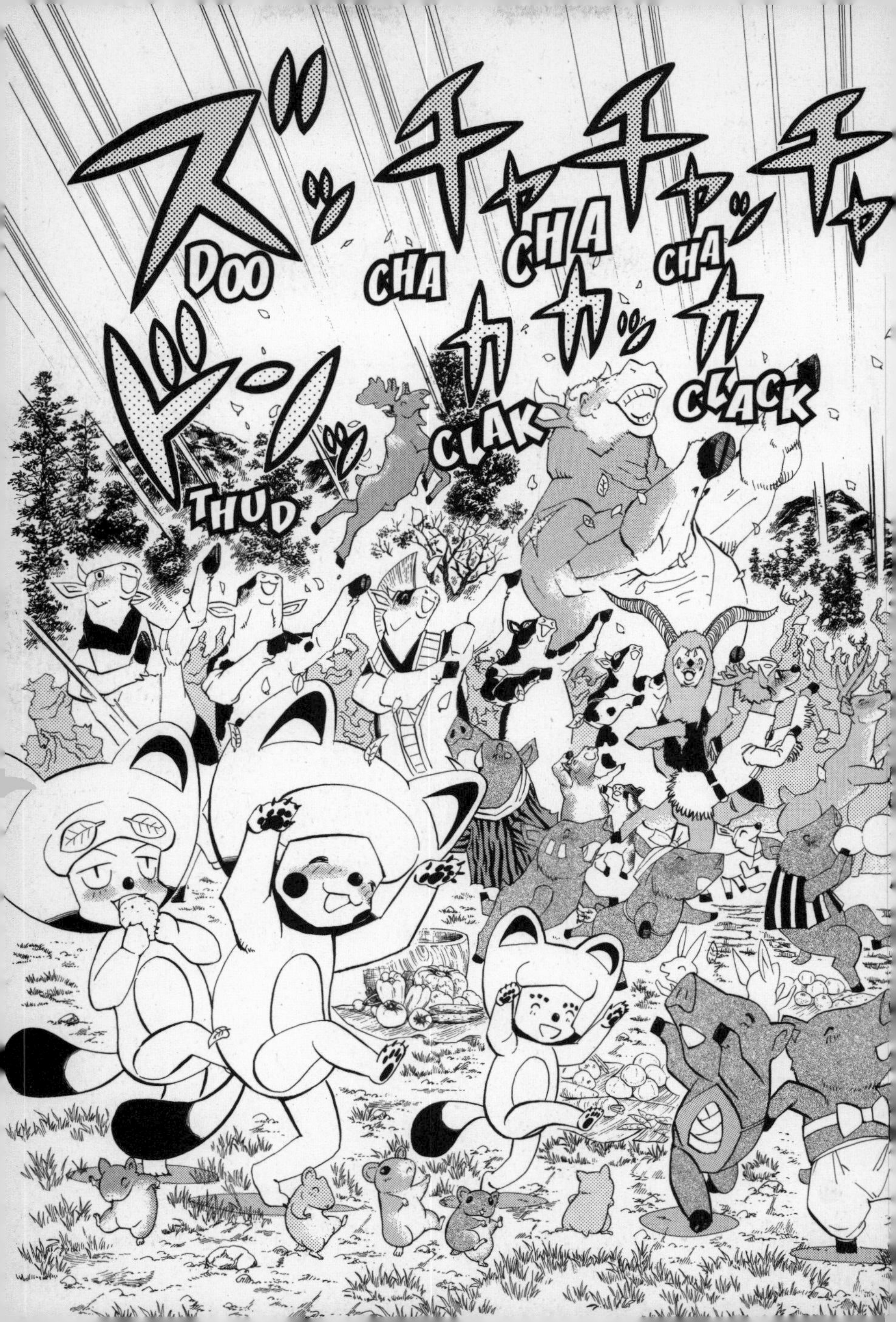
DOO
CHA
CHA
CHA
THUD
CLAK
CLACK

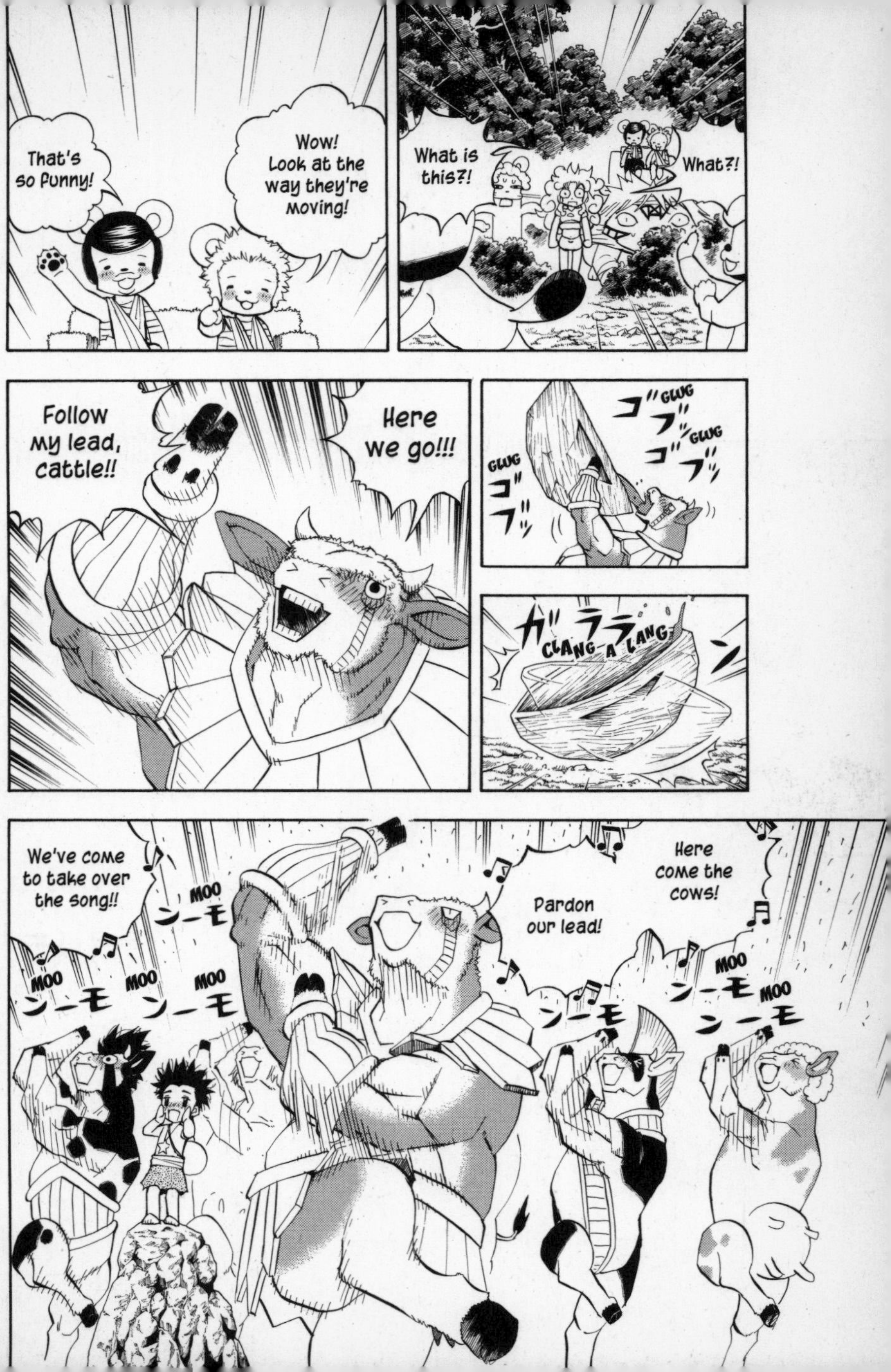
What?!
What is this?!
Wow! Look at the way they're moving!
That's so funny!
GWG
GWG
GWG
CLANG-A-LANG
Here we go!!!
Follow my lead, cattle!!
Here come the cows!
Pardon our lead!
We've come to take over the song!!
MOO
MOO
MOO
MOO
MOO
MOO

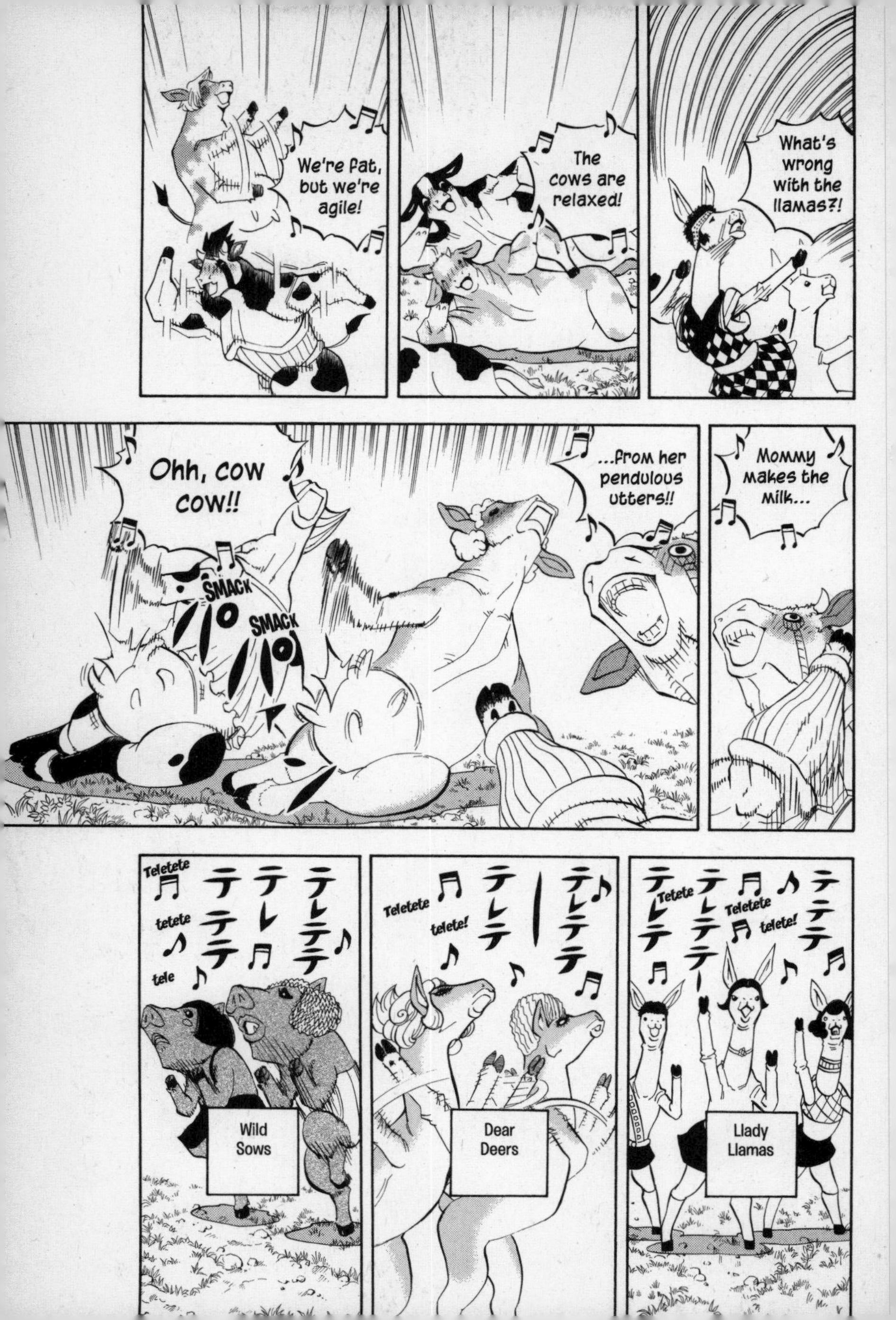
What's wrong with the llamas?!
The cows are relaxed!
We're fat, but we're agile!
Mommy makes the milk...
...from her pendulous utters!!
Ohh, cow cow!!
SMACK
SMACK
Teletete
telete!
Tetete
Llady Llamas
Teletete
telete!
Dear Deers
Teletete
tetete
tele
Wild Sows

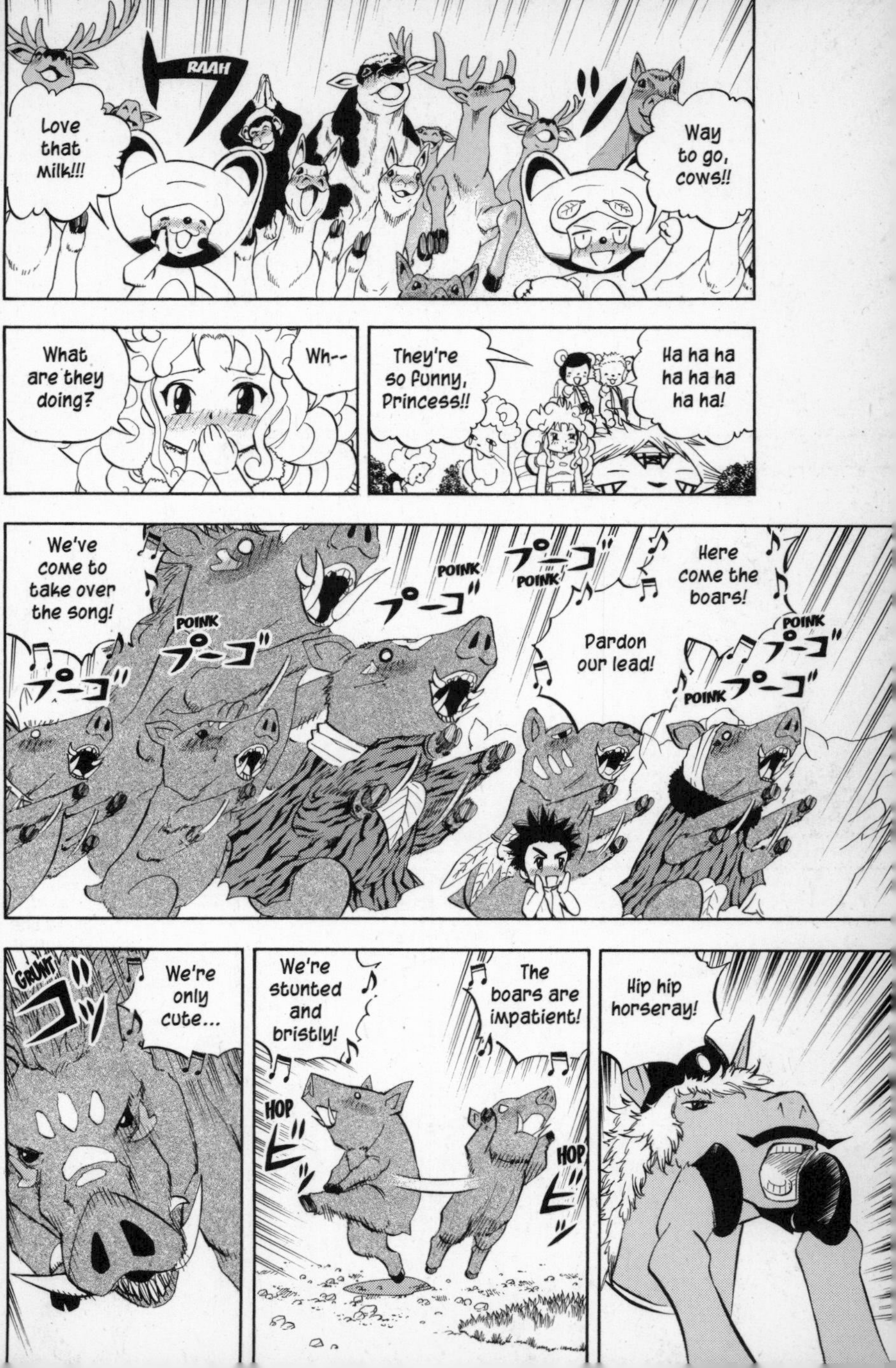
Way to go, cows!!
RAAH
Love that Milk!!!
Ha ha ha ha ha ha ha ha!
They're so funny, Princess!!
Wh--
What are they doing?
Here come the boars!
POINK
POINK
Pardon our lead!
POINK
POINK
POINK
We've come to take over the song!
Hip hip horseray!
The boars are impatient!
HOP
We're stunted and bristly!
HOP
We're only cute...
GRUNT

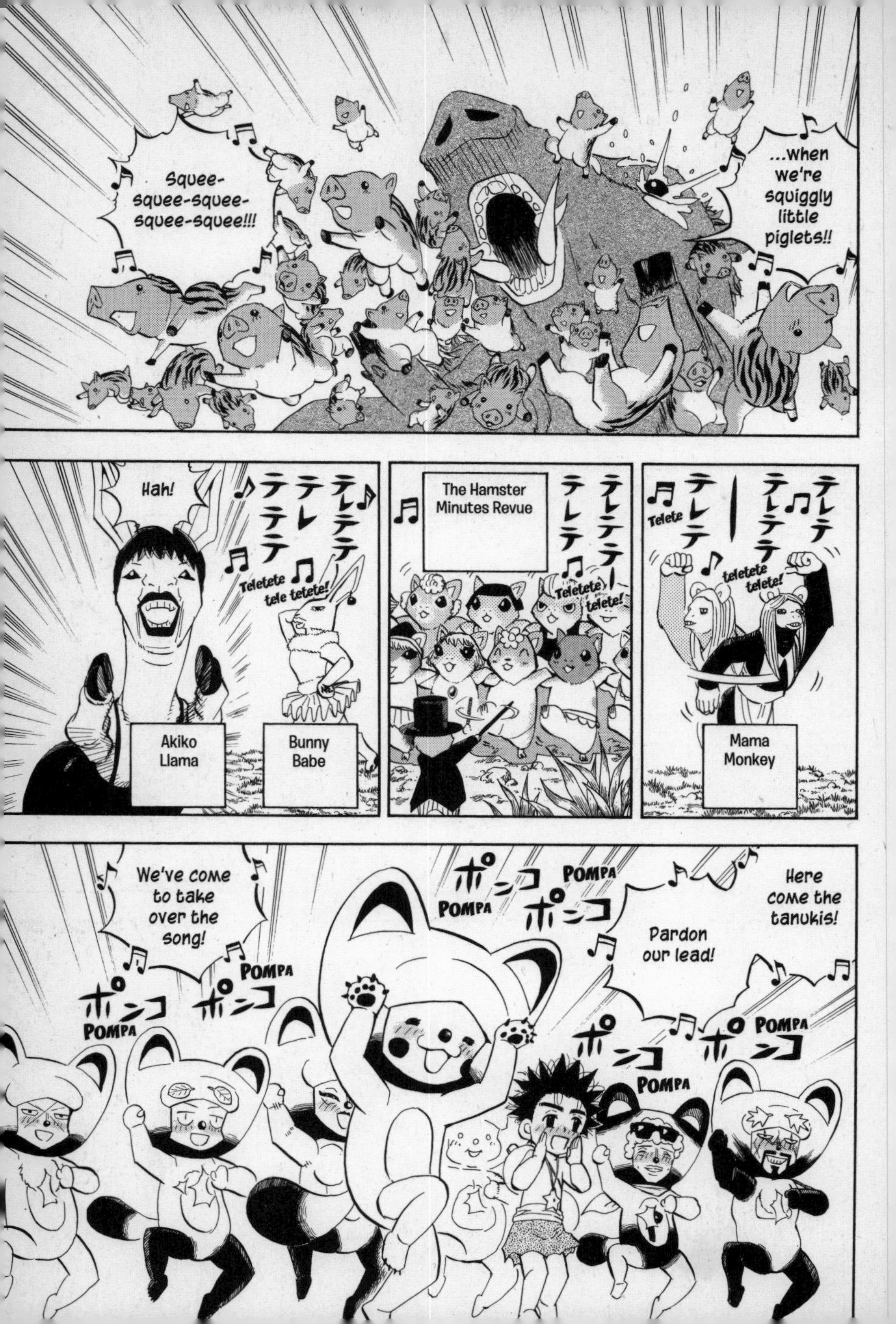
...when we're squiggly little piglets!!
Squee-squee-squee-squee-squee!!!
テレテ
テレテテ
ー
テレテ
Telete
teletete telete!
Mama Monkey
テレテテー
テレテ
Teletete telete!
The Hamster Minutes Revue
テレテテ
テレ
テテテ
Teletete tele tetete!
Bunny Babe
Hah!
Akiko Llama
Here come the tanukis!
Pardon our lead!
ポンコ POMPA
ポンコ POMPA
ポンコ POMPA
ポンコ POMPA
We've come to take over the song!
ポンコ POMPA
ポンコ POMPA

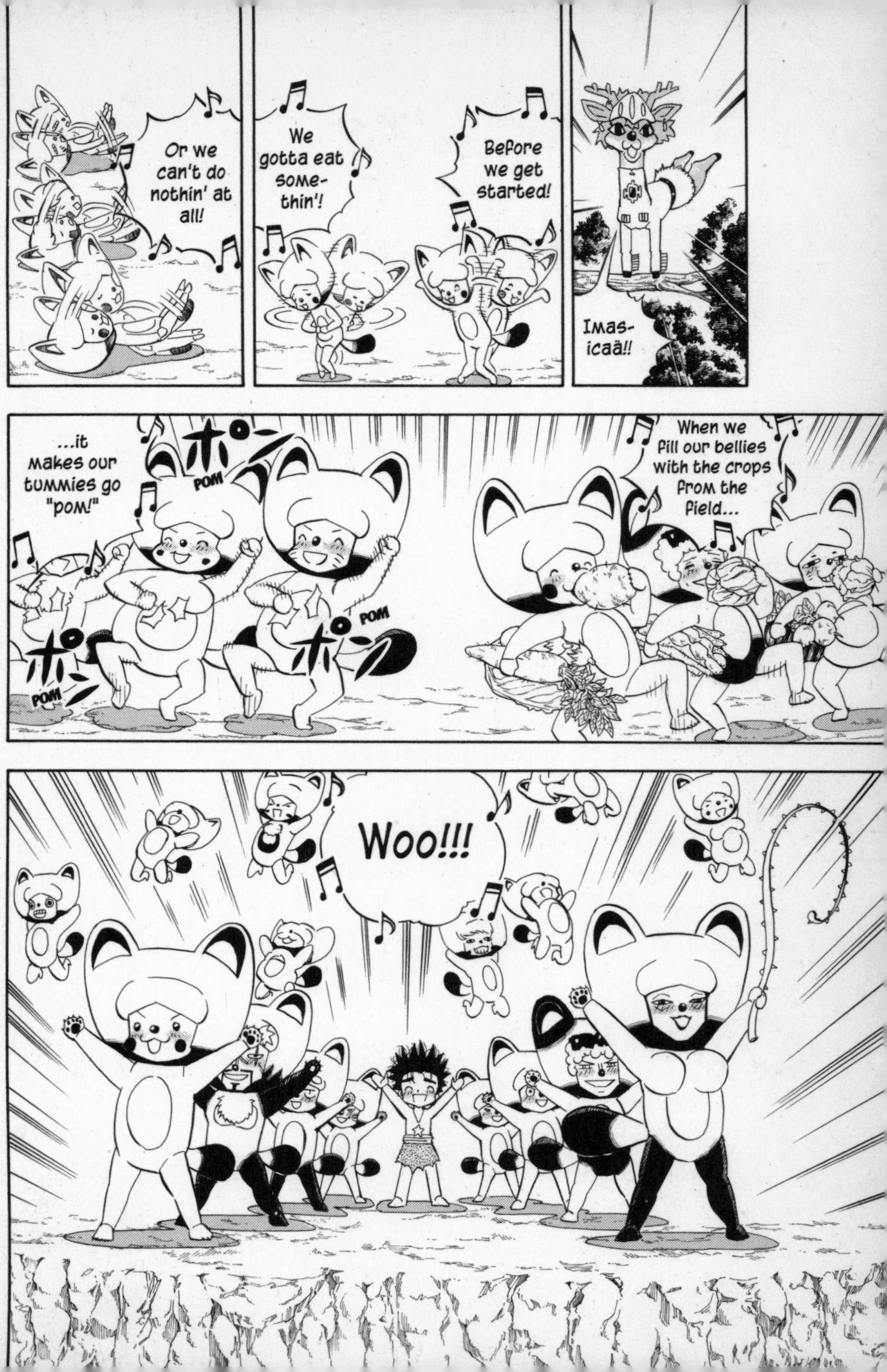
Imas-icaä!!
Before we get started!
We gotta eat some-thin'!
Or we can't do nothin' at all!
When we fill our bellies with the crops from the field...
...it makes our tummies go "pom!"
POM
POM
POM
Woo!!!

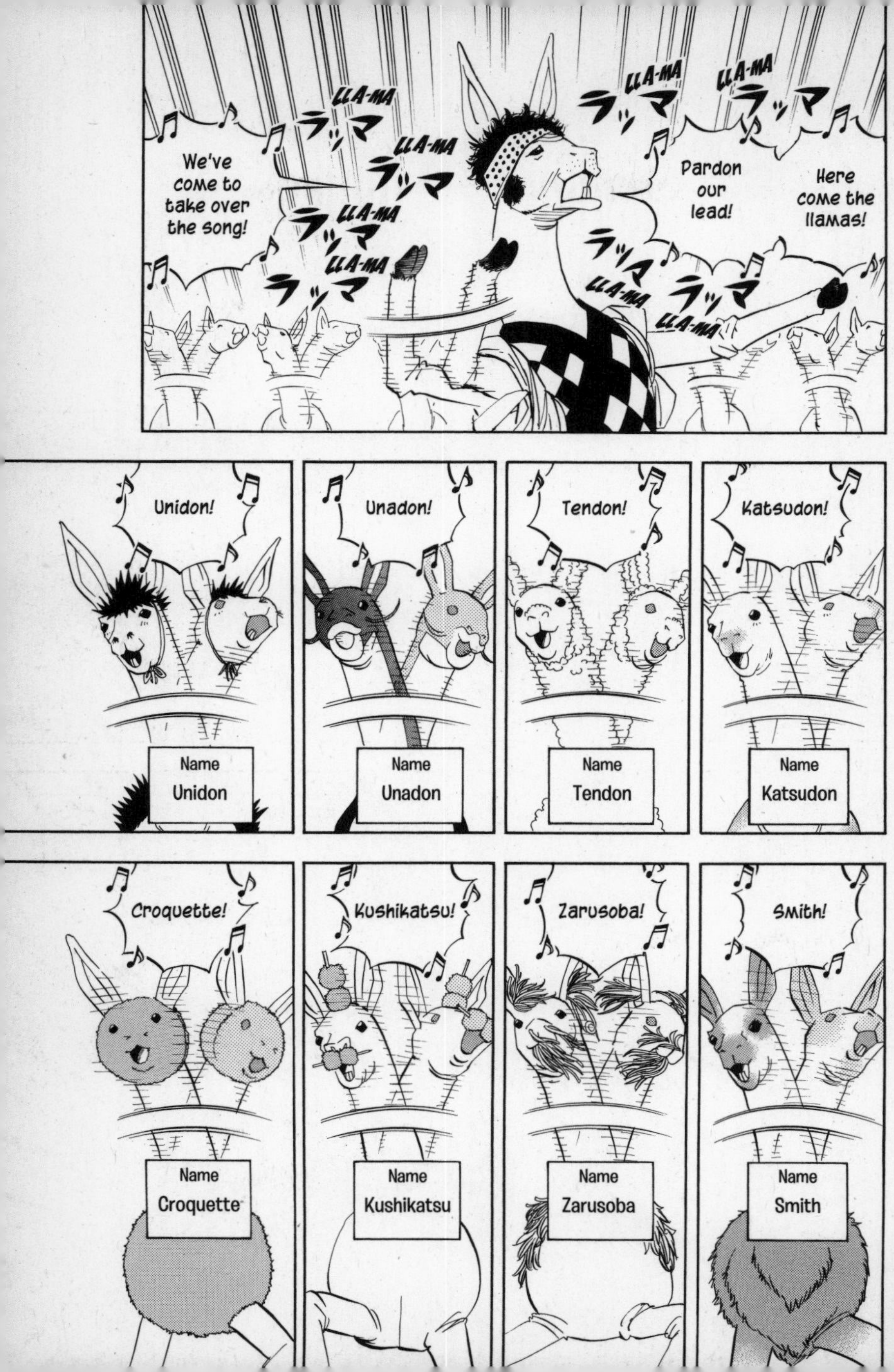
Here come the llamas!
ラッマ
LLA-MA
ラッマ
LLA-MA
Pardon our lead!
ラッマ
LLA-MA
ラッマ
LLA-MA
ラッマ
LLA-MA
ラッマ
LLA-MA
ラッマ
LLA-MA
ラッマ
LLA-MA
We've come to take over the song!
Katsudon!
Name
Katsudon
Tendon!
Name
Tendon
Unadon!
Name
Unadon
Unidon!
Name
Unidon
Smith!
Name
Smith
Zarusoba!
Name
Zarusoba
Kushikatsu!
Name
Kushikatsu
Croquette!
Name
Croquette

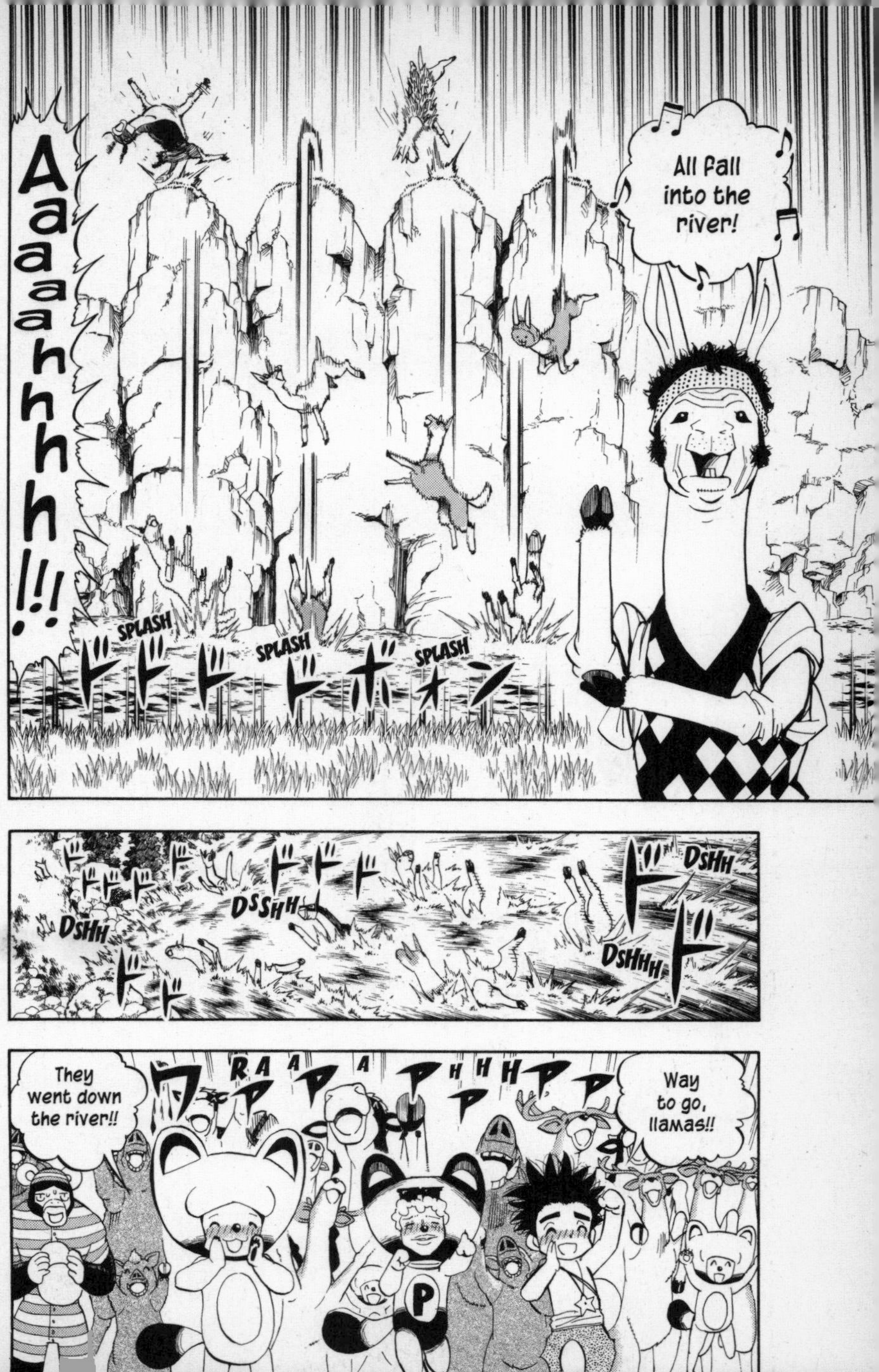
All fall into the river!
Aaaaahhhh!!!
SPLASH
SPLASH
SPLASH
DSHH
DSHHH
DSSHH
DSHH
Way to go, llamas!!
RAAAAHHHH
They went down the river!!

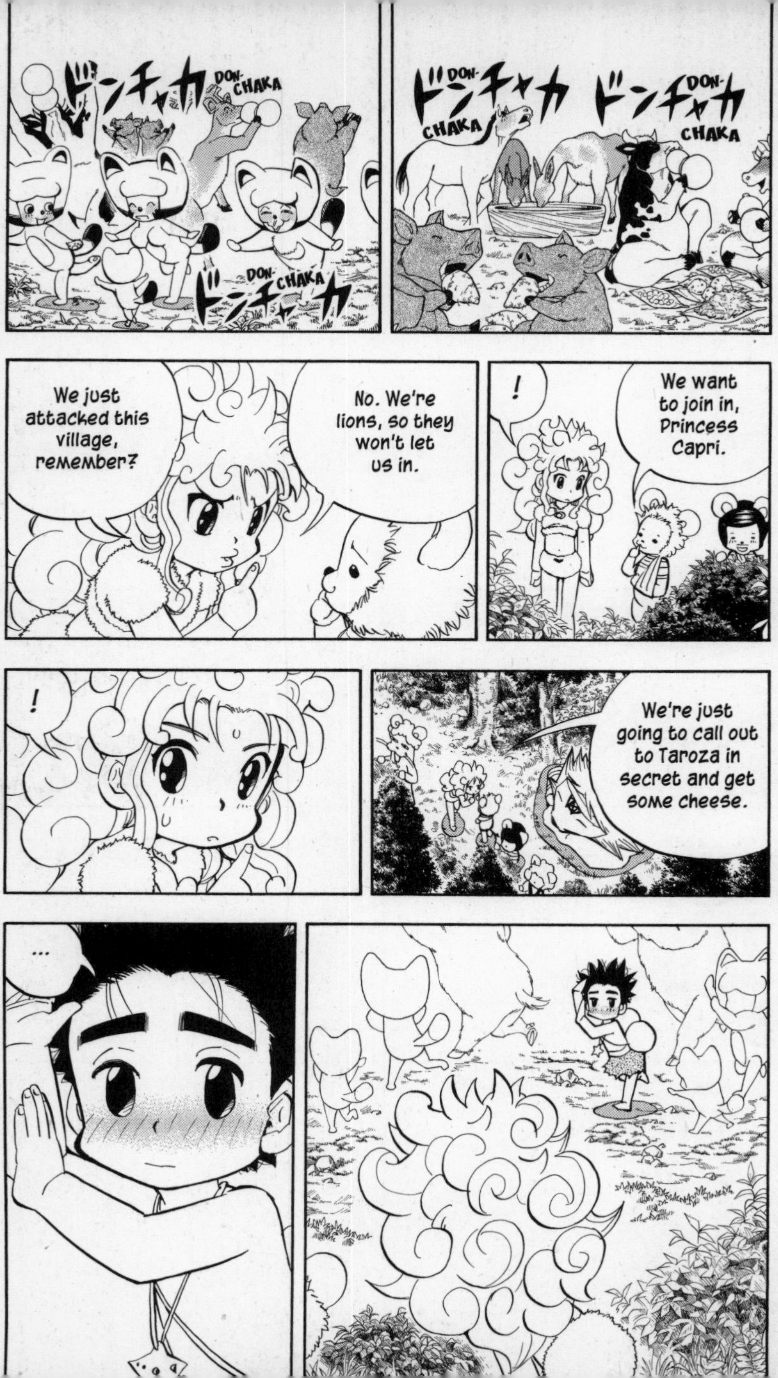

ドンチャカ DON-CHAKA
ドンチャカ DON-CHAKA
ドンチャカ DON-CHAKA
ドンチャカ DON-CHAKA
!
We want to join in, Princess Capri.
No. We're lions, so they won't let us in.
We just attacked this village, remember?
We're just going to call out to Taroza in secret and get some cheese.
!
...

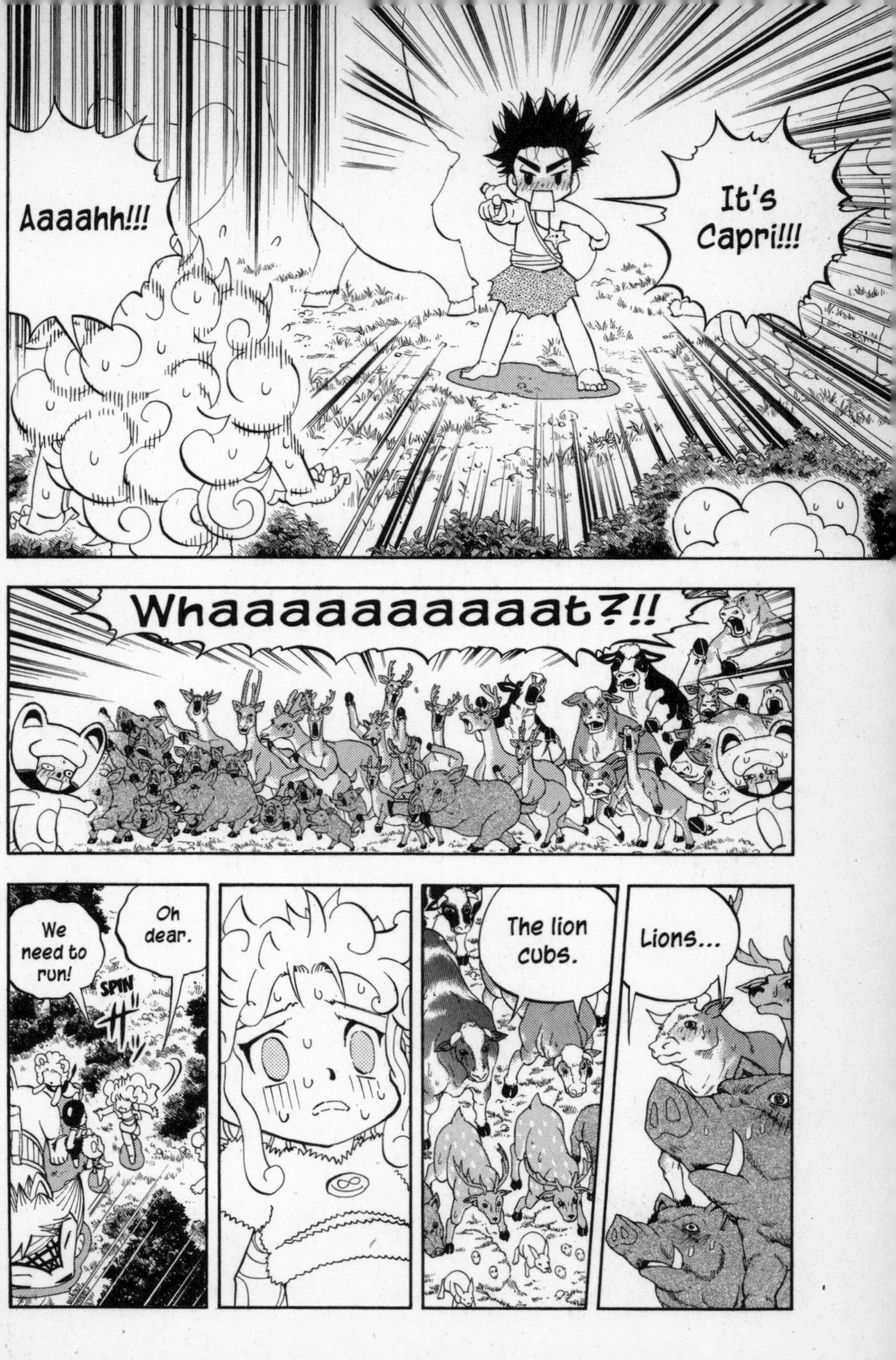
It's Capri!!!
Aaaahh!!!
Whaaaaaaaaaat?!!
Lions...
The lion cubs.
Oh dear.
We need to run!
SPIN

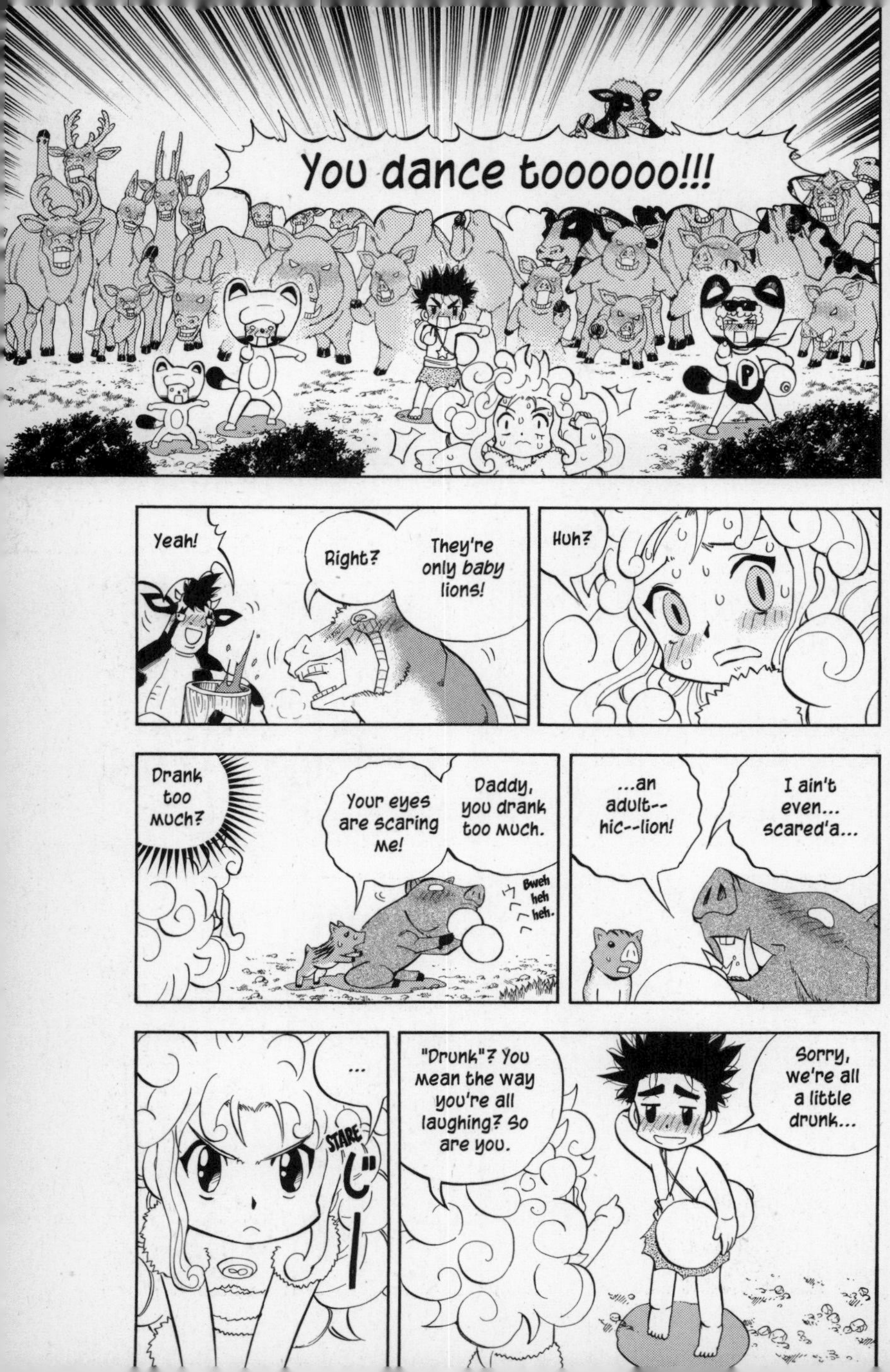
You dance tooooooo!!!
Huh?
They're only baby lions!
Right?
Yeah!
I ain't even... scared'a...
...an adult--hic--lion!
Daddy, you drank too much.
Your eyes are scaring me!
Bweh heh heh.
Drank too much?
Sorry, we're all a little drunk...
"Drunk"? You mean the way you're all laughing? So are you.
...
STARE

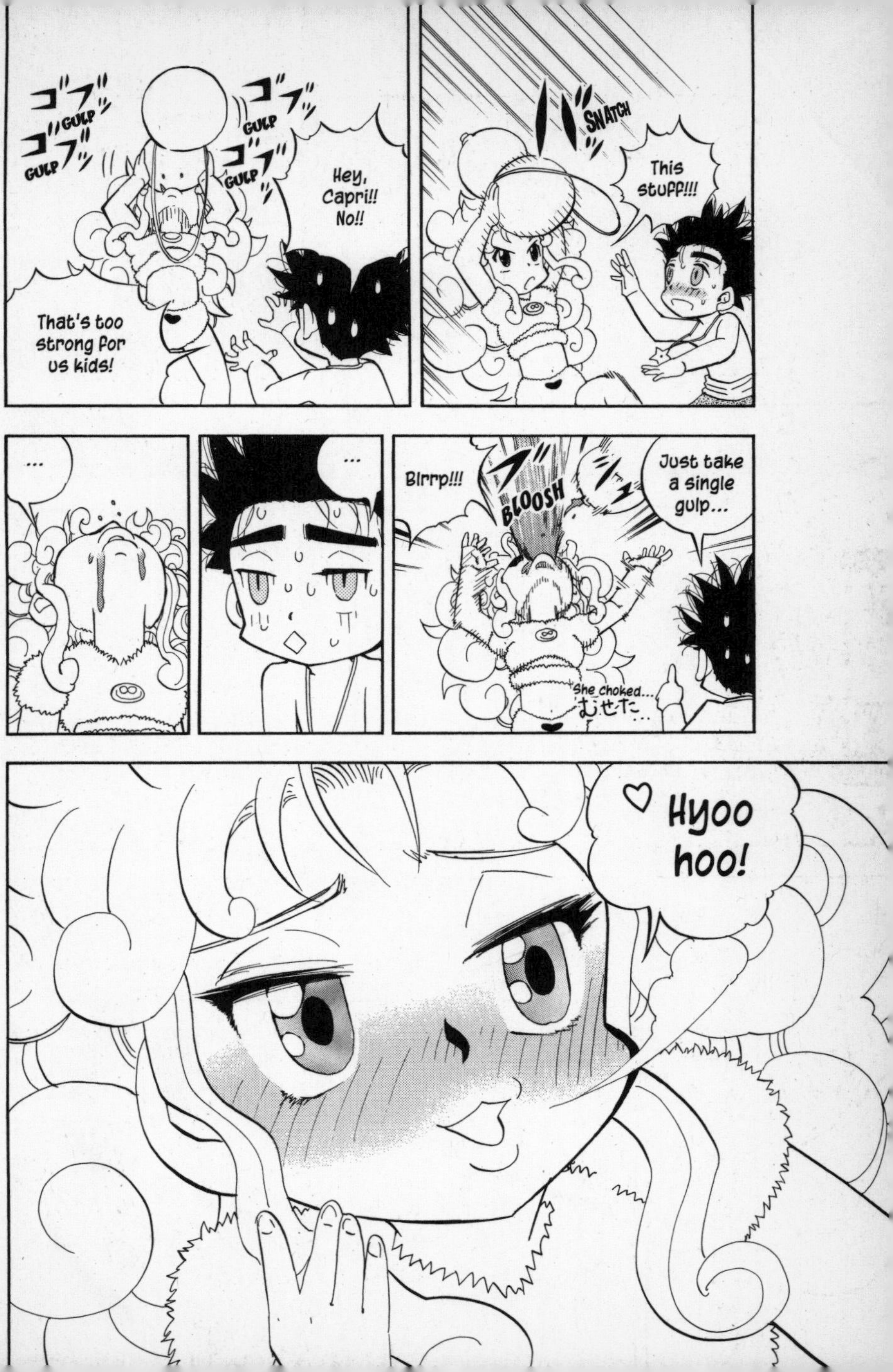
SNATCH
This stuff!!!
ゴブ
GULP
ゴブ
GULP
ゴブ
GULP
ゴブ
GULP
Hey, Capri!! No!!
That's too strong for us kids!
Just take a single gulp...
BLOOSH
Birrp!!!
She choked...
むせた...
...
...
♡ Hyoo hoo!

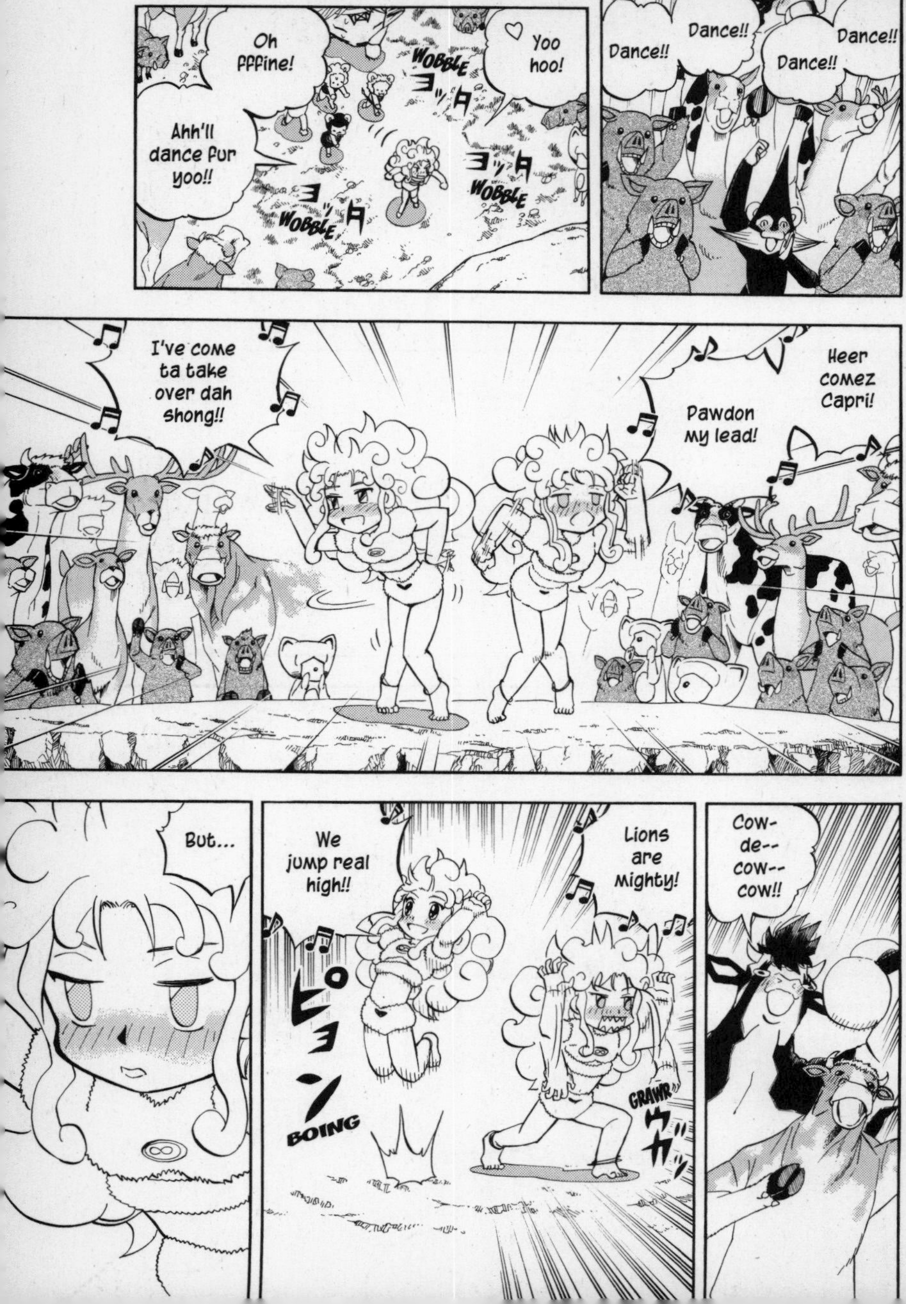

Dance!!
Dance!!
Dance!!
Dance!!
Yoo hoo!
WOBBLE
WOBBLE
WOBBLE
Oh fffine!
Ahh'll dance fur yoo!!
Heer comez Capri!
Pawdon my lead!
I've come ta take over dah shong!!
Cow-de--cow--cow!!
Lions are mighty!
GRAWR
We jump real high!!
BOING
But...

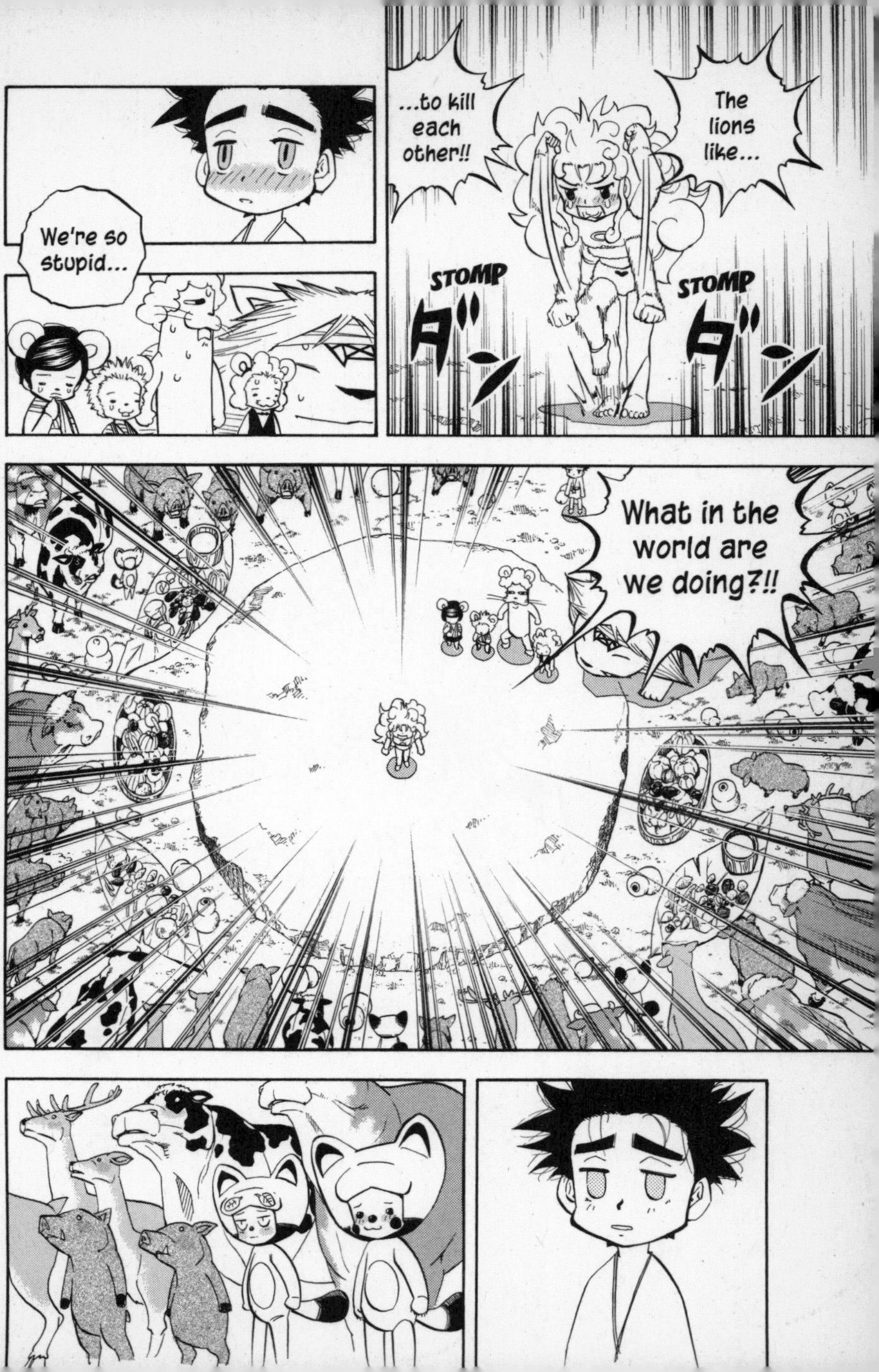
The lions like...
...to kill each other!!
STOMP
ダン
STOMP
ダン
We're so stupid...
What in the world are we doing?!!

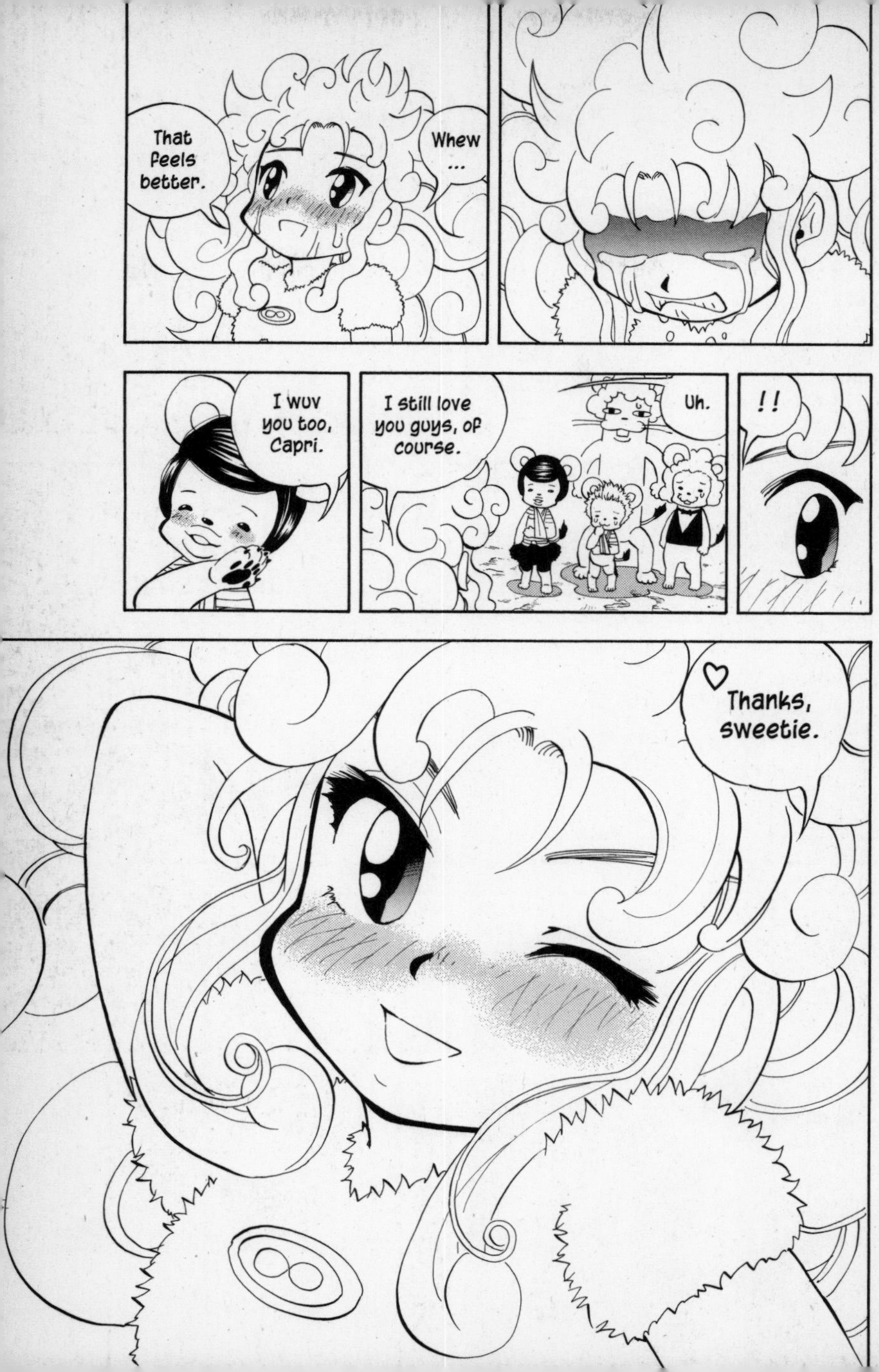
Whew ...
That feels better.
!!
Uh.
I still love you guys, of course.
I wuv you too, Capri.
Thanks, sweetie.

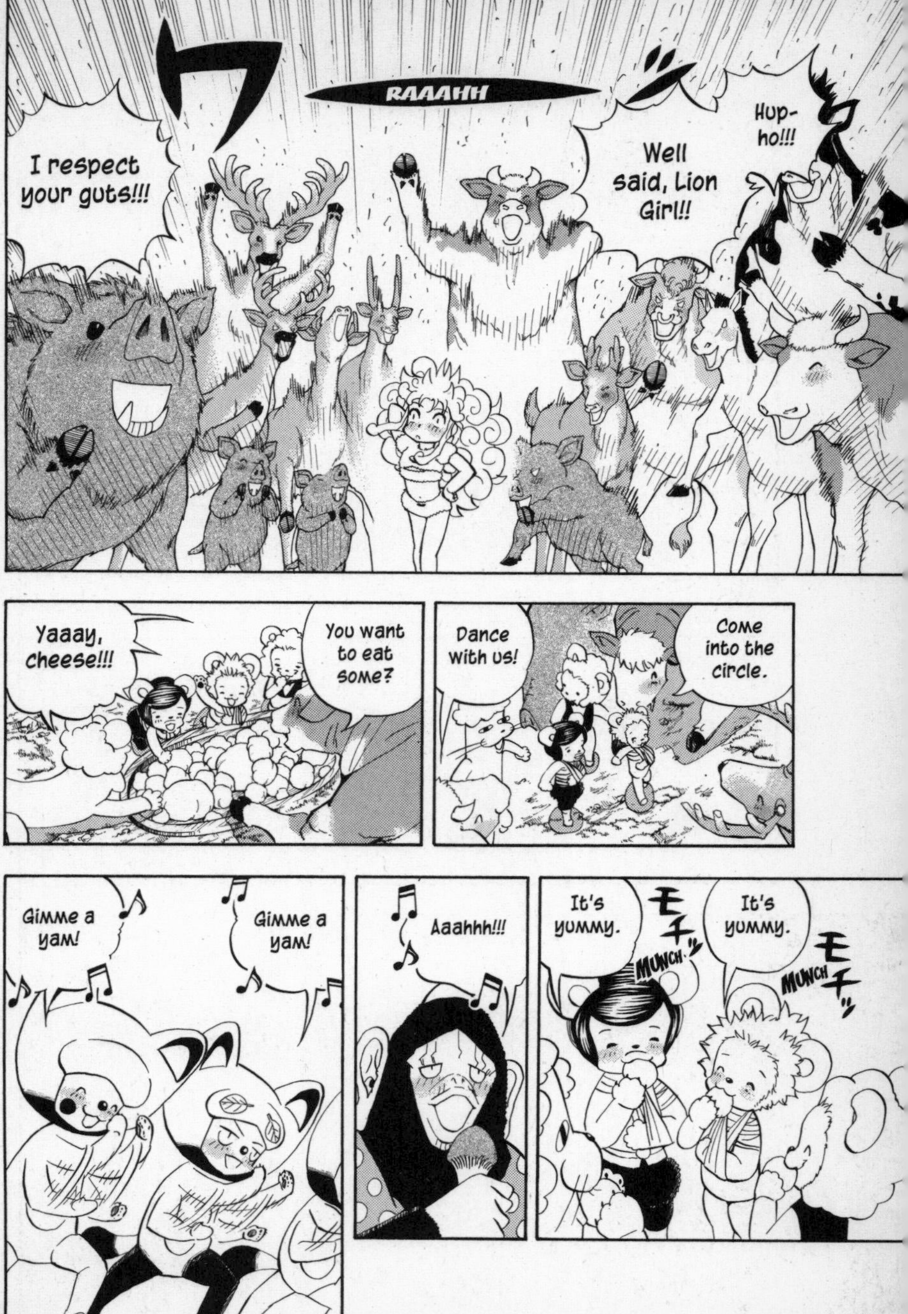
Hup-ho!!!
Well said, Lion Girl!!
RAAAHH
I respect your guts!!!
Come into the circle.
Dance with us!
You want to eat some?
Yaaay, cheese!!!
It's yummy.
MUNCH
It's yummy.
MUNCH
Aaahhh!!!
Gimme a yam!
Gimme a yam!

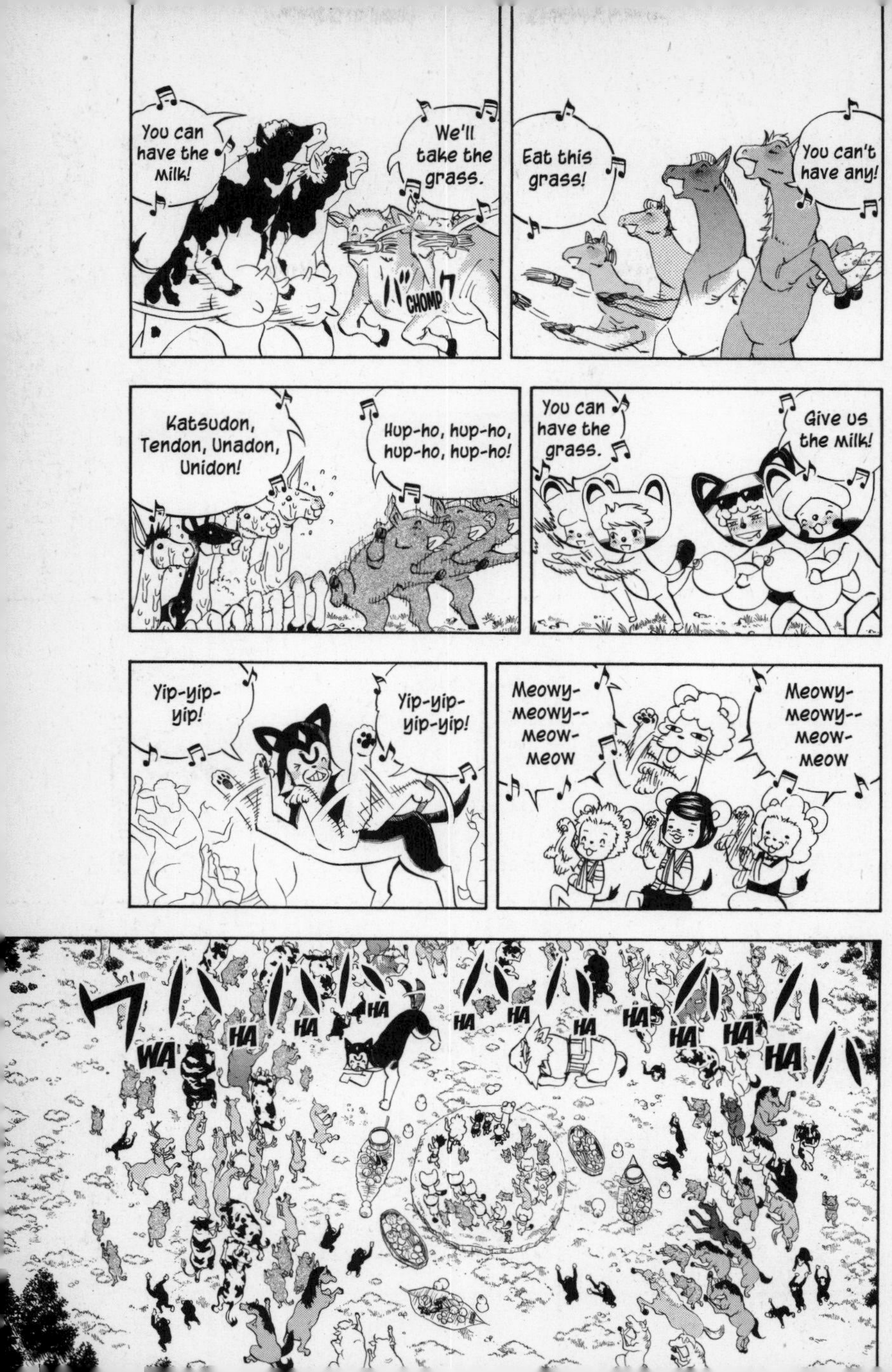
You can't have any!
Eat this grass!
We'll take the grass.
CHOMP
You can have the milk!
Give us the milk!
You can have the grass.
Hup-ho, hup-ho, hup-ho, hup-ho!
Katsudon, Tendon, Unadon, Unidon!
Meowy-meowy--meow-meow
Meowy-meowy--meow-meow
Yip-yip-yip-yip!
Yip-yip-yip!
WA HA HA HA HA HA HA HA HA HA HA

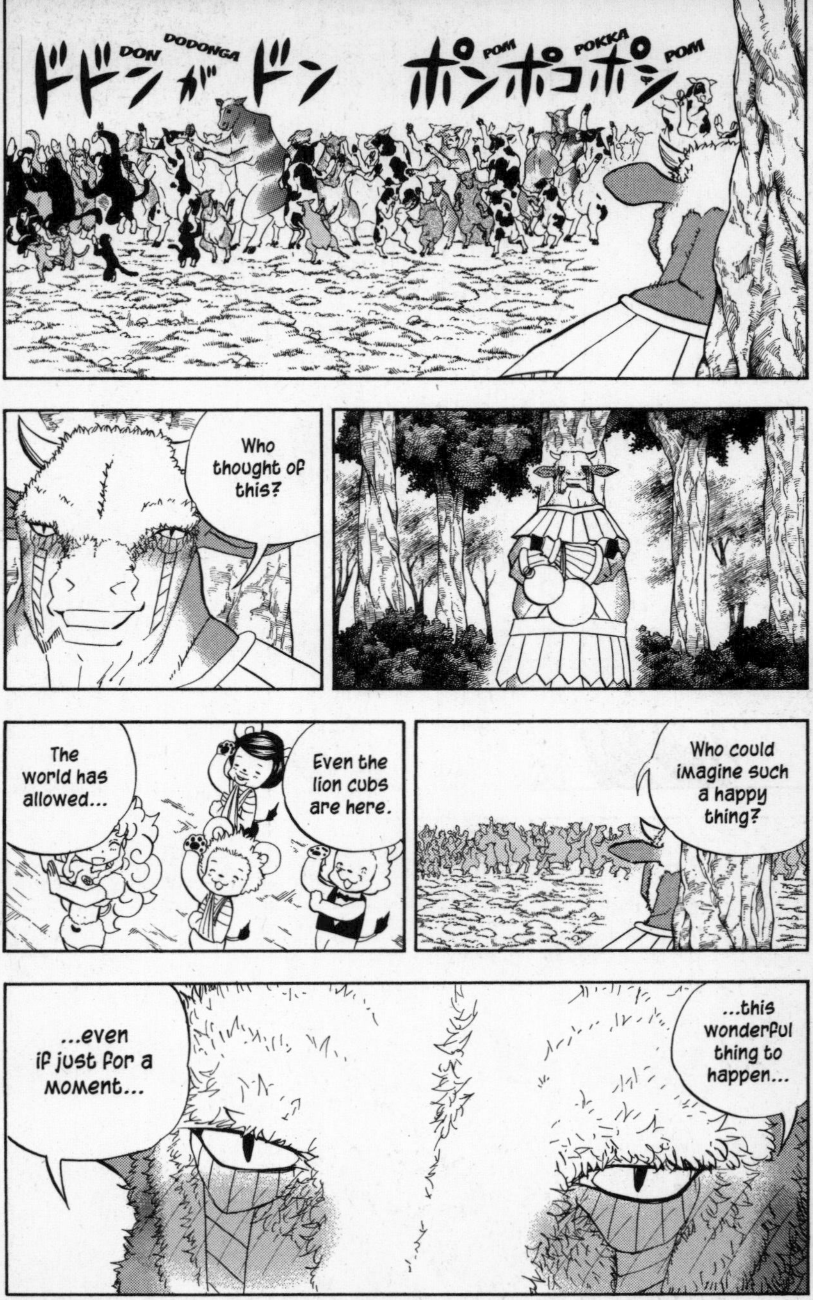
ポンポコポン
POM POKKA POM
ドドンガドン
DON DODONGA
Who thought of this?
Who could imagine such a happy thing?
Even the lion cubs are here.
The world has allowed...
...this wonderful thing to happen...
...even if just for a moment...

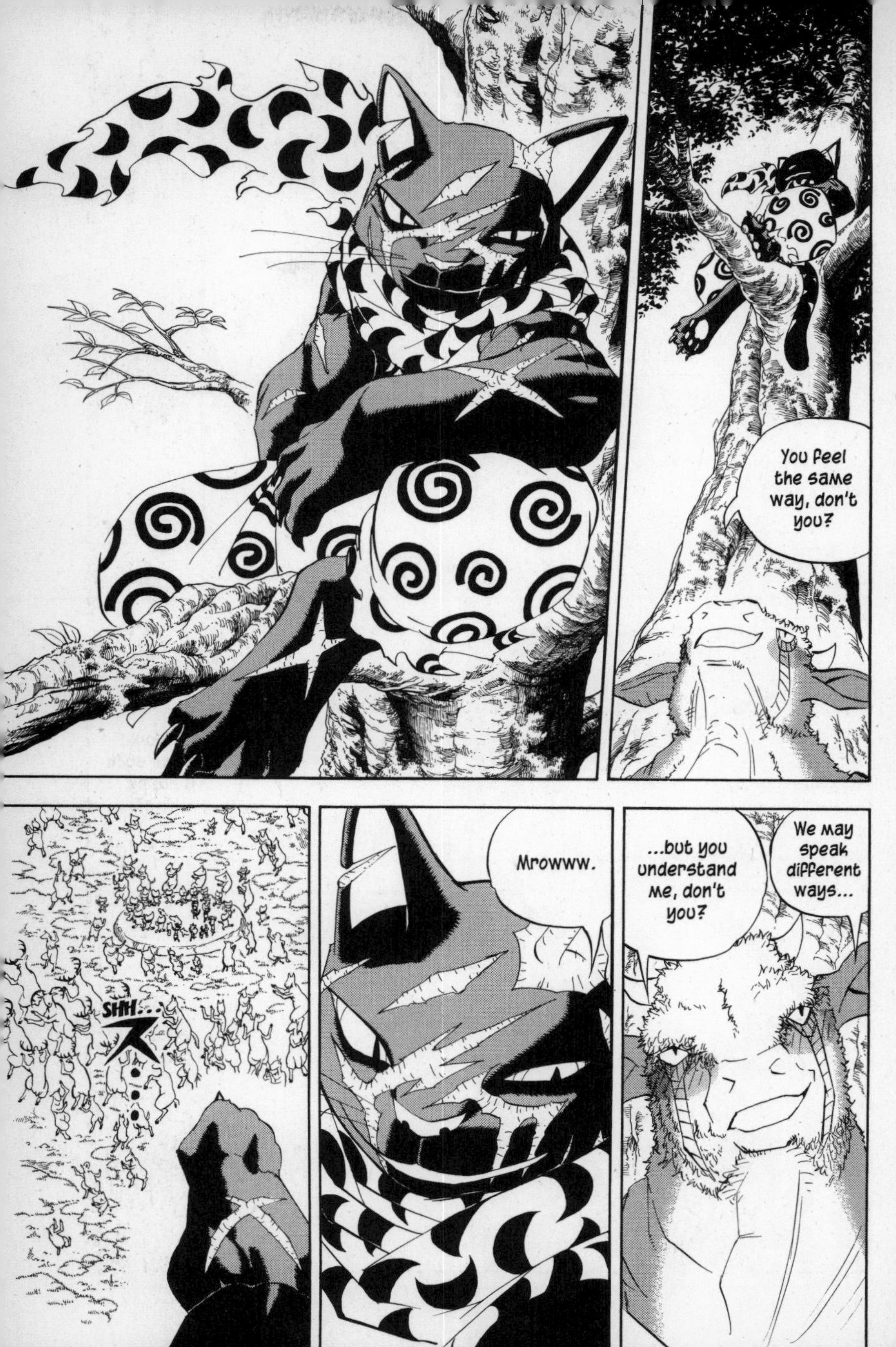
You feel the same way, don't you?
We may speak different ways...
...but you understand me, don't you?
Mrowww.
SHH...

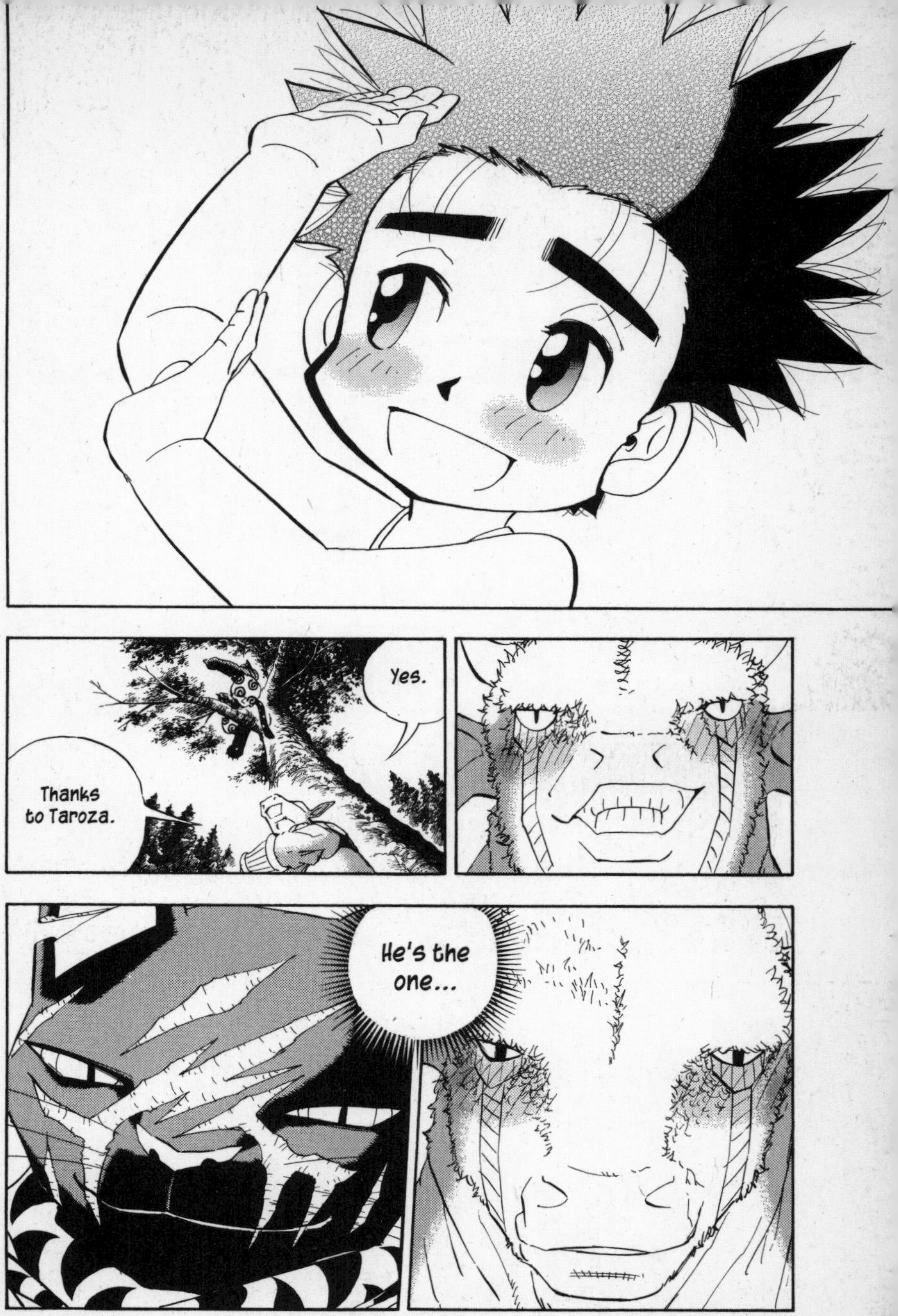
Yes.
Thanks to Taroza.
He's the one...

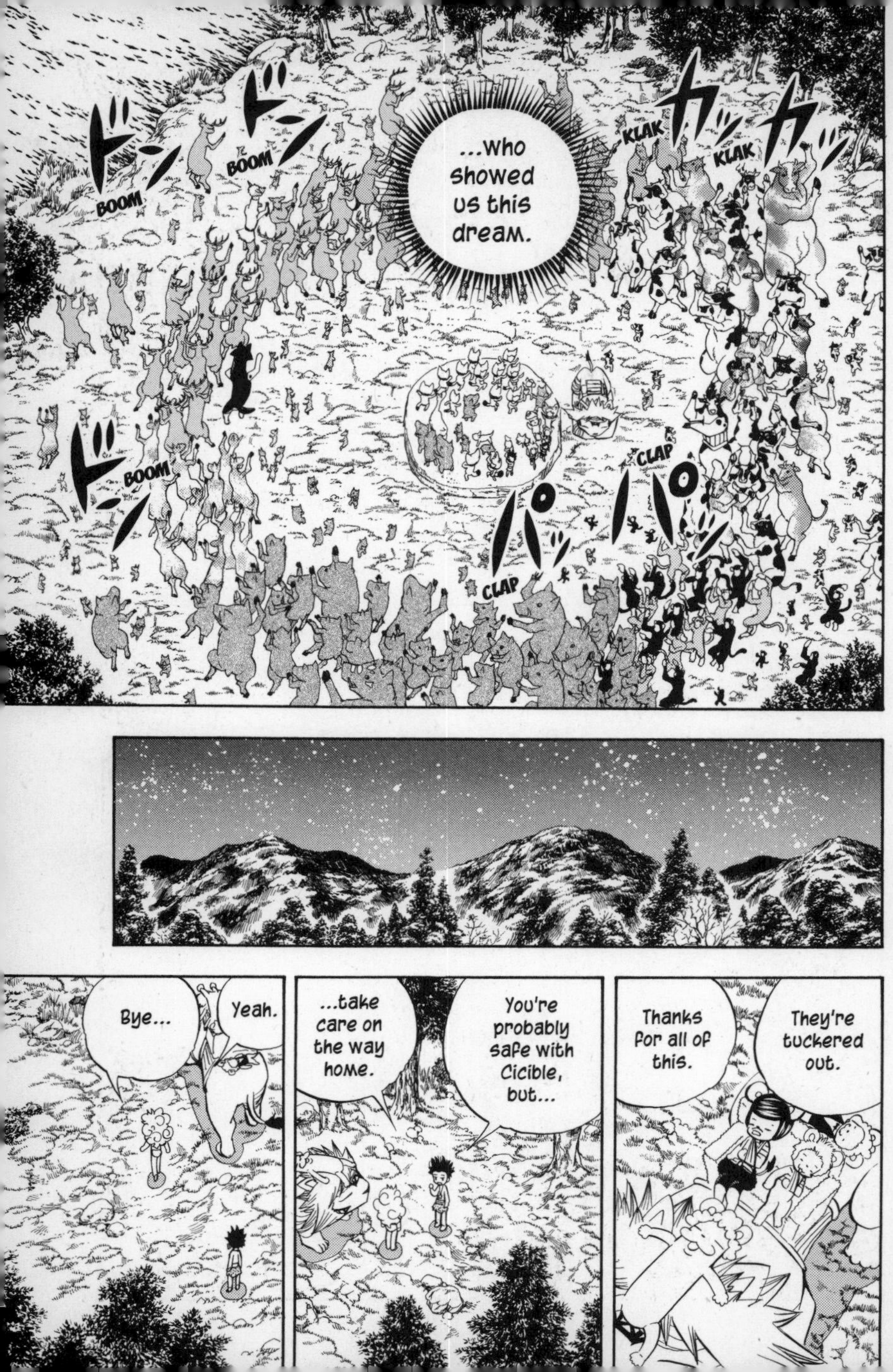
KLAK
KLAK
...who showed us this dream.
BOOM
BOOM
CLAP
CLAP
BOOM
They're tuckered out.
Thanks for all of this.
You're probably safe with Cicible, but...
...take care on the way home.
Yeah.
Bye...

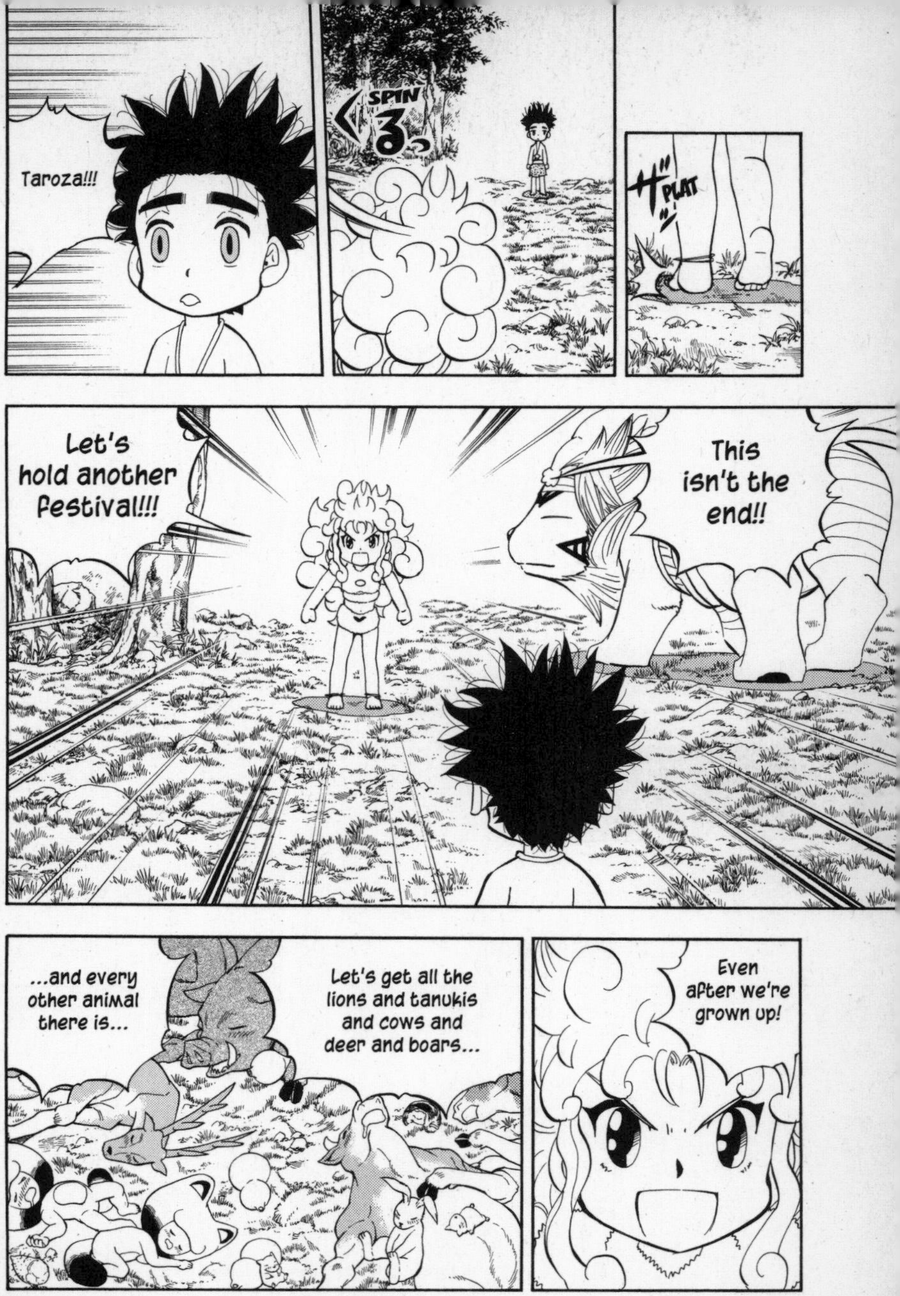
PLAT
SPIN
Taroza!!!
This isn't the end!!
Let's hold another festival!!!
Even after we're grown up!
Let's get all the lions and tanukis and cows and deer and boars...
...and every other animal there is...

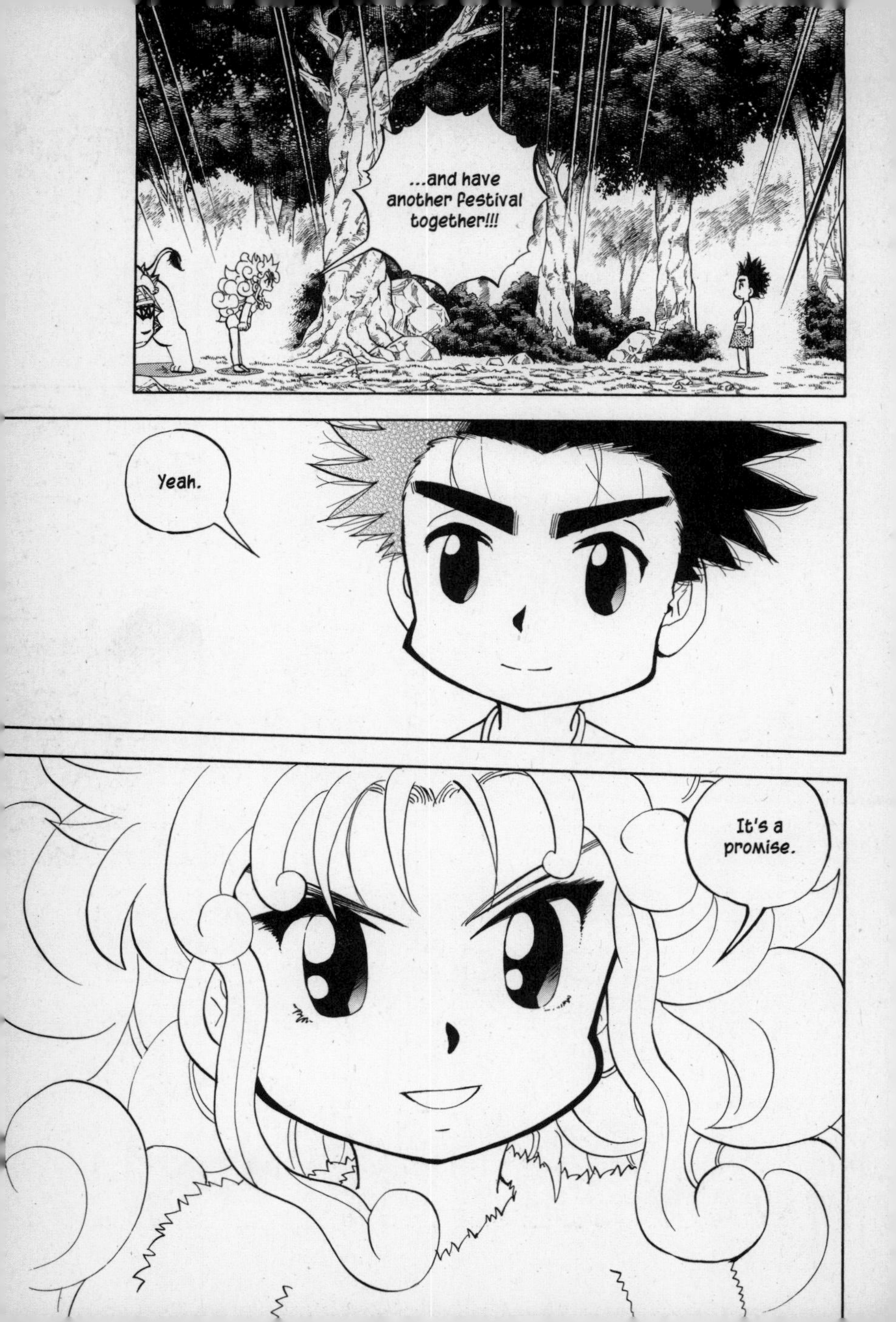
...and have another festival together!!!
Yeah.
It's a promise.

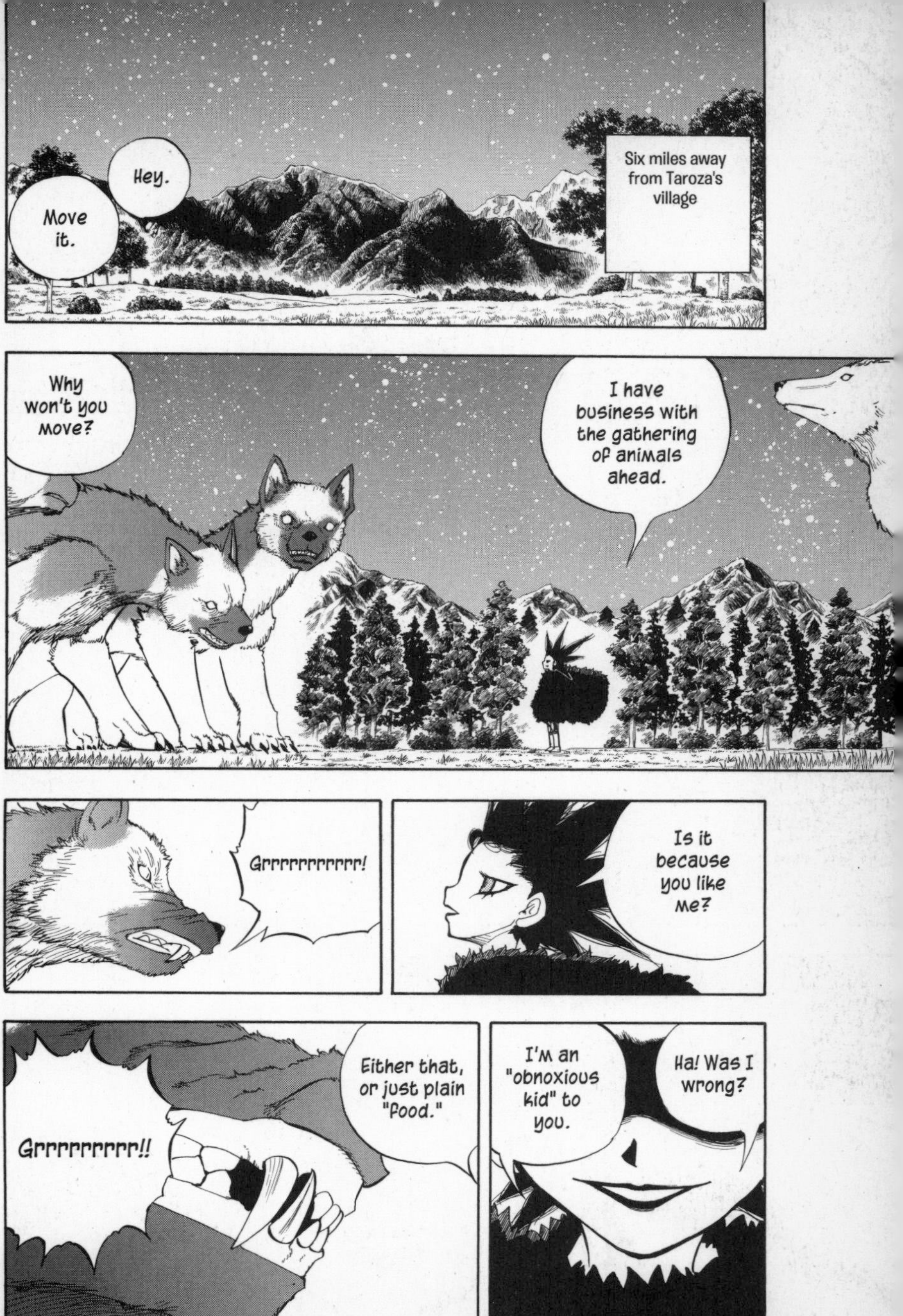
Six miles away from Taroza's village
Hey.
Move it.
I have business with the gathering of animals ahead.
Why won't you move?
Is it because you like me?
Grrrrrrrrrrr!
Ha! Was I wrong?
I'm an "obnoxious kid" to you.
Either that, or just plain "food."
Grrrrrrrrr!!

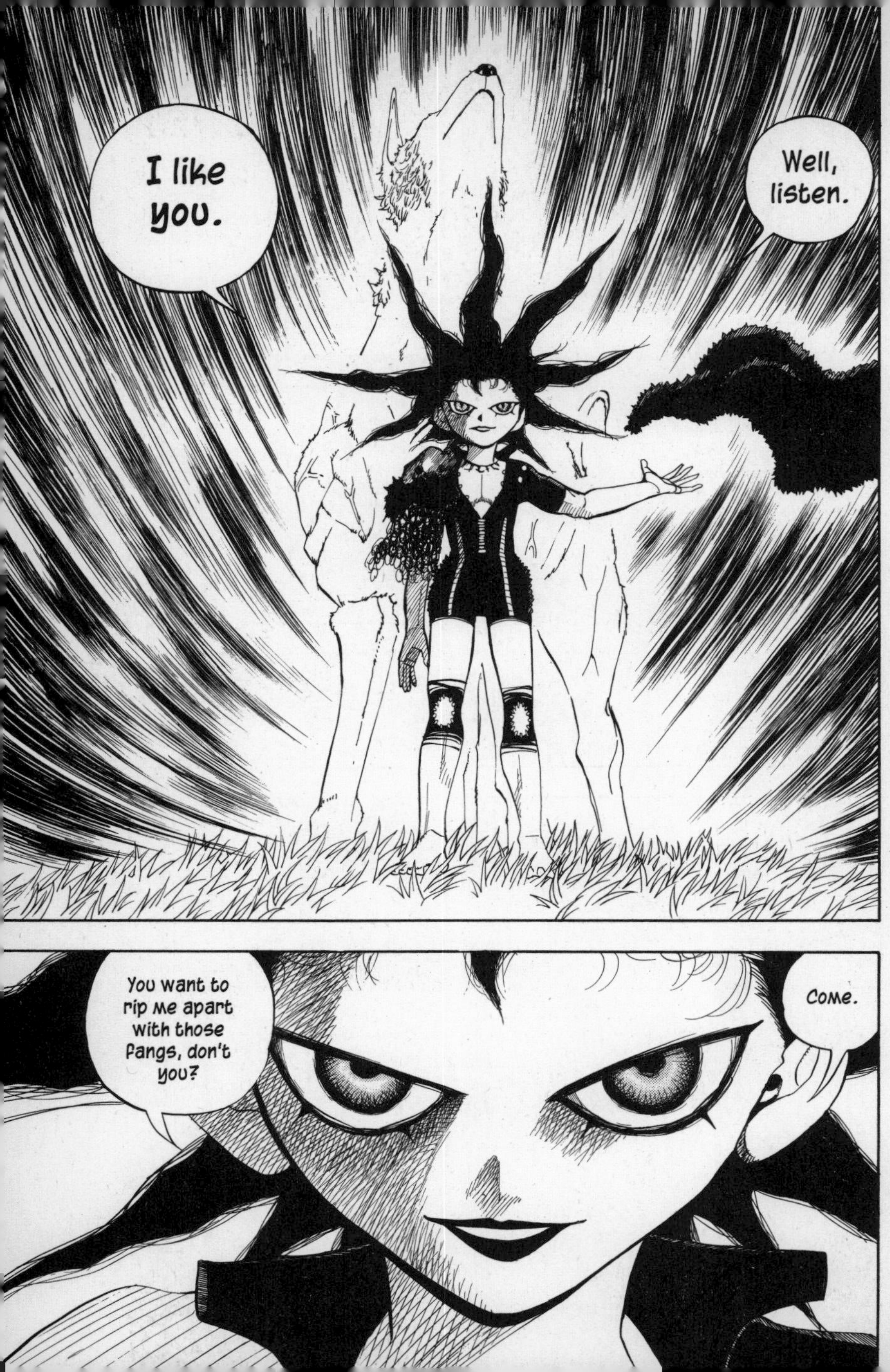
Well, listen.
I like you.
Come.
You want to rip me apart with those fangs, don't you?

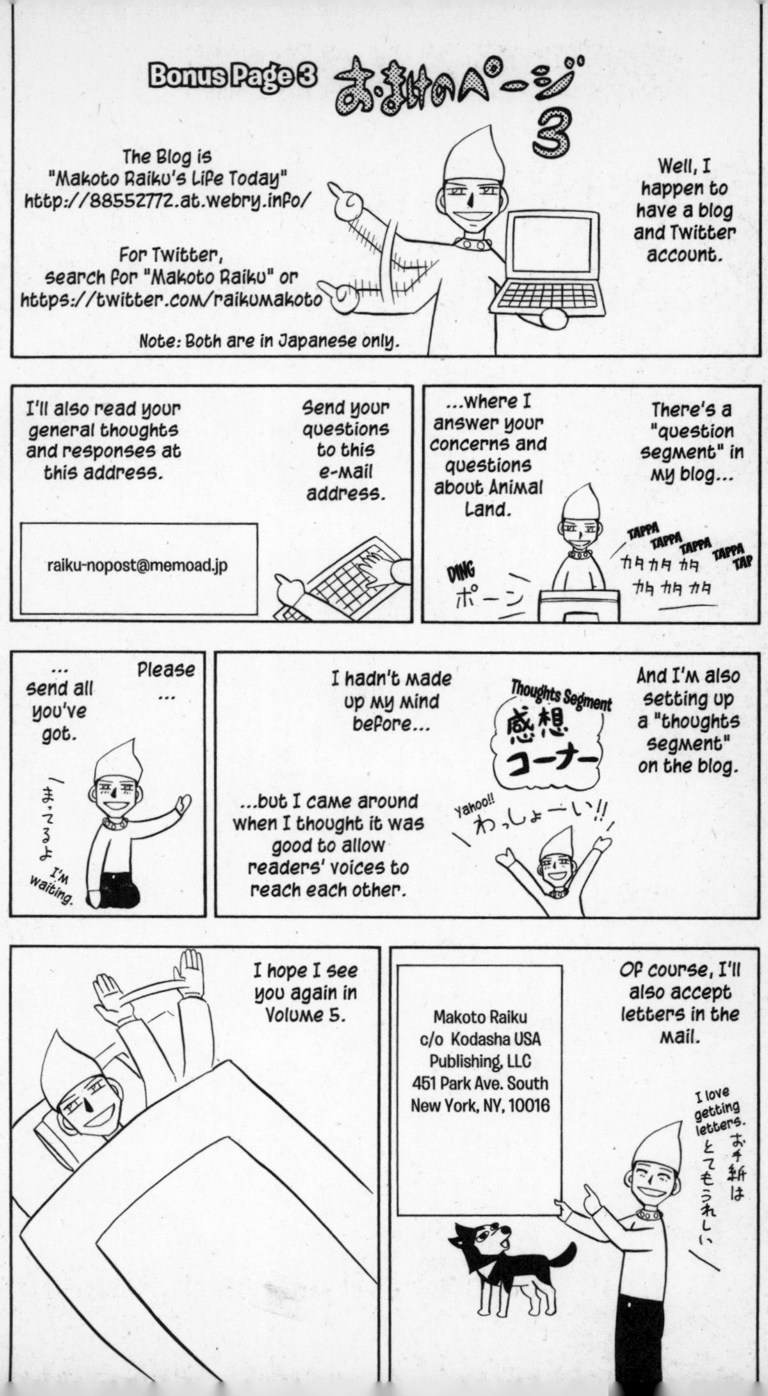
おまけのページ 3
Bonus Page 3
Well, I happen to have a blog and Twitter account.
The Blog is "Makoto Raiku's Life Today" http://88552772.at.webry.info/
For Twitter, search for "Makoto Raiku" or https://twitter.com/raikumakoto
Note: Both are in Japanese only.
There's a "question segment" in my blog...
...where I answer your concerns and questions about Animal Land.
TAPPA TAPPA TAPPA TAPPA TAP
カタカタ カタ カタ カタ カタ
DING
ポーン
Send your questions to this e-mail address.
I'll also read your general thoughts and responses at this address.
raiku-nopost@memoad.jp
And I'm also setting up a "thoughts segment" on the blog.
Thoughts Segment
感想コーナー
I hadn't made up my mind before...
...but I came around when I thought it was good to allow readers' voices to reach each other.
Yahoo!!
わっしょーい!!
Please ...
... send all you've got.
まってるよ
I'm waiting.
Of course, I'll also accept letters in the mail.
Makoto Raiku
c/o Kodasha USA
Publishing, LLC
451 Park Ave. South
New York, NY, 10016
I love getting letters.
お手紙はとてもうれしい
I hope I see you again in Volume 5.

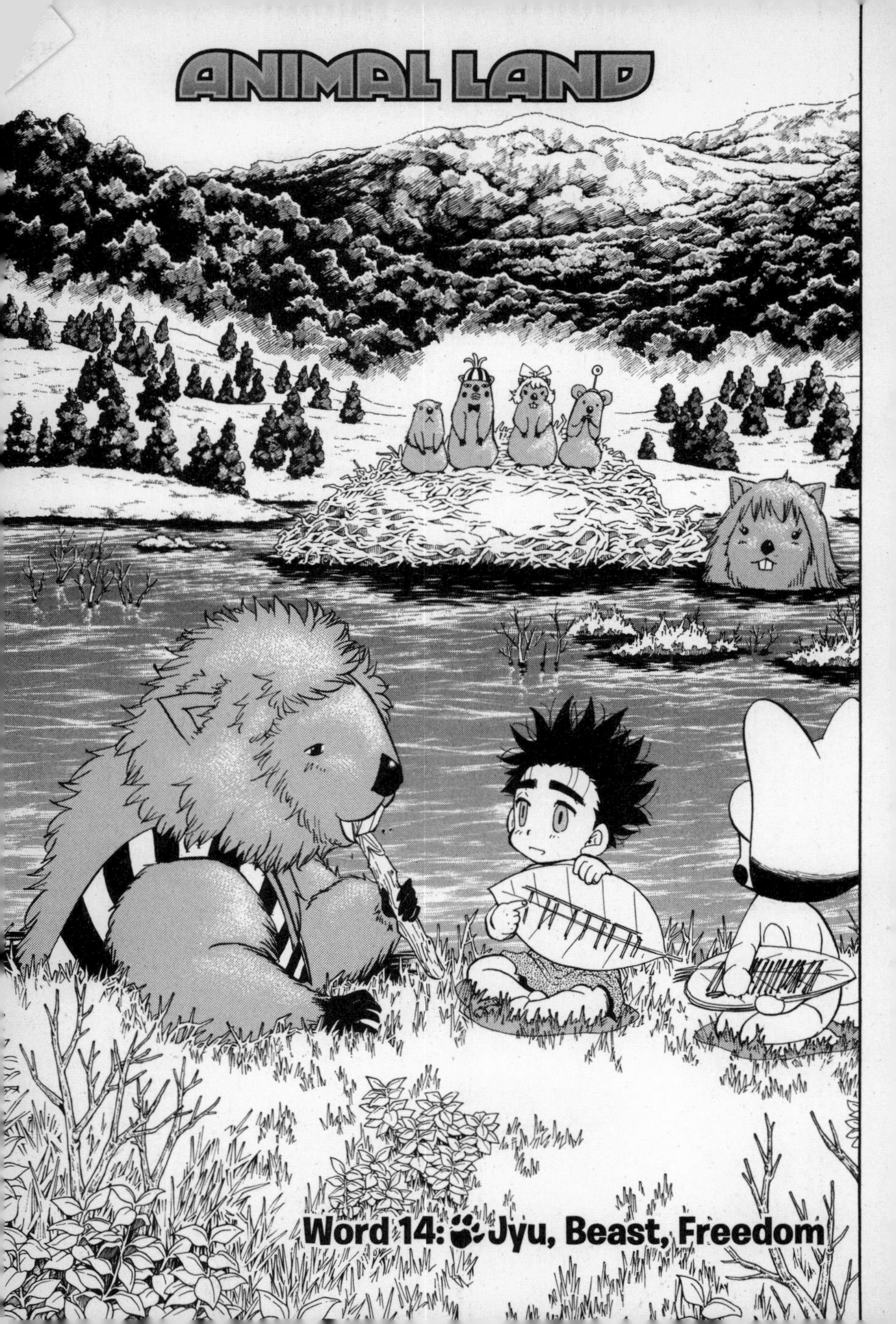
ANIMAL LAND
Word 14: Jyu, Beast, Freedom

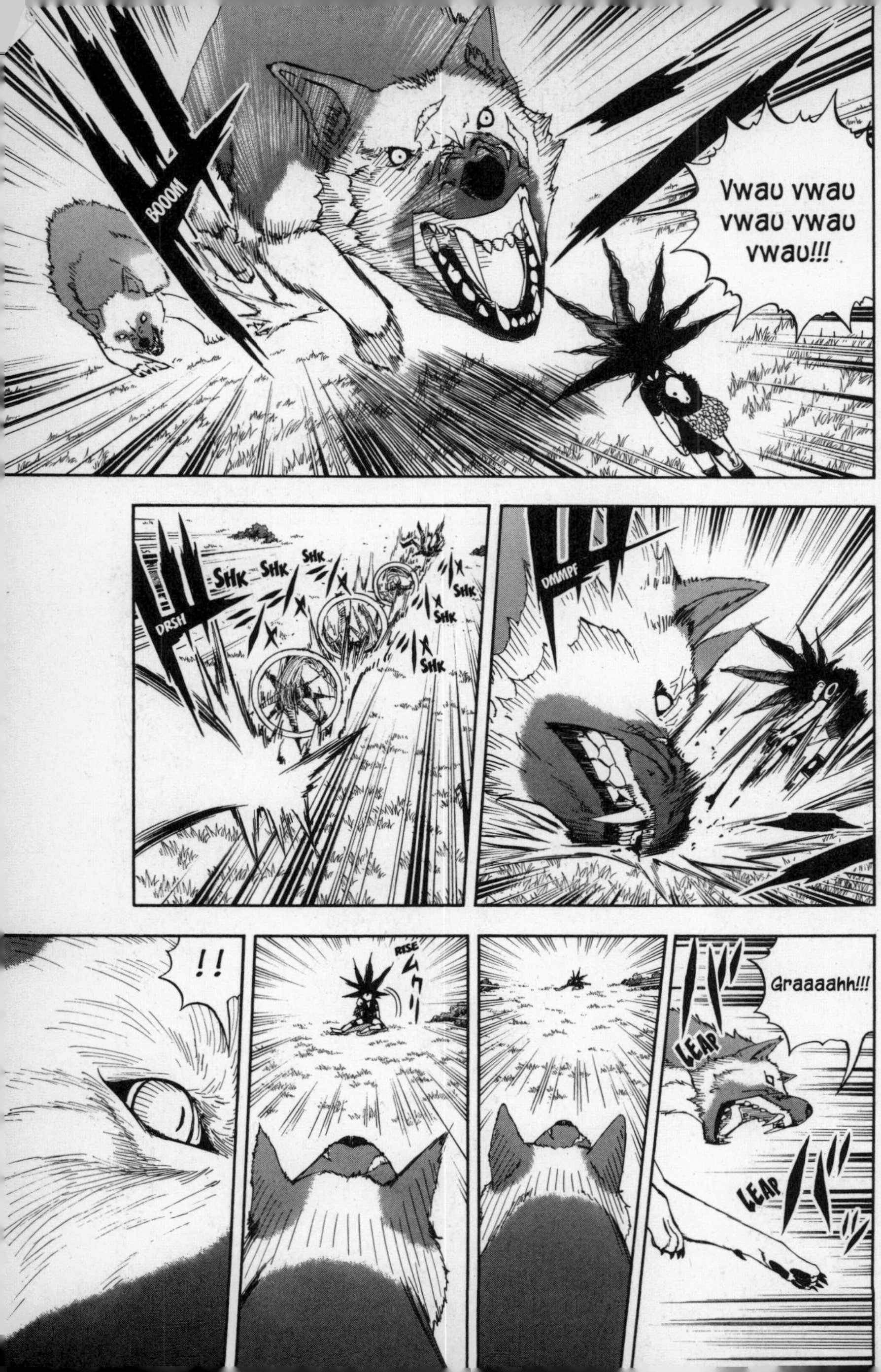
Vwau vwau vwau vwau vwau!!!
BOOOM
DMMPF
SHK
SHK
SHK
SHK
SHK
SHK
SHK
DRSH
Graaaahh!!!
LEAP
LEAP
RISE
!!

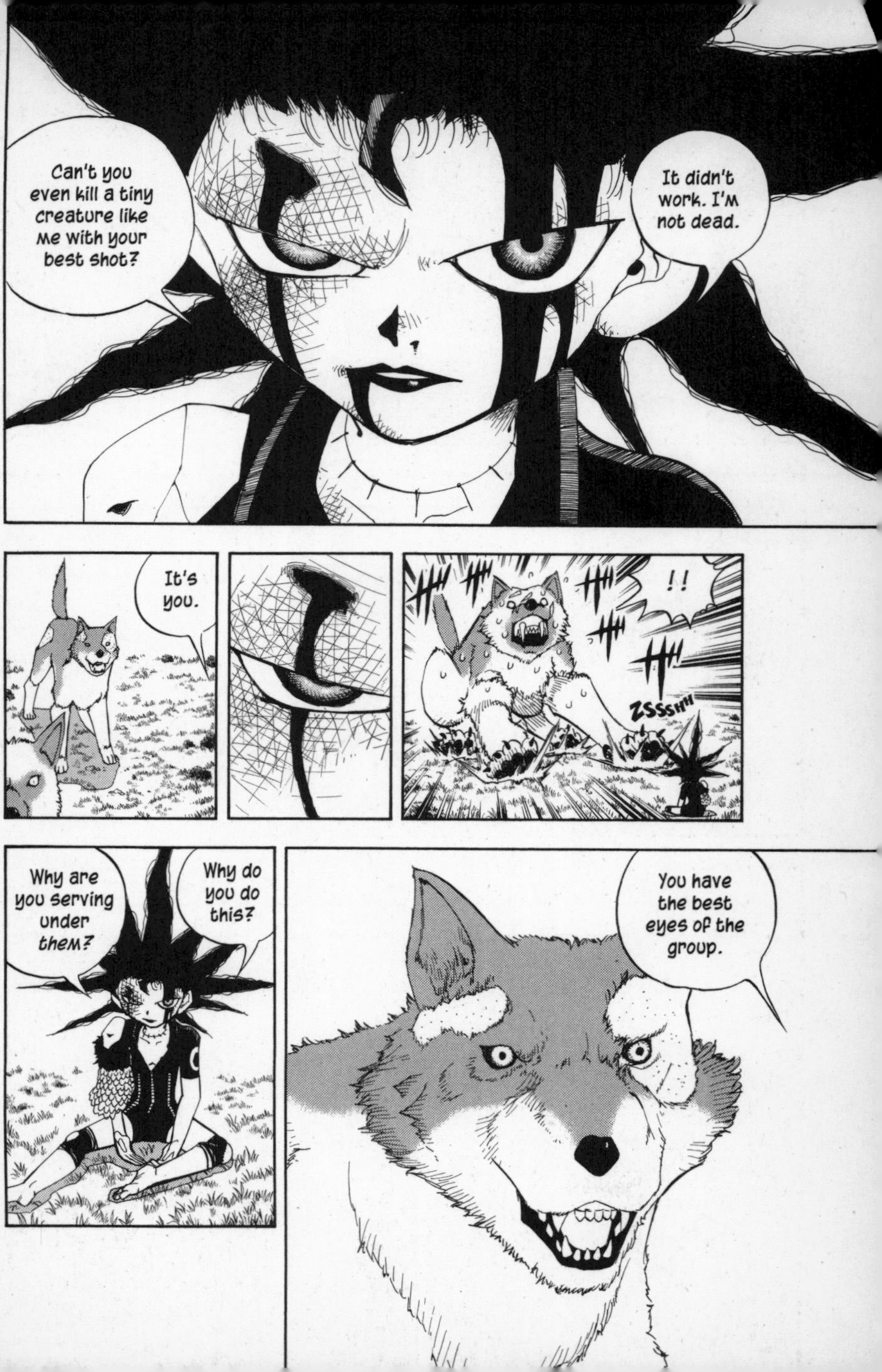
It didn't work. I'm not dead.
Can't you even kill a tiny creature like me with your best shot?
!!
ZSSSHH
It's you.
You have the best eyes of the group.
Why do you do this?
Why are you serving under them?

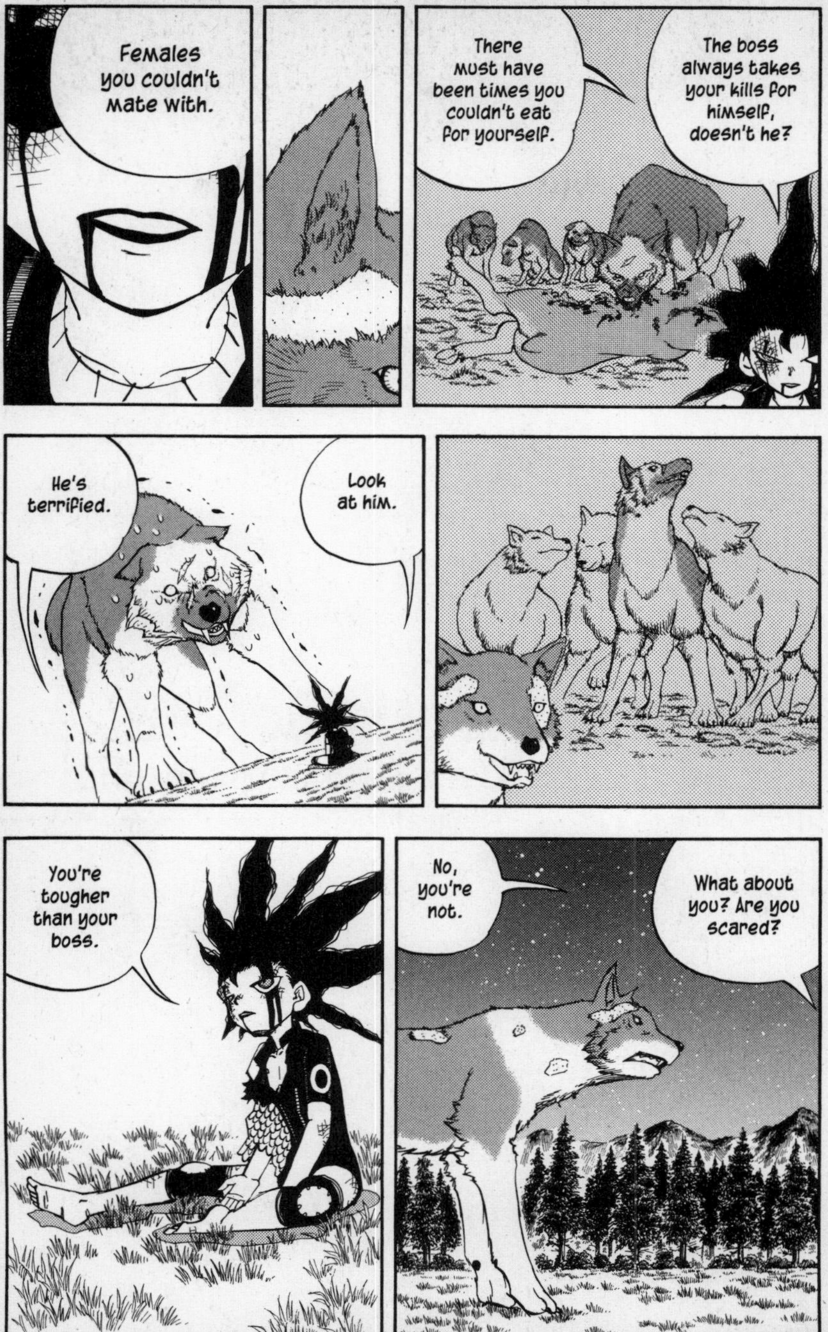
The boss always takes your kills for himself, doesn't he?
There must have been times you couldn't eat for yourself.
Females you couldn't mate with.
Look at him.
He's terrified.
What about you? Are you scared?
No, you're not.
You're tougher than your boss.

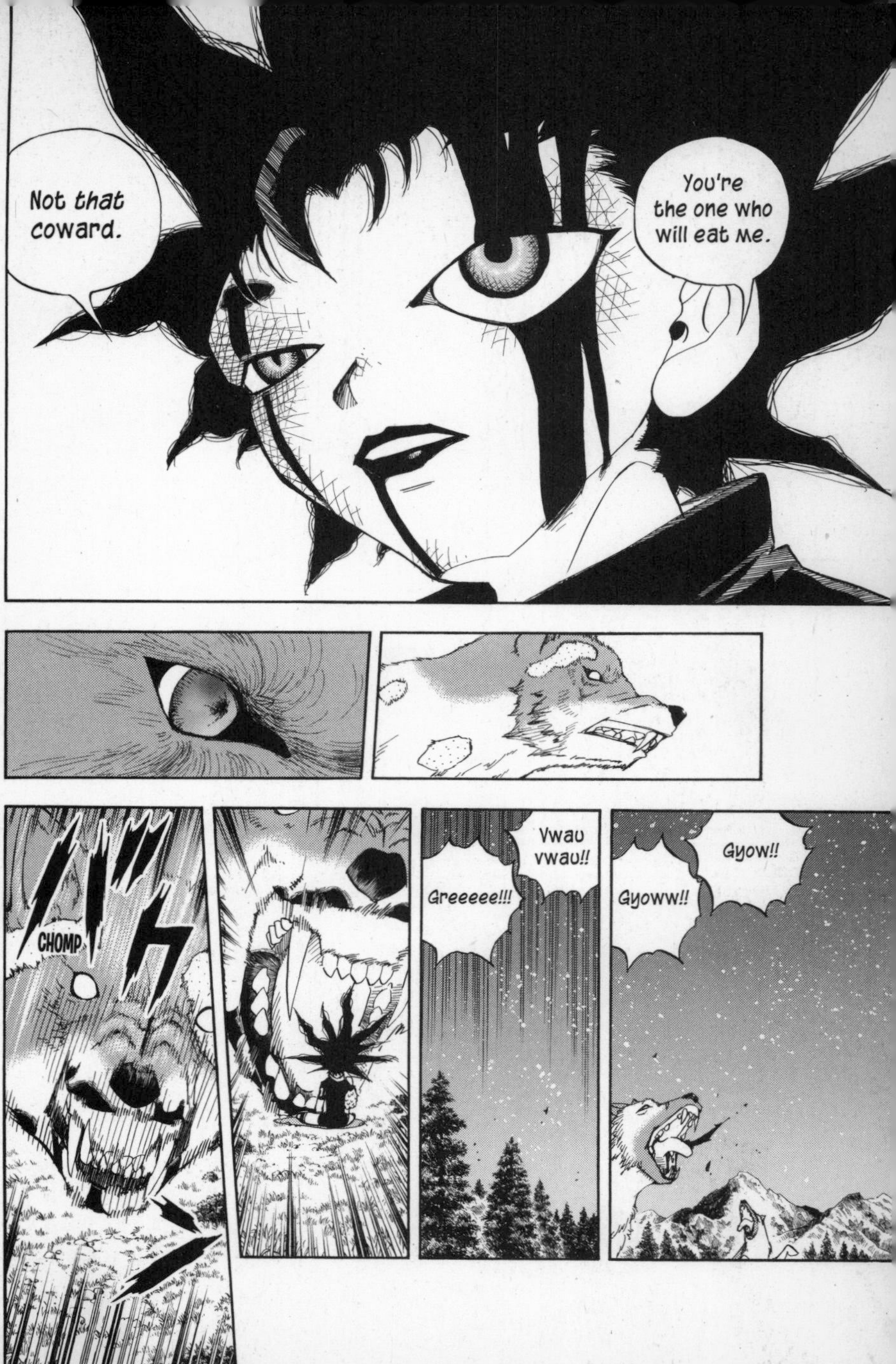
You're the one who will eat me.
Not that coward.
Gyow!!
Gyoww!!
Vwau vwau!!
Greeeee!!!
CHOMP

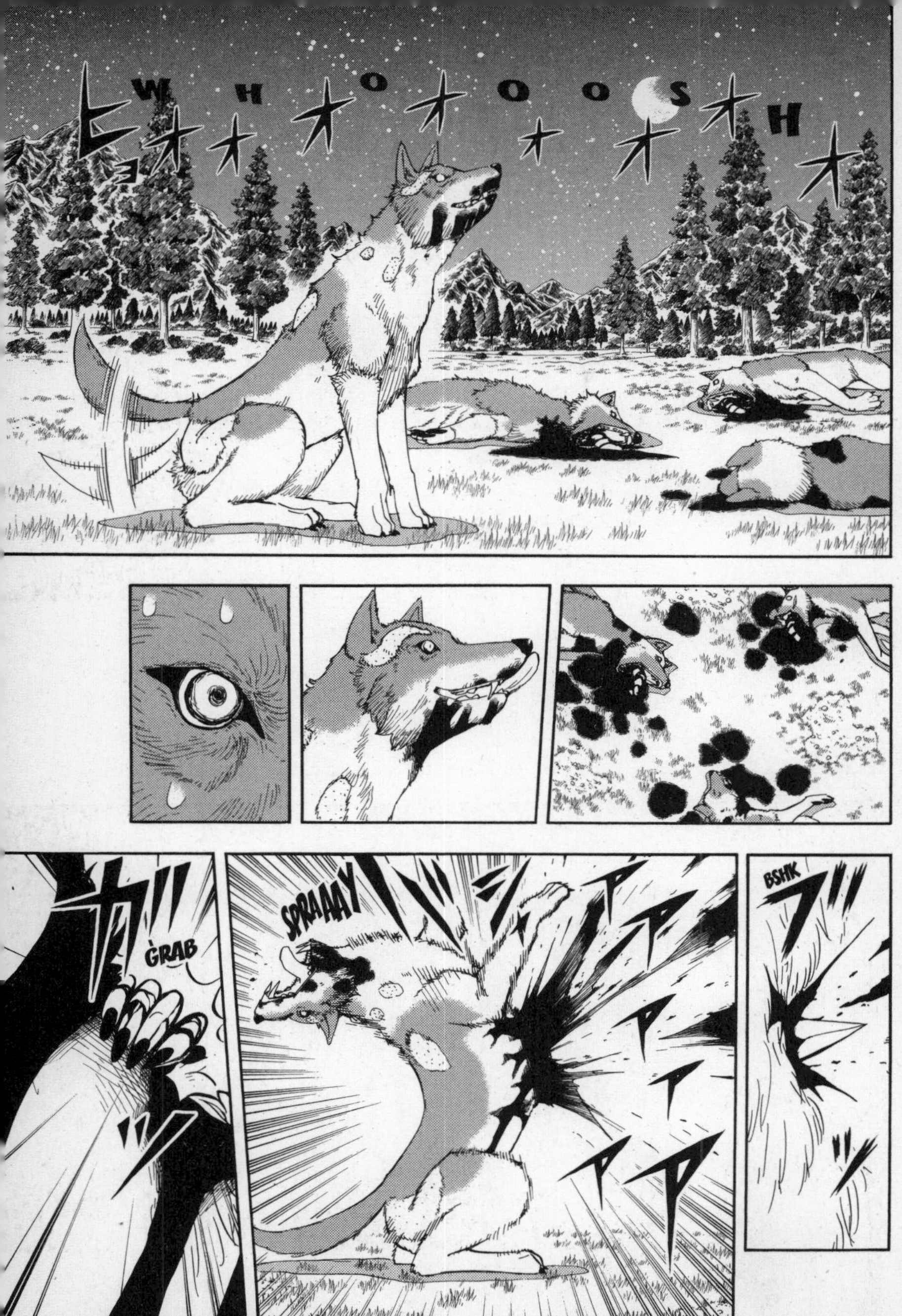
WHOOOSH
BSHK
SPRAAAY
GRAB

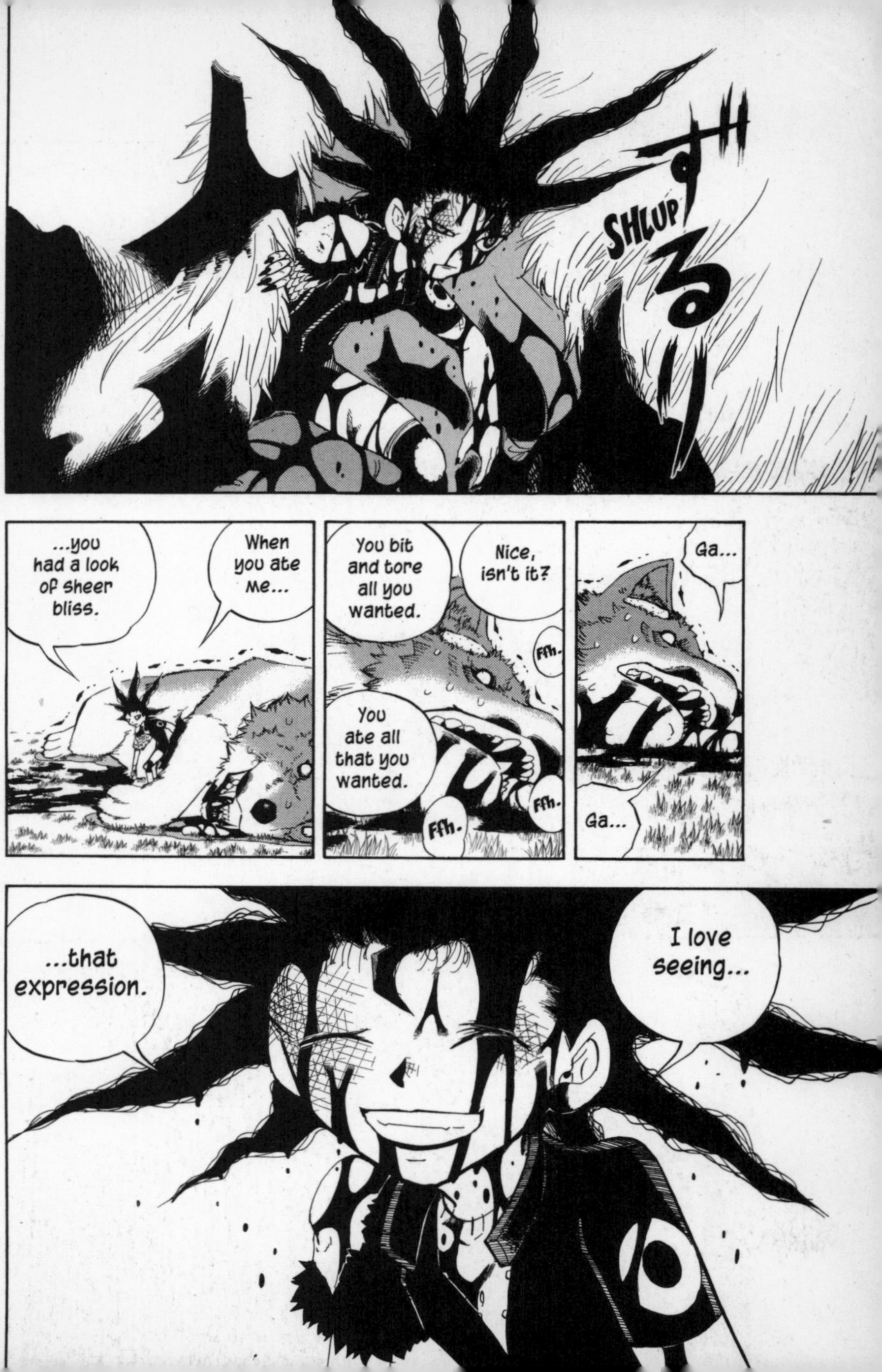
ずる
SHLUP
Ga...
Ga...
Nice, isn't it?
You bit and tore all you wanted.
Ffh.
You ate all that you wanted.
Ffh.
Ffh.
When you ate me...
...you had a look of sheer bliss.
I love seeing...
...that expression.

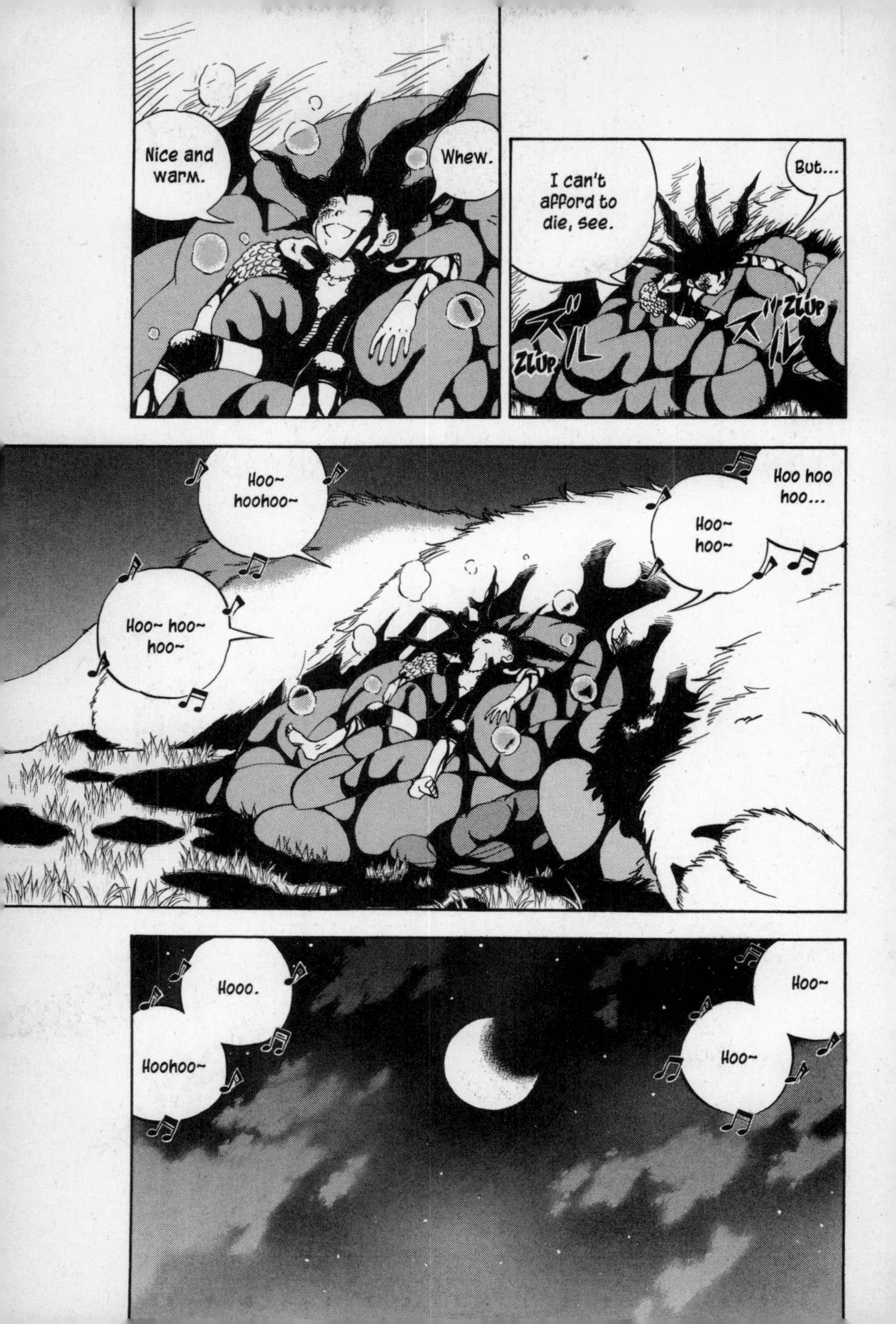
But...
I can't afford to die, see.
ズル
ZLUP
ズル
ZLUP
Whew.
Nice and warm.
Hoo hoo hoo...
Hoo~ hoo~
Hoo~ hoohoo~
Hoo~ hoo~ hoo~
Hoo~
Hoo~
Hooo.
Hoohoo~

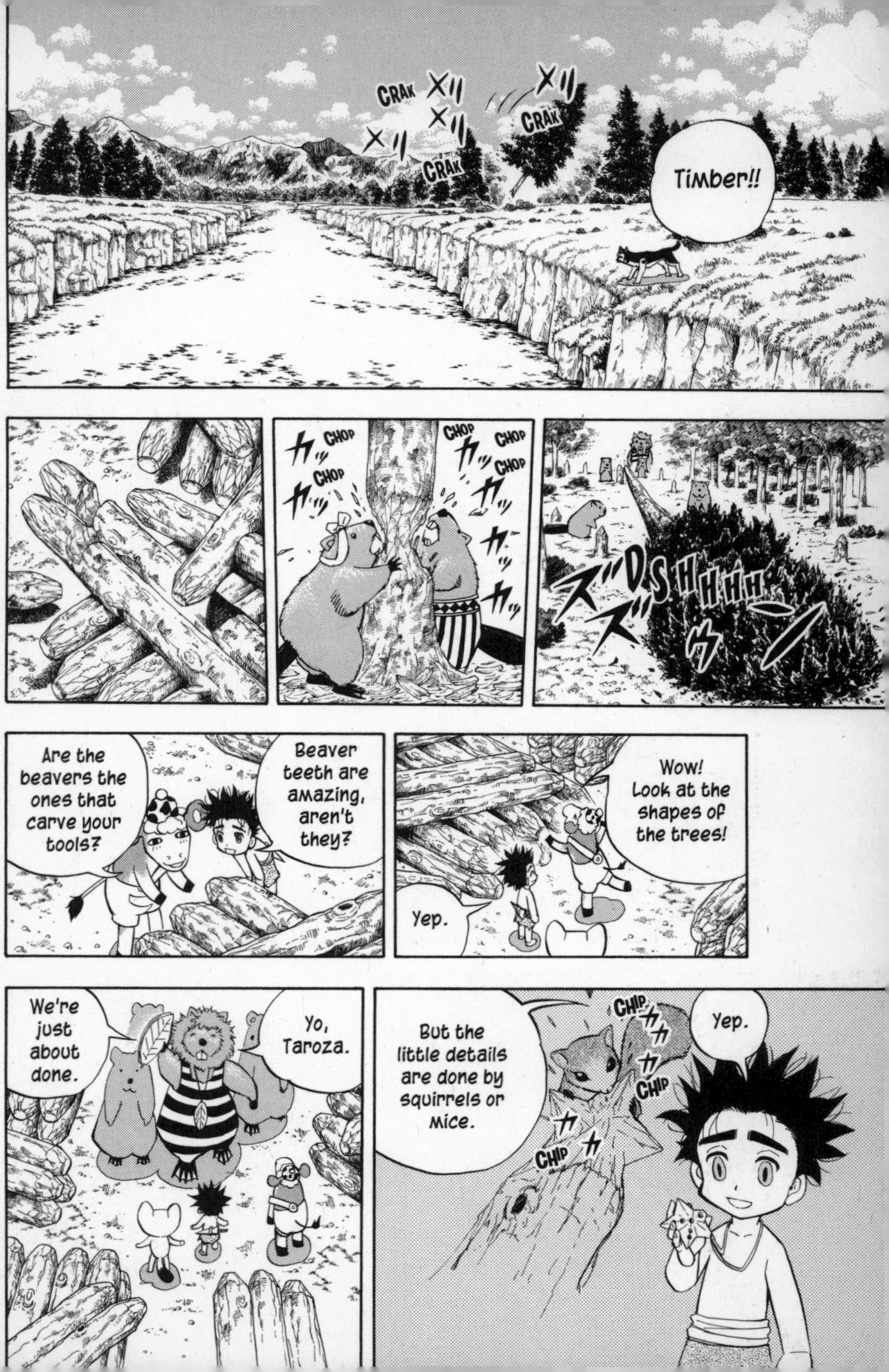
CRAK
CRAK
CRAK
Timber!!
DSHHHH
CHOP
CHOP
CHOP
CHOP
Wow! Look at the shapes of the trees!
Yep.
Beaver teeth are amazing, aren't they?
Are the beavers the ones that carve your tools?
Yep.
CHIP
CHIP
But the little details are done by squirrels or mice.
CHIP
Yo, Taroza.
We're just about done.

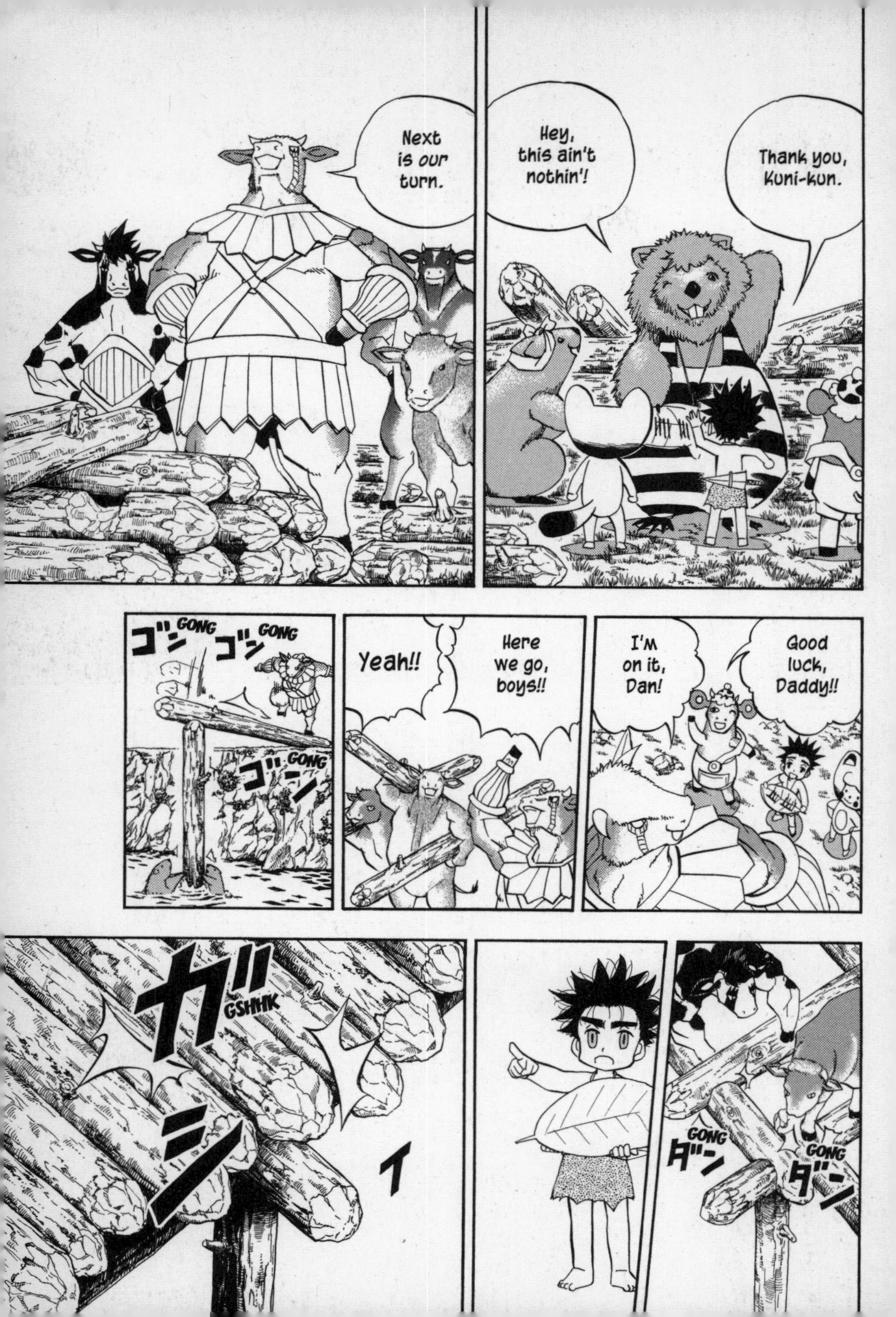
Thank you, Kuni-kun.
Hey, this ain't nothin'!
Next is our turn.
Good luck, Daddy!!
I'm on it, Dan!
Here we go, boys!!
Yeah!!
GONG
GONG
GONG
GONG
GONG
GSHHK

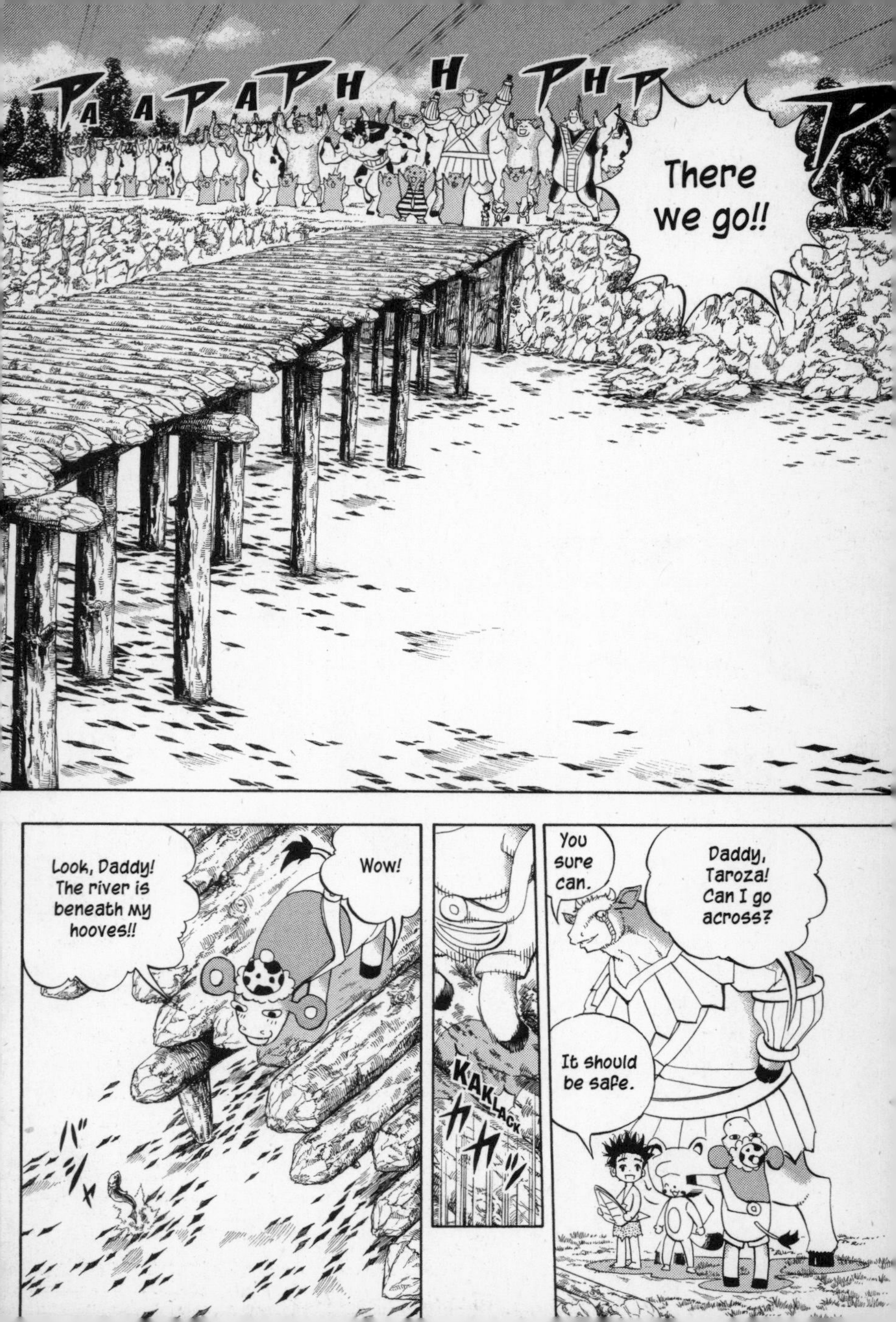
PAAPAPH H PHP P
There we go!!
Daddy, Taroza! Can I go across?
You sure can.
It should be safe.
KAKLACK
Wow!
Look, Daddy! The river is beneath my hooves!!

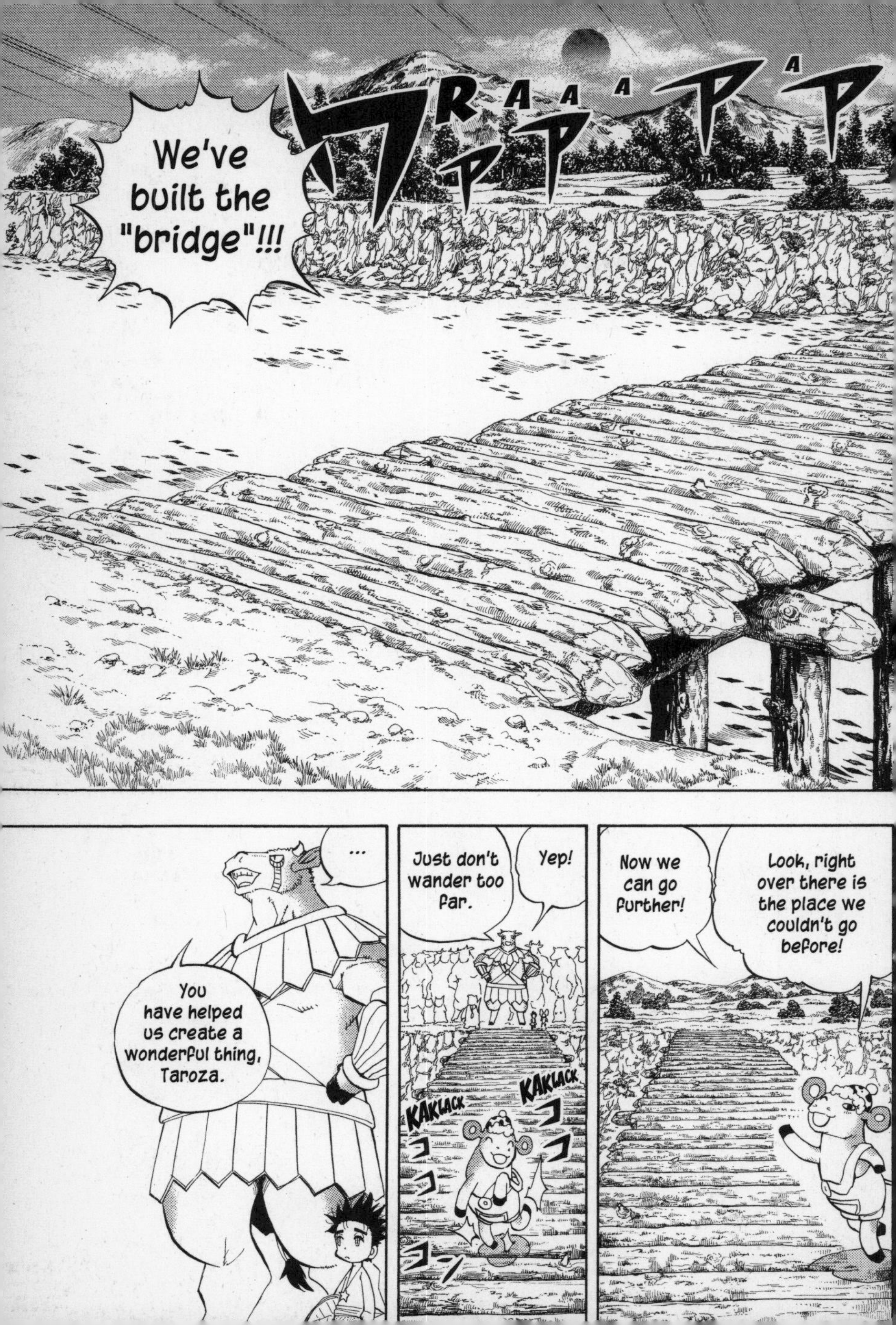
We've built the "bridge"!!!
RAAAA
Look, right over there is the place we couldn't go before!
Now we can go further!
Yep!
Just don't wander too far.
KAKLACK
KAKLACK
...
You have helped us create a wonderful thing, Taroza.

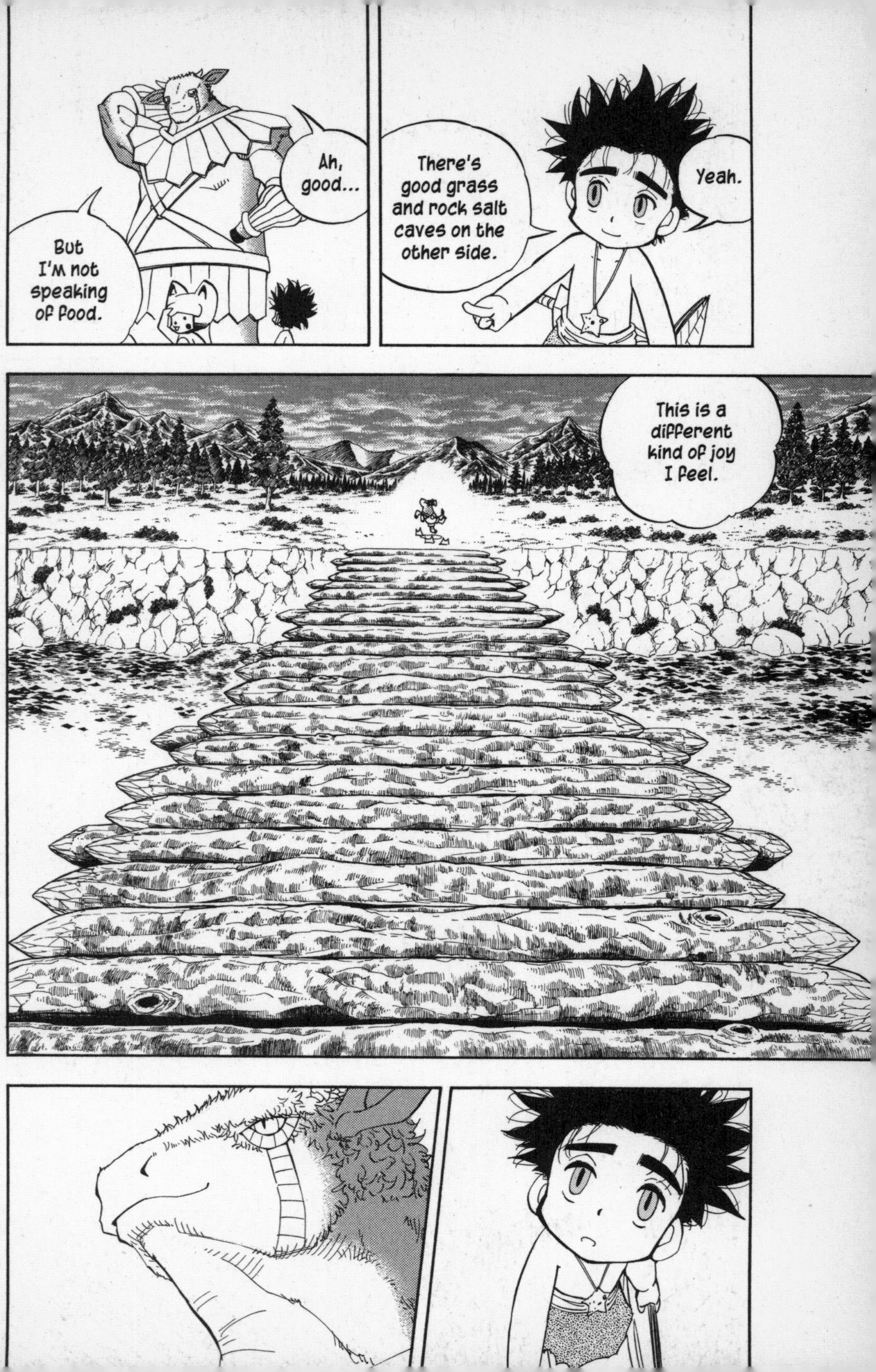
Yeah.
There's good grass and rock salt caves on the other side.
Ah, good...
But I'm not speaking of food.
This is a different kind of joy I feel.

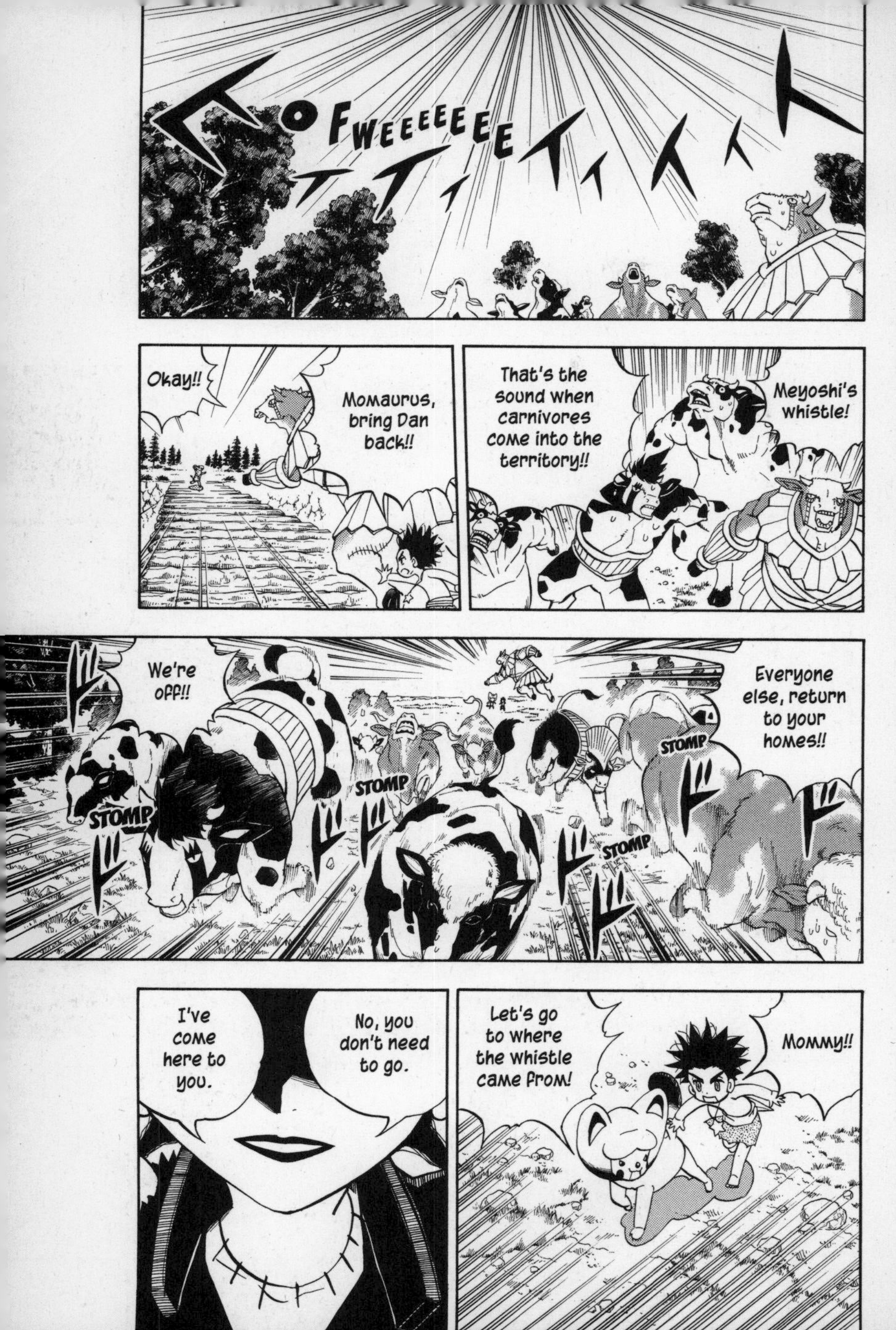
FWEEEEEEE
Meyoshi's whistle!
That's the sound when carnivores come into the territory!!
Momaurus, bring Dan back!!
Okay!!
Everyone else, return to your homes!!
STOMP
STOMP
STOMP
STOMP
We're off!!
Mommy!!
Let's go to where the whistle came from!
No, you don't need to go.
I've come here to you.

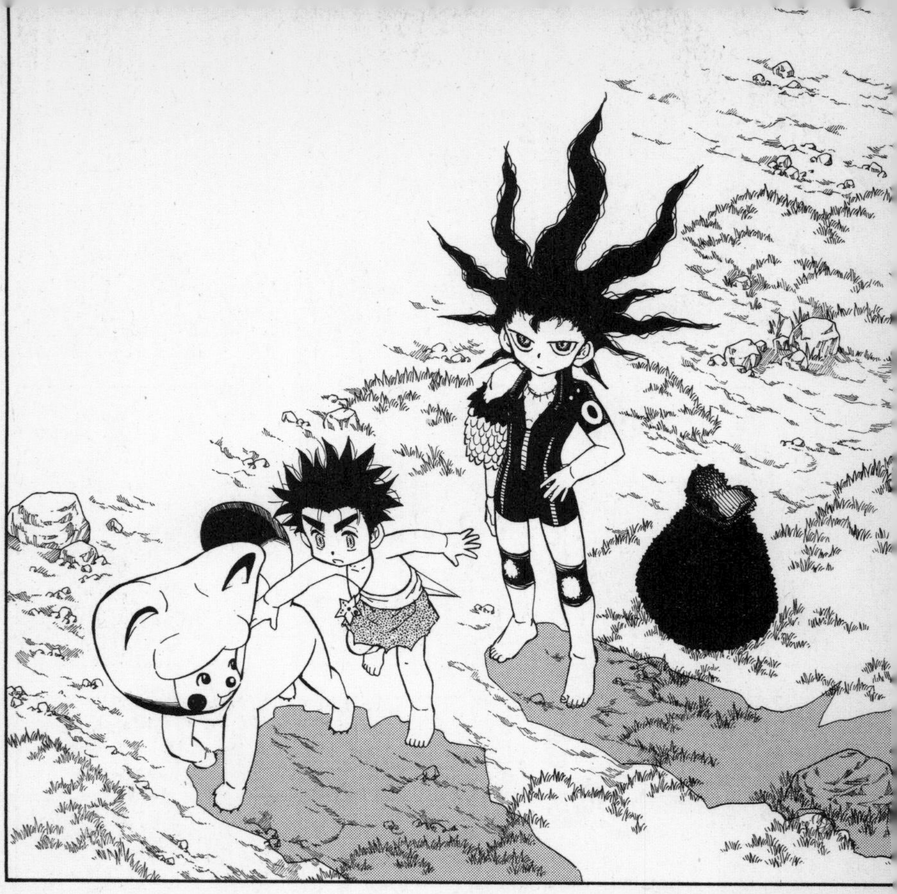

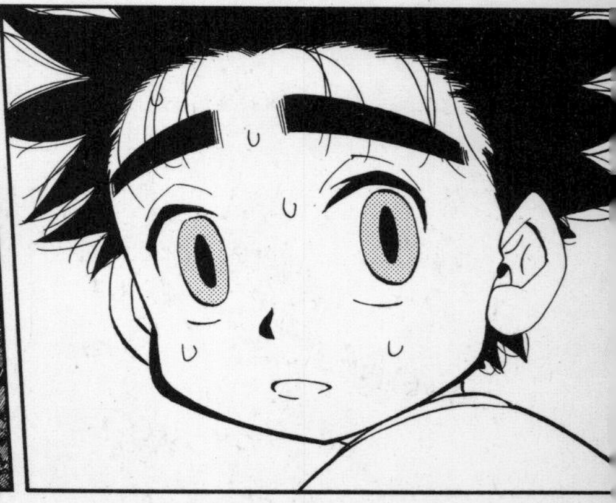

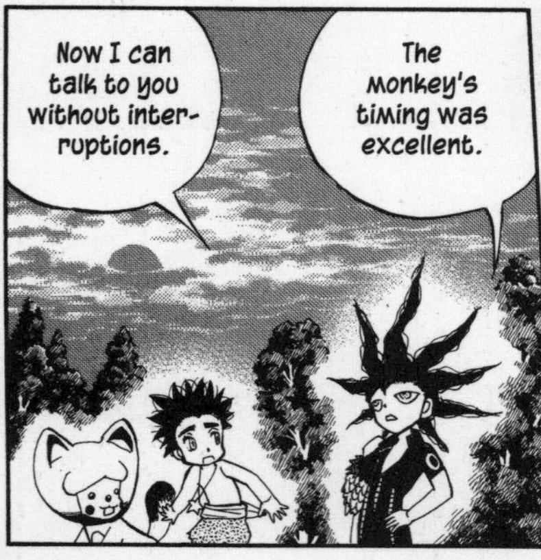
The monkey's timing was excellent.
Now I can talk to you without interruptions.

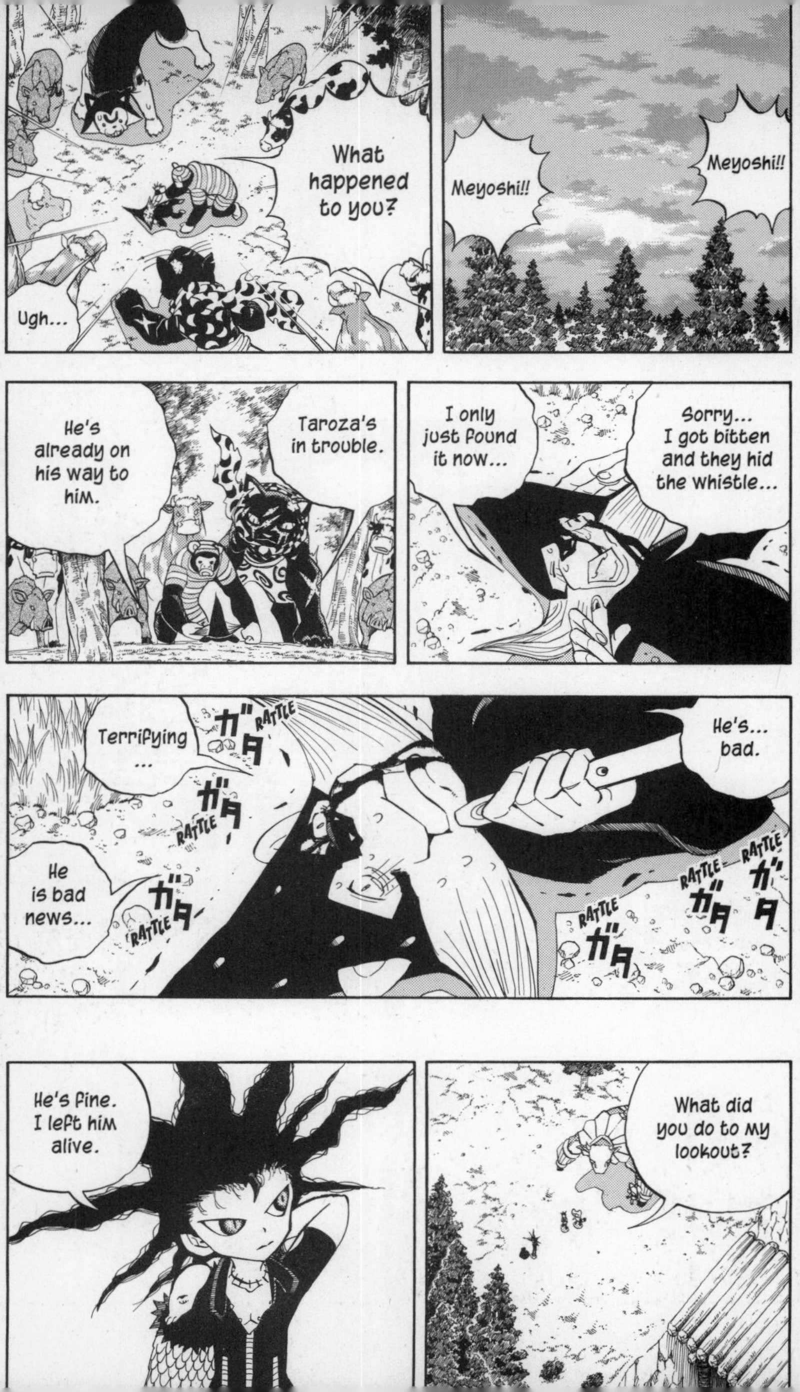
Meyoshi!!
Meyoshi!!
What happened to you?
Ugh...
Sorry... I got bitten and they hid the whistle...
I only just found it now...
Taroza's in trouble.
He's already on his way to him.
He's... bad.
ガタ RATTLE
ガタ RATTLE
ガタ RATTLE
Terrifying...
ガタ RATTLE
ガタ RATTLE
He is bad news...
ガタ RATTLE
What did you do to my lookout?
He's fine. I left him alive.

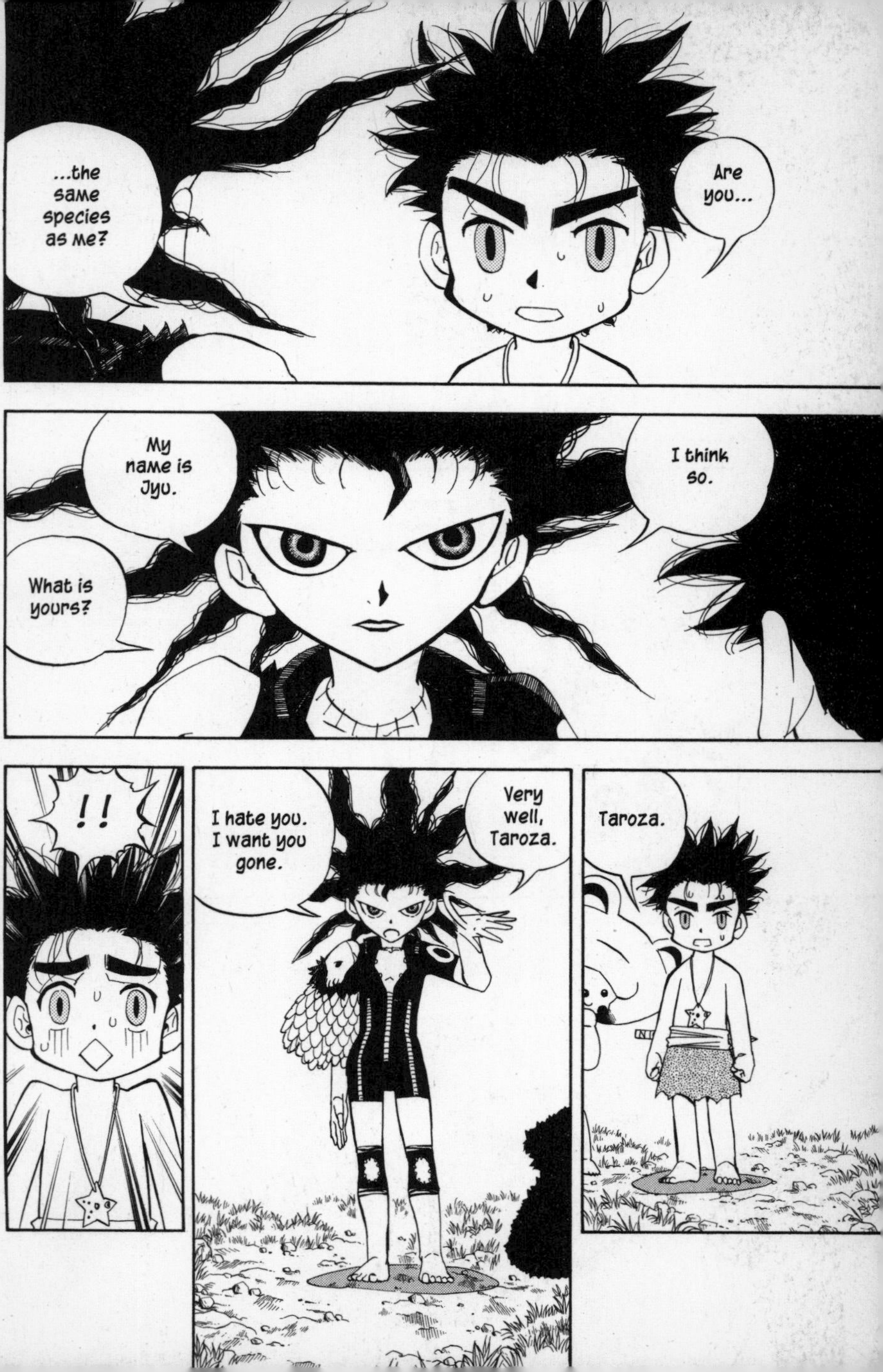
Are you...
...the same species as me?
I think so.
My name is Jyu.
What is yours?
Taroza.
Very well, Taroza.
I hate you. I want you gone.
!!

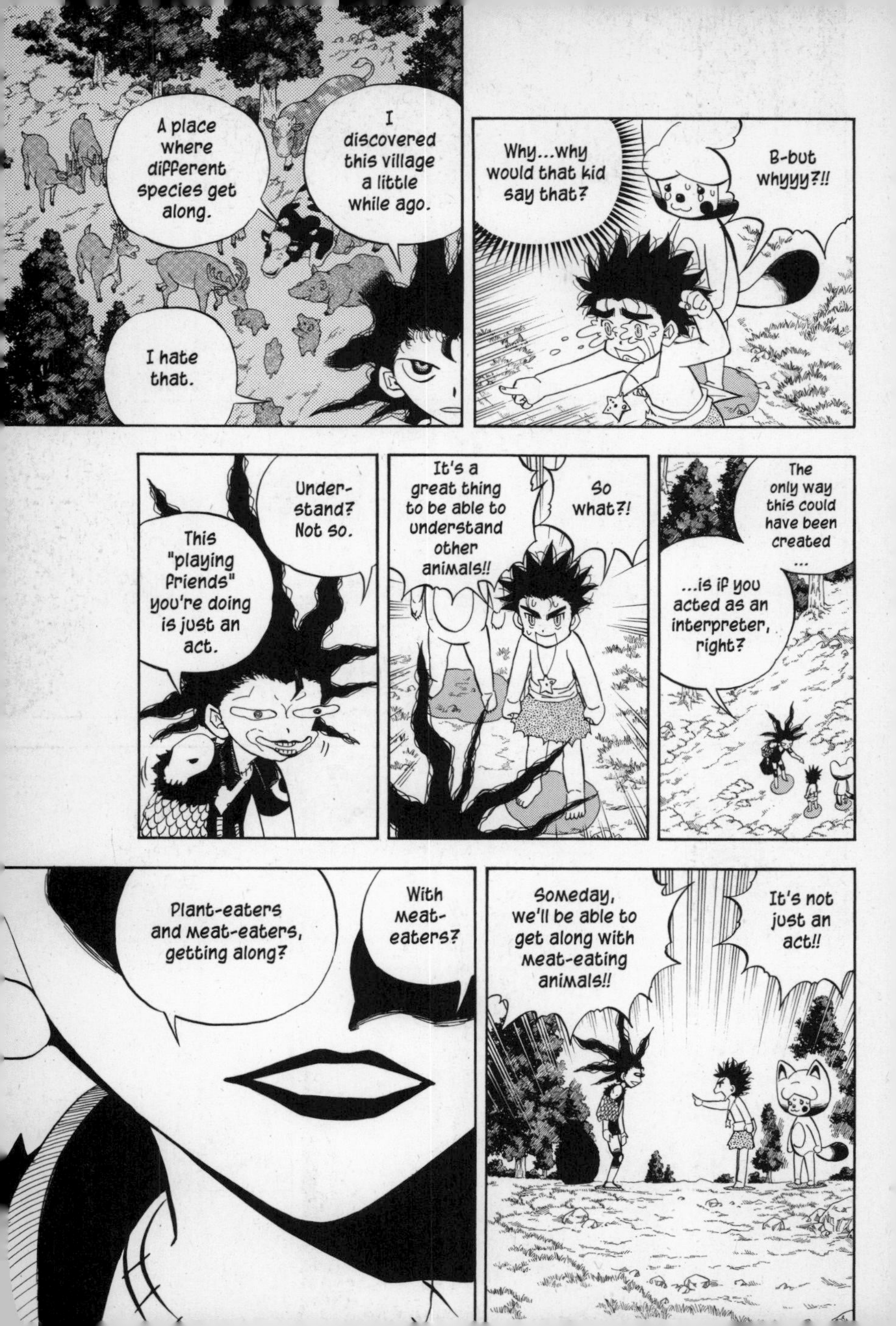
B-but whyyy?!!
Why...why would that kid say that?
I discovered this village a little while ago.
A place where different species get along.
I hate that.
The only way this could have been created ...
...is if you acted as an interpreter, right?
So what?!
It's a great thing to be able to understand other animals!!
Under-stand? Not so.
This "playing friends" you're doing is just an act.
It's not just an act!!
Someday, we'll be able to get along with meat-eating animals!!
With meat-eaters?
Plant-eaters and meat-eaters, getting along?

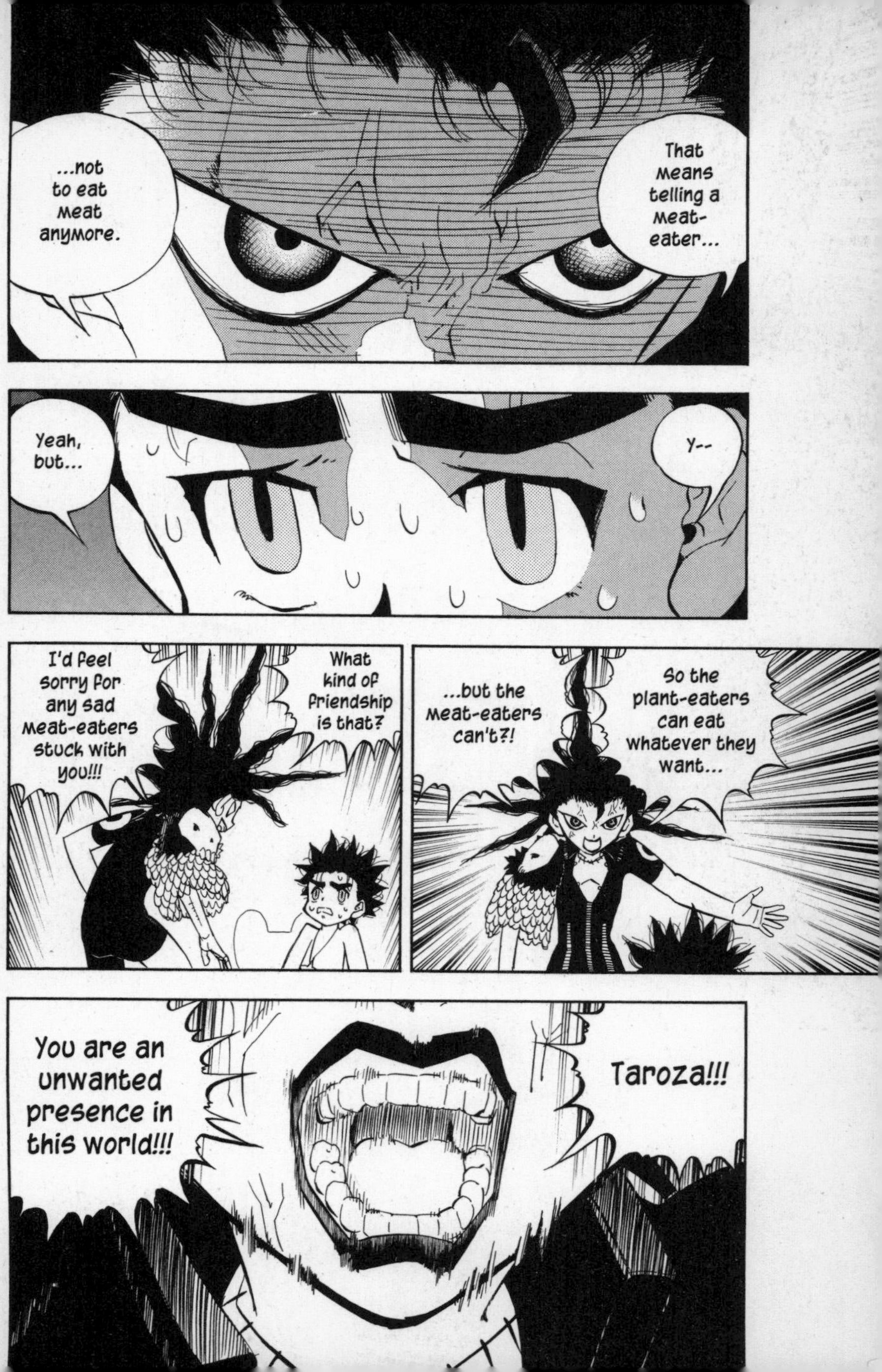
That means telling a meat-eater...
...not to eat meat anymore.
Y--
Yeah, but...
So the plant-eaters can eat whatever they want...
...but the meat-eaters can't?!
What kind of friendship is that?
I'd feel sorry for any sad meat-eaters stuck with you!!!
Taroza!!!
You are an unwanted presence in this world!!!

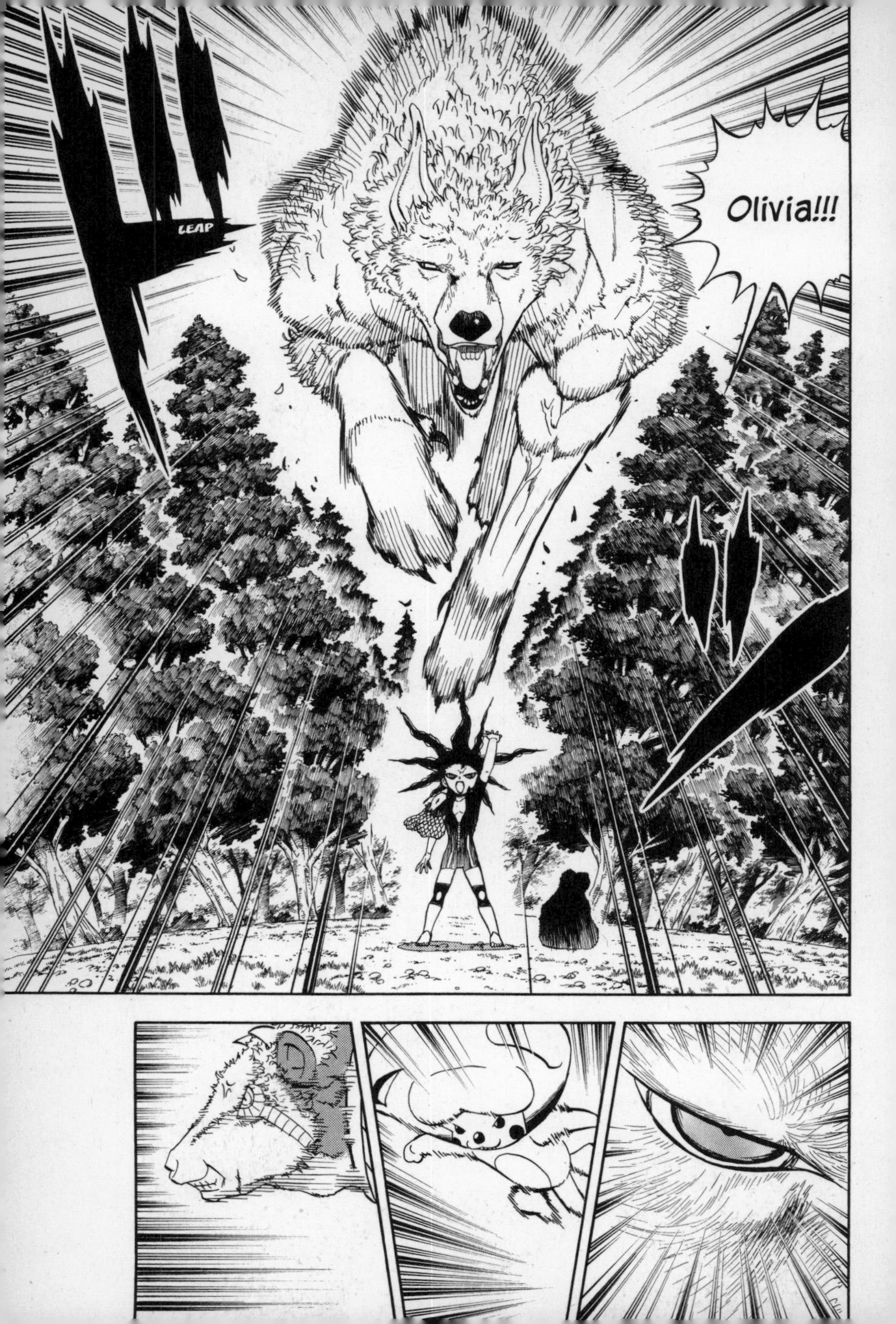
Olivia!!!
LEAP

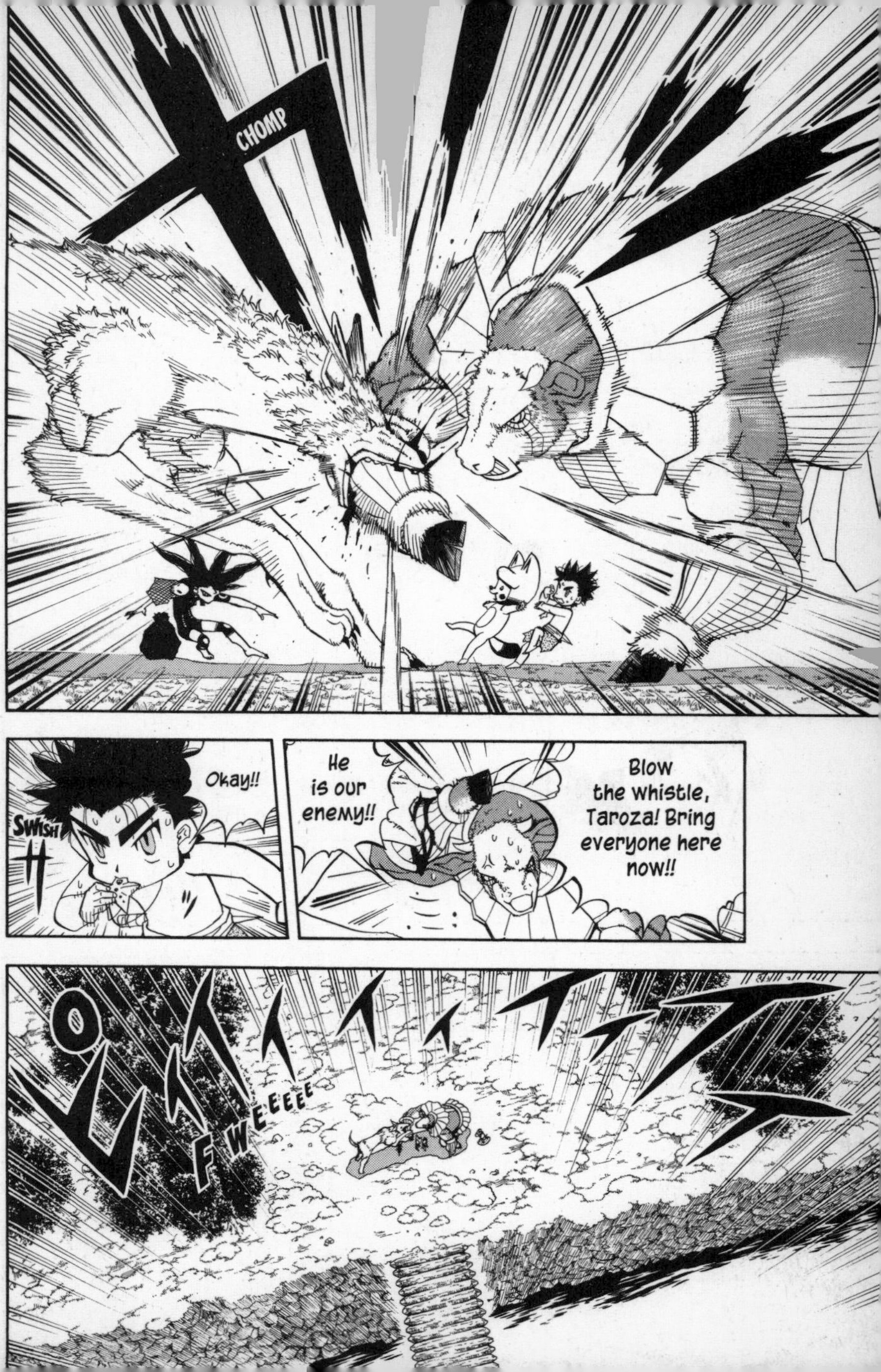
CHOMP
Blow the whistle, Taroza! Bring everyone here now!!
He is our enemy!!
Okay!!
SWISH
FWEEEEE

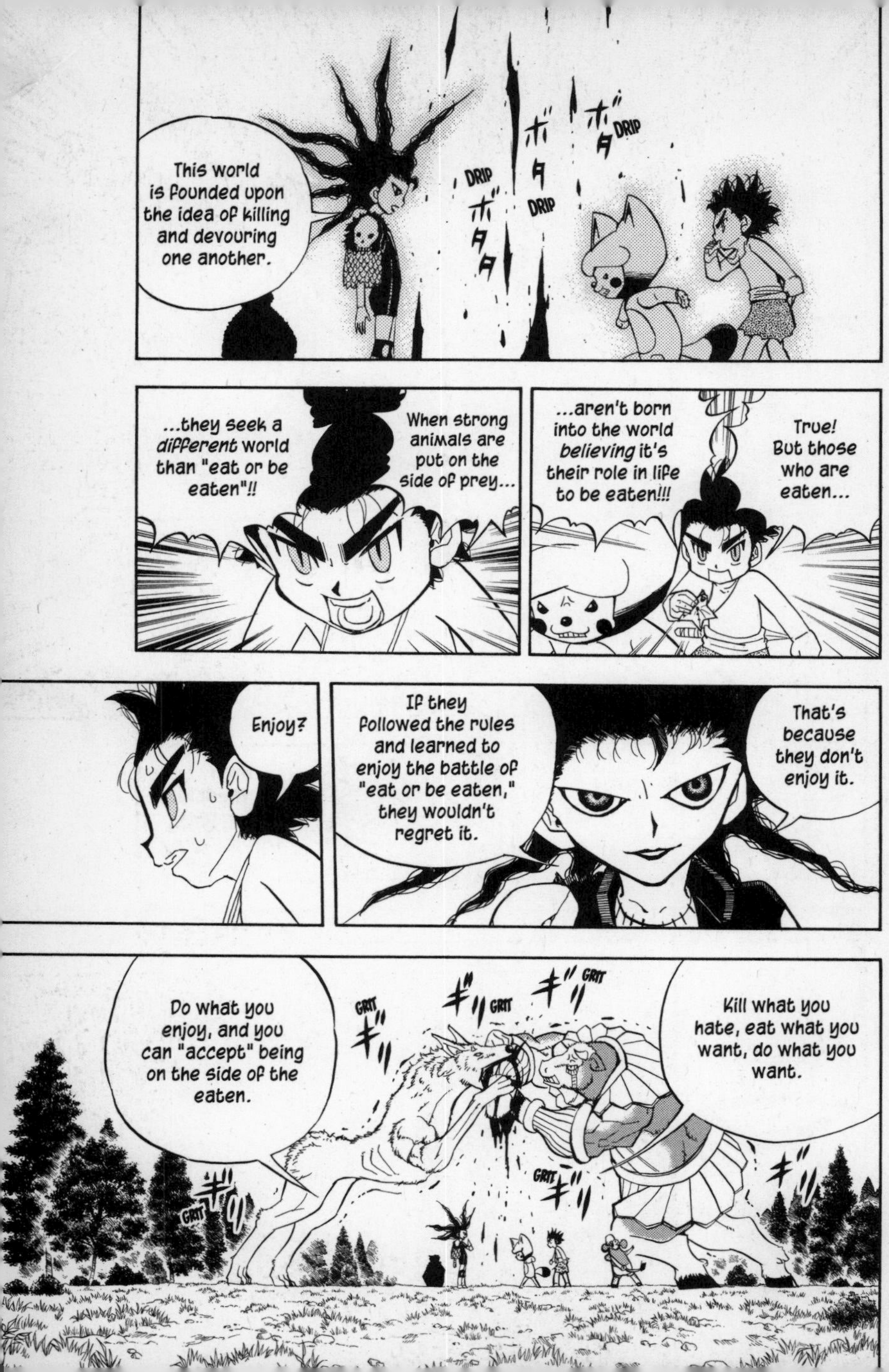
ボタ DRIP
ボタ DRIP
DRIP ボタタ
This world is founded upon the idea of killing and devouring one another.
True! But those who are eaten...
...aren't born into the world *believing* it's their role in life to be eaten!!!
When strong animals are put on the side of prey...
...they seek a *different* world than "eat or be eaten"!!
That's because they don't enjoy it.
If they followed the rules and learned to enjoy the battle of "eat or be eaten," they wouldn't regret it.
Enjoy?
Kill what you hate, eat what you want, do what you want.
GRIT
GRIT
GRIT
Do what you enjoy, and you can "accept" being on the side of the eaten.
GRIT
GRIT

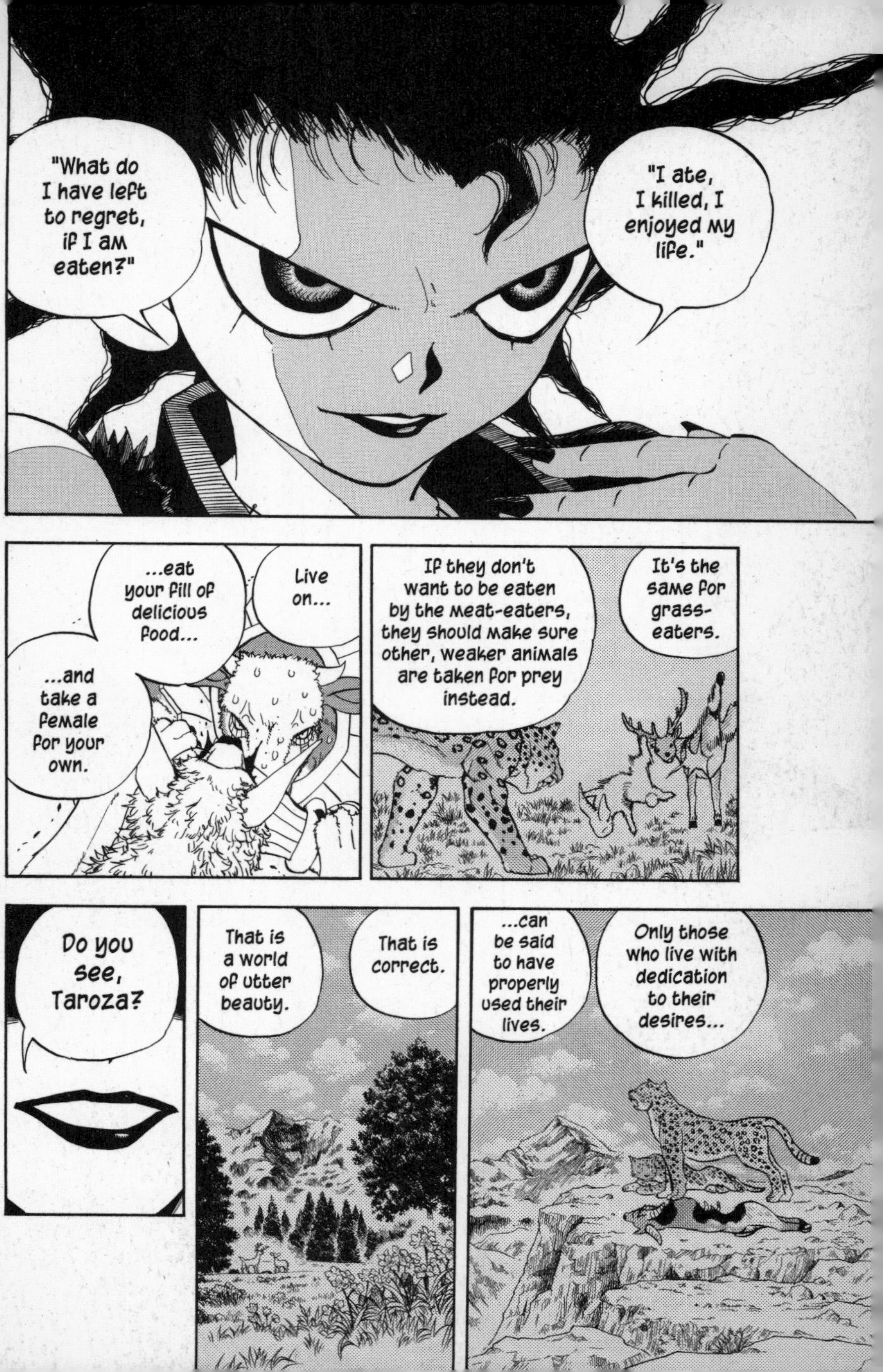
"I ate, I killed, I enjoyed my life."
"What do I have left to regret, if I am eaten?"
It's the same for grass-eaters.
If they don't want to be eaten by the meat-eaters, they should make sure other, weaker animals are taken for prey instead.
Live on...
...eat your fill of delicious food...
...and take a female for your own.
Only those who live with dedication to their desires...
...can be said to have properly used their lives.
That is correct.
That is a world of utter beauty.
Do you see, Taroza?

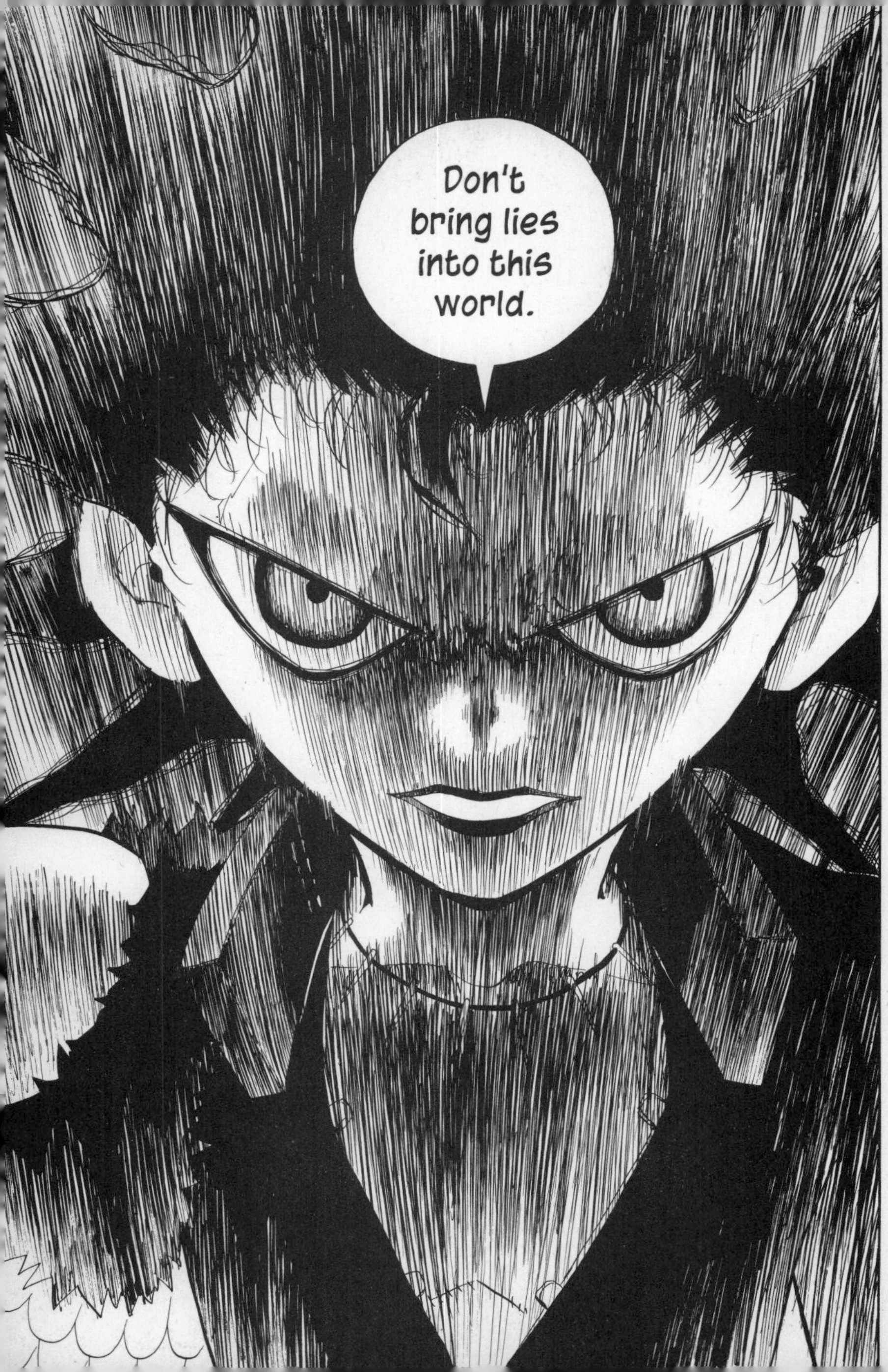
Don't bring lies into this world.

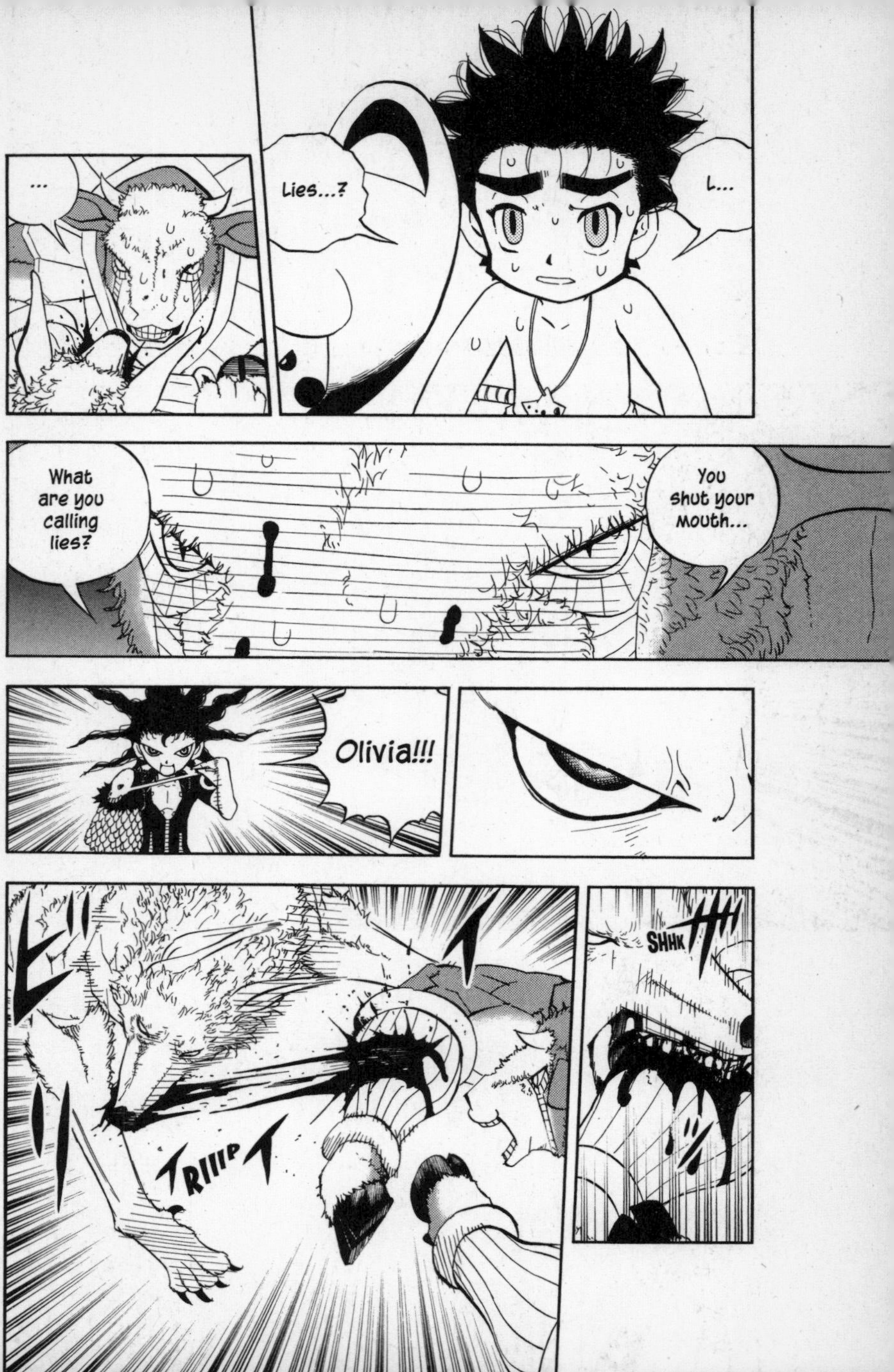
L...
Lies...?
...
You shut your mouth...
What are you calling lies?
Olivia!!!
SHHK
TRIIIP

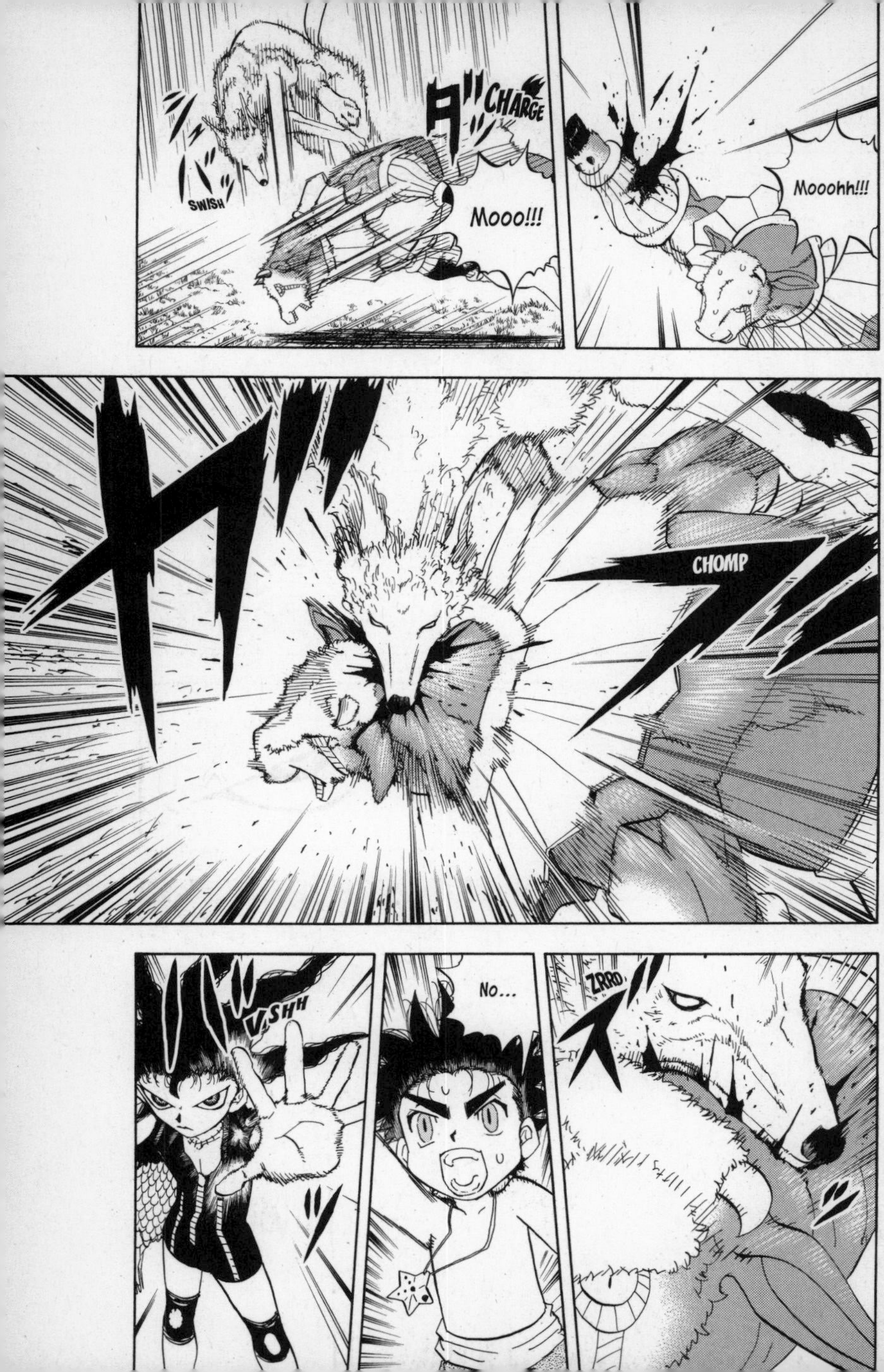
Mooohh!!!
CHARGE
Mooo!!!
SWISH
CHOMP
ZRRD
No...
VSHH

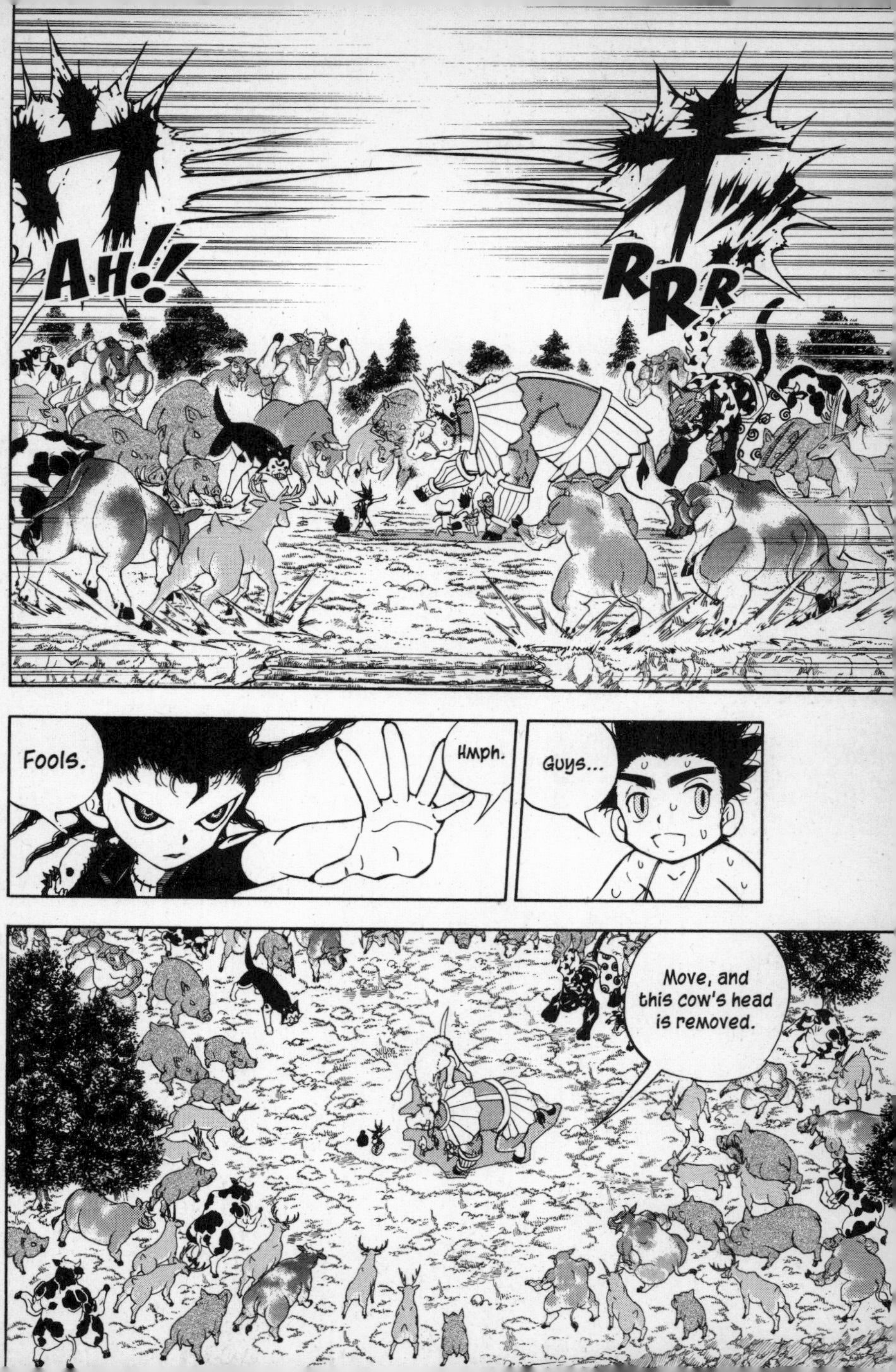
RRR
AH!!
Guys...
Hmph.
Fools.
Move, and this cow's head is removed.

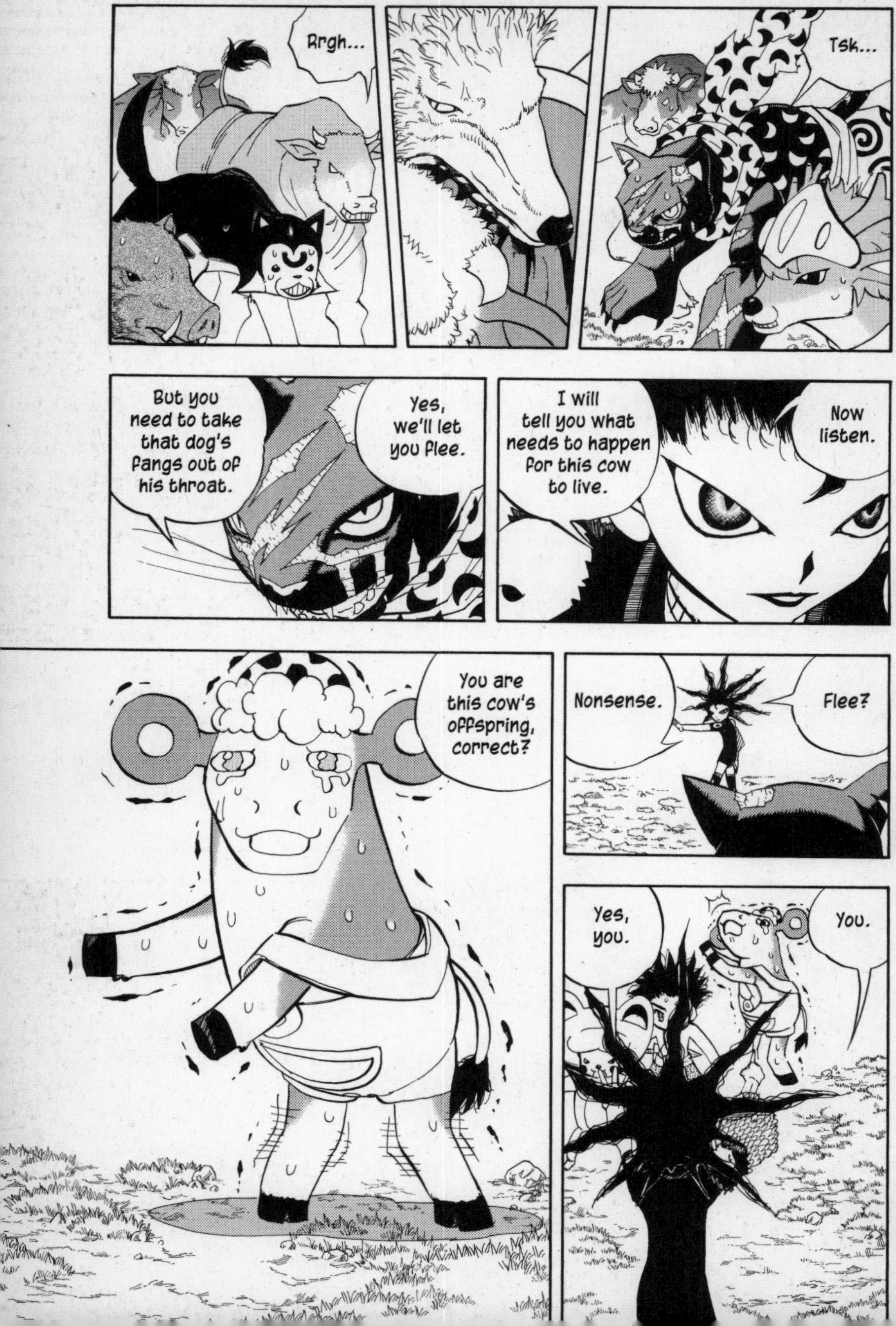

Tsk...
Rrgh...
Now listen.
I will tell you what needs to happen for this cow to live.
Yes, we'll let you flee.
But you need to take that dog's fangs out of his throat.
Flee?
Nonsense.
You.
Yes, you.
You are this cow's offspring, correct?

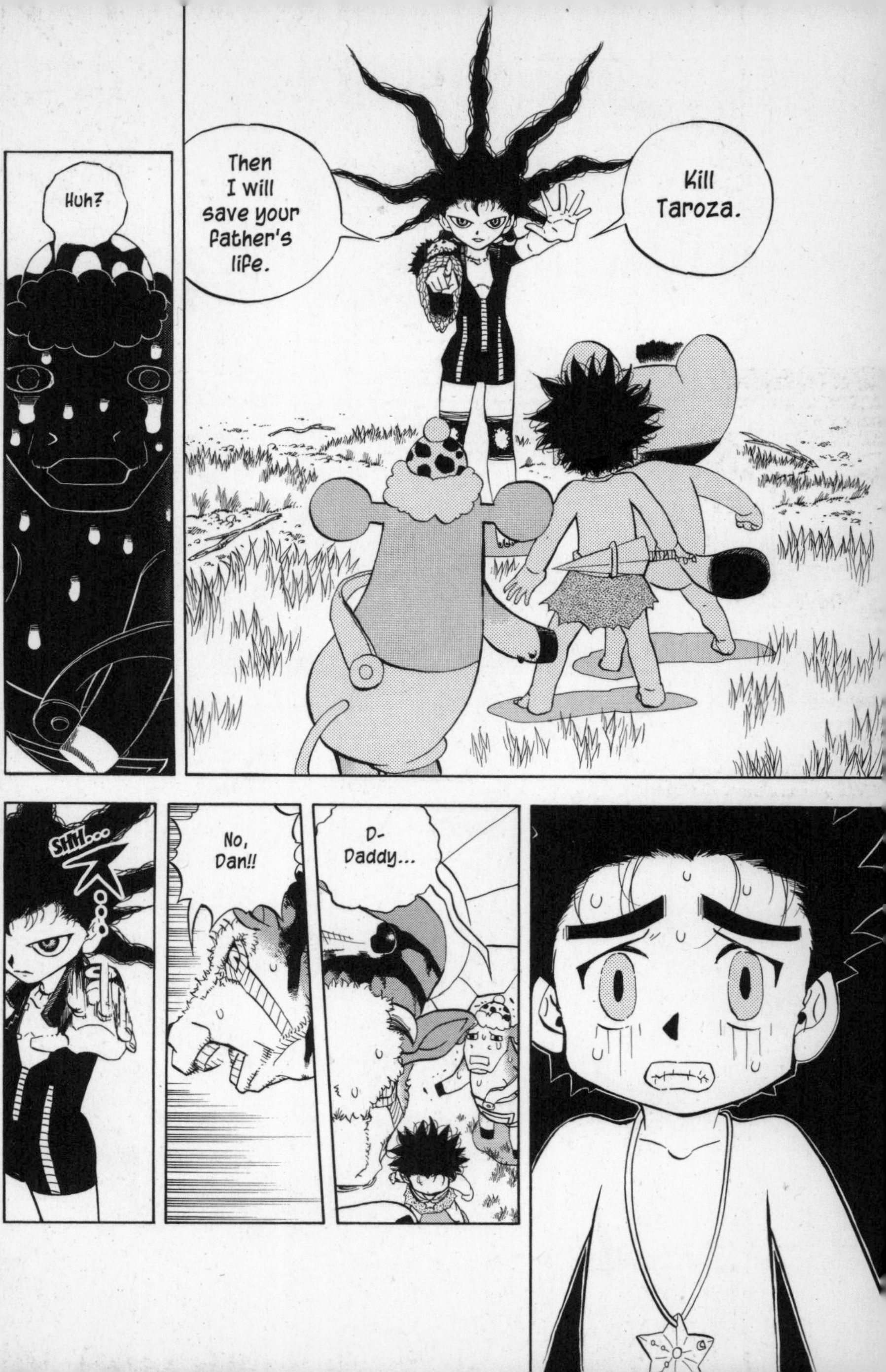
Kill Taroza.
Then I will save your father's life.
Huh?
D- Daddy...
No, Dan!!
SHH...

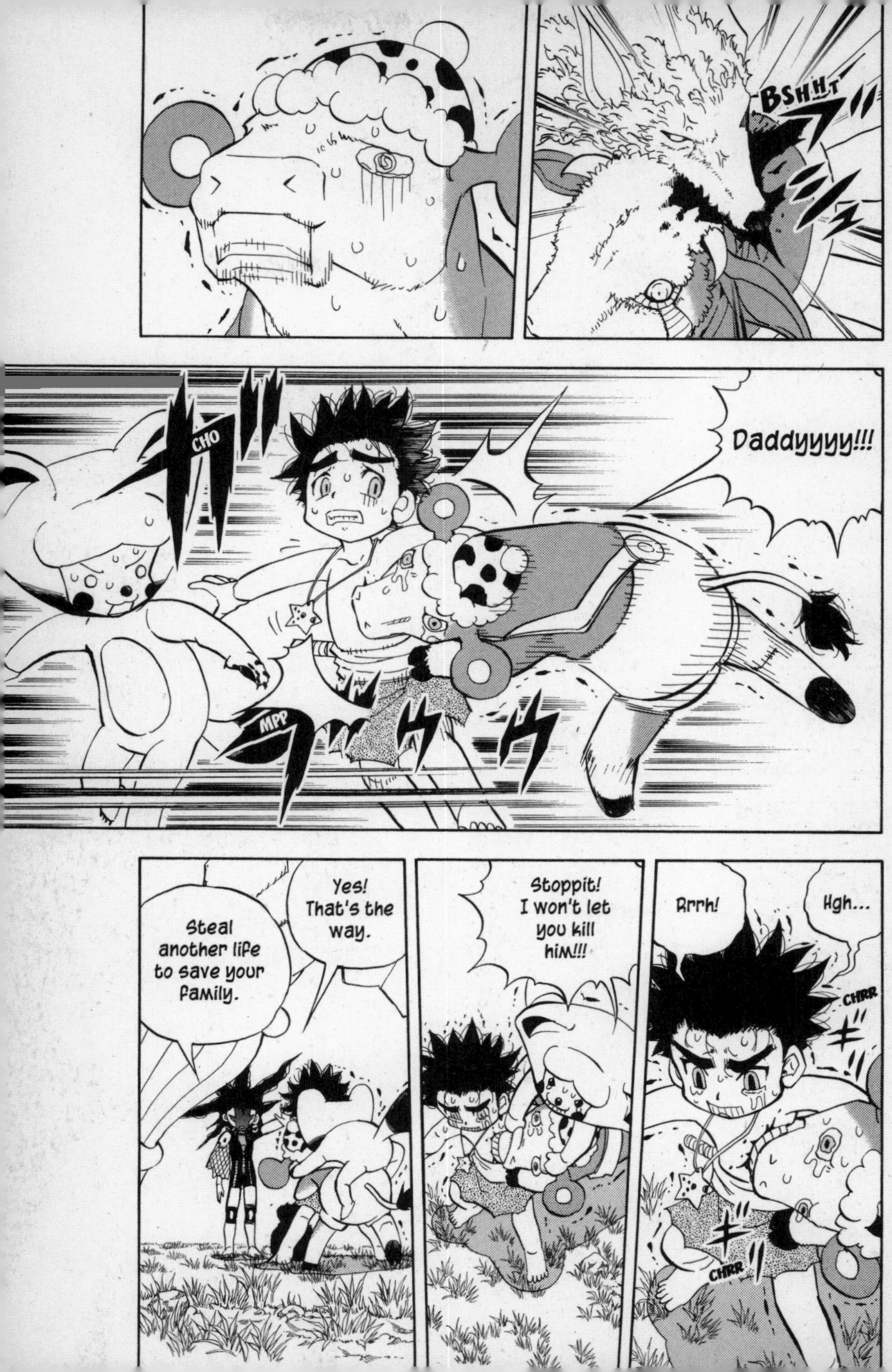
BSHHT
Daddyyyy!!!
CHO
MPP
Hgh...
Rrrh!
CHRR
CHRR
Stoppit! I won't let you kill him!!!
Yes! That's the way.
Steal another life to save your family.

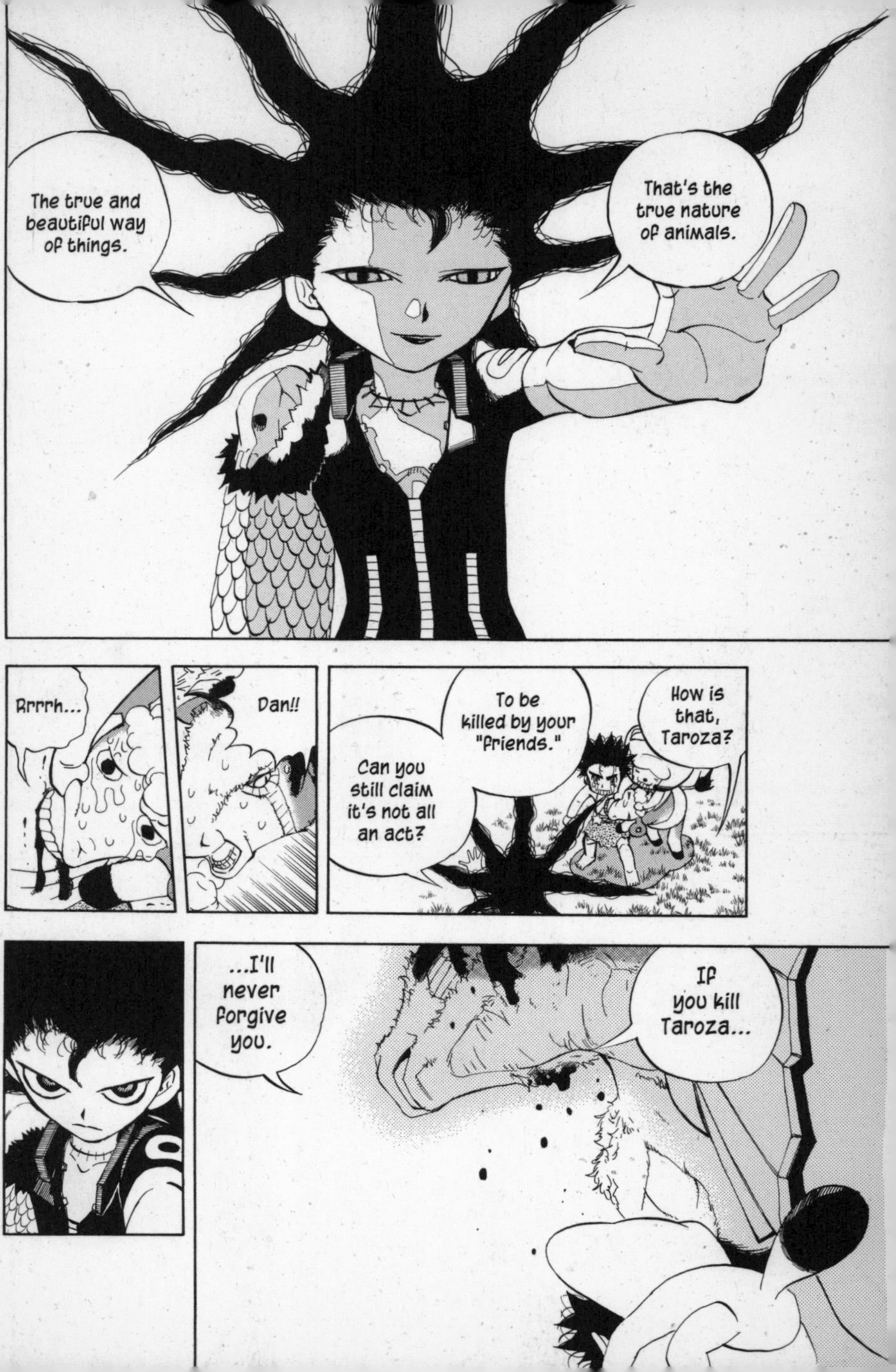
That's the true nature of animals.
The true and beautiful way of things.
How is that, Taroza?
To be killed by your "friends."
Can you still claim it's not all an act?
Dan!!
Rrrrh...
If you kill Taroza...
...I'll never forgive you.

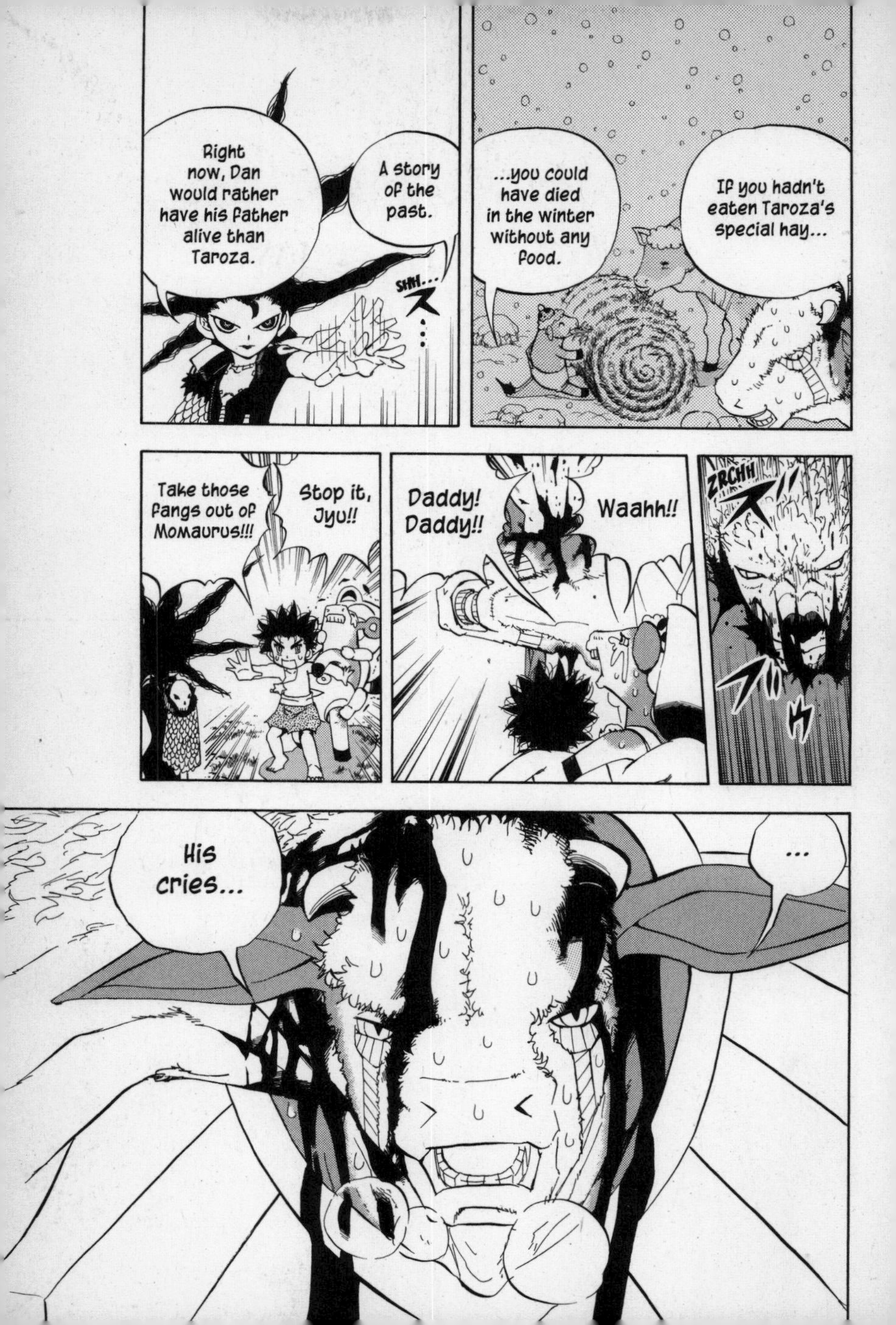
If you hadn't eaten Taroza's special hay...
...you could have died in the winter without any food.
A story of the past.
Right now, Dan would rather have his father alive than Taroza.
SHH...
ZRCHH
Waahh!!
Daddy! Daddy!!
Stop it, Jyu!!
Take those fangs out of Momaurus!!!
...
His cries...

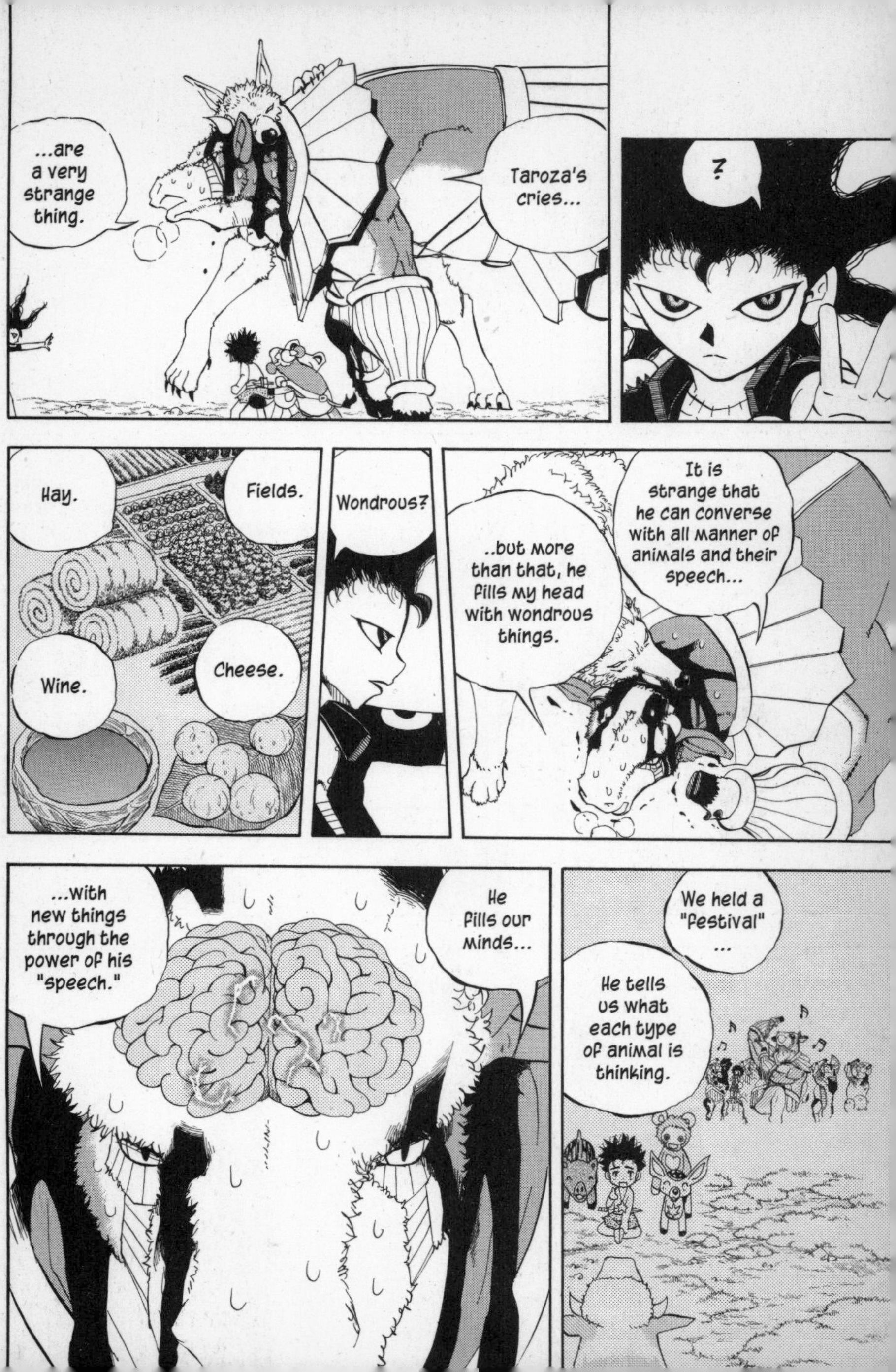
?
Taroza's cries...
...are a very strange thing.
It is strange that he can converse with all manner of animals and their speech...
..but more than that, he fills my head with wondrous things.
Wondrous?
Fields.
Hay.
Cheese.
Wine.
We held a "festival" ...
He tells us what each type of animal is thinking.
He fills our minds...
...with new things through the power of his "speech."

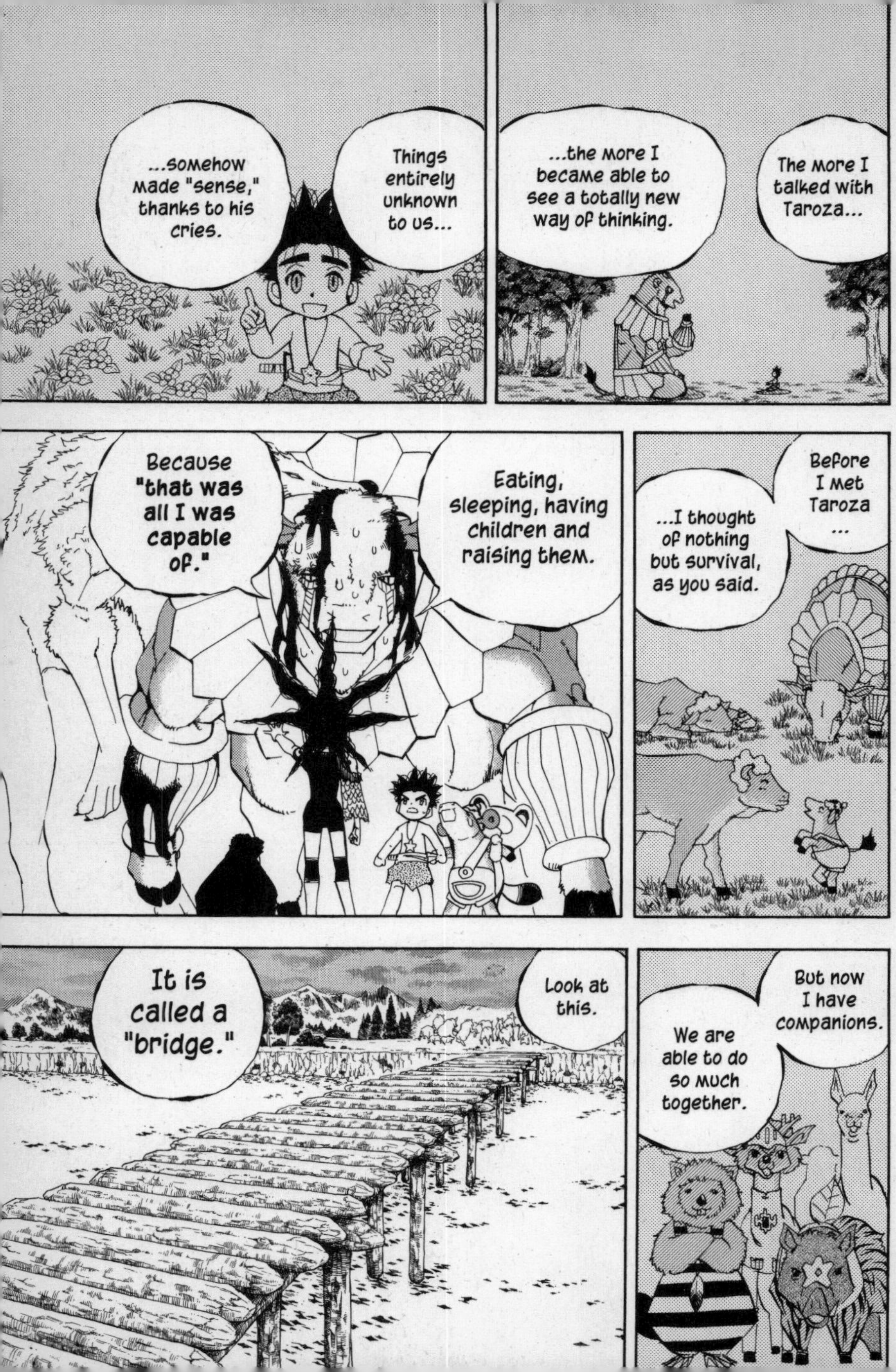
The more I talked with Taroza...
...the more I became able to see a totally new way of thinking.
Things entirely unknown to us...
...somehow made "sense," thanks to his cries.
Before I met Taroza ...
...I thought of nothing but survival, as you said.
Eating, sleeping, having children and raising them.
Because "that was all I was capable of."
But now I have companions.
We are able to do so much together.
Look at this.
It is called a "bridge."

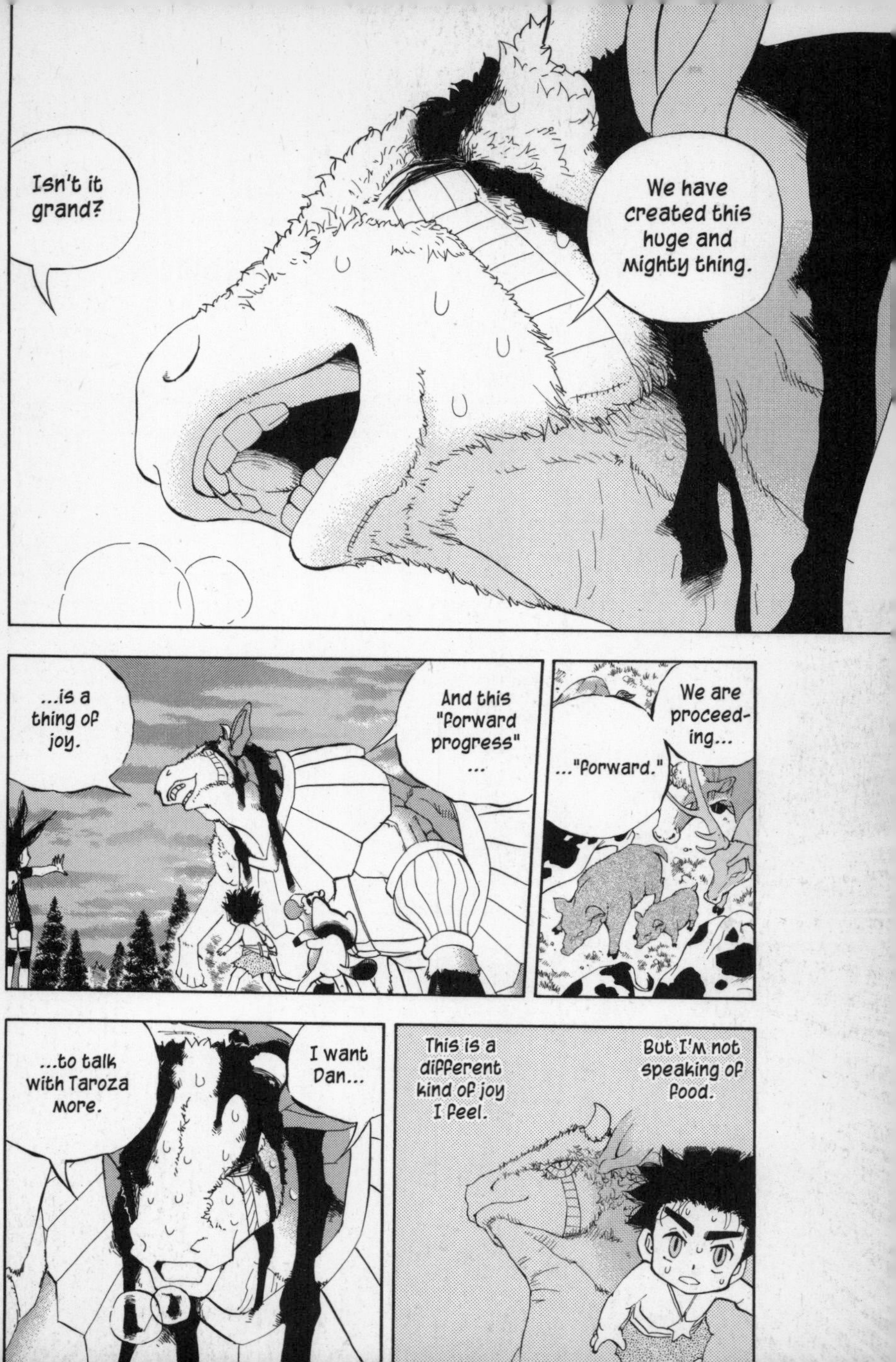
We have created this huge and mighty thing.
Isn't it grand?
We are proceeding...
..."forward."
And this "forward progress" ...
...is a thing of joy.
But I'm not speaking of food.
This is a different kind of joy I feel.
I want Dan...
...to talk with Taroza more.

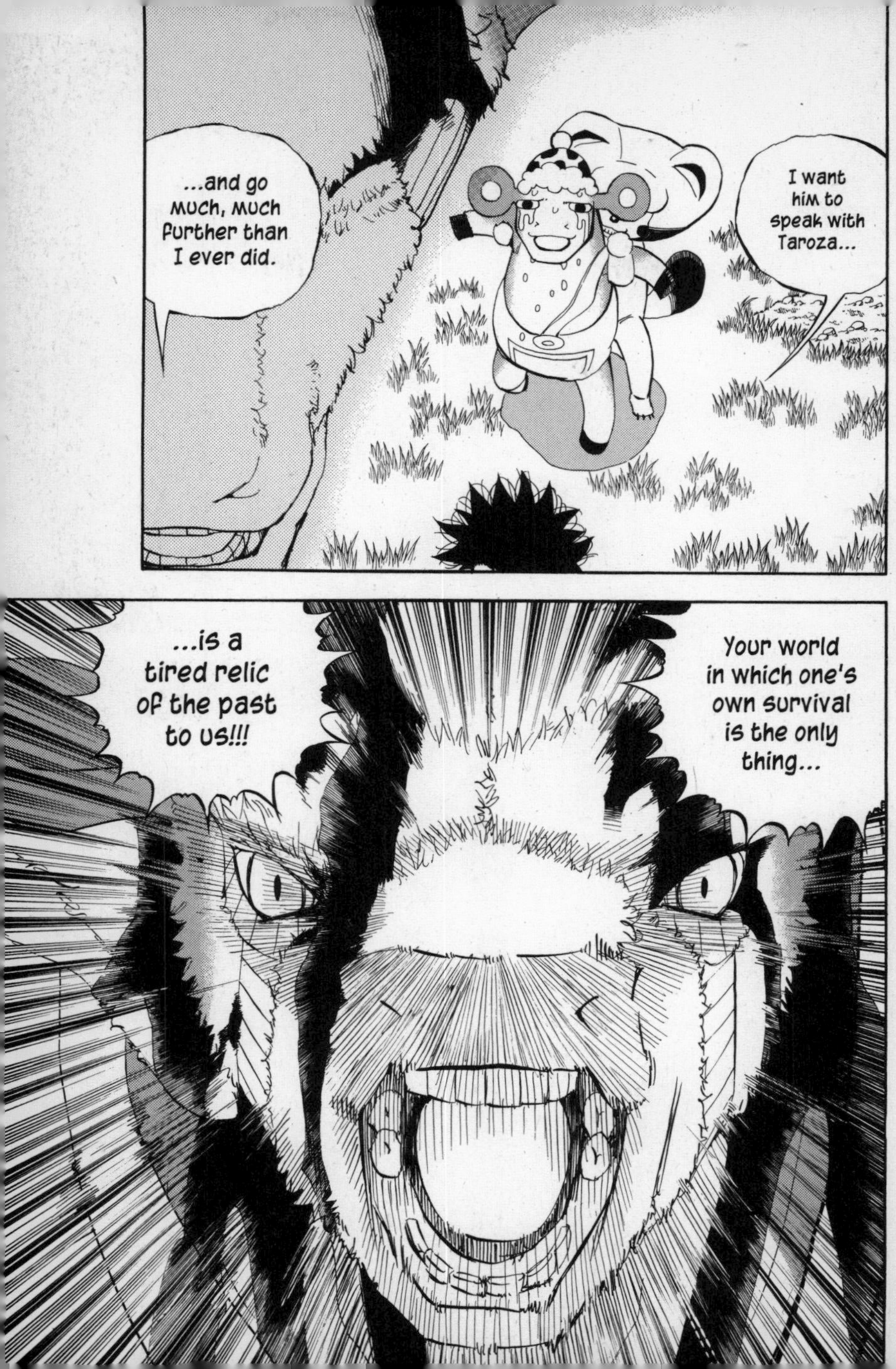
I want him to speak with Taroza...
...and go much, much further than I ever did.
Your world in which one's own survival is the only thing...
...is a tired relic of the past to us!!!

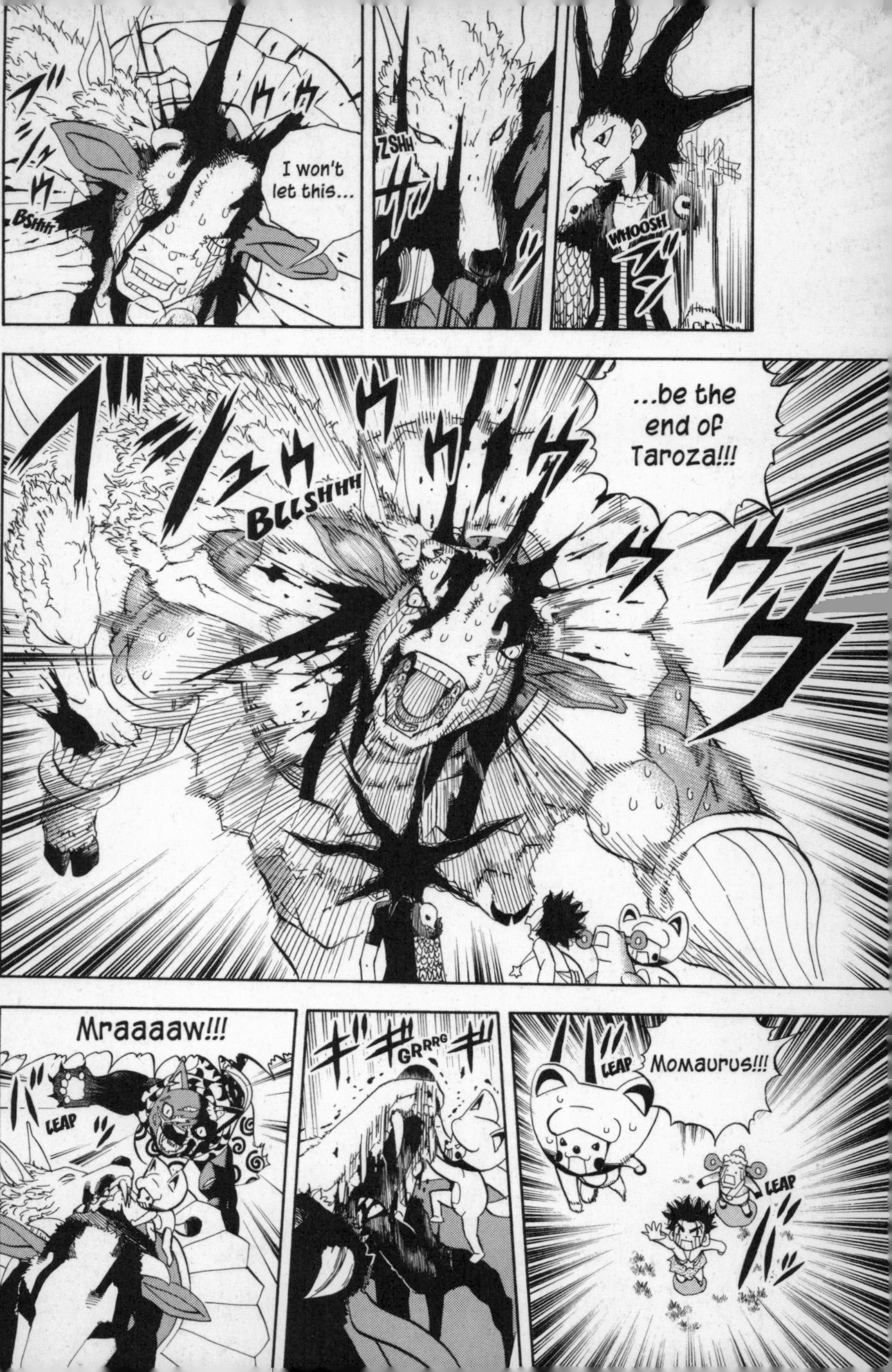
WHOOSH
ZSHH
I won't let this...
BSHHH
...be the end of Taroza!!!
BLLSHHH
LEAP
Momaurus!!!
LEAP
GRRRG
Mraaaaw!!!
LEAP

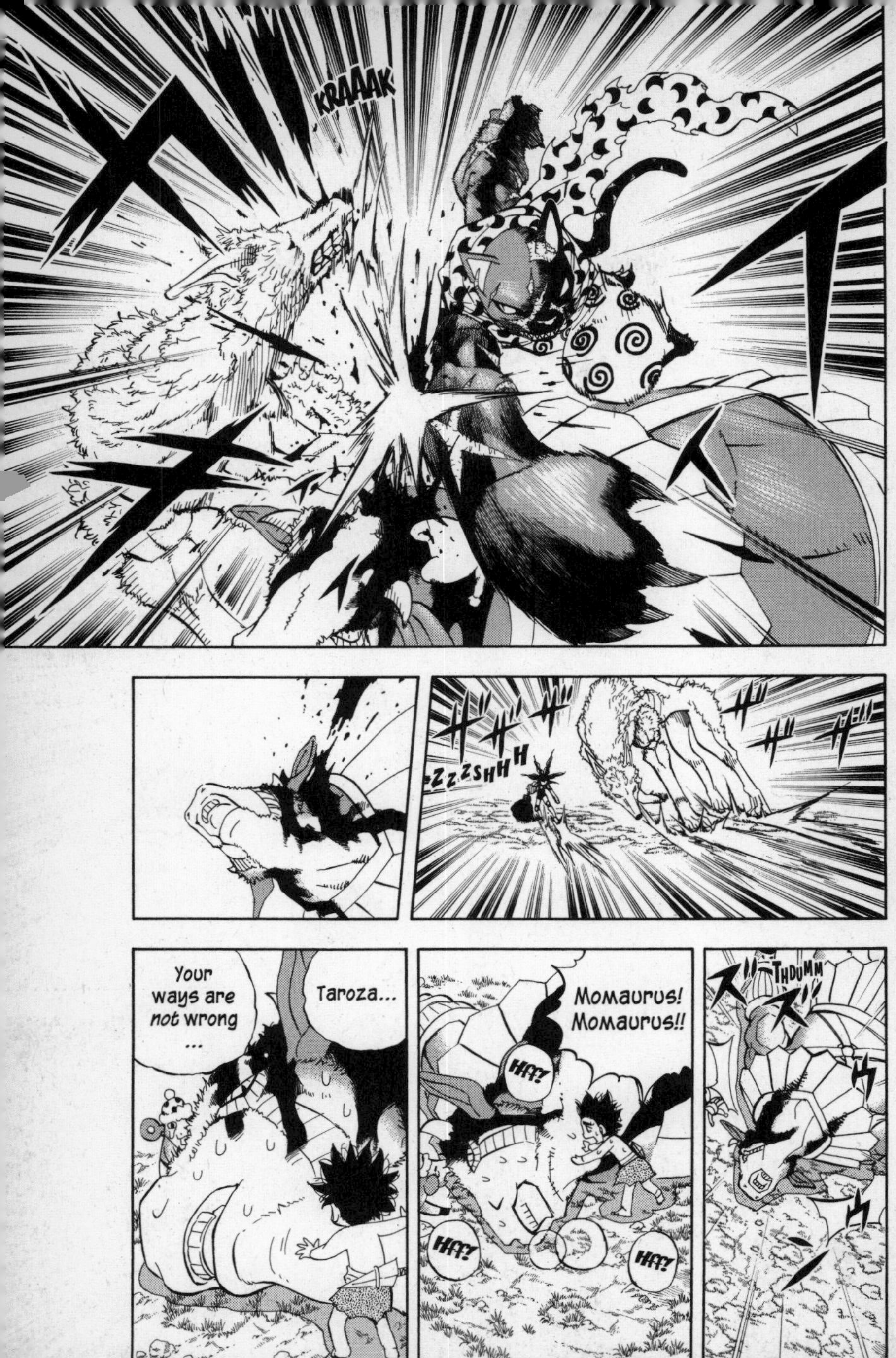

KRAAAK
ZZZSHHH
THDUMM
Momaurus! Momaurus!!
Hff?
Hff?
Hff?
Taroza...
Your ways are *not* wrong ...

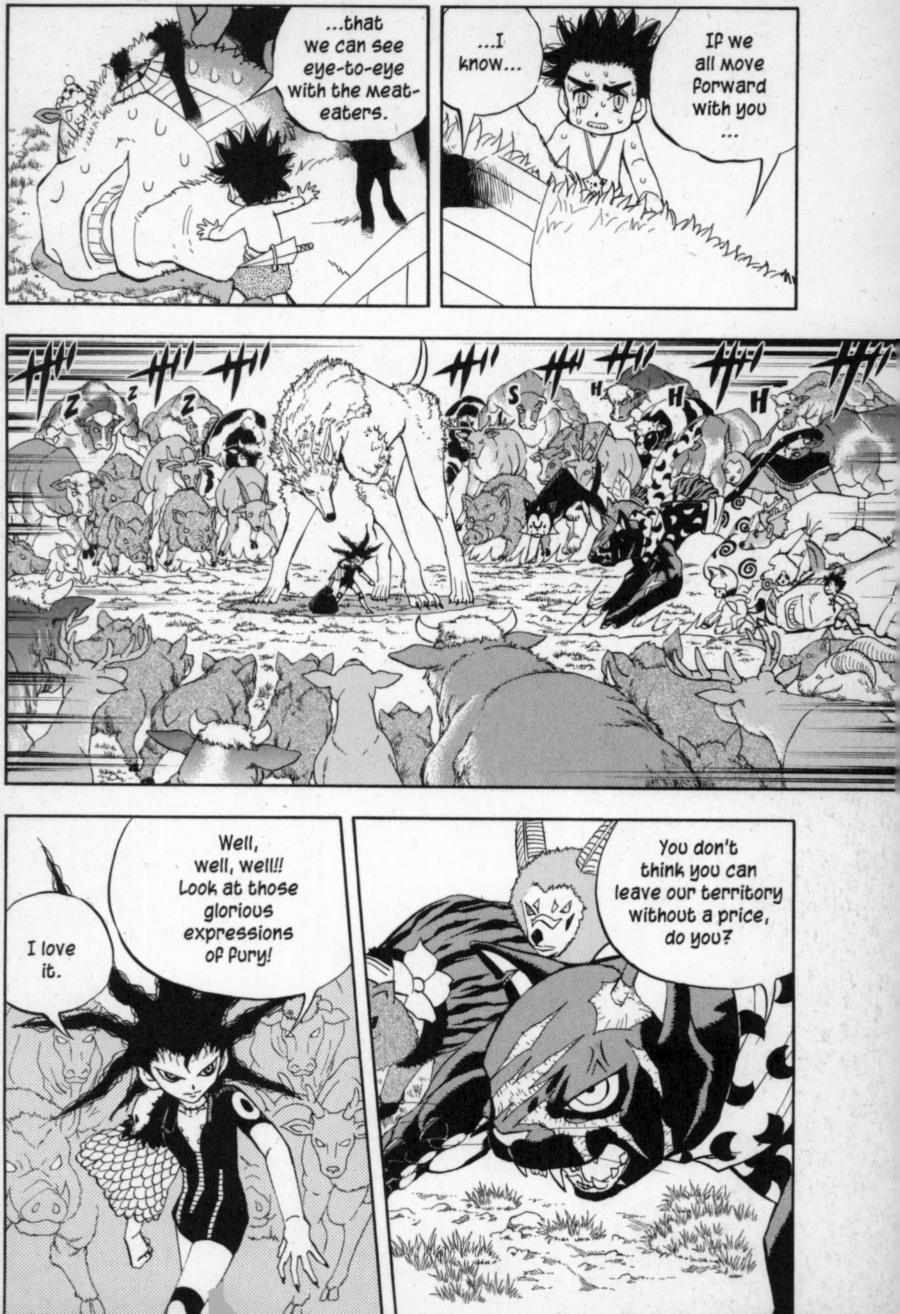
If we all move forward with you ...
...I know...
...that we can see eye-to-eye with the meat-eaters.
You don't think you can leave our territory without a price, do you?
Well, well, well!! Look at those glorious expressions of fury!
I love it.

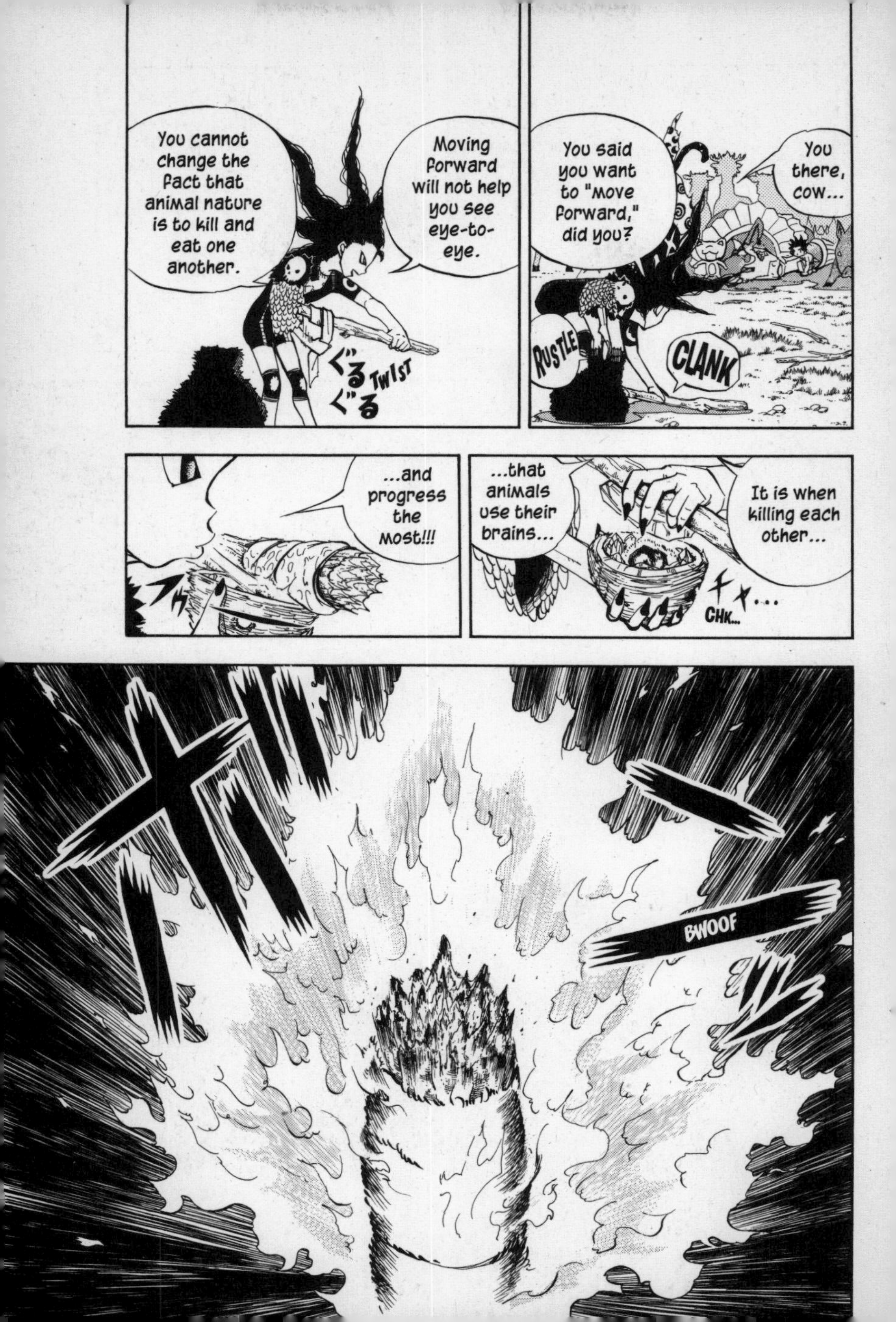
You there, cow...
You said you want to "move forward," did you?
RUSTLE
CLANK
Moving forward will not help you see eye-to-eye.
You cannot change the fact that animal nature is to kill and eat one another.
ぐる TWIST ぐる
It is when killing each other...
...that animals use their brains...
CHK...
...and progress the most!!!
BWOOF

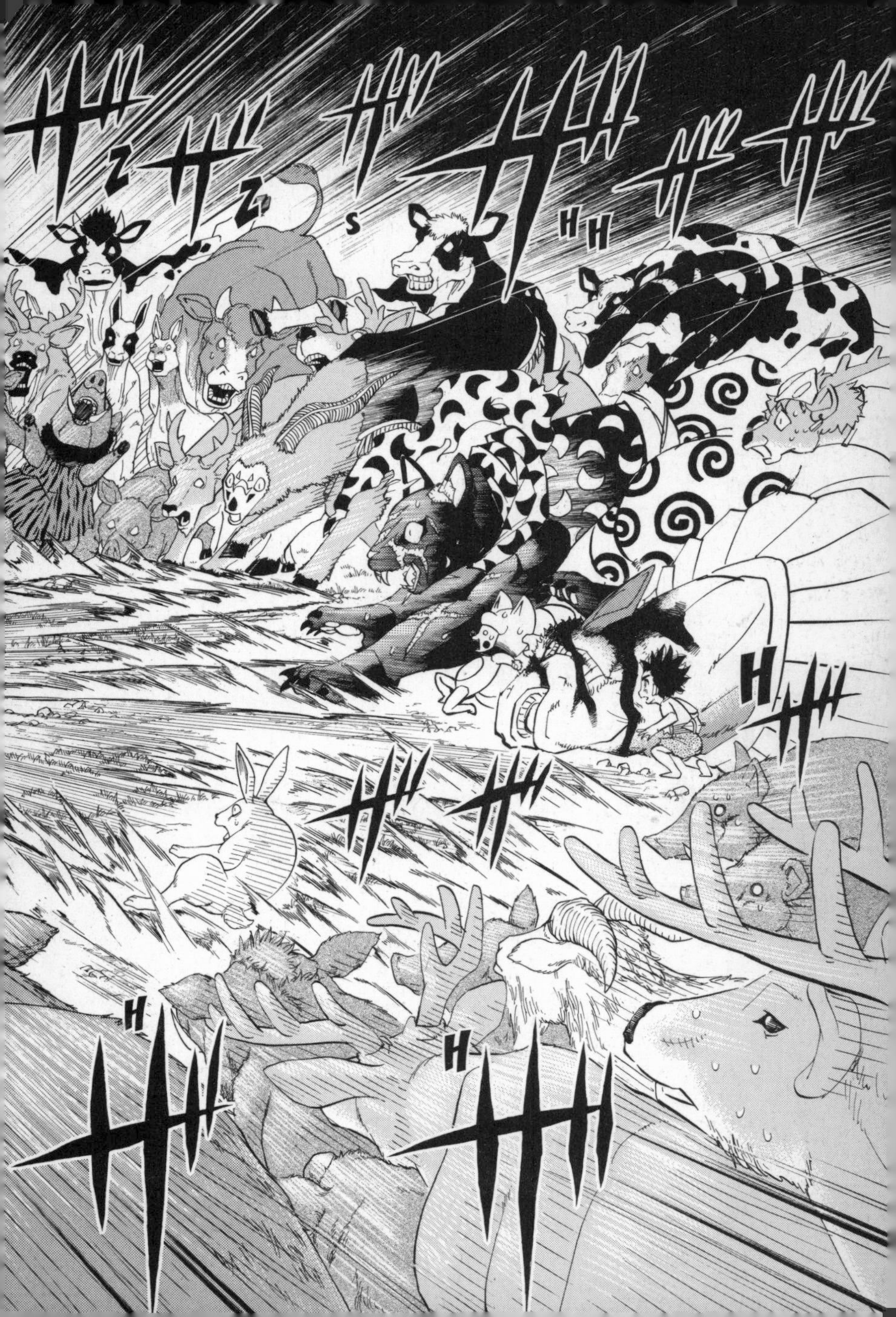
ザザザ
Z
Z
ザ
S
ザザ
H H
ザザ
H
ザザ
H
ザザ
H
ザザ

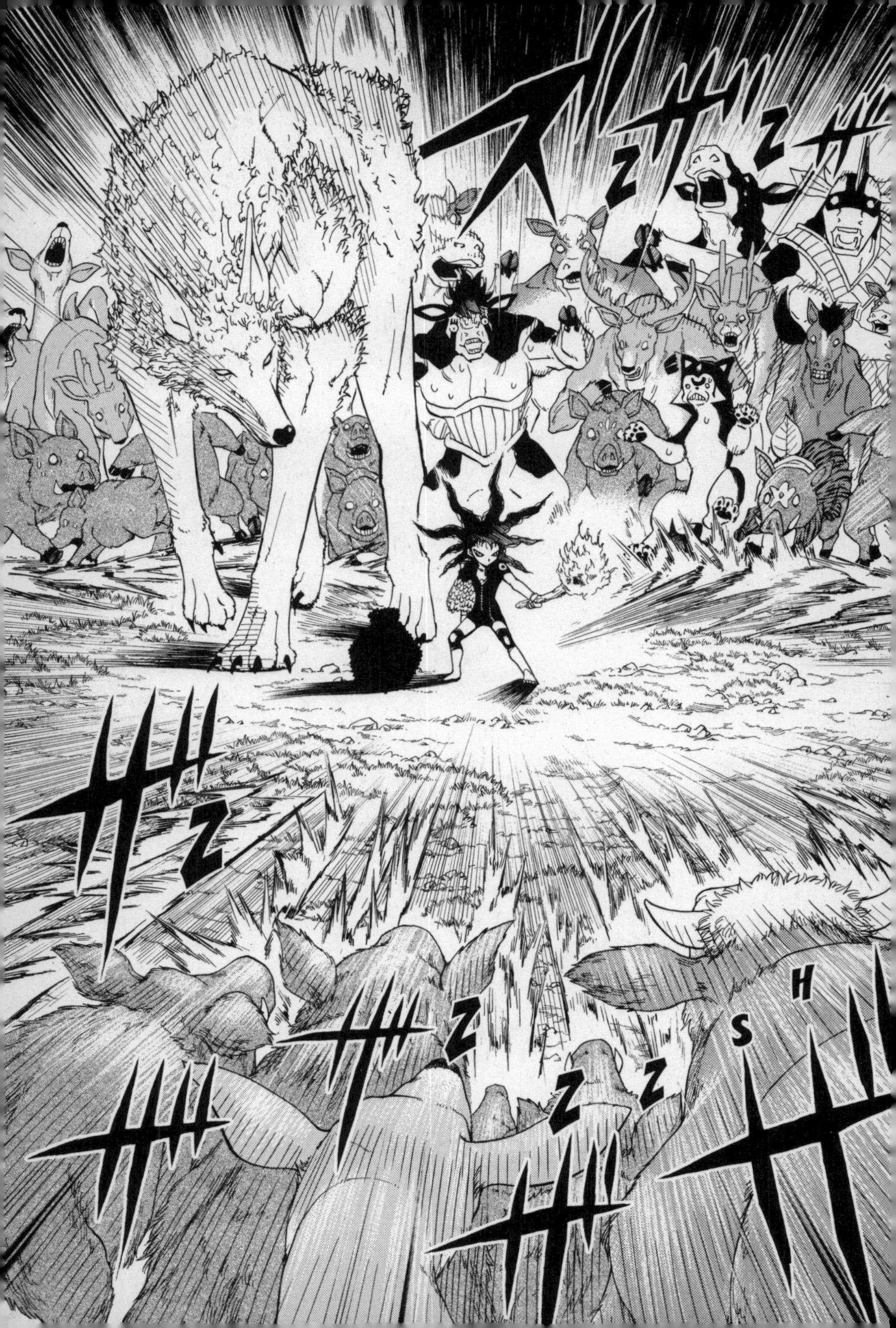
ZZ
Z
ZZZSH

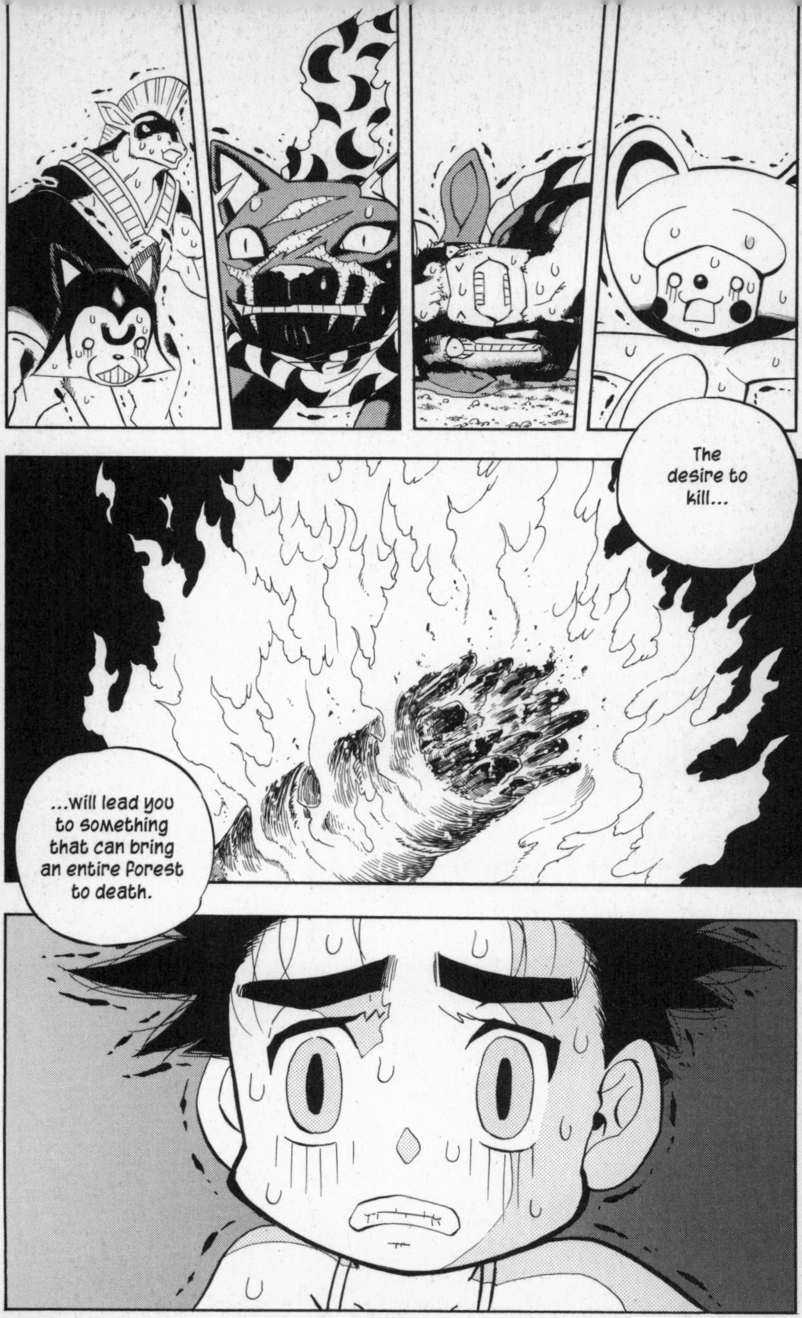
The desire to kill...
...will lead you to something that can bring an entire forest to death.

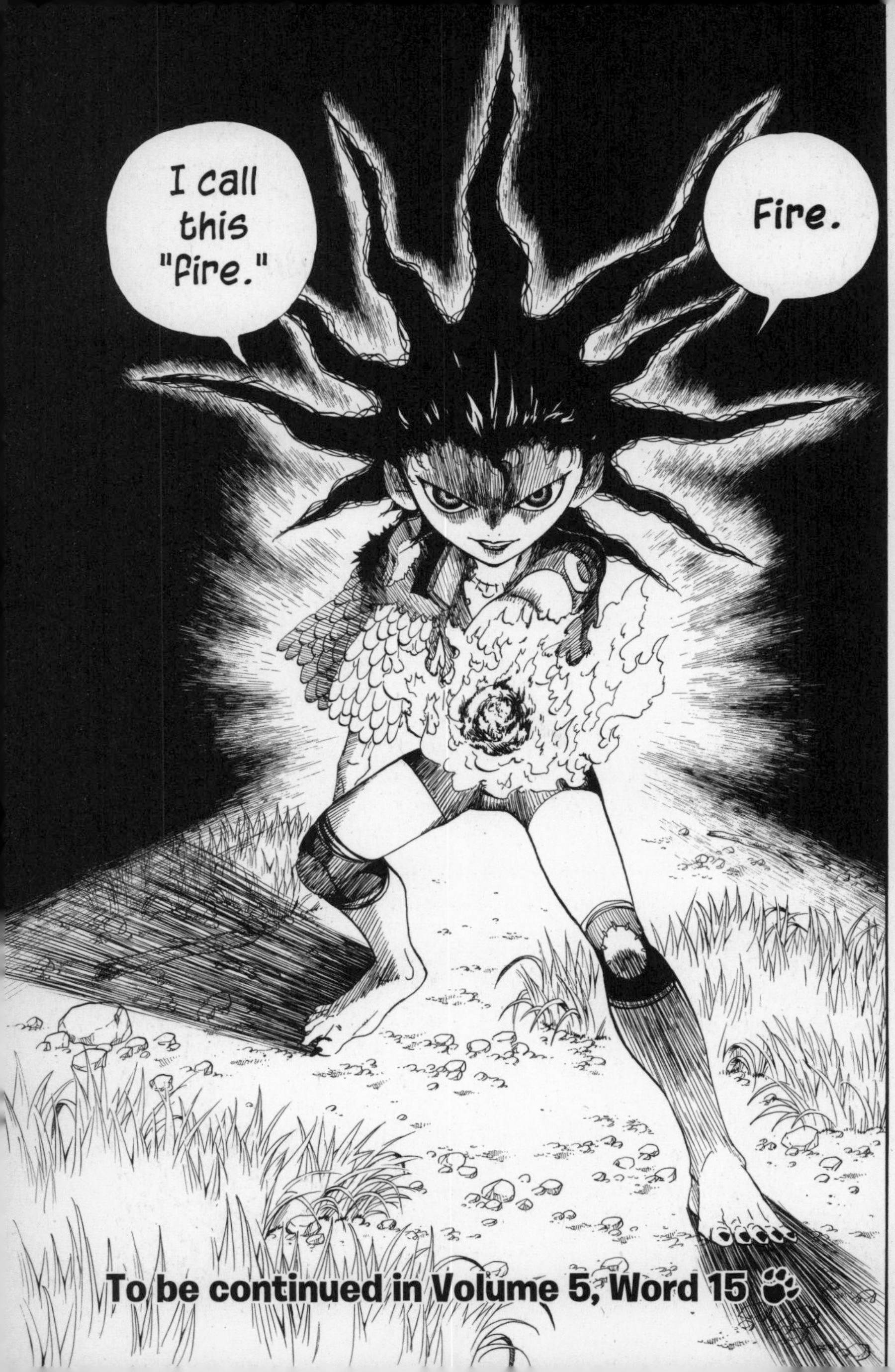
Fire.
I call this "fire."
To be continued in Volume 5, Word 15

Translation Notes

Japanese is a tricky language for most Westerners, and translation is often more art than science. For your edification and reading pleasure, here are notes on some of the places where we could have gone in a different direction with our translation of the work, or where a Japanese cultural reference is used.

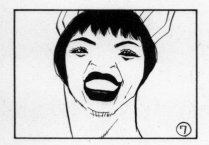

Akiko Llama, page 50

This character is a parody of real life singer and entertainer Akiko Wada, who is known for her short haircut, imposing height and sharp opinions.

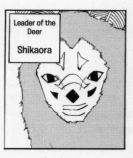

Leader of the Deer
Shikaora

Shikaora, page 115

The word *shika* is Japanese for "deer."

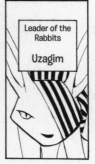

Leader of the Rabbits
Uzagim

Uzagim, page 116

This name bears a strong similarity to *usagi,* the word for "rabbit."

Leader of the Hamsters
Director

Hamster Director, page 116

This pun may be related to the fact that the Japanese pronunciation for "ham-ster" ends the same way as "star," a fitting sign for aspiring rodent actors.

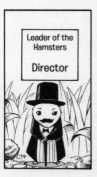

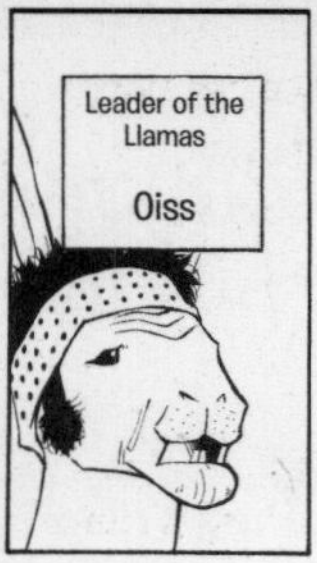
Leader of the Llamas
Oiss

Oiss, page 116

The leader of the llamas' name sounds a lot like a slangy way of saying, "wassup?"

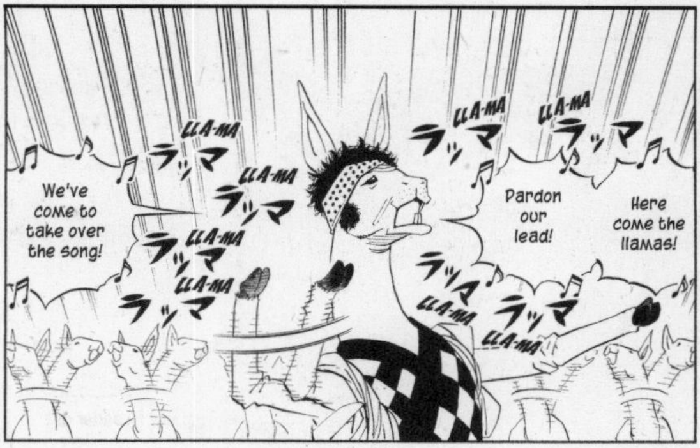
LLA-MA
ラッマ
LLA-MA
ラッマ
Here come the llamas!
Pardon our lead!
LLA-MA
ラッマ
LLA-MA
ラッマ
LLA-MA
ラッマ
LLA-MA
ラッマ
LLA-MA
ラッマ
LLA-MA
ラッマ
We've come to take over the song!

Llamas, page 125

Nearly all of the llamas listed are named (and designed) after food dishes. *Katsudon* is a "pork bowl," or breaded pork cutlet served on top of rice. Tendon is a "tenpura bowl." *Unadon* is "eel bowl." *Unidon* is "sea urchin bowl." *Zarusoba* is a type of cool *soba* (buckwheat) noodles eaten in the summertime with a strong broth. *Kushikatsu* is pork cutlet on skewers, and of course, a croquette is a croquette.

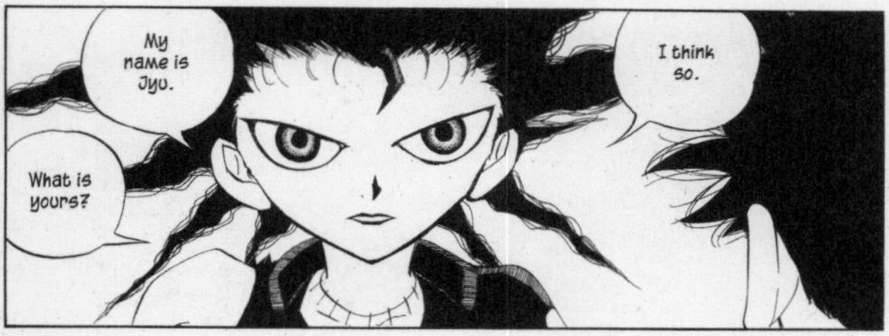
I think so.
My name is Jyu.
What is yours?

Jyu, page 162

The title of Chapter 14, "Jyu, Beast, Freedom," is a list of homophones in Japanese. "Beast" is spelled *ju* in Japanese, and "freedom" is *jiyu,* which is very close in the Japanese syllabary. Though Jyu's name doesn't have any *kanji* that would assign it a specific meaning (as with "beast" or "freedom") the similarity is quite intentional.

Next Volume Preview

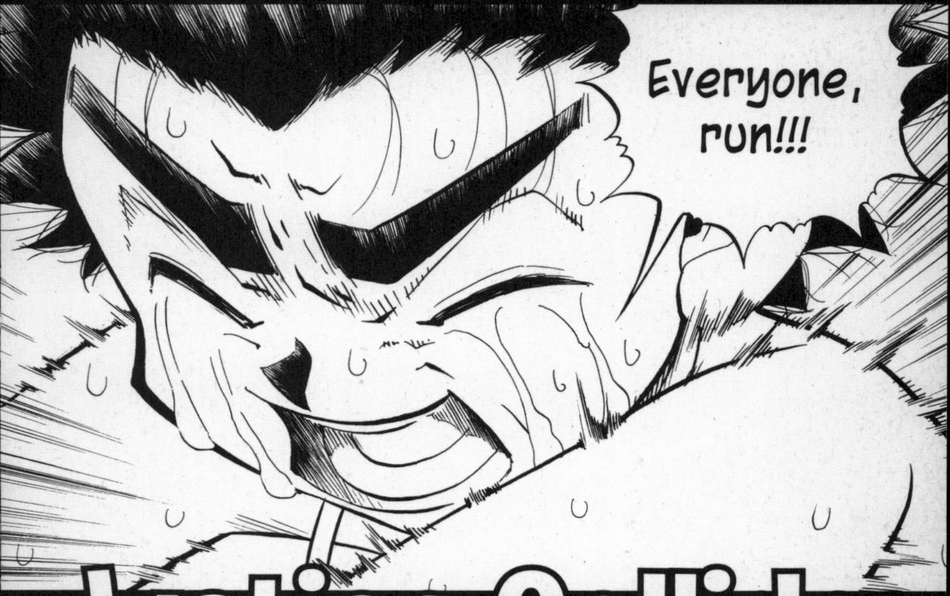
Everyone, run!!!

Justice Collide

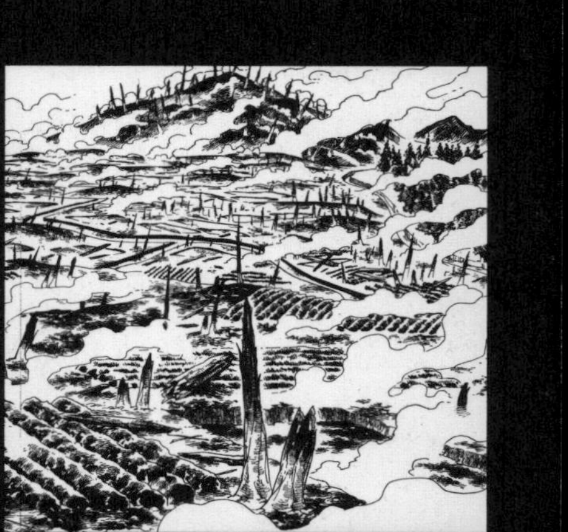

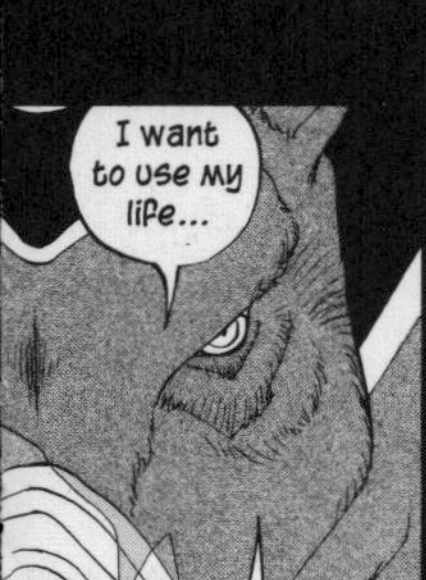
I want to use my life...

A conflict of beliefs as to the rightful state of the planet. Two human beings who will never share the other's views.

Two Forms of

This is the true form of our "Animal Land."

The unknown violence of fire is unleashed. After a clash of souls, who should stand before Taroza, but...?

...in the pursuit of joy, as you do.

What is "truth"?

Enjoy these preview pages of *Animal Land* 5! On sale soon!

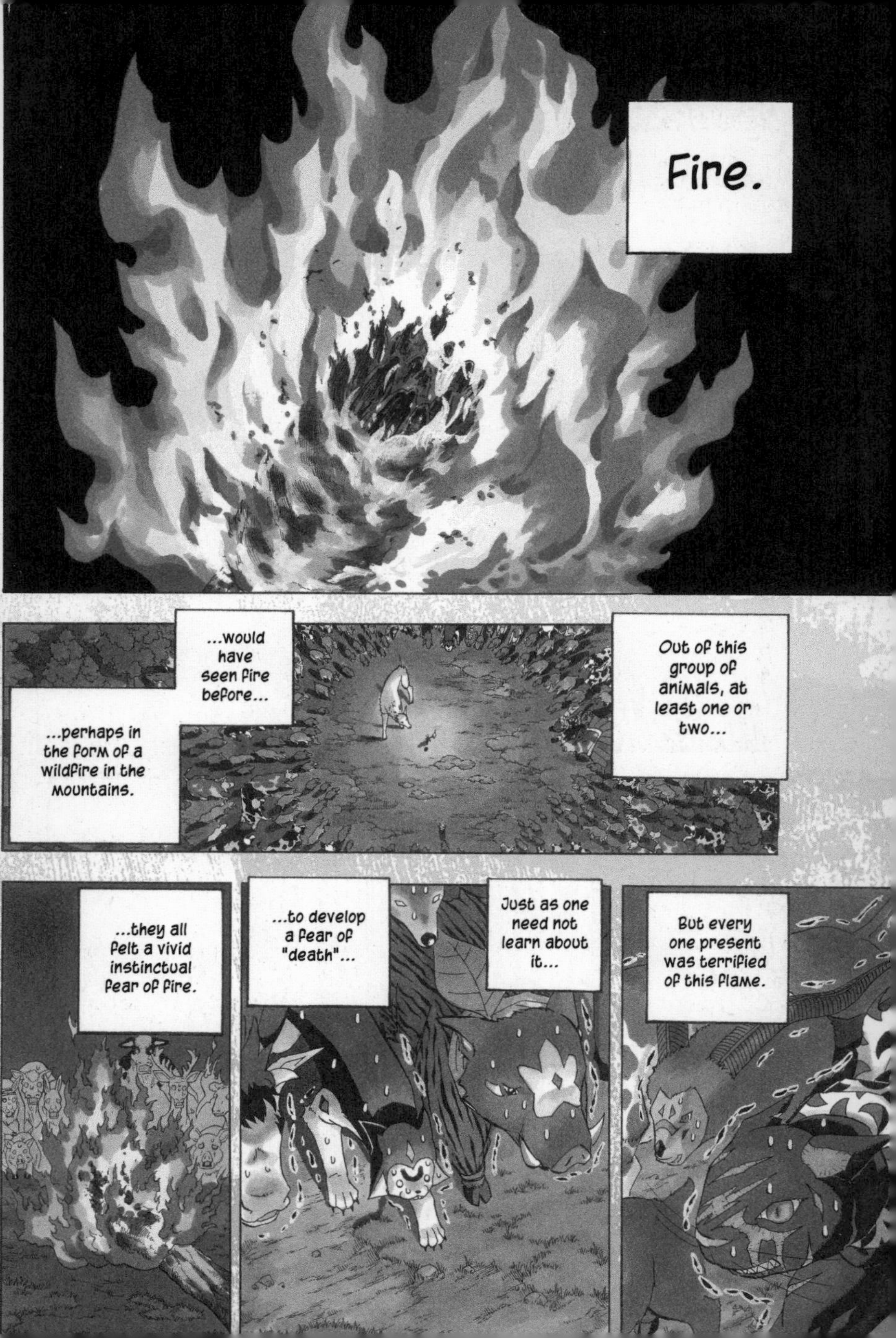
Fire.
Out of this group of animals, at least one or two...
...would have seen fire before...
...perhaps in the form of a wildfire in the mountains.
But every one present was terrified of this flame.
Just as one need not learn about it...
...to develop a fear of "death"...
...they all felt a vivid instinctual fear of fire.

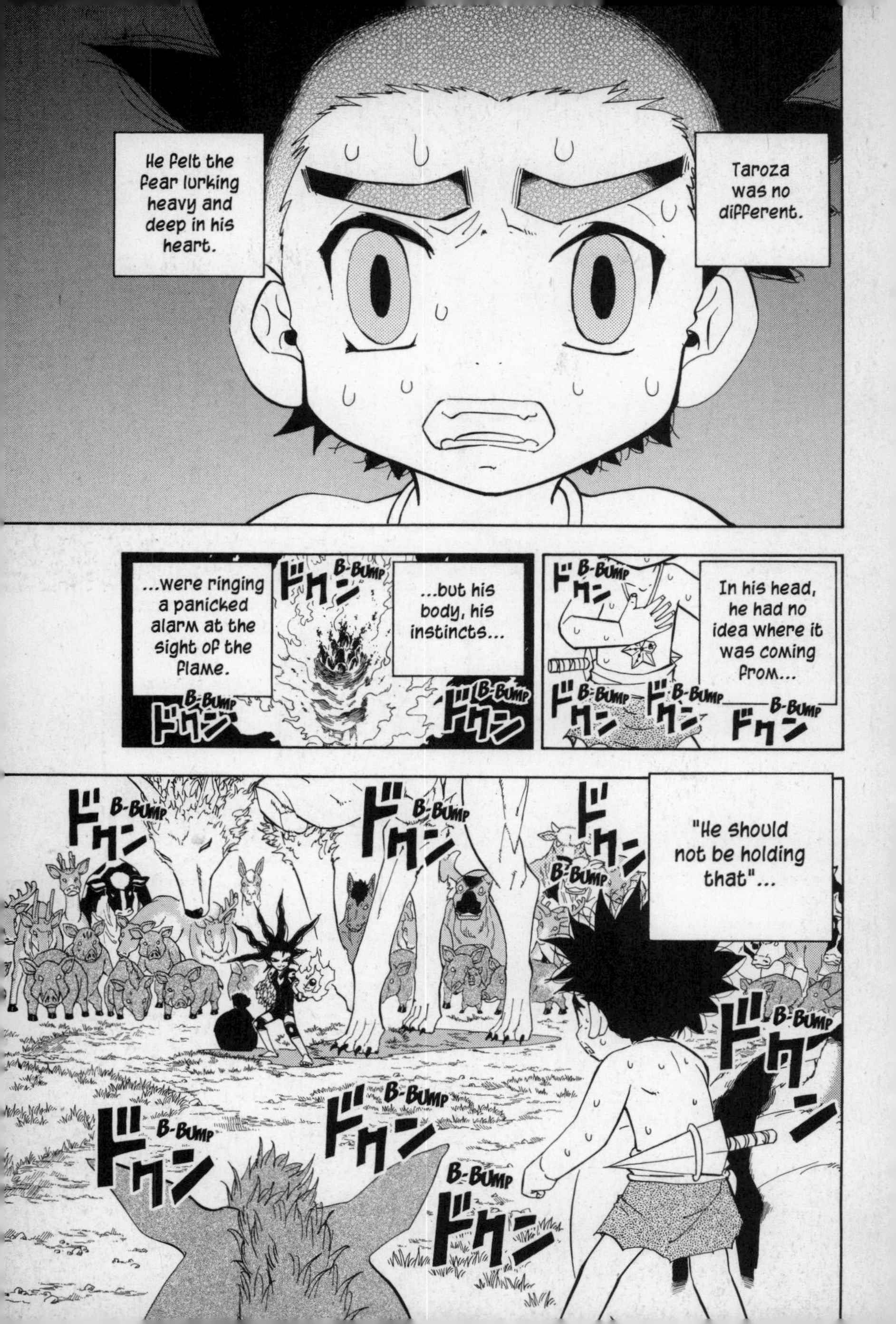
Taroza was no different.
He felt the fear lurking heavy and deep in his heart.
In his head, he had no idea where it was coming from...
ドクン B-BUMP
ドクン B-BUMP
ドクン B-BUMP
ドクン B-BUMP
...but his body, his instincts...
ドクン B-BUMP
ドクン B-BUMP
...were ringing a panicked alarm at the sight of the flame.
ドクン B-BUMP
"He should not be holding that"...
ドクン B-BUMP
ドクン B-BUMP
ドクン B-BUMP
ドクン B-BUMP
ドクン B-BUMP
ドクン B-BUMP
ドクン B-BUMP

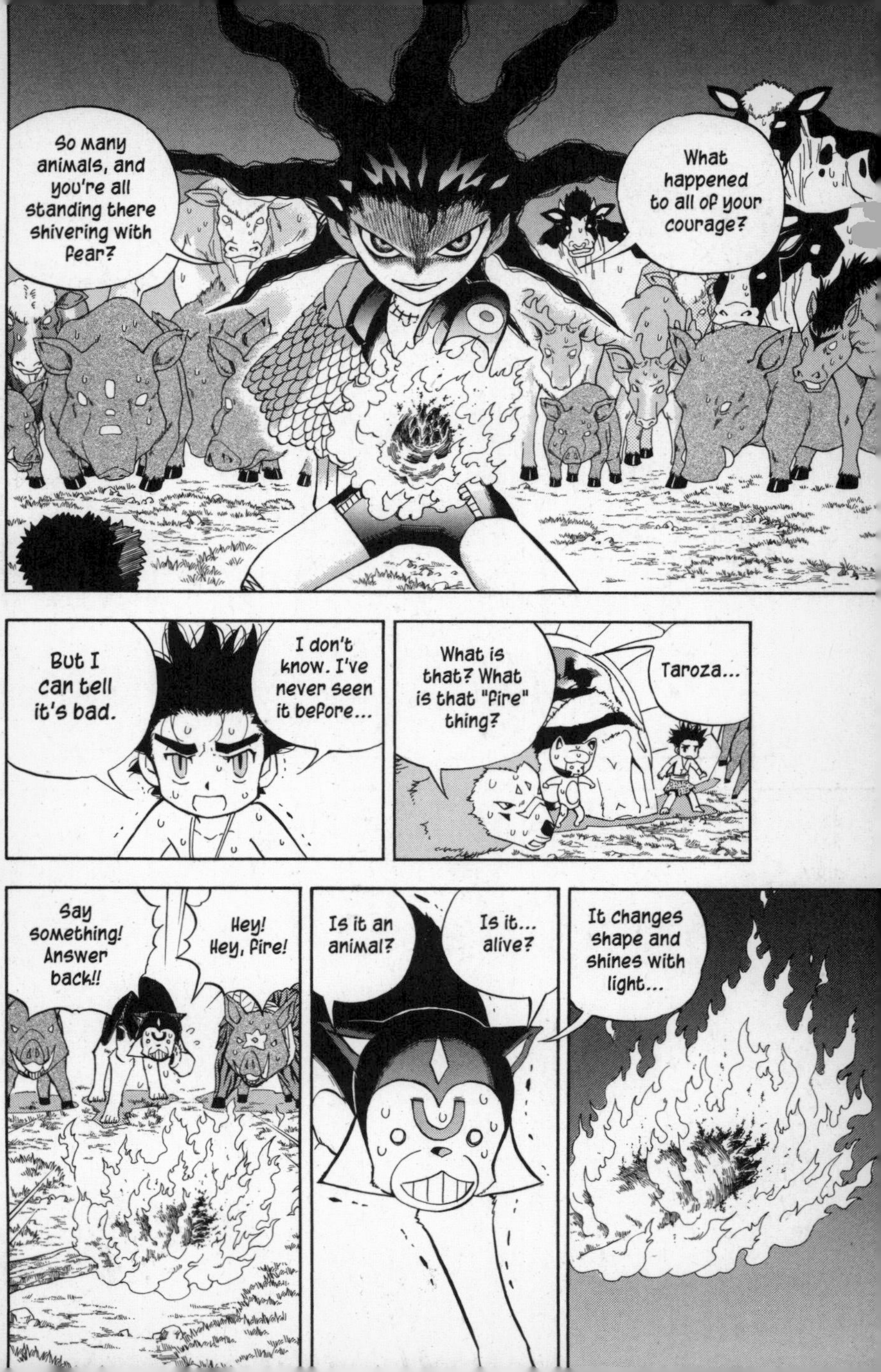
What happened to all of your courage?
So many animals, and you're all standing there shivering with fear?
Taroza...
What is that? What is that "fire" thing?
I don't know. I've never seen it before...
But I can tell it's bad.
It changes shape and shines with light...
Is it... alive?
Is it an animal?
Hey! Hey, fire!
Say something! Answer back!!

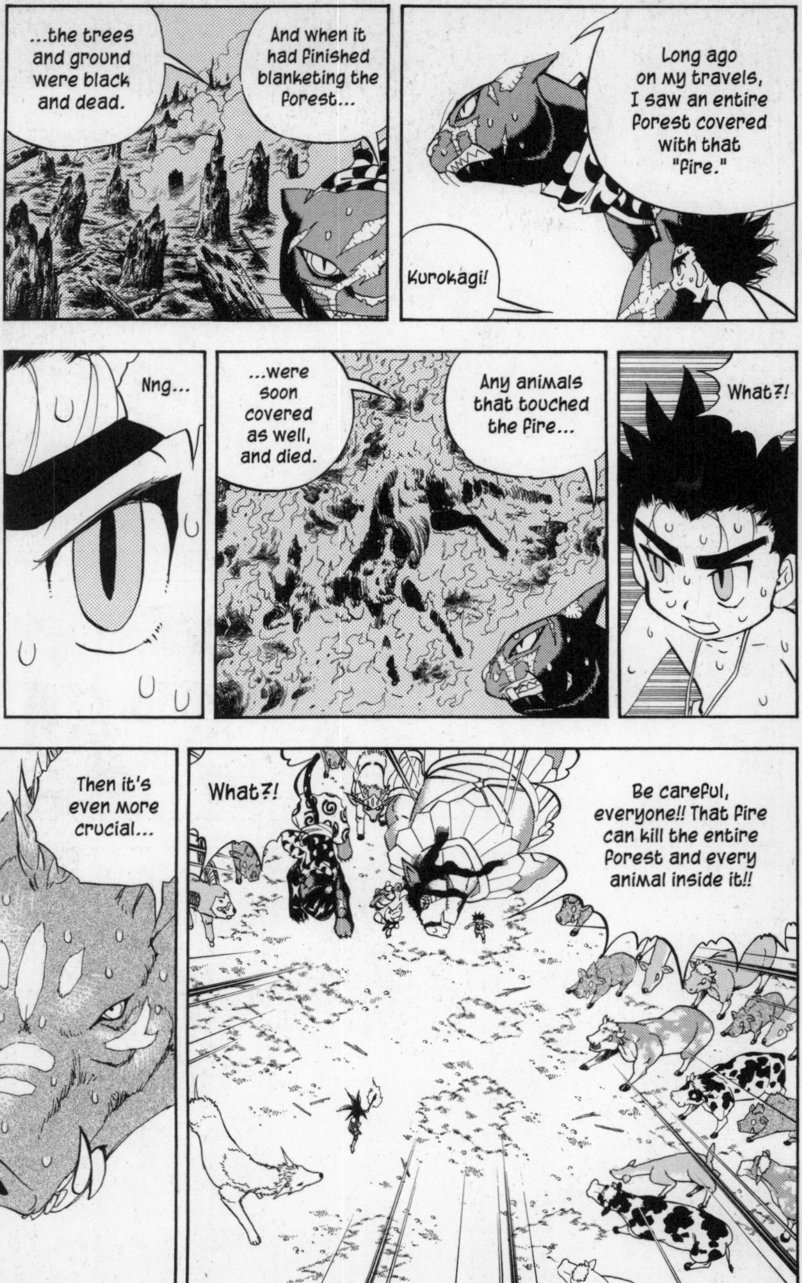
Long ago on my travels, I saw an entire forest covered with that "fire."
Kurokagi!
And when it had finished blanketing the forest...
...the trees and ground were black and dead.
What?!
Any animals that touched the fire...
...were soon covered as well, and died.
Nng...
Be careful, everyone!! That fire can kill the entire forest and every animal inside it!!
What?!
Then it's even more crucial...

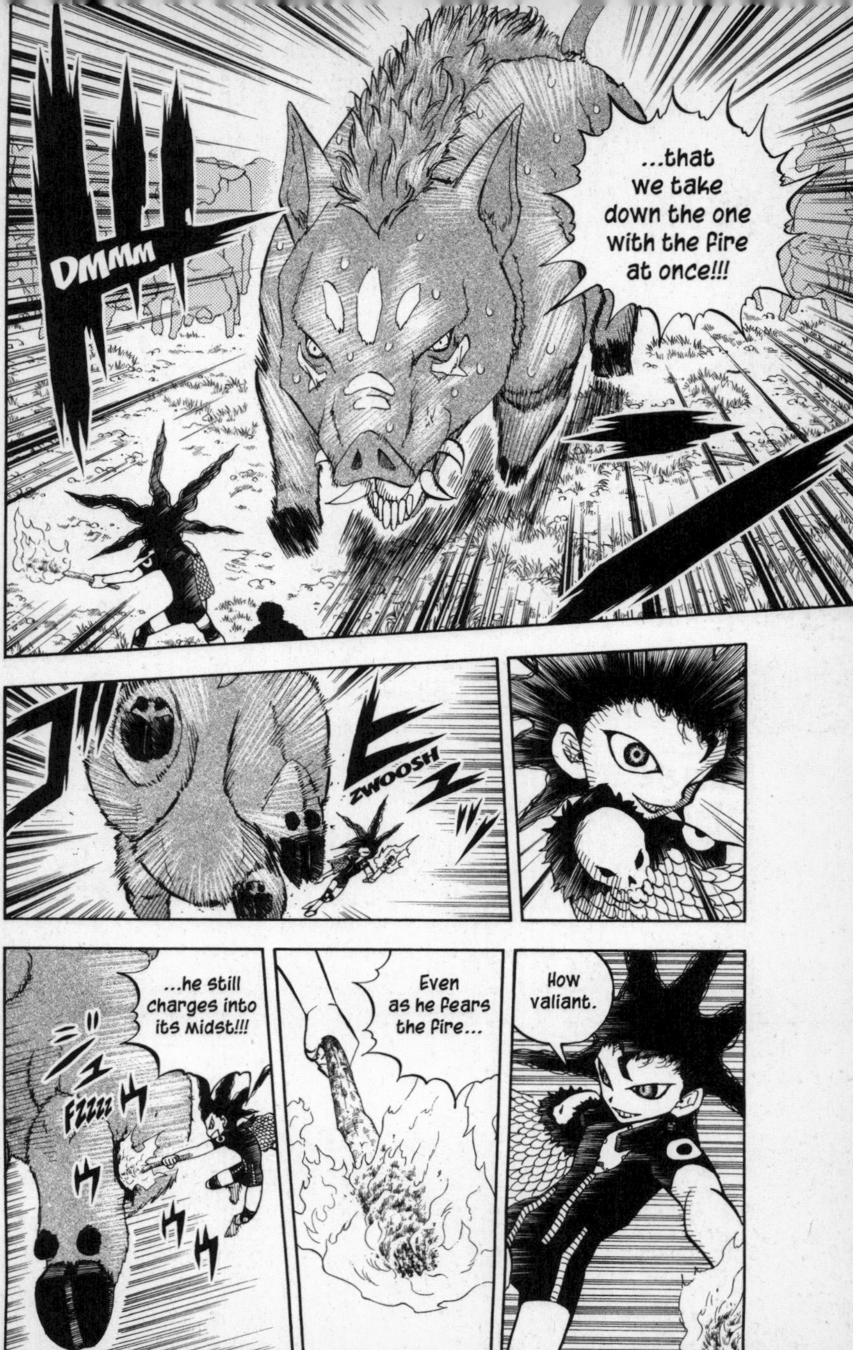
...that we take down the one with the fire at once!!!
DMMM
ZWOOSH
How valiant.
Even as he fears the fire...
...he still charges into its midst!!!
Fzzzz

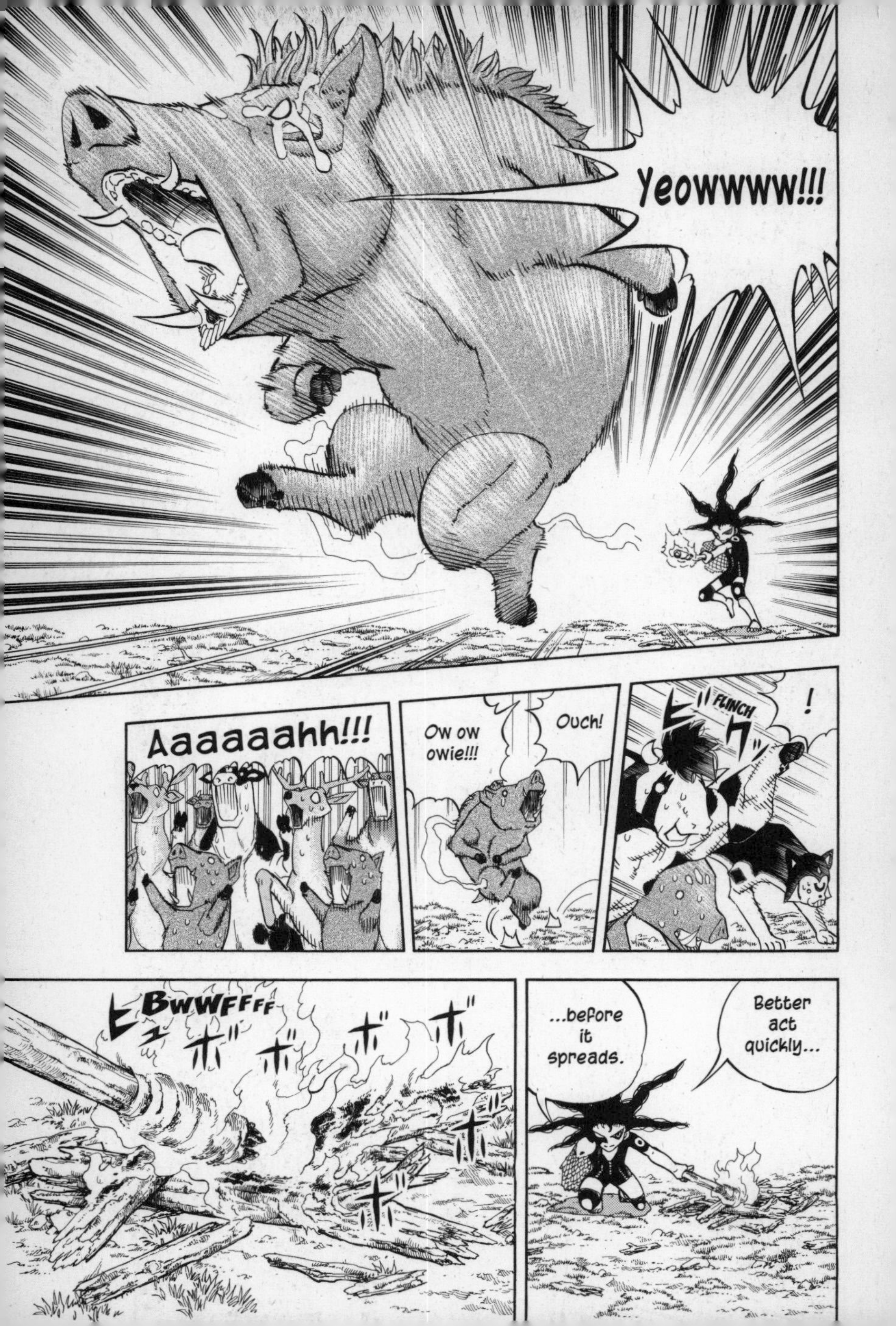
Yeowwww!!!
FLINCH
!
Ouch!
Ow ow owie!!!
Aaaaaahh!!!
Better act quickly...
...before it spreads.
BWWFFFF

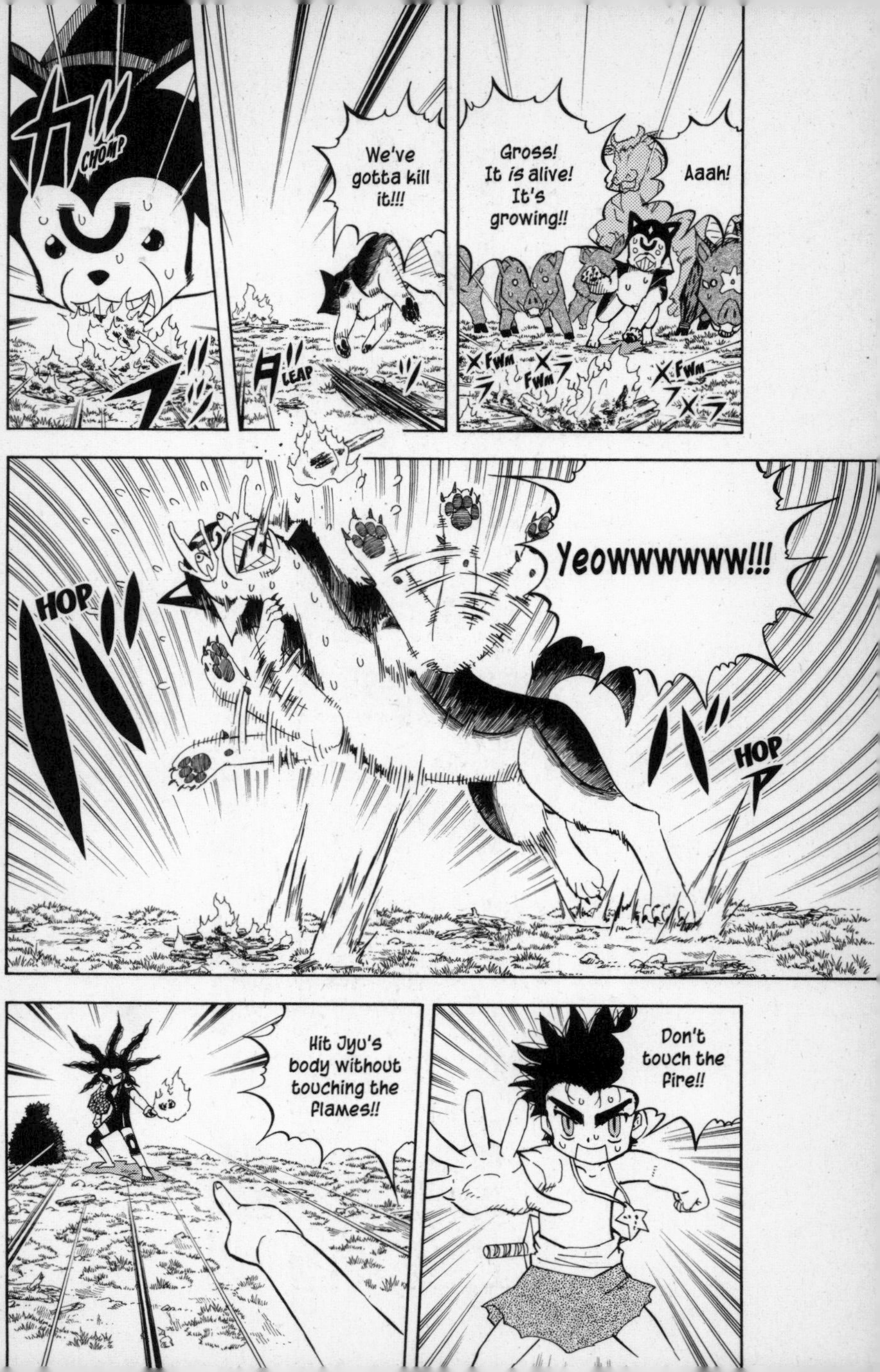
Aaah!
Gross! It *is* alive! It's growing!!
Fwm
Fwm
Fwm
We've gotta kill it!!!
LEAP
CHOMP
Yeowwwwww!!!
HOP
HOP
Don't touch the fire!!
Hit Jyu's body without touching the flames!!

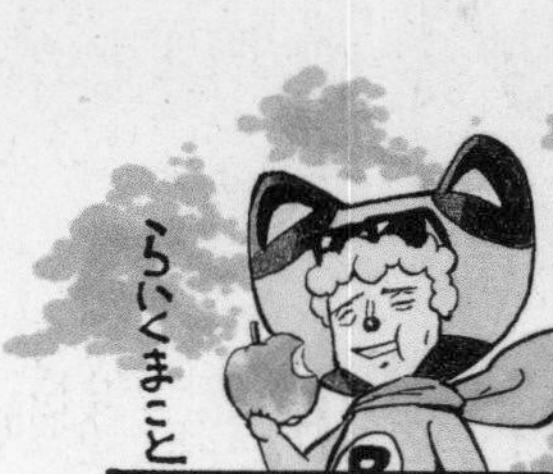

Pepper's Life

らいくまこと

by Makoto Raiku

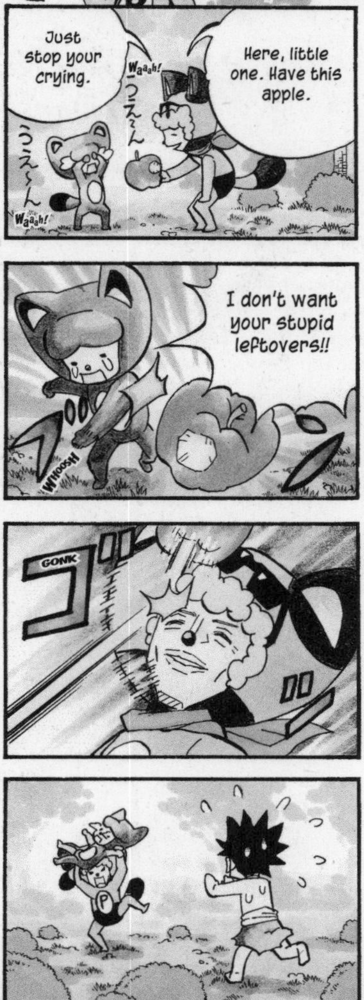
Here, little one. Have this apple.
Just stop your crying.
Waaah!
うえ~ん
Waaah!
うえ~ん
I don't want your stupid leftovers!!
WHOOSH
GONK

Animal Land volume 4 is a work of fiction. Names, characters, places, and incidents are the products of the author's imagination or are used fictitiously. Any resemblance to actual events, locales, or persons, living or dead, is entirely coincidental.

A Kodansha Comics Trade Paperback Original

Published in the United States by Kodansha Comics, an imprint of Kodansha USA Publishing, LLC, New York.

Publication rights for this English edition arranged through Kodansha Ltd., Tokyo.

First published in Japan in 2010 by Kodansha Ltd., Tokyo, as Doubutsu no Kuni, volume 4.

ISBN 978-1-61262-036-7

Printed in the United States of America.

www.kodanshacomics.com

9 8 7 6 5 4 3 2 1

Translator/Adapter: Stephen Paul
Lettering: Eve Grandt

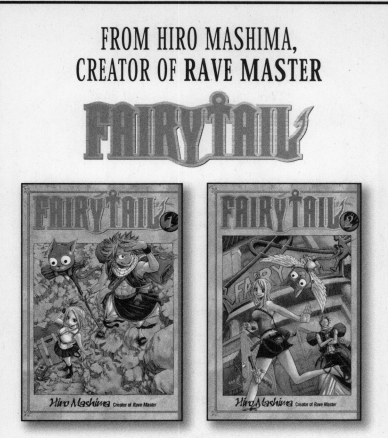

TOMARE!
[STOP!]

You are going the wrong way!

Manga is a completely different type of reading experience.

To start at the beginning, go to the end!

That's right! Authentic manga is read the traditional Japanese way—from right to left, exactly the opposite of how American books are read. It's easy to follow: Just go to the other end of the book, and read each page—and each panel—from right side to left side, starting at the top right. Now you're experiencing manga as it was meant to be.